Overcoming Personality Disorders

Other Books in the Series

Resolving Difficult Clinical Syndromes: A Personalized Psychotherapy Approach
Theodore Millon and Seth Grossman

Moderating Severe Personality Disorders: A Personalized Psychotherapy Approach
Theodore Millon and Seth Grossman

Overcoming Resistant Personality Disorders

A Personalized Psychotherapy Approach

Theodore Millon   **Seth Grossman**

John Wiley & Sons, Inc.

Published by John Wiley & Sons, Inc., Hoboken, New Jersey.
Published simultaneously in Canada.

Wiley Bicentennial Logo: Richard J. Pacifico

Library of Congress Cataloging-in-Publication Data:

Millon, Theodore.
Overcoming resistant personality disorders. A personalized psychotherapy approach. /
    Theodore Millon, Seth Grossman.
        p. ; cm.
    Rev. ed. in part of: Personality-guided therapy / Theodore Millon. c1999.
    Includes bibliographical references.
    ISBN 978–0–471–71771-3 (pbk.: alk. paper)
    1. Personality disorders. 2. Personality. 3. Psychotherapy.
  I. Grossman, Seth.   II. Millon, Theodore. Personality-guided therapy.   III. Title.
    IV. Title: Overcoming resistant personality cases.
    [DNLM: 1. Psychotherapy—methods. 2. Personality Disorders—therapy. WM 420 M656p 2007]
RC554.M547 2007
616.85′82—dc22

                                                                        2006031289

Printed in the United States of America.

10 9 8 7 6 5 4 3 2 1

To our patients of the past 50 years

CONTENTS

PREFACE

Would it not be a great step forward in our field if diagnosis or psychological assessment, following a series of interviews, tests, or laboratory procedures, actually pointed clearly to what a clinician should do in therapy? Would it not be good if evaluations could spell out which specific features of a patient's psychological makeup are fundamentally problematic—biological, cognitive, interpersonal—and therefore deserved primary therapeutic attention? Is it not time for clinicians to recognize that diagnosis can lead directly to the course of therapy?

This diagnosis-to-therapy goal can be achieved by employing treatment-oriented assessment tools (e.g., the Millon Clinical Multiaxial Inventory III Facet Scales, the Millon-Grossman Personality Disorder Checklist).

"Personalized psychotherapy" is not a vague concept or a platitudinous buzzword in our treatment approach, but an explicit commitment to focus first and foremost on the *unique composite* of a patient's psychological makeup. That focus should be followed by a precise formulation and specification of therapeutic rationales and techniques to remedy those personal attributes that are assessed as problematic.

Therapists should take cognizance of the *person* from the start, for the psychic parts and environmental contexts take on different meanings and call for different responses depending on the specific person to whom they are anchored. To focus on one social structure or one psychological realm of expression, without understanding its undergirding or reference base, is to engage in potentially misguided, if not random, therapeutic techniques.

Fledgling therapists should learn further that the *symptoms and disorders we diagnose represent but one or another segment of a complex of organically interwoven psychological elements.* The significance of each clinical feature can best be grasped by reviewing a patient's unique psychological experiences and his or her overall psychic pattern or configurational dynamics, of which any one component is but a single part.

Therapies that conceptualize clinical disorders from a single perspective, be it psychodynamic, cognitive, behavioral, or physiological, may be useful, and even necessary, but are not sufficient in themselves to undertake a therapy of the patient, disordered or not. The revolution we propose asserts that clinical disorders are not exclusively behavioral or cognitive or unconscious, that is, confined to a particular expressive form. The overall pattern of a person's traits and psychic expressions are systemic and multioperational. No part of the system exists in complete isolation from the others. Every part is directly or indirectly tied to every other, such that there is an emergent synergism that accounts for a disorder's clinical tenacity.

Personality is real; it is a composite of intertwined elements whose totality must be reckoned with in all therapeutic enterprises. The key to treating our patients, therefore, lies in *therapy that is designed to be as organismically complex as the person himself or herself;* this form of therapy should generate more than the sum of its parts. Difficult as this may appear, we hope to demonstrate its ease and utility.

If our wish takes root, this book will serve as a revolutionary call, a renaissance that brings therapy back to the natural reality of patients' lives.

It is our hope that the book will lead all of us back to reality by exploring both the unique intricacy and the wide diversity of the patients we treat. Despite frequent brilliance, most single-focus schools of therapy (e.g., behavioral, psychoanalytic) have become inbred. Of more concern, they persist in narrowing the clinicians' attention to just one or another facet of their patients' psychological makeup, thereby wandering ever farther from human reality. They cease to represent the full richness of their patients' lives, considering as significant only one of several psychic spheres: the unconscious, biochemical processes, cognitive schemas, or some other. In effect, what has been taught to most fledgling therapists is an artificial reality, one that may have been formulated in its early stages as an original perspective and insightful methodology, but has drifted increasingly from its moorings over time, no longer anchored to the complex clinical reality from which it was abstracted.

How does our therapeutic approach differ from others? In essence, we come to the treatment task not with a favored theory or technique, but with the patient's unique constellation of personality attributes given center stage. *Only after* a thorough evaluation of the nature and prominence of these personal attributes do we think through which combination and sequence of treatment orientations and methodologies we should employ.

It should be noted that a parallel personalized approach to physical treatment has currently achieved recognition in what is called *genomic medicine.* Here medical scientists have begun to tinker with a particular patient's DNA so as to decipher and remedy existing, missing, or broken genes, thereby enabling the physician to tailor treatment in a highly personalized manner, that is, specific to the underlying or core genetic defects of that particular patient. Anomalies that are etched into a patient's unique DNA are screened and assessed to determine their source, the vulnerabilities they portend, and the probability of the patient's succumbing to specific manifest diseases.

As detailed in the first chapter of the first book of this *Personalized Psychotherapy* series, we have formulated eight personality components or domains comprising what we might term a *psychic DNA,* a framework that conceptually parallels the four chemical elements composing biologic DNA. Deficiencies, excesses, defects, or dysfunctions in these psychic domains (e.g., mood/temperament, intrapsychic mechanisms) effectively result in a spectrum of 15 manifestly different variants of personality styles and pathology (e.g., avoidant style, borderline disorder). It is the unique constellation of vulnerabilities as expressed in and traceable to one or several of these eight potentially problematic psychic domains that become the object and focus of personalized psychotherapy (in the same manner as the vulnerabilities in biologic DNA result in a variety of different genomically based diseases).

In the first book of the personalized series, we attempt to show that *all the clinical syndromes that constitute Axis I can be understood more clearly and treated more effectively when conceived as an outgrowth of a patient's overall personality style.* To say that depression is experienced and expressed differently from one patient to the next is a truism; so general a statement, however, will not suffice for a book such as this. Our task requires much more.

The first book focuses on resolving difficult clinical syndromes of Axis I of the *Diagnostic and Statistical Manual of Mental Disorders;* it provides extensive information and illustrations on how patients with different personality vulnerabilities react to and cope with life's stressors. With this body of knowledge in hand, therapists should be guided to undertake more precise and effective treatment plans. For example, a dependent person will often respond to a divorce situation with feelings of helplessness and hopelessness, whereas a narcissist faced with similar circumstances may respond in a disdainful and cavalier way. Even when both a dependent and a narcissist exhibit depressive symptoms in common, the precipitant of these symptoms will likely have been quite different; furthermore, treatment—its goals and methods—should likewise differ. In effect, similar symptoms do not call for the same treatment *if* the pattern of patient vulnerabilities and coping styles differ. In the case of dependents, the emotional turmoil may arise from their feelings of lower self-esteem and their inability to function autonomously; in narcissists, depression may be the outcropping of failed cognitive denials as well as a consequent collapse of their habitual interpersonal arrogance.

Whether we work with a clinical syndrome's "part functions" as expressed in behavior (social isolation), or cognitions (a delusional belief), or affect (depression), or a biological defect (appetite loss) *or* we address contextual systems that focus on the larger environment, the family, or the group, or the socioeconomic and political conditions of life, the crossover point, the place that links the varieties of clinical expression to the individual's social context, is the person. The person is the intersecting medium that brings functions and systems together. Persons, however, are more than just crossover mediums. As we elaborate in the first book of the series, they are the only organically integrated system in the psychological domain, inherently created from birth as natural entities. Moreover, it is the person who lies at the heart of the therapeutic experience, the substantive being who gives meaning and coherence to symptoms and traits—be they behaviors, affects, or mechanisms—as well as that being, that singular entity, who gives life and expression to family interactions and social processes.

Looking at a patient's totality can present a bewildering if not chaotic array of therapeutic possibilities, potentially driving even the most motivated young clinician to back off into a more manageable and simpler worldview, be it cognitive or pharmacologic. But as we contend here, complexity need not be experienced as overwhelming; nor does it mean chaos, if we can create a logic and order to the treatment plan. We try to provide logic and order by illustrating that the systematic integration of an Axis I syndrome into its foundation in an Axis II disorder is not only feasible, but is one that is conducive to both briefer and more effective therapy. We should note, however, that a therapeutic method, no matter how logical and rational it may be, can never achieve the precision of the physical sciences. In our field we must be ever alert to the many subtle variations and sequences, as well as the constantly evolving forces, that compose the natural course of human life.

We are pleased to report that an excellent 240-minute videotape entitled "*DSM-IV Personality Disorders: The Subtypes*" has been produced and is distributed by Insight Media (800-233-9910, www.Insight-Media.com), psychology's premier publisher of videos and CD-Roms. It is available for purchase by instructors and clinicians who wish to view over 60 case vignettes that illustrate all *DSM-IV* personality prototypes and subtypes, as interviewed by psychologists and discussed by the senior author of this book.

THEODORE MILLON
SETH D. GROSSMAN

Coral Gables, Florida

PART **ONE**

Personalized Psychotherapy: A Recapitulation

This chapter is written for readers not fully acquainted with Chapter 1 of the first book, *Resolving Difficult Clinical Syndromes*, of this *Personalized Psychotherapy* series (Millon & Grossman, 2007). It provides a brief synopsis of the essential themes and rationale of this new approach to psychotherapy.

Are not all psychotherapies personalized? Do not all therapists concern themselves with the person who is the patient they are treating? What justifies our appropriating the name "personalized" to the treatment approach we espouse? Are we not usurping a universal, laying claim to a title that is commonplace, routinely shared, and employed by most (all?) therapists?

We think not. In fact, we believe most therapists only incidentally or secondarily attend to the *specific personal qualities* of their patients. The majority come to their treatment task with a distinct if implicit bias, a preferred theory or technique they favor, one usually encouraged, sanctioned, and promoted in their early training, be it cognitive, group, family, eclectic, pharmacologic, or what have you.

How does our therapeutic approach differ? In essence, we come to the treatment task not with a favored theory or technique, but giving center stage to the patient's unique constellation of personality attributes. *Only after* a thorough evaluation of the nature and prominence of these personal attributes do we think through which combination and sequence of treatment orientations and methodologies we should employ.

"Personalized" is therefore not a vague concept or a platitudinous buzzword in our approach, but an explicit commitment to focus first and foremost on the unique composite of a patient's psychological makeup, followed by a precise formulation and specification of therapeutic rationales and techniques suitable to remedying those personal attributes that are assessed as problematic.

We have drawn on two concepts from our earlier writings, namely, personality-guided therapy (Millon, 1999) and synergistic therapy (Millon, 2002), integrating them into what we have now labeled "personalized psychotherapy." Both prior concepts remain core facets of our current treatment formulations in that, first, they are *guided* by the patient's overall personality makeup and, second, they are methodologically *synergistic* in that they utilize a combinational approach that employs reciprocally interacting and mutually reinforcing treatment modalities that produce a greater total result than the sum of their individual effects.

The preface recorded a parallel "personalized" approach to physical treatment in what is called *genomic medicine.* Here medical scientists have begun to investigate a particular patient's DNA so as to decipher and remedy existing, missing or broken genes, thereby enabling the physician to tailor treatment in a highly personalized manner, that is, specific to the underlying or core genetic defects of that particular patient. Anomalies that are etched into a patient's unique DNA are screened and assessed to determine their source, the vulnerabilities they portend, and the probability of the patient's succumbing to specific manifest diseases.

Personalized psychological *assessment* is *therapy-guiding;* it undergirds and orients personalized psychotherapy. Together, they should be conceived as corresponding to genomic medicine in that they seek to identify the unique constellation of *underlying vulnerabilities* that characterize a particular mental patient and the consequent likelihood of his or her succumbing to specific mental clinical syndromes. In personalized assessment, we seek to employ *customized instruments,* such as the Grossman Facet Scales of the Millon Clinical Multiaxial Inventory (MCMI-III), to identify the patient's vulnerable psychic domains (e.g., cognitive style, interpersonal conduct). These assessment data furnish a foundation and a guide for implementing the distinctive individualized goals we seek to achieve in personalized psychotherapy.

As will be detailed in later sections, we have formulated eight personality components or domains constituting what we term a *psychic DNA,* a framework that conceptually parallels the four chemical elements composing biologic DNA. Deficiencies, excesses, defects, or dysfunctions in these psychic domains (e.g., mood/temperament, intrapsychic mechanisms) effectively result in a spectrum of 15 manifestly different variants of personality pathology (e.g., Avoidant Disorder, Borderline Disorder). It is the unique constellation of vulnerabilities as expressed in and traceable to one or several of these eight potentially problematic psychic domains that becomes the object and focus of personalized psychotherapy (in the same manner as the vulnerabilities in biologic DNA result in a variety of different genomically based diseases).

Psychotherapy has been dominated until recently by what might be termed domain- or modality-oriented therapy. That is, therapists identified themselves with a single-realm focus or a theoretical school (behavioral, intrapsychic) and attempted to practice within whatever prescriptions for therapy it made. Rapid changes in the therapeutic milieu, all interrelated through economic pressures, conceptual shifts, and diagnostic innovations, have taken place in the past few decades. For better or worse, these changes show no sign of decelerating and have become a context to which therapists, far from reversing, must now themselves adapt.

The simplest way to practice psychotherapy is to approach all patients as possessing essentially the same disorder, and then utilize one standard modality of therapy for their treatment. Many therapists still employ these simplistic models. Yet everything we have learned in the past 2 or 3 decades tells us that this approach is only minimally effective and deprives patients of other, more sensitive and effective approaches to treatment. In the past 2 decades, we have come to recognize that patients differ substantially in the clinical syndromes and personality disorders they present. It is clear that not all treatment modalities are equally effective for all patients, be it pharmacologic, cognitive, intrapsychic, or another mode. The task set before us is to maximize our effectiveness, beginning with efforts to abbreviate treatment, to recognize significant cultural considerations, to combine treatment, and to outline an integrative model for selective therapeutics. When the selection is based on each patient's personal trait configuration, integration becomes what we have termed *personalized psychotherapy,* to be discussed in the next section.

Present knowledge about combinational and integrative therapeutics has only begun to be developed. In this section we hope to help overcome the resistance that many psychotherapists possess to the idea of utilizing treatment combinations of modalities that they have not been trained to exercise. Most therapists have worked long and hard to become experts in a particular technique or two. Though they are committed to what they know and do best, they are likely to approach their patients' problems with techniques consonant with their prior training. Unfortunately, most modern therapists have become expert in only a few of the increasingly diverse approaches to treatment and are not open to exploring interactive combinations that may be suitable for the complex configuration of symptoms most patients bring to treatment.

In line with this theme, Frances, Clarkin, and Perry (1984, p. 195) have written:

> The proponents of the various developing schools of psychotherapy tended to maintain the pristine and competitive purity of their technical innovations, rather than attempt to determine how these could best be combined with one another. There have always been a few synthesizers and bridgebuilders (often derided from all sides as "eclectic") but, for the most part, clinicians who were trained in one form of therapy tended to regard other types with disdain and suspicion.

The inclination of proponents of one or another modality of therapy to remain separate was only in part an expression of treatment rivalries. During the early phases of a treatment's development, innovators, quite appropriately, sought to establish a measure of effectiveness without having their investigations confounded by the intrusion of other modalities. No less important was that each treatment domain was but a single dimension in the complex of elements that patients bring to us. As we move away from a simple medical model to one that recognizes the psychological complexity of patients' symptoms and causes, it appears wise to mirror the patients' complexities by developing therapies that are comparably complex.

As will be elaborated throughout the text, certain combinational approaches have an additive effect; others may prove to possess a synergistic effect (Klerman, 1984). The term additive describes a situation in which the combined benefits of two or more treatments are at least equal to the sum of their individual benefits. The term synergistic describes a situation in which the combined benefits of several treatment modalities exceed the sum of their individual components; that is, their effects are potentiated. This entire book series is intended to show that several modalities—pharmacotherapy, cognitive therapy, family therapy, intrapsychic therapy—may be combined and integrated to achieve additive, if not synergistic, effects.

It is our view that psychopathology itself contains structural implications that legislate the form of any therapy one would propose to remedy its constituents. Thus, the philosophy we present derives from several implications and proposes a new integrative model for therapeutic action, an approach that we have called *personalized psychotherapy*. This model, which is guided by the psychic makeup of a patient's personality—and not a preferred theory or modality or technique—gives promise, we believe, of a new level of efficacy and may, in fact, contribute to making therapy briefer. Far from being merely a theoretical rationale or a justification for adhering to one or another treatment modality, it should optimize psychotherapy by tailoring treatment interventions to fit the patient's specific form of pathology. It is not a ploy to be adopted or dismissed as congruent or incongruent with established therapeutic preferences or modality styles. Despite its name, we believe that what we have termed a personalized approach will be effective not only with Axis II personality disorders, but also with Axis I clinical syndromes.

Integration should be more than the coexistence of two or three previously discordant orientations or techniques. We cannot simply piece together the odds and ends of several theoretical schemas, each internally consistent and oriented to different data domains. Such a hodgepodge will lead only to illusory syntheses that cannot long hold together (Messer, 1986, 1992). Efforts such as these, meritorious as they may be in some regards, represent the work of peacemakers, not innovators and not integrationists. Integration is eclectic, of course, but more.

As we will argue further, it is our belief that integration should be a synthesized system to mirror the problematic configuration of traits (personality) and symptoms (clinical syndromes) of a specific patient at hand. In the next section, we discuss integration from this view. Many in the past have sought to coalesce differing theoretical orientations and treatment modalities with interconnecting bridges. By contrast, those of us in the *personalized* therapeutic persuasion bypass the synthesis of theory. Rather, primary attention should be given to the *natural synthesis or inherent integration that may be found within patients* themselves.

As Arkowitz (1997) has noted, efforts to create a theoretical synthesis are usually not fully integrative in that most theorists do not draw on component approaches equally. Most are oriented to one particular theory or modality, and then seek to assimilate other strategies and notions to that core approach. Moreover, assimilated theories and techniques are invariably changed by the core model into which they have been imported. In other words, the assimilated orientation or methodology is frequently transformed from its original intent. As Messer (1992, p. 151) wrote, "When incorporating elements of other therapies into one's own, a procedure takes its meaning not only from its point of origin, but even more so from the structure of the therapy into which it is imported." Messer illustrates this point by describing a two-chair gestalt procedure that is brought into a primary social-learning model; in this assimilation, the two-chair procedure will likely be utilized differently and achieve different goals than would occur in the hands of a gestalt therapist using the same technique.

Furthermore, by seeking to impose a theoretical synthesis, therapists may lose the context and thematic logic that each of the standard theoretical approaches has built up over its history. In essence, intrinsically coherent theories are usually disassembled in the effort to interweave their diverse bits and pieces. Such an integrative model composed of alternative models (behavioral, psychoanalytic) may be pluralistic, but it reflects separate modalities with varying conceptual networks and their unconnected studies and findings. As such, integrative models *do not* reflect that which is inherent in nature, but *invent* a schema for interweaving that which is, in fact, essentially discrete.

As will be discussed in the following section, intrinsic unity cannot be invented, but can be discovered in nature by focusing on the intrinsic unity of the person, that is, the full scope of a patient's psychic being. Integration based on the natural order and unity of the person avoids the rather arbitrary efforts at synthesizing disparate and sometimes disjunctive theoretical schemas.

Efforts at synthesizing therapeutic models have been most successful in desegregating the field rather than truly integrating it. As Arkowitz (1997, pp. 256–257) explains:

> Integrative perspectives have been catalytic in the search for new ways of thinking about and doing psychotherapy that go beyond the confines of single-school approaches. Practitioners and researchers are examining what other theories and therapies have to offer. . . .
>
> Several promising starts have been made in clinical proposals for integrative therapies, but it is clear that much more work needs to be done.

As noted, it is the belief of the authors that integration cannot stem from an intellectual synthesis of different theories, but from the inherent integration that is discovered in each patient's personal style of functioning, a topic to which we now turn.

Unlike eclecticism, integration insists on the primacy of an overarching gestalt that gives coherence, provides an interactive framework, and creates an organic order among otherwise discrete units or elements. Whereas the theoretical syntheses previously discussed attempt to provide an intellectual bridge across several theories or modalities, personalized integrationists assert that a natural synthesis already exists within the patient. As we better understand the configuration of traits that characterize each patient's psyche, we can better devise a treatment plan that will mirror these traits and, we believe, will provide an optimal therapeutic course and outcome.

As noted previously, integration is an important concept in considering not only the psychotherapy of the individual case but also the place of psychotherapy in clinical science. For the treatment of a particular patient to be integrated, the elements of a clinical science—theory, taxonomy, assessment, and therapy—should be integrated as well (Millon, 1996b). One of the arguments advanced earlier against empirically based eclecticism is that it further insulates psychotherapy from a broad-based clinical science. In contrast to eclecticism, where techniques are justified empirically, *personalized psychotherapeutic integration* should take its shape and character from an integrative theory of human nature. Such a grand theory should be inviting because it attempts to explain all of the natural variations of human behavior, normal or otherwise; moreover, personalized psychotherapy will grow naturally out of such a personalized theory. Theory of this nature will not be disengaged from therapeutic technique; rather, it will inform and guide it.

Murray (1983) has suggested that the field must develop a new, higher order theory to help us better understand the interconnections among cognitive, affective, self, and interpersonal psychic systems. It is the belief of personalized therapeutic theorists, such as ourselves, who claim that interlinked configurations of pathology deduced from such a theory can serve to guide psychotherapy.

Although differential treatment gives special weight to the specific problem areas of the patient, most theorists and therapists pay little attention to the particular domains composing different diagnostic categories. We argue for considering the configuration of personality traits that characterize each specific patient. Differential treatment recognizes that current diagnostic information, such as listed in the *Diagnostic and Statistical Manual of Mental Disorders* (*DSM-IV*), provides only a surface coverage of the complex elements that are associated with a patient's inner and outer worlds.

As noted previously, whether we work with "part functions" that focus on behaviors, cognitions, unconscious processes, or biological defects, or whether we address contextual systems that focus on the larger environment, the family, the group, or the socioeconomic and political conditions of life, the crossover point, the place that links parts to contexts, is the person. The individual is the intersecting medium that brings them together.

Persons, however, are more than crossover mediums. They are the only organically integrated system in the psychological domain, inherently created from birth as natural entities, rather than experience-derived gestalts constructed via cognitive attribution. Moreover, it is persons who lie at the heart of the psychotherapeutic experience, the substantive beings that give meaning and coherence to symptoms and traits—be they behaviors, affects, or mechanisms—as well as those beings, those singular entities, that give life and expression to family interactions and social processes.

The cohesion (or lack thereof) of intrinsically interwoven psychic structures and functions is what distinguishes most complex disorders of psychopathology; likewise, the orchestration of diverse, yet synthesized modalities of intervention is what differentiates synergistic from other variants of psychotherapy. These two parallel constructs, emerging from different traditions and conceived in different venues, reflect shared philosophical perspectives, one oriented toward the understanding of mental disorders, the other toward effecting their remediation.

It is not that one-modality or school-oriented psychotherapies are inapplicable to more focal or simple syndrome pathologies, but rather that synergistically planned therapies are required for the intricate relationships that interconnect personality and clinical syndromes (whereas depression may successfully be treated either cognitively or pharmacologically); it is the very interwoven nature of the components that compose such complex disorders that makes a multifaceted and synthesized approach a necessity.

In the following pages we present a few ideas in sequence. First, personalized therapies require a foundation in a coordinating theory of nature, that is, they must be more than a schema of eclectic techniques, a hodgepodge of diverse alternatives assembled de novo with each case. Second, although the diagnostic criteria that make up *DSM* syndromes are a decent first step, these criteria must become comprehensive and comparable, that is, be systematically revised so as to be genuinely useful for treatment planning. Third, a logical rationale can be formulated as to how one can and should integrate diverse modality-focused therapies when treating complex psychopathologies.

Before turning to these themes, we would like to comment briefly on some philosophical issues. They bear on a rationale for developing a wide-ranging theory of nature to serve as a basis for treatment techniques, that is, universal principles that transcend the merely empirical (e.g., electroconvulsive therapy for depressives). It is our conviction that the theoretical foundations of our personologic science must be advanced further if we are to succeed in constructing a personalized approach to psychotherapy.

Obviously, a tremendous amount of knowledge, both about the nature of the patient's disorders and about diverse modes of intervention, is required to perform personalized therapy. To maximize synergism among numerous modalities requires that the therapist be a little like a jazz soloist. Not only should the professional be fully versed in the various musical keys, that is, in techniques of psychotherapy that span all trait domains, but he or she should also be prepared to respond to subtle fluctuations in the patient's thoughts, actions, and emotions, any of which could take the composition in a wide variety of directions, and integrate these with the overall plan of therapy as it evolves. After the instruments have been packed away and the band goes home, a retrospective account of the entire process should reveal a level of thematic continuity and logical order commensurate with that which would have existed had all relevant constraints been known in advance.

The integrative processes of personalized therapy should be dictated by the nature of personality itself. The actual logic and foundation of this therapy, however, must be grounded on some other basis. Psychopathology is by definition a patterning of intraindividual variables, but the nature of these variables must be supplied by a set of fundamental principles or on some basis beyond the personologic construct. In our view, for example, the structure and functions of personality and psychopathology are grounded in evolutionary theory, a discipline that informs but exists apart from our clinical subject. In and of itself, pathologic personality is a structural-functional concept that refers to the intraorganismic patterning of variables; it does not in itself say what these variables are or how they relate, nor can it.

We believe that several elements characterize all mature clinical sciences: (a) They embody *conceptual theories* based on universal principles of nature from which their propositional deductions can be derived; (b) these theories provide the basis for *coherent taxonomies* that specify and characterize the central features of their subject domain (in our case, that of personality and psychopathology, the substantive realm within which scientific psychotherapeutic techniques are applied); (c) these taxonomies are associated with a variety of *empirically oriented assessment instruments* that can identify and quantify the concepts that constitute their theories (in psychopathology, methods that uncover developmental history and furnish cross-sectional assessments); and (d) in addition to natural theory, clinical taxonomy, and empirically anchored assessment tools, mature clinical sciences possess *change-oriented intervention* techniques that are therapeutically optimal in modifying the pathological elements of their domain.

Most current therapeutic schools share a common failure to coordinate these four components of a mature science. What differentiates them has less to do with their scientific grounding than with the fact that they attend to different levels of data in the natural world. It is to the credit of those of an eclectic persuasion that they have recognized, albeit in a fuzzy way, the arbitrary if not illogical character of single-focus positions, as well as the need to bridge schisms among these approaches that have evolved less by philosophical considerations or pragmatic goals than by the accidents of history (Millon, 2004). There are numerous other knotty issues with which the nature of psychic pathology and personalized therapy must contend (e.g., differing worldviews concerning the essential nature of psychological experience). There is no problem, as we see it, in encouraging active dialectics among these contenders.

However, there are two important barriers that stand in the way of personalized psychotherapy as a treatment philosophy. The first is the *DSM*. The idea of diagnostic prototypes was a genuine innovation when the *DSM-III* was published in 1980. The development of diagnostic criteria work groups was intended to provide broad representation of various points of view, while preventing any single perspective from foreclosing on the others. Even some 25 years later, however, the *DSM* has yet to officially endorse an underlying set of principles that would interrelate and differentiate the categories in terms of their deeper principles. Instead, progress proceeds mainly by way of committee consensus, cloaked by the illusion of empirical research.

The second barrier is the human habit system. The admonition that different therapeutic approaches should be pursued with different patients and different problems has become almost self-evident. But given no logical basis from which to design effective therapeutic sequences and composites, even the most self-consciously antidogmatic clinician must implicitly lean toward one orientation or another.

What specifically are the procedures that distinguish personalized therapy from other models of an eclectic nature?

The integrative model labeled 2 decades ago by the senior author as "personologic psychotherapy" (Millon, 1988) insisted on the primacy of an overarching gestalt that gave coherence, provided an interactive framework, and created an organic order among otherwise discrete polarities and attributes. It was eclectic, but more. It was derived from a substantive theory whose overall utility and orientation derives from that old chestnut "The whole is greater than the sum of its parts." The problems our patients bring to us are often an inextricably linked nexus of interpersonal behaviors, cognitive styles, regulatory processes, and so on. They flow through a tangle of feedback loops and serially unfolding concatenations that emerge at different times in dynamic and changing configurations. Each component of these configurations has its role and significance altered by virtue of its place in these continually evolving constellations. *In parallel form, personalized therapy should be conceived as an integrated configuration of strategies and tactics in which each intervention technique is selected not only for its efficacy in resolving particular pathological attributes, but also for its contribution to the overall constellation of treatment procedures of which it is but one integral part.*

Although the admonition that we should *not* employ the same therapeutic approach with all patients is self-evident, it appears that therapeutic approaches accord more with where training occurred than with the nature of the patients' pathologies. To paraphrase Millon (1969/1985), there continues to be a disinclination among clinical practitioners to submit their cherished techniques to detailed study or to revise them in line with critical empirical findings. Despite the fact that most of our therapeutic research leaves much to be desired in the way of proper controls, sampling, and evaluative criteria, one overriding fact comes through repeatedly: Therapeutic techniques must be suited to the patient's problem. Simple and obvious though this statement is, it is repeatedly neglected by therapists who persist in utilizing and arguing heatedly in favor of a particular approach to *all* variants of psychopathology. No school of therapy is exempt from this notorious attitude.

Why should we formulate a personalized therapeutic approach to psychopathology? The answer may be best grasped if we think of the psychic elements of a person as analogous to the sections of an orchestra, and the trait domains of a patient as a clustering of discordant instruments that exhibit imbalances, deficiencies, or conflicts within these sections. To extend this analogy, therapists may be seen as conductors whose task is to bring forth a harmonious balance among all the sections, as well as their specifically discordant instruments, muting some here, accentuating others there, all to the end of fulfilling the conductor's knowledge of how the composition can best be made consonant. The task is not that of altering one instrument, but of altering all, in concert. What is sought in music, then, is a balanced score, one composed of harmonic counterpoints, rhythmic patterns, and melodic combinations. What is needed in therapy is a likewise balanced program, a coordinated strategy of counterpoised techniques designed to optimize sequential and combinatorial treatment effects.

If clinical syndromes were anchored exclusively to one particular trait domain (as phobias are thought to be primarily behavioral in nature), modality-bound psychotherapy would always be appropriate and desirable. Psychopathology, however, is not exclusively behavioral, cognitive, biologic, or intrapsychic, that is, confined to a particular clinical data level. Instead, it is multioperational and systemic. No part of the system exists in complete isolation. Instead, every part is directly or indirectly tied to every other, such that a synergism lends the whole a tenacity that makes the full system of pathology "real"—a complex that needs to be fully reckoned with in a comprehensive therapeutic endeavor. Therapies should mirror the configuration of as many trait and clinical domains as the syndromes and disorders they seek to remedy. If the scope of the therapy is insufficient relative to the scope of the pathology, the treatment system will have considerable difficulty fulfilling its meliorative and adaptive goals. Both unstructured intrapsychic therapy and highly structured behavioral techniques, to note the extremes, share this deficiency.

Psychopathology is neither exclusively behavioral, exclusively cognitive, nor exclusively interpersonal, but is instead a genuine integration of each of its subsidiary domains. Far from overturning established paradigms, such a broad perspective simply allows a given phenomenon to be treated from several angles, so to speak. Even agnostic therapists, with no strong allegiance to any one point of view, may avail themselves of a kaleidoscope of modalities. By turning the kaleidoscope, by shifting paradigmatic sets, the same phenomenon can be viewed from any of a variety of internally consistent perspectives. Eclecticism becomes a first step toward synthesizing modalities that correspond to the natural configuration of each patient's traits and disorders.

The open-minded therapist is left, however, with several different modality combinations, each with some currency for understanding the patient's pathology, but no real means of bringing these diverse conceptions together in a coherent model of what, exactly, to do. The therapist's plight is understandable, but not acceptable. For example, modality techniques considered fundamental in one perspective may not be so regarded in another. The interpersonal model of Lorna Benjamin and the neurobiological model of Robert Cloninger are both structurally strong approaches to understanding personality and psychopathology. Yet their fundamental constructs are different. Rather than inherit the modality tactics of a particular perspective, then, a theory of psychotherapy as a total system should seek some set of principles that can be addressed to the patient's whole psyche, thereby capitalizing on the naturally organic system of the person. The alternative is an uncomfortable eclecticism of unassimilated partial views. Perhaps believing that nothing more is possible, most psychotherapists have accepted this state of affairs as an inevitable reality.

Fortunately, modality-bound psychotherapies are increasingly becoming part of the past. In growing numbers, clinicians are identifying themselves, not as psychodynamic or behavioral, but as eclectic or integrative. As noted earlier, eclecticism is an insufficient guide to personalized therapy. As a movement, and not a construct, it cannot prescribe the particular form of those modalities that will remedy the pathologies of persons and their syndromes. Eclecticism is too open with regard to content and too imprecise to achieve focused goals. The intrinsically configurational nature of psychopathology, its multioperationalism, and the interwoven character of clinical domains simply are not as integrated in eclecticism as they need be in treating psychopathology.

The following text, figures. and tables will provide the reader with a brief synopsis of a personality-based evolutionary model; other sources should be pursued for a more

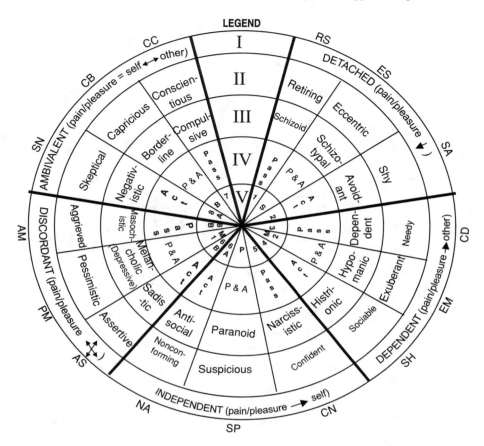

FIGURE 1.1   Personality spectra circulargram I: Normal and abnormal personality patterns. Evolutionary foundations of the normal and abnormal extremes of each personality prototype of the 15 spectra. I: Evolutionary Orientation; II: Normal Prototype; III: Abnormal Prototype; IV: Adaptation Style; V: MCMI-III-E Scale number/letter.

extensive elaboration of these ideas (Millon, Bloom, & Grossman, in press; Millon & Davis, 1996a; Millon & Grossman, 2006; Millon & Grossman, in press).

Three figures, 1.1, 1.2, and 1.3, present circumplex representations of the overall theoretically derived personality spectra of normal and abnormal patterns and their associated clinical domains. Figure 1.1, the Personality Spectra Circulargram, portrays the 15 prototypal variants derived from the theory. Legend I of Figure 1.1 relates to the prototype's primary evolutionary foundation (e.g., the retiring/schizoid reflects a detached pattern that stems from deficiencies in the pain-pleasure polarity). Figure 1.2 represents the four *functional* domains for each of the 15 personality prototype patterns. Legend II of Figure 1.2, for example, relates to the prototype's characteristic

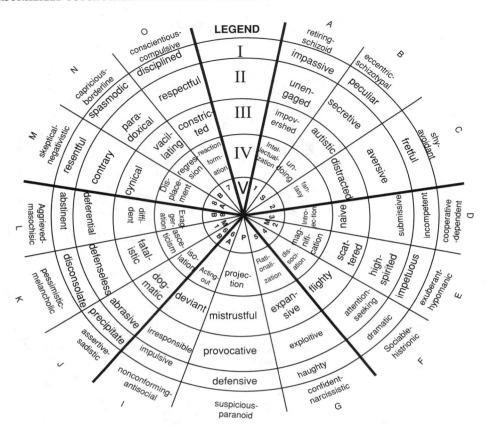

FIGURE 1.2 Personality circulargram IIA: Functional personologic domains.
I: Expressive Behavior; II: Interpersonal Conduct; III: Cognitive Style/Content;
IV: Intrapsychic Mechanisms; V: MCMI-III Scale.

interpersonal conduct (e.g., the retiring/schizoid's conduct is noted as unengaged).
Figure 1.3 portrays the four *structural* domains for all of the 15 personality prototypes. Legend IV of Figure 1.3, to illustrate, concerns the prototypal fundamental
mood/affect (e.g., the retiring/schizoid's typical mood is recorded as apathetic).

Scores on these functional and structural domains, as calculated by MCMI-III
analyses and/or obtained on the Millon-Grossman Personality Domain Checklist
(MG-PDC), to be described shortly, serve as the basis for identifying, selecting, and
coordinating the major foci and techniques of therapeutic action. Thus, high ratings on
the pessimistic/melancholic interpersonal and mood/affect domains may identify the
more problematic realms of a patient's psychological makeup. It also suggests the use of
a combination of two therapeutic techniques: interpersonal methods (e.g., Benjamin's
approach) and pharmacologic medications (e.g., daily regimen of Prozac).

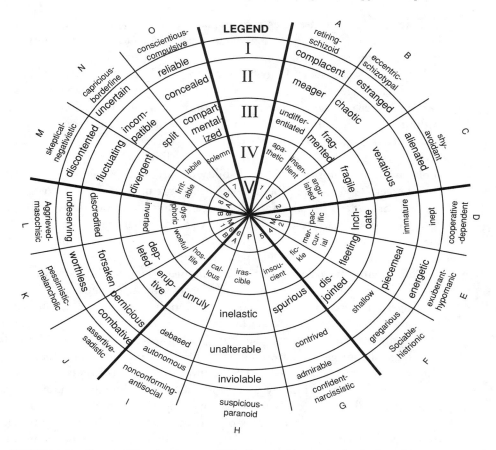

FIGURE 1.3   Personality circulargram IIB: Structural personologic domains.
I: Self-Image; II: Intrapsychic Content; III: Intrapsychic Structure; IV: Mood-Affect;
V: MCMI-III Scale.

Several words may usefully be said regarding the newly devised MG-PDC instrument (Millon & Grossman, in press). Clinicians and personologists employ numerous sources to obtain assessment data on both persons in general and their patients. These range from incidental to well-structured observations, casual to highly systematic interviews, and cursory to formal analyses of biographic history; also employed are a variety of laboratory tests, self-report inventories, and performance-based or projective techniques. All of these have proven to be useful grounds for diagnostic study.

How do we put these diverse data sources together to systematize and quantify the information we have gathered? It is toward the end of organizing and maximizing the clinical utility of our personality findings that the MG-PDC has been developed.

On their own, observations and projective techniques are viewed as excessively subjective. Laboratory procedures (e.g., brain imaging) are not yet sufficiently developed, and biographical data are often too unreliable to depend on. And despite their popularity with many a distinguished psychometrician, the utility of self-report inventories is far from universally accepted.

Whether assessment tools are based on empirical investigations, epidemiologic research, mathematical analyses, or theoretical deductions, they often fail to characterize persons in the language and concepts traditionally employed by clinical personologists. Although many instruments have proven of value in numerous research studies, such as demonstrating reasonable intercorrelations or a correspondence with established diagnostic systems (e.g., the *DSM*), many an astute clinician has questioned whether these tools yield anything beyond the reliability of surface impressions. Some (Westen & Weinberger, 2004) doubt whether self-report instruments, for example, successfully tap into or unravel the diverse, complex, and hidden relationships among difficult-to-fathom processes. Other critics have contended that patient-generated responses may contain *no* clinically relevant information beyond the judgments of nonscientists employing the vocabulary of a layperson's lexicon.

Data obtained from patient-based self-judgments may be contrasted with the sophisticated clinical appraisals of mental health professionals. We must ask whether clinical language, concepts, and instruments encoded in the evolving professional language of the past 100 years or so generate information incremental to the naive descriptions of an ordinary person's everyday lexicon. We know that clinical languages differ from laypersons' languages because they serve different and more sophisticated purposes (Livesley, Jackson, & Schroeder, 1989). Indeed, clinical concepts reflect the experienced contributions of numerous historical schools of thought (Millon, 2004). Each of these clinical schools (e.g., psychodynamic, cognitive, interpersonal) have identified a multitude of diverse and complex psychic processes that operate in our mental life. Surely the concepts of these historical professional lexicons are not reducible to the superficial factors drawn from the everyday vocabulary of nonscientists.

It is to represent and integrate the insights and concepts of the several major schools of thought that has led us to formulate a domain-based clinician-rated assessment (Millon, 1969/1985, 1981, 1984, 1990, 1996b; Tringone, 1997), and now to develop, following numerous empirical and theoretical refinements, the MG-PDC. In contrast with the five-factor method, popular among research-oriented psychologists, the Personality Domain Checklist (PDC) is based on the contributions of five of the major *clinical traditions;* the behavioral, the interpersonal, the self, the cognitive, and the biological. Three optional domains are listed additionally in the instrument to reflect the psychoanalytic tradition; the use of these intrapsychic domains has diminished in recent decades and they are therefore included as elective, that is, not required components of the instrument.

Several criteria were used to select and develop the clinical domains listed in the checklist: (a) that they be *broad-based and varied* in the features they embody, that is, not limited just to biological temperaments or cognitive processes, but instead encompass a full range of personality characteristics that are based on frequently used clinical terms and concepts; (b) that they correspond to the major *therapeutic modalities* employed by contemporary mental health professionals to treat their patients (e.g., *cognitive* techniques for altering dysfunctional beliefs, group procedures for modifying *interpersonal* conduct) and, hence, are readily employed by practicing therapeutic clinicians; (c) that they be *coordinated with* and reflect the official personality disorder prototypes established by the *International Classification of Diseases* (*ICD*) and *DSM* and, thereby, be understood by insurance and other management professionals; (d) that a *distinctive psychological trait* can be identified and operationalized in each of the clinical trait domains for each personality prototype, assuring thereby both scope and comparability among personological criteria; (e) that they lend themselves to the appraisal of domain characteristics for both *normal and abnormal* personalities and, hence, further promote advances in the field of normality, one of growing interest in the psychological literature; and (f) that they can serve as an *educational clinical tool* to sensitize mental heath workers in training (psychologists, psychiatrists, clinical social workers, etc.) to the many distinctions, subtleties, and domain interactions that are worth considering in appraising personality attributes.

The *integrative perspective* encouraged in the MG-PDC views personalities as a multidetermined and multireferential construct. One, albeit problematic, means by some clinical researchers of dealing with the conceptual alternatives that characterizes personality study today is to oversimplify the task. They choose to assess the patient in accord with a single conceptual orientation, eliminating thereby the integration of divergent perspectives by an act of regressive dogmatism. A truly effective assessment, however, one that is logically consonant with the modern integrative character of personality, both as a construct and as a reality, requires that the individual be assessed systematically across multiple characterological domains, thereby ensuring that the assessment is comprehensive, useful to a broad range of clinicians, and more likely valid. In assessing with the MG-PDC, clinicians should refrain, therefore, from regarding each domain as an independent entity, and thereby falling into a naive, single-minded approach. Each of the domains is a legitimate but highly contextualized part of a unified or integrated whole, a necessary composite that ensures that the full integrity of the person is represented.

As noted previously, the domains of the instrument can be organized in a manner similar to distinctions drawn in the biological realm; that is, they may be divided and characterized as *structural* and *functional* attributes. The functional domains of the instrument represent dynamic processes that transpire between the individual and his or her psychosocial environment. These transactions take place through what we have termed the person's *modes of regulatory action,* that is, his or her demeanor, social relations, and thought processes, each of which serve to manage, adjust, transform, coordinate, and control the give-and-take of inner and outer life. Several functional domains relevant to each personality are included among the major components of the MG-PDC.

In contrast to the functional characteristics, structural domains represent templates of deeply embedded affect dispositions and imprinted memories, attitudes, needs, and conflicts that guide experience and orient ongoing life events. These domains may be conceived as *quasi-permanent substrates for identity and temperament.* These residues of the past and relatively enduring affects effectively constrain and even close off innovative learnings and limit new possibilities to already established habits and dispositions. Their persistent and preemptive character perpetuates the maladaptive behavior and vicious circles of a patient's extant personality pathology.

Of course, individuals differ with respect to the domains they enact most frequently. People vary not only in the degree to which they approximate each personality prototype but also in the extent to which each domain dominates their behavior. In conceptualizing personality as a system, we must recognize that different parts of the system will be dominant in different individuals, even when those individuals are patients who share the same prototypal diagnosis. It is the goal of the MG-PDC to *differentiate, operationalize,* and *measure quantitatively* those domain features that are primary in contributing to the person's functioning. Thus identified, the instrument should help orient the clinical therapist to modify the person's problematic features (e.g., interpersonal conduct, cognitive beliefs), and thereby enable the patient to acquire a greater variety of adaptive behaviors in his or her life circumstances.

The reader may wish to review the trait options that constitute the choices for each of the domains. While reading and thinking about the several domain descriptions, and to help guide your choices, feel comfortable in moving freely, back and forth, as you proceed. For example, while working on reviewing the trait options for the Expressive Behavior domain, do not hesitate to look at the trait descriptions for any of the other domains (e.g., Interpersonal Conduct) if by doing so you may be aided in understanding the characteristics of the Expressive Behavior group of choices.

For each of the domains in Tables 1.1 through 1.8, beginning with Expressive Behavior, you will see 15 descriptive trait choices. Locate the descriptive choice that appears to you to *best fit* in characterizing the patient you are thinking about. You would fill in that choice in the 1 box column.

Because most people can be characterized by more than one expressive behavior trait, locate a second-best-fit descriptive characteristic, one not as applicable to this person as the first best fit you selected, but notable nonetheless. Fill in the 2 box, the second-best-fit column.

Should there be other listed descriptive trait features that are applicable to this person, but less so than the one selected as second best, fill in the 3 box in the third-best-fit column. You may fill in up to three boxes in the third-best-fit column. (Note that only one trait description may be marked in each of the first- and second-best-fit columns.)

Consider the following points as you proceed. The 15 descriptive traits for each domain were written to characterize patients. Further, each trait is illustrated with several clinical characteristics and examples. Note that the person you are rating need not display precisely the characteristics that are listed; they need only be the best fit of the listed group of features. It is important to note also that for rated persons of a nonclinical character, that is, normal personalities who display only minor or mild aspects of the trait characteristic, you should, nevertheless, fully mark the best-fit columns (even though the descriptor is characterized with a more serious clinical description than suits the person). In short, *do not* leave any of the best-fit columns blank. Fill them in, in rank best-fit order, even when the features of the trait are only marginally present.

After completing ratings for the Expressive Behavior domain, you would proceed to fill in your choices for the next seven domains, one at a time, using the same first, second, and third ratings you followed previously.

Because readers of this text are not actually completing the following MG-PDC judgment forms, it will be useful for them to know which personality prototype corresponds to the letters that precede each of the descriptors. For example, in the Expressive Behavior domain, note that the letter A precedes the first descriptor, "Impassive." The letter A signifies that this descriptor characterizes the Retiring/Schizoid Prototype. Each of the following letters on all eight domains corresponds to the following associated prototypes:

A. Retiring/Schizoid

B. Eccentric/Schizotypal

C. Shy/Avoidant

D. Needy/Dependent

E. Exuberant/Hypomanic

F. Sociable/Histrionic

G. Confident/Narcissistic

H. Suspicious/Paranoid

I. Nonconforming/Antisocial

J. Assertive/Sadistic

K. Pessimistic/Melancholic (Depressive)

L. Aggrieved/Masochistic

M. Skeptical/Negativistic

N. Capricious/Borderline

O. Conscientious/Compulsive

On the basis of your knowledge of the person you have evaluated, using the domain categories listed in Tables 1.1 through 1.8, summarize your judgments by making an overall 1st, 2nd, and 3rd best fit personality spectrum diagnosis on Table 1.9.

Empirical and theoretical developments of the past decade have led to an expansion in the number of personality disorder types and subtypes in the recent and forthcoming literature. Likewise, there has been a growing interest in refining the disorders into a continuum or spectrum from normal to abnormal personalities. Toward the end of contributing further to these advances, we would like you to select, as best you can,

Table 1.1 *MG-PDC* I. Expressive Behavior DOMAIN

These attributes relate to observables at the *behavioral level* of emotion and are usually recorded by noting how the patient acts. Through inference, observations of overt behavior enable us to deduce what the patient unknowingly reveals about his or her emotions or, often conversely, what he or she wants others to think about him or her. The range and character of expressive actions are wide and diverse and they convey distinctive and worthwhile clinical information, from communicating a sense of personal incompetence to exhibiting emotional defensiveness to demonstrating disciplined self-control, and so on.

1st Best Fit	2nd Best Fit	3rd Best Fit	Characteristic Behavior
1	2	3	**A. Impassive:** Is colorless, sluggish, displaying deficits in activation and emotional expressiveness; appears to be in a persistent state of low energy and lack of vitality (e.g., phlegmatic and lacking in spontaneity).
1	2	3	**B. Peculiar:** Is perceived by others as eccentric, disposed to behave in an unobtrusively aloof, curious, or bizarre manner; exhibits socially gauche habits and aberrant mannerisms (e.g., manifestly odd or eccentric).
1	2	3	**C. Fretful:** Fearfully scans environment for social derogation; overreacts to innocuous events and judges them to signify personal derision and mockery (e.g., anxiously anticipates ridicule/humiliation).
1	2	3	**D. Incompetent:** Ill-equipped to assume mature and independent roles; is passive and lacking functional competencies, avoiding self-assertion and withdrawing from adult responsibilities (e.g., has difficulty doing things on his or her own).
1	2	3	**E. Impetuous:** Is forcefully energetic and driven, emotionally excitable, and overzealous; often worked up, unrestrained, rash, and hotheaded (e.g., is restless and socially intrusive).
1	2	3	**F. Dramatic:** Is histrionically overreactive and stimulus-seeking, resulting in unreflected and theatrical responsiveness; describes penchant for sensational situations and short-sighted hedonism (e.g., overly emotional and artificially affected).
1	2	3	**G. Haughty:** Manifests an air of being above conventional rules of shared social living, viewing them as naive or inapplicable to self; reveals an egocentric indifference to the needs of others (e.g., acts arrogantly self-assured and confident).

Table 1.1 *(Continued)*

1st Best Fit	2nd Best Fit	3rd Best Fit	Characteristic Behavior
1	2	3	**H. Defensive:** Is vigilantly guarded, hyperalert to ward off anticipated deception and malice; is tenaciously resistant to sources of external influence (e.g., disposed to be wary, envious, and jealous).
1	2	3	**I. Impulsive:** Since adolescence, acts thoughtlessly and irresponsibly in social matters; is shortsighted, heedless, incautious, and imprudent, failing to plan ahead or consider legal consequences (e.g., Conduct Disorder evident before age 15).
1	2	3	**J. Precipitate:** Is stormy and unpredictably abrupt, reckless, thick-skinned, and unflinching, seemingly undeterred by pain; is attracted to challenge, as well as undaunted by punishment (e.g., attracted to risk, danger, and harm).
1	2	3	**K. Disconsolate:** Appearance and posture convey an irrelievably forlorn, heavy-hearted, if not grief-stricken quality; markedly dispirited and discouraged (e.g., somberly seeks others to be protective).
1	2	3	**L. Abstinent:** Presents self as nonindulgent, frugal, and chaste, refraining from exhibiting signs of pleasure or attractiveness; acts in an unpresuming and self-effacing manner, placing self in an inferior light (e.g., undermines own good fortune).
1	2	3	**M. Resentful:** Exhibits inefficiency, erratic, contrary, and irksome behaviors; reveals gratification in undermining the pleasures and expectations of others (e.g., uncooperative, contrary, and stubborn).
1	2	3	**N. Spasmodic:** Displays a desultory energy level with sudden, unexpected self-punitive outbursts; endogenous shifts in emotional state places behavioral equilibrium in constant jeopardy (e.g., does impulsive, self-damaging acts).
1	2	3	**O. Disciplined:** Maintains a regulated, emotionally restrained, and highly organized life; often insists that others adhere to personally established rules and methods (e.g., meticulous and perfectionistic).

Table 1.2 *MG-PDC* II. Interpersonal Conduct DOMAIN

A patient's style of relating to others may be captured in a number of ways, such as how his or her actions affect others, intended or otherwise; the attitudes that underlie, prompt, and give shape to these actions; the methods by which he or she engages others to meet his or her needs; and his or her way of coping with social tensions and conflicts. Extrapolating from these observations, the clinican may construct an image of how the patient functions in relation to others.

1st Best Fit	2nd Best Fit	3rd Best Fit	Characteristic Conduct
1	2	3	**A. Unengaged:** Is indifferent to the actions or feelings of others, possessing minimal "human" interests; ends up with few close relationships and a limited role in work and family settings (e.g., has few desires or interests).
1	2	3	**B. Secretive:** Strives for privacy, with limited personal attachments and obligations; drifts into increasingly remote and clandestine social activities (e.g., is enigmatic and withdrawn).
1	2	3	**C. Aversive:** Reports extensive history of social anxiety and isolation; seeks social acceptance, but maintains careful distance to avoid anticipated humiliation and derogation (e.g., is socially pan-anxious and fearfully guarded).
1	2	3	**D. Submissive:** Subordinates needs to a stronger and nurturing person, without whom will feel alone and anxiously helpless; is compliant, conciliatory, and self-sacrificing (e.g., generally docile, deferential, and placating).
1	2	3	**E. High-Spirited:** Is unremittingly full of life and socially buoyant; attempts to engage others in an animated, vivacious, and lively manner; often seen by others, however, as intrusive and needlessly insistent (e.g., is persistently overbearing).
1	2	3	**F. Attention-Seeking:** Is self-dramatizing, and actively solicits praise in a showy manner to gain desired attention and approval; manipulates others and is emotionally demanding (e.g., seductively flirtatious and exhibitionistic).
1	2	3	**G. Exploitive:** Acts entitled, self-centered, vain, and unempathic; expects special favors without assuming reciprocal responsibilities; shamelessly takes others for granted and uses them to enhance self and indulge desires (e.g., egocentric and socially inconsiderate).

Table 1.2   *(Continued)*

1st Best Fit	2nd Best Fit	3rd Best Fit	Characteristic Conduct
1	2	3	**H. Provocative:** Displays a quarrelsome, fractious, and distrustful attitude; bears serious grudges and precipitates exasperation by a testing of loyalties and a searching preoccupation with hidden motives (e.g., unjustly questions fidelity of spouse/friend).
1	2	3	**I. Irresponsible:** Is socially untrustworthy and unreliable, intentionally or carelessly failing to meet personal obligations of a marital, parental, employment, or financial nature; actively violates established civil codes through duplicitous or illegal behaviors (e.g., shows active disregard for rights of others).
1	2	3	**J. Abrasive:** Reveals satisfaction in competing with, dominating, and humiliating others; regularly expresses verbally abusive and derisive social commentary, as well as exhibiting harsh, if not physically brutal behavior (e.g., intimidates, coerces, and demeans others).
1	2	3	**K. Defenseless:** Feels and acts vulnerable and guilt-ridden; fears emotional abandonment and seeks public assurances of affection and devotion (e.g., needs supportive relationships to bolster hopeless outlook).
1	2	3	**L. Deferential:** Relates to others in a self-sacrificing, servile, and obsequious manner, allowing, if not encouraging others to exploit or take advantage; is self-abasing, accepting undeserved blame and unjust criticism (e.g., courts others to be exploitive and mistreating).
1	2	3	**M. Contrary:** Assumes conflicting roles in social relationships, shifting from dependent acquiescence to assertive independence; is obstructive toward others, behaving either negatively or erratically (e.g., sulky and argumentative in response to requests).
1	2	3	**N. Paradoxical:** Needing extreme attention and affection, but acts unpredictably and manipulatively and is volatile, frequently eliciting rejection rather than support; reacts to fears of separation and isolation in angry, mercurial, and often self-damaging ways (e.g., is emotionally needy, but interpersonally erratic).
1	2	3	**O. Respectful:** Exhibits unusual adherence to social conventions and proprieties; prefers polite, formal, and "correct" personal relationships (e.g., interpersonally proper and dutiful).

Table 1.3 *MG-PDC* III. Cognitive Style/Content DOMAIN

How the patient focuses and allocates attention, encodes and processes information, organizes thoughts, makes attributions, and communicates reactions and ideas to others represents key cognitive functions of clinical value. These characteristics are among the most useful indices of the patient's distinctive way of thinking. By synthesizing his or her beliefs and attitudes, it may be possible to identify indications of problematic cognitive functions and assumptions.

1st Best Fit	2nd Best Fit	3rd Best Fit	Characteristic Cognitive Style
1	2	3	**A. Impoverished:** Seems deficient in human spheres of knowledge and evidences vague thought processes about everyday matters that are below intellectual level; social communications are easily derailed or conveyed via a circuitous logic (e.g., lacks awareness of human relations).
1	2	3	**B. Autistic:** Intrudes social communications with personal irrelevancies; there is notable circumstantial speech, ideas of reference, and metaphorical asides; is ruminative, appears self-absorbed and lost in occasional magical thinking; there is a marked blurring of fantasy and reality (e.g., exhibits peculiar ideas and superstitious beliefs).
1	2	3	**C. Distracted:** Is bothered by disruptive and often distressing inner thoughts; the upsurge from within of irrelevant and digressive ideation upsets thought continuity and interferes with social communications (e.g., withdraws into reveries to fulfill needs).
1	2	3	**D. Naive:** Is easily persuaded, unsuspicious, and gullible; reveals a Pollyanna attitude toward interpersonal difficulties, watering down objective problems and smoothing over troubling events (e.g., childlike thinking and reasoning).
1	2	3	**E. Scattered:** Thoughts are momentary and scrambled in an untidy disarray with minimal focus to them, resulting in a chaotic hodgepodge of miscellaneous and haphazard beliefs expressed randomly with no logic or purpose (e.g., intense and transient emotions disorganize thoughts).
1	2	3	**F. Flighty:** Avoids introspective thought and is overly attentive to trivial and fleeting external events; integrates experiences poorly, resulting in shallow learning and thoughtless judgments (e.g., faddish and responsive to superficialities).
1	2	3	**G. Expansive:** Has an undisciplined imagination and exhibits a preoccupation with illusory fantasies of success, beauty, or love; is minimally constrained by objective reality; takes liberties with facts and seeks to redeem boastful beliefs (e.g., indulges fantasies of repute/power).

Table 1.3 (*Continued*)

1st Best Fit	2nd Best Fit	3rd Best Fit	Characteristic Cognitive Style
1	2	3	**H. Mistrustful:** Is suspicious of the motives of others, construing innocuous events as signifying conspiratorial intent; magnifies tangential or minor social difficulties into proofs of duplicity, malice, and treachery (e.g., wary and distrustful).
1	2	3	**I. Deviant:** Construes ordinary events and personal relationships in accord with socially unorthodox beliefs and morals; is disdainful of traditional ideals and conventional rules (e.g., shows contempt for social ethics and morals).
1	2	3	**J. Dogmatic:** Is strongly opinionated, as well as unbending and obstinate in holding to his or her preconceptions; exhibits a broad social intolerance and prejudice (e.g., closed-minded and bigoted).
1	2	3	**K. Fatalistic:** Sees things in their blackest form and invariably expects the worst; gives the gloomiest interpretation of current events, believing that things will never improve (e.g., conceives life events in persistent pessimistic terms).
1	2	3	**L. Diffident:** Is hesitant to voice his or her views; often expresses attitudes contrary to inner beliefs; experiences contrasting and conflicting thoughts toward self and others (e.g., demeans own convictions and opinions).
1	2	3	**M. Cynical:** Skeptical and untrusting, approaching current events with disbelief and future possibilities with trepidation; has a misanthropic view of life, expressing disdain and caustic comments toward those who experience good fortune (e.g., envious or disdainful of those more fortunate).
1	2	3	**N. Vacillating:** Experiences rapidly changing, fluctuating, and antithetical perceptions or thoughts concerning passing events; contradictory reactions are evoked in others by virtue of his or her behaviors, creating, in turn, conflicting and confusing social feedback (e.g., erratic and contrite over own beliefs and attitudes).
1	2	3	**O. Constricted:** Constructs world in terms of rules, regulations, time schedules, and social hierarchies; is unimaginative, indecisive, and notably upset by unfamiliar or novel ideas and customs (e.g., preoccupied with lists, details, rules, etc.).

Table 1.4 *MG-PDC* **IV. Self-Image DOMAIN**

As the inner world of symbols is mastered through development, one major configuration emerges to impose a measure of sameness on an otherwise fluid environment: the perception of self-as-object, a distinct, ever-present identity. Self-image is significant in that it serves as a guidepost and lends continuity to changing experience. Most patients have an implicit sense of who they are but differ greatly in the clarity, accuracy, and complexity of their introspection of the psychic elements that make up this image.

1st Best Fit	2nd Best Fit	3rd Best Fit	Characteristic Self-Image
1	2	3	**A. Complacent:** Reveals minimal introspection and awareness of self; seems impervious to the emotional and personal implications of his or her role in everyday social life (e.g., minimal interest in own personal life).
1	2	3	**B. Estranged:** Possesses permeable ego boundaries, exhibiting acute social perplexities and illusions as well as experiences of depersonalization, derealization, and dissociation; sees self as "different," with repetitive thoughts of life's confusions and meaninglessness (e.g., self-perceptions are haphazard and fragmented).
1	2	3	**C. Alienated:** Sees self as a socially isolated person, one rejected by others; devalues self-achievements and reports feelings of aloneness and undesirability (e.g., feels injured and unwanted by others).
1	2	3	**D. Inept:** Views self as weak, fragile, and inadequate; exhibits lack of self-confidence by belittling own aptitudes and competencies (e.g., sees self as childlike and/or fragile).
1	2	3	**E. Energetic:** Sees self as full of vim and vigor, a dynamic force, invariably hardy and robust, a tireless and enterprising person whose ever-present energy galvanizes others (e.g., proud to be active and animated).
1	2	3	**F. Gregarious:** Views self as socially stimulating and charming; enjoys the image of attracting acquaintances and pursuing a busy and pleasure-oriented social life (e.g., perceived as appealing and attractive, but shallow).
1	2	3	**G. Admirable:** Confidently exhibits self, acts in a self-assured manner, and publicly displays achievements, despite being seen by others as egotistic, inconsiderate, and arrogant (e.g., has a sense of high self-worth).

Table 1.4 (*Continued*)

1st Best Fit	2nd Best Fit	3rd Best Fit	Characteristic Self-Image
1	2	3	*H. Inviolable:* Is highly insular, experiencing intense fears of losing identity, status, or powers of self-determination; nevertheless, has persistent ideas of self-reference, asserting as personally derogatory and scurrilous entirely innocuous actions and events (e.g., sees ordinary life events as invariably referring to self).
1	2	3	*I. Autonomous:* Values the sense of being free, unencumbered, and unconfined by persons, places, obligations, or routines; sees self as unfettered by the restrictions of social customs and the restraints of personal loyalties (e.g., values being independent of social responsibilities).
1	2	3	*J. Combative:* Values aspects of self that present tough, domineering, and power-oriented image; is proud to characterize self as unsympathetic and unsentimental (e.g., proud to be stern and feared by others).
1	2	3	*K. Worthless:* Sees self as valueless, of no account, a person who should be overlooked, owing to having no praiseworthy traits or achievements (e.g., sees self as insignificant or inconsequential).
1	2	3	*L. Undeserving:* Focuses on and amplifies the very worst features of self; judges self as worthy of being shamed, humbled, and debased; has failed to live up to the expectations of others and, hence, should be reproached and demeaned (e.g., sees self as deserving to suffer).
1	2	3	*M. Discontented:* Sees self as unjustly misunderstood and unappreciated; recognizes that he or she is characteristically resentful, disgruntled, and disillusioned with life (e.g., sees self as unfairly treated).
1	2	3	*N. Uncertain:* Experiences the marked confusions of a nebulous or wavering sense of identity and self-worth; seeks to redeem erratic actions and changing self-presentations with expressions of contrition and self-punitive behaviors (e.g., has persistent identity disturbances).
1	2	3	*O. Reliable:* Sees self as industrious, meticulous, and efficient; fearful of error or misjudgment and, hence, overvalues aspects of self that exhibit discipline, perfection, prudence, and loyalty (e.g., sees self as reliable and conscientious).

Table 1.5   *MG-PDC* **V. Mood/Affect DOMAIN**

Few observables are more clinically relevant than the predominant character of an individual's affect and the intensity and frequency with which he or she expresses it. The meaning of extreme emotions is easy to decode. This is not so with the more subtle moods and feelings that insidiously and repetitively pervade the patient's ongoing relationships and experiences. The expressive features of mood/affect may be revealed, albeit indirectly, in activity level, speech quality, and physical appearance.

1st Best Fit	2nd Best Fit	3rd Best Fit	Characteristic Mood
1	2	3	**A. Apathetic:** Is emotionally impassive, exhibiting an intrinsic unfeeling, cold, and stark quality; reports weak affectionate or erotic needs, rarely displaying warm or intense feelings, and apparently unable also to experience either sadness or anger (e.g., unable to experience pleasure in depth).
1	2	3	**B. Distraught or Insentient:** Reports being *either* apprehensive and ill at ease, particularly in social encounters; anxiously watchful, distrustful of others, and wary of their motives; *or* manifests drab, sluggish, joyless, and spiritless appearance; reveals marked deficiencies in emotional expression and in face-to-face encounters (e.g., highly agitated and/or affectively flat).
1	2	3	**C. Anguished:** Vacillates between desire for affection, fear of rebuff, and numbness of feeling; describes constant and confusing undercurrents of tension, sadness, and anger (e.g., unusually fearful of new social experiences).
1	2	3	**D. Pacific:** Quietly and passively avoids social tension and interpersonal conflicts; is typically pleasant, warm, tender, and noncompetitive (e.g., characteristically timid and uncompetitive).
1	2	3	**E. Mercurial:** Volatile and quicksilverish, at times unduly ebullient, charged up, and irrepressible; at other times, flighty and erratic emotionally, blowing hot and cold (e.g., has marked penchant for momentary excitements).
1	2	3	**F. Fickle:** Displays short-lived and superficial emotions; is dramatically overreactive and exhibits tendencies to be easily enthused and as easily bored (e.g., impetuously pursues pleasure-oriented social life).

Table 1.5 (*Continued*)

1st Best Fit	2nd Best Fit	3rd Best Fit	Characteristic Mood
1	2	3	**G. Insouciant:** Manifests a general air of nonchalance and indifference; appears coolly unimpressionable or calmly optimistic, except when self-centered confidence is shaken, at which time either rage, shame, or emptiness is briefly displayed (e.g., generally appears imperturbable and composed).
1	2	3	**H. Irascible:** Displays a sullen, churlish, and humorless demeanor; attempts to appear unemotional and objective, but is edgy, touchy, surly, quick to react angrily (e.g., ready to take personal offense).
1	2	3	**I. Callous:** Exhibits a coarse incivility, as well as a ruthless indifference to the welfare of others; is unempathic, as expressed in wide-ranging deficits in social charitableness, human compassion, or personal remorse (e.g., experiences minimal guilt or contrition for socially repugnant actions).
1	2	3	**J. Hostile:** Has an overtly rough and pugnacious temper, which flares periodically into contentious argument and physical belligerence; is fractious, willing to do harm, even persecute others to get own way (e.g., easily embroiled in brawls).
1	2	3	**K. Woeful:** Is typically mournful, tearful, joyless, and morose; characteristically worrisome and brooding; low spirits rarely remit (e.g., frequently feels dejected or guilty).
1	2	3	**L. Dysphoric:** Intentionally displays a plaintive and gloomy appearance, occasionally to induce guilt and discomfort in others (e.g., drawn to relationships in which he or she will suffer).
1	2	3	**M. Irritable:** Is often petulant, reporting being easily annoyed or frustrated by others; typically obstinate and resentful, followed in turn by sulky and grumpy withdrawal (e.g., impatient and easily provoked into oppositional behavior).
1	2	3	**N. Labile:** Fails to accord unstable moods with external reality; has marked shifts from normality to depression to excitement, or has extended periods of dejection and apathy, interspersed with brief spells of anger, anxiety, or euphoria (e.g., mood changes erratically from sadness to bitterness to torpor).
1	2	3	**O. Solemn:** Is unrelaxed, tense, joyless, and grim; restrains overtly warm or covertly antagonistic feelings, keeping most emotions under tight control (e.g., affect is constricted and confined).

Table 1.6   *MG-PDC* **VI. Intrapsychic Mechanisms DOMAIN**

Although mechanisms of self-protection, need gratification, and conflict resolution are consciously recognized at times, they represent data derived primarily at the intrapsychic level. Because the ego or defense mechanisms are internal regulatory processes, they are more difficult to discern and describe than processes that are anchored closer to the observable world. As such, they are not directly amenable to assessment by self-reflective appraisal in their pure form but only as derivatives that are potentially many levels removed from their core conflicts and their dynamic resolution. Despite the methodological problems they present, the task of identifying which mechanisms are most characteristic of a patient and the extent to which they are employed is extremely useful in a comprehensive clinical assessment.

1st Best Fit	2nd Best Fit	3rd Best Fit	Characteristic Mechanism
1	2	3	**A. Intellectualization:** Describes interpersonal and affective experiences in a matter-of-fact, abstract, impersonal, or mechanical manner; pays primary attention to formal and objective aspects of social and emotional events.
1	2	3	**B. Undoing:** Bizarre mannerisms and idiosyncratic thoughts appear to reflect a retraction or reversal of previous acts or ideas that have stirred feelings of anxiety, conflict, or guilt; ritualistic or "magical" behaviors serve to repent for or nullify assumed misdeeds or "evil" thoughts.
1	2	3	**C. Fantasy:** Depends excessively on imagination to achieve need gratification and conflict resolution; withdraws into reveries as a means of safely discharging affectionate as well as aggressive impulses.
1	2	3	**D. Introjection:** Is firmly devoted to another to strengthen the belief that an inseparable bond exists between them; jettisons any independent views in favor of those of another to preclude conflicts and threats to the relationship.
1	2	3	**E. Magnification:** Engages in hyperbole, overstating and overemphasizing ordinary matters so as to elevate their importance, especially features that enhance not only his or her own virtues but those of others who are valued.
1	2	3	**F. Dissociation:** Regularly alters self presentations to create a succession of socially attractive but changing façades; engages in self-distracting activities to avoid reflecting on/integrating unpleasant thoughts/emotions.
1	2	3	**G. Rationalization:** Is self-deceptive and facile in devising plausible reasons to justify self-centered and socially inconsiderate behaviors; offers alibis to place self in the best possible light, despite evident shortcomings or failures.

Table 1.6 (*Continued*)

1st Best Fit	2nd Best Fit	3rd Best Fit	Characteristic Mechanism
1	2	3	**H. Projection:** Actively disowns undesirable personal traits and motives and attributes them to others; remains blind to own unattractive behaviors and characteristics, yet is overalert to and hypercritical of the defects of others.
1	2	3	**I. Acting Out:** Inner tensions that might accrue by postponing the expression of offensive thoughts and malevolent actions are rarely constrained; socially repugnant impulses are not refashioned in sublimated forms, but are discharged directly in precipitous ways, usually without guilt.
1	2	3	**J. Isolation:** Can be cold-blooded and remarkably detached from an awareness of the impact of his or her destructive acts; views objects of violation impersonally, often as symbols of devalued groups devoid of human sensibilities.
1	2	3	**K. Asceticism:** Engages in acts of self-denial, self-tormenting, and self-punishment, believing that one should exhibit penance and not be rewarded with life's bounties; not only is there a repudiation of pleasures but there are harsh self-judgments and minor self-destructive acts.
1	2	3	**L. Exaggeration:** Repetitively recalls past injuries and seeks out future disappointments as a means of raising distress to troubled homeostatic levels; misconstrues, if not sabotages, personal good fortunes to enhance or maintain preferred suffering and pain.
1	2	3	**M. Displacement:** Discharges anger and other troublesome emotions either indirectly or by shifting them from their true objective to settings or persons of lesser peril; expresses resentments by substitute or passive means, such as acting inept or perplexed, or behaving in a forgetful or indolent manner.
1	2	3	**N. Regression:** Retreats under stress to developmentally earlier levels of anxiety tolerance, impulse control, and social adaptation; is unable or disinclined to cope with responsible tasks and adult issues, as evident in immature, if not increasingly childlike behaviors.
1	2	3	**O. Reaction Formation:** Repeatedly presents positive thoughts and socially commendable behaviors that are diametrically opposite to his or her deeper, contrary, and forbidden feelings; displays reasonableness and maturity when faced with circumstances that normally evoke anger or dismay in most persons.

Table 1.7 *MG-PDC* **VII. Intrapsychic Content DOMAIN**

Significant experiences from the past leave an inner imprint, a structural residue composed of memories, attitudes, and affects that serve as a substrate of dispositions for perceiving and reacting to life's events. Analogous to the various organ systems in the body, both the character and the substance of these internalized representations of significant figures and relationships from the past can be differentiated and analyzed for clinical purposes. Variations in the nature and content of this inner world, or what are often called *object relations*, can be identified with one or another personality and lead us to employ the following descriptive terms to represent them.

1st Best Fit	2nd Best Fit	3rd Best Fit	Characteristic Content
1	2	3	**A. Meager:** Inner representations are few in number and minimally articulated, largely devoid of the manifold percepts and memories, or the dynamic interplay among drives and conflicts that typify even well-adjusted persons.
1	2	3	**B. Chaotic:** Inner representations consist of a jumble of miscellaneous memories and percepts, random drives and impulses, and uncoordinated channels of regulation that are only fitfully competent for binding tensions, accommodating needs, and mediating conflicts.
1	2	3	**C. Vexatious:** Inner representations are composed of readily reactivated, intense, and anxiety-ridden memories, limited avenues of gratification, and few mechanisms to channel needs, bind impulses, resolve conflicts, or deflect external stressors.
1	2	3	**D. Immature:** Inner representations are composed of unsophisticated ideas and incomplete memories, rudimentary drives and childlike impulses, as well as minimal competencies to manage and resolve stressors.
1	2	3	**E. Piecemeal:** Inner representations are disorganized and dissipated, a jumble of diluted and muddled recollections that are recalled by fits and starts, serving only as momentary guideposts for dealing with everyday tensions and conflicts.
1	2	3	**F. Shallow:** Inner representations are composed largely of superficial yet emotionally intense affects, memories, and conflicts, as well as facile drives and insubstantial mechanisms.
1	2	3	**G. Contrived:** Inner representations are composed far more than usual of illusory ideas and memories, synthetic drives and conflicts, and pretentious, if not simulated, percepts and attitudes, all of which are readily refashioned as the need arises.

Table 1.7 (*Continued*)

1st Best Fit	2nd Best Fit	3rd Best Fit	Characteristic Content
1	2	3	**H. Unalterable:** Inner representations are arranged in an unusual configuration of rigidly held attitudes, unyielding percepts, and implacable drives, which are aligned in a semidelusional hierarchy of tenacious memories, immutable cognitions, and irrevocable beliefs.
1	2	3	**I. Debased:** Inner representations are a mix of revengeful attitudes and impulses oriented to subvert established cultural ideals and mores, as well as to debase personal sentiments and conventional societal attainments.
1	2	3	**J. Pernicious:** Inner representations are distinguished by the presence of aggressive energies and malicious attitudes, as well as by a contrasting paucity of sentimental memories, tender affects, internal conflicts, shame, or guilt feelings.
1	2	3	**K. Forsaken:** Inner representations have been depleted or devitalized, either drained of their richness and joyful elements or withdrawn from memory, leaving the person to feel abandoned, bereft, discarded.
1	2	3	**L. Discredited:** Inner representations are composed of disparaged past memories and discredited achievements, of positive feelings and erotic drives transposed onto their least attractive opposites, of internal conflicts intentionally aggravated, of mechanisms of anxiety reduction subverted by processes that intensify discomforts.
1	2	3	**M. Fluctuating:** Inner representations compose a complex of opposing inclinations and incompatible memories that are driven by impulses designed to nullify his or her own achievements and/or the pleasures and expectations of others.
1	2	3	**N. Incompatible:** Rudimentary and expediently devised, but repetitively aborted, inner representations have led to perplexing memories, enigmatic attitudes, contradictory needs, antithetical emotions, erratic impulses, and opposing strategies for conflict reduction.
1	2	3	**O. Concealed:** Only those inner affects, attitudes, and actions that are socially approved are allowed conscious awareness or behavioral expression, resulting in gratification being highly regulated, forbidden impulses sequestered and tightly bound, personal and social conflicts defensively denied, kept from awareness, all maintained under stringent control.

Table 1.8 *MG-PDC* VIII. Intrapsychic Structure DOMAIN

The overall architecture that serves as a framework for an individual's psychic interior may display weakness in its structural cohesion, exhibit deficient coordination among its components, and possess few mechanisms to maintain balance and harmony, regulate internal conflicts, or mediate external pressures. The concept of intrapsychic structure refers to the organizational strength, interior congruity, and functional efficacy of the personality system, a concept almost exclusively derived from inferences at the *intrapsychic* level of analysis. Psychoanalytic usage tends to be limited to quantitative degrees of integrative pathology, not to *qualitative variations* in either integrative structure or configuration. Stylistic variants of this structural attribute, such as the following, may be employed to characterize each of the personality prototypes.

1st Best Fit	2nd Best Fit	3rd Best Fit	Characteristic Structure
1	2	3	**A. Undifferentiated:** Given an inner barrenness, a feeble drive to fulfill needs, and minimal pressures to defend against or resolve internal conflicts, or to cope with external demands, internal structures may best be characterized by their limited coordination and deficient organization.
1	2	3	**B. Fragmented:** Coping and defensive operations are haphazardly organized in a fragile assemblage, leading to spasmodic and desultory actions in which primitive thoughts and affects are directly discharged, with few reality-based sublimations, leading to significant further structural disintegrations.
1	2	3	**C. Fragile:** Tortuous emotions depend almost exclusively on a single modality for their resolution and discharge, that of avoidance, escape, and fantasy; hence, when faced with unanticipated stress, there are few resources available to deploy and few positions to revert to, short of a regressive decompensation.
1	2	3	**D. Inchoate:** Owing to entrusting others with the responsibility to fulfill needs and to cope with adult tasks, there is both a deficit and a lack of diversity in internal structures and controls, leaving a miscellany of relatively undeveloped and immature adaptive abilities and elementary systems for independent functioning.
1	2	3	**E. Fleeting:** Structures are highly transient, existing in momentary forms that are cluttered and disarranged, making effective coping efforts temporary at best. Affect and action are unconstrained owing to the paucity of established controls and purposeful goals.

Table 1.8 (*Continued*)

1st Best Fit	2nd Best Fit	3rd Best Fit	Characteristic Structure
1	2	3	**F. Disjointed:** A loosely knit structural conglomerate exists in which processes of internal regulation and control are scattered and unintegrated, with few methods for restraining impulses, coordinating defenses, and resolving conflicts, leading to broad and sweeping mechanisms to maintain psychic cohesion and stability and, when employed, only further disarrange thoughts, feelings, and actions.
1	2	3	**G. Spurious:** Coping and defensive strategies tend to be flimsy and transparent, appear more substantial and dynamically orchestrated than they are, regulating impulses only marginally, channeling needs with minimal restraint, and creating an egocentric inner world in which conflicts are dismissed, failures are quickly redeemed, and self-pride is effortlessly reasserted.
1	2	3	**H. Inelastic:** A markedly constricted and inflexible pattern of coping and defensive methods exists, as well as rigidly fixed channels of conflict mediation and need gratification, creates an overstrung and taut frame that is so uncompromising in its accommodation to changing circumstances that unanticipated stressors are likely to precipitate either explosive outbursts or inner shatterings.
1	2	3	**I. Unruly:** Inner defensive operations are noted by their paucity, as are efforts to curb irresponsible drives and attitudes, leading to easily transgressed social controls, low thresholds for impulse discharge, few subliminatory channels, unfettered self-expression, and a marked intolerance of delay or frustration.
1	2	3	**J. Eruptive:** Despite a generally cohesive structure of routinely modulating controls and expressive channels, surging, powerful, and explosive energies of an aggressive and sexual nature produce precipitous outbursts that periodically overwhelm and overrun otherwise reasonable restraints.
1	2	3	**K. Depleted:** The scaffold for structures is markedly weakened, with coping methods enervated and defensive strategies impoverished and devoid of vigor and focus, resulting in a diminished if not exhausted capacity to initiate action and regulate affect.
1	2	3	**L. Inverted:** Structures have a dual quality, one more or less conventional, the other its obverse—resulting in a repetitive undoing of affect and intention, of a transposing of channels of need gratification with those leading to their frustration, and of actions that produce antithetical, if not self-sabotaging consequences.

(*continued*)

Table 1.8 *(Continued)*

1st Best Fit	2nd Best Fit	3rd Best Fit	Characteristic Structure
1	2	3	**M. Divergent:** There is a clear division in the pattern of internal elements such that coping and defensive maneuvers are often directed toward incompatible goals, leaving major conflicts unresolved and psychic cohesion impossible, as fulfillment of one drive or need inevitably nullifies or reverses another.
1	2	3	**N. Split:** Inner cohesion constitutes a sharply segmented and conflictful configuration with a marked lack of consistency among elements; levels of consciousness occasionally blur; a rapid shift occurs across boundaries separating unrelated memories/affects, results in schisms upsetting limited extant psychic order.
1	2	3	**O. Compartmentalized:** Psychic structures are rigidly organized in a tightly consolidated system that is clearly partitioned into numerous distinct and segregated constellations of drive, memory, and cognition, with few open channels to permit any interplay among these components.

Table 1.9 Spectra that Best Characterize the Person

1st Best Fit	2nd Best Fit	3rd Best Fit	Normal to Abnormal Personality Spectrum
1	2	3	Retiring—Schizoid
1	2	3	Eccentric—Schizotypal
1	2	3	Shy—Avoidant
1	2	3	Needy—Dependent
1	2	3	Exuberant—Hypomanic
1	2	3	Sociable—Histrionic
1	2	3	Confident—Narcissistic
1	2	3	Suspicious—Paranoid
1	2	3	Nonconforming—Antisocial
1	2	3	Assertive—Sadistic
1	2	3	Pessimistic—Melancholic
1	2	3	Aggrieved—Masochistic
1	2	3	Skeptical—Negativistic
1	2	3	Capricious—Borderline
1	2	3	Conscientious—Compulsive

three of the personality spectra listed in Table 1.9 that you believe may best characterize the person you have just evaluated. As before, select the 1st best fit, the 2nd best fit, and the 3rd best fit. If you wish, you may go back to review your eight domain "first best" choices and *double encircle* the three that you judge most important for therapeutic intervention.

As earlier, we would like you to further evaluate the person you have just rated using the preceding eight domain characteristics. In Table 1.10 please assess his or her current overall level of social and occupational functioning. Make your judgment using the 7-point continuum, which ranges from Excellent to Markedly Impaired. Focus your rating on the individual's present mental state and social competencies, overlooking where possible physical impairments or socioeconomic considerations. Circle the number on the chart that closely approximates your best judgment.

We will return to many of the numerous guiding principles and issues touched on in this extensive chapter as we proceed to the following chapters of this and the third book in the personalized psychotherapy series. Many themes characterizing our rationale for personalized psychotherapy have been presented and argued in the preceding pages. It is hoped that these themes and justifications will become more clearly evident to the reader as we move forward to the next chapters and books.

Potentiated Pairings and Catalytic Sequences

What procedures contributed to making personalized therapy individualized and synergized rather than eclectic?

To restate from earlier paragraphs, there is a separateness among eclectically designed techniques, just a wise selectivity of what works best. In personalized therapy there are psychologically designed *composites* and *progressions* among diverse techniques. In an attempt to formulate them in current writings (Millon, 1988), terms such as "catalytic sequences" and "potentiated pairings" are employed to represent the nature and intent of theory-based polarity- and domain-oriented treatment plans. In essence, they comprise therapeutic arrangements and timing series that will resolve each patient's distinctive polarity imbalances and effect targeted clinical domain changes that would otherwise not occur by the use of several essentially uncoordinated techniques.

The first of the *personalized procedures* we recommended some years ago (Millon, 1988, 1990) was termed "potentiated pairings"; these are treatment methods that are *combined simultaneously* to overcome problematic characteristics that might be refractory to each technique if administered separately. These composites pull and push for change on many different fronts, so that the therapy becomes as multioperational and as tenacious as the disorder itself. A recent and popular illustration of treatment pairings is found in what has been referred to as cognitive-behavior therapy, one of the first of the combinatorial therapies (Craighead, Craighead, Kazdin, & Mahoney, 1994; Rasmussen, 2005).

Table 1.10 Overall Level of Social and Occupational Functioning

Judgment	Rating Number	Description
Excellent	1	Clearly manifests an effective, if not superior level of functioning in relating to family and social peers, even to helping others in resolving their difficulties, as well as demonstrating high occupational performance and success.
Very Good	2	Exhibits considerable social and occupational skills on a reasonably consistent basis, evidencing few if any major areas of interpersonal stress or occupational difficulty.
Good	3	Displays a higher than average level of social and occupational competence in ordinary matters of everyday life. He or she does experience intermittent difficulties in interpersonal relationships and in efforts to achieve work satisfaction.
Fair	4	Functions about average for a typical patient seen in outpatient clinical work. Although able to meet everyday family, social, and occupational responsibilities adequately, there remain problematic or extended periods of occupational stress and/or interpersonal conflict.
Poor	5	Able to be maintained on an outpatient basis, but often precipitates severe conflicts with others that upset his or her equanimity in either or both interpersonal relationships and occupational settings.
Very Poor	6	There is an inability to function competently in most social and occupational settings. Difficulties are precipitated by the patient, destabilizing job performance and upsetting relationships with significant others. Inpatient hospitalization may be necessary to manage periodic severe psychic disruptions.
Markedly Impaired	7	A chronic and marked disintegration is present across most psychic functions. The loss of physical and behavioral controls necessitate extended stays in residential or hospital settings, requiring both sustained care and self-protection.

In the second personalized procedure, termed "catalytic sequences," one might seek first to alter a patient's humiliating and painful stuttering by *behavior modification* procedures, which, if achieved, may facilitate the use of *cognitive or self-actualizing* methods to produce changes in self-confidence, which may, in its turn, foster the utility of *interpersonal* techniques in effecting improvements in relationships with others. Catalytic sequences are timing series that should optimize the impact of changes that would be less effective if the sequential combination were otherwise arranged.

A more recent example has begun to show up in numerous clinical reports this past decade (Slater, 1998). It relates to the fact that patients with depressive personalities or long-term dysthymic disorders have their clinical symptoms markedly reduced by virtue of pharmacologic medications (e.g., selective serotonin reuptake inhibitors [SSRIs]). Although these patients are greatly comforted by the reduction of their clinical symptoms, "depressiveness" has over time become a core part of their overall psychological makeup. Because their depressiveness is no longer a part of their everyday experience, many may now feel empty and confused, not knowing who they are, not knowing to what they may aspire, or how to relate to the world. It is here where a catalytic sequence of psychotherapies may come into play constructively. Patients may no longer be depressed, but they may require therapy for their new self-image and its valuation. No less important to their subsequent treatment will be opportunities to alter their formerly habitual interpersonal styles and attitudes, substituting in their stead social behaviors and cognitions that are more consonant with their current state. Former cognitive assumptions and expectations will no longer be infused with depressogenic elements calling for substantial psychic reformulations.

As the great neurological surgeon and psychologist Kurt Goldstein (1940) stated, patients whose brains have been altered to remedy a major neurological disorder do not simply lose the function that the extirpated area subserved. Rather, patients restructure and reorganize their brain capacities so that they can maintain an integrated sense of self. In a similar way, when one or another major domain of patients' habitual psychological makeup is removed or diminished (e.g., depression), the patients must reorganize themselves, not only to compensate for the loss, but also *to formulate a new self.*

Similarly, the neurologist Oliver Sacks in his 1973 book *Awakenings* describes what happens to patients who had been immobile for decades with encephalitis lethargica who suddenly "unfroze" when given the drug L-Dopa. Although these patients were restored to life, they had to learn to function in a world that had long passed them by. For them, their immobile state had an element of familiarity in which they had learned to cope, miserable though it was, for 10, 20, or 30 years. With the elimination of their adaptive lifestyle, they now had to deal with the new world in which they found themselves, a task that rarely can be managed without considerable guidance and encouragement. Catalytic sequences represent the steps that should be employed in succession to facilitate these relearning and reintegrative processes.

There are no discrete boundaries between potentiated pairings and catalytic sequences, just as there is no line between their respective pathological analogues, that is, adaptive inflexibility and vicious circles (Millon, 1969/1985). Nor should therapists be concerned about when to use one rather than another. Instead, they are intrinsically interdependent phenomena whose application is intended to foster increased flexibility and, hopefully, a virtuous rather than a vicious circle. Potentiated pairings and catalytic sequences represent the logic of combinatorial therapies. The idea of a potentiated sequence or a catalytic pairing recognizes that these logical composites may build on each other in proportion to what the tenacity of the patient's interwoven disorder domains require.

One question concerns the limits to which the content of personalized therapy can be specified in advance, that is, the extent to which specific potentiated pairings and catalytic sequences can be identified for each of the typical complex syndromes and personality disorders that exist. Many of the chapters of this and later texts of this series contain charts that present the salience of each of the clinical domains for that syndrome or disorder. To the extent that each patient's presentations are prototypal, the potentiated pairings and catalytic sequences that may be used should derive from the more or less typical modality tactics that are optimal for their problematic domains, for example, pharmacology for mood/affect. That, however, probably represents the limits to which theory or "therapies that work" can guide clinical practice, that is, without knowing anything about the history and characteristics of the *specific individual case*. Patient individuality is so rich and special that it cannot fit into any ideal taxonomic schema; personalized therapy, properly practiced, is full of specificities that cannot readily be resolved by classification generalities. Potentiated pairings, catalytic sequences, and whatever other higher order composites therapists may evolve are best conducted at an idiographic person level rather than at a nomothetic taxonomic level. Accordingly, their precise content is specified as much by the logic of the individual case as by the logic of the syndrome or disorder. At an idiographic level, each of us must ultimately be artful and open-minded therapists, using simultaneous or alternately focused methods. The synergism and enhancement produced by such catalytic and potentiating processes are what constitute genuinely innovative personalized treatment strategies.

Personalized therapists will be more efficacious if they think about the likely utility of treatment choices in probabilistic terms; that is, they should make concurrent and sequential modality arrangements, knowing that the effectiveness of each component is only partial, and that the probability of success will be less than perfect. To generate a high-probability estimate, therapists must gather all available assessment information and, as do mathematicians, calculate which combination of modalities will have the highest overall probability of being effective. Note that no combinational approach can automatically be judged "best." With each new patient, a therapist should recognize that he or she is dealing with a person whose composite of dispositions and vulnerabilities has never before existed in this exact form. Moreover, it is important that the personalized therapist never think in treatment absolutes, or in black-and-white results; all treatment modalities have reasonable probabilities of success.

There will be many cases in which the pattern of a patient's characteristics does not lend itself to an intelligent estimate of treatment success probabilities. Under such circumstances, therapists should not feel that they must create a long-term or overall plan. Available options in the early stages of treatment may not provide a good, no less an excellent, course of action. Such indeterminate states favor selecting a rather tentative or conservative course—until such time as greater clarity emerges. It should be evident from the foregoing comments that a personalized therapist will be challenged to make a series of difficult judgments, one more demanding and possibly with less assurance as to outcome than if the therapist routinely selected a specific modality for all or most of his or her cases. The latter course will be easier for the therapist, but not necessarily best for the patient. The remainder of this and other books of this series will seek to make the probabilistic task less indeterminate and less onerous. We provide a rationale for which modalities and which combinations are likely to be most effective, given the pattern of the patient's clinical syndromes and personality disorders.

Turning to the specific domains in which clinical problems exhibit themselves, we can address dysfunctions in the realm of interpersonal conduct by employing any number of family or group therapeutic methods, as well as a series of recently evolved and explicitly formulated interpersonal techniques. Methods of classical analysis or its more contemporary schools may be especially suited to the realm of object representations, as would the methods of Beck and Ellis be well chosen to modify difficulties of cognitive beliefs and self-esteem.

Tactics and *strategies* keep in balance the two conceptual ingredients of therapy; the first refers to what goes on with a particular focused intervention, and the second refers to the overall plan or design that characterizes the entire course of therapy. Both are required. Tactical specificity without strategic goals implies doing without knowing why in the big picture, and goals without specificity implies knowing where to go, but having no way to get there. Obviously, one uses short-term modality tactics to accomplish higher level strategies or goals over the long term.

Psychotherapies seem to vary in the amounts of tactical specificity and strategic goals they prefer. This is not often merely an accident of history, but can be tied back to assumptions latent in the therapies themselves. Historically, a progression seems to be toward both greater specificity and clearer goals. More modern approaches to psychotherapy, such as the cognitive-behavioral, put into place highly detailed elements (e.g., agreed upon goals, termination criteria, and ongoing assessments) in which therapy itself becomes a self-regulating system. Ongoing assessments ensure the existence of a feedback process that is open to inspection and negotiation by both therapist and patient. The mode is one of action rather than talk. Talk is viewed as incapable of realizing possibilities in and of itself, but is merely a prerequisite for action, used to reframe unfortunate circumstances so that obstacles to action are removed or minimized. Action is more transactive than talk, and therapy is forward-looking and concentrates on realizing present possibilities as a means of creating or opening up new possibilities. Persons are often changed more through exposure and action than by focusing and unraveling the problems of the past. Insight may be a useful, even necessary but limited goal in itself.

It must be remembered that the primary function of any system is homeostasis. In an early book (Millon, 1981), personality was likened to an immune system for the psyche, such that stability, constancy, and internal equilibrium become the goals of a personality. Obviously, these run directly in opposition to the explicit goal of therapy, which is change. Usually, the dialogue between patient and therapist is not so directly confrontational that it is experienced as particularly threatening. When the patient does feel threatened, the personality system functions for the patient as a form of passive resistance, albeit one that may be experienced as a positive force (or trait) by the therapist. In fact, the structural grounding of a patient's self-image and object representations are so preemptive and confirmation-seeking that the true meaning of the therapist's comments may never reach the level of conscious processing. Alternatively, even if a patient's equilibrium is initially up-ended by a particular interpretation, his or her defensive mechanisms may kick in to ensure that a therapist's comments are somehow distorted, misunderstood, interpreted in a less threatening manner, or even ignored. The first is a passive form of resistance, the second an active form. No wonder, then, that effective therapy is often considered anxiety provoking, for it is in situations where the patient really has no effective response, where the functioning of the psychic immune system is temporarily suppressed, that the scope of his or her response repertoire is most likely to be broadened. Personality goes with what it knows, and it is with the unknown where learning is most possible.

If the psychic makeup of a person is regarded as a system, then the question becomes: How can the characteristics that define systems be co-opted to facilitate rather than retard change? A coordinated schema of strategic goals and tactical modalities for treatment that seeks to accomplish these ends are what we expect to achieve in personalized psychotherapy. Through various coordinated approaches that mirror the system-based composition of the patient's complex clinical syndrome and personality disorder, an effort is made to select domain-focused tactics that will fulfill the strategic goals of treatment.

If interventions are unfocused, rambling, and diffuse, the patient will merely lean forward a little, passively resisting change by using his or her own weight, that is, habitual characteristics already intrinsic to the system. Although creating rapport is always important, nothing happens unless the system is eventually shaken up in some way. Therapists should not always be toiling to expose their patient's defenses, but sooner or later, something must happen that cannot be readily fielded by habitual processes, something that often will be experienced as uncomfortable or even threatening.

In fact, personalized therapy appears in many ways to be like a "punctuated equilibrium" (Eldridge & Gould, 1972) rather than a slow and continuous process. This evolutionary insight argues for periods of rapid growth during which the psychic system reconfigures itself into a new gestalt, alternating with periods of relative constancy. The purpose of keeping to a domain or tactical focus, or knowing clearly what you are doing and why you are doing it, is to keep the whole of the therapeutic enterprise from becoming diffused. The person-focused systems model runs counter to the deterministic universe-as-machine model of the late nineteenth century, which features slow but incremental gains. In the prepunctuated evolutionary model as applied to therapy, moderate interventions become an input that is processed gradually and homeostatically, producing minor, if not zero change. In these earlier procedures, conservation laws play a prominent role; mild interventions produce small increments of change, with the hope that therapeutic goals will be reached, given enough time and effort. In contrast, in a focused, "punctuated" personalized model, therapeutic advances may clearly be spelled out to have genuine transformational potential, a potential optimized through procedures such as those we have termed potentiated pairings and catalytic sequences.

Tactical specificity is required in part because the psychic level in which therapy is practiced is fairly explicit. Most often, the in-session dialogue between patient and therapist is dominated by a discussion of specific domain behaviors, specific domain feelings, and specific domain cognitions, not by an abstract discussion of personality disorders or clinical syndromes. When the latter are discussed, they are often perceived by the patient as an ego-alien or intrusive characterization. A statement such as "You have a negativistic personality that should be changed" conceives the patient as a vessel to be filled or altered by some noxious substance. Under these conditions, the professional is expected to empty the vessel and refill it with something more desirable; the patient has relinquished control and responsibility and simply waits passively for the therapist to perform some mystical ritual, one of the worst assumptive sets in which to carry out psychotherapy.

For the therapist, operationalizing clinical syndromes and personality disorders as domain clusters of expressive behaviors or cognitive styles can be especially beneficial in selecting tactical modalities. The *avoidant's* social withdrawal can be seen as having enough pride in oneself to leave a humiliating situation. The *dependent's* clinging to a significant other can be seen as having the strength to devote oneself to another's care. Of course, these reframes will not be sufficient in and of themselves to produce change. They do, however, seek a bond with the patient by way of making positive attributions and thereby raising self-esteem, while simultaneously working to disconfirm or make the patient reexamine other beliefs that lower esteem and function to keep the person closed off from trying on new roles and behaviors.

Understanding traits as domain clusters of behaviors and/or cognitions is just as beneficial for the therapist as for the patient when it comes to overturning the medical model of syndromal and personality pathology and replacing it with a personalized model. One of the problems of complex syndromes and personality disorders is that their range of attributions and perceptions is too narrow to characterize the richness that in fact exists in their social environment. As a result, they end up perpetuating old problems by interpreting even innocuous behaviors and events as noxious. Modern therapists have a similar problem, in that the range of paradigms they have to bring to their syndromal and disordered patients is too narrow to describe the rich set of possibilities that exist for every individual. The belief that mental difficulties are medical diseases, monolithically fixed and beyond remediation, should itself be viewed as a form of iatrogenic pathology.

As has been noted previously, there are *strategic goals* of therapy, that is, those that endure across numerous sessions and against which progress is measured, and there are specific *domain modality* tactics by which these goals are pursued. Ideally, strategies and tactics should be integrated, with the tactics chosen to accomplish strategic goals, and the strategies chosen on the basis of what tactics might actually achieve, given other constraints, such as the number of therapy sessions and the nature of the problem. To illustrate, intrapsychic therapies are highly strategic but tactically impoverished; pure behavioral therapies are highly tactical but strategically narrow and inflexible. There are, in fact, many different ways that strategies might be operationalized. Just as diagnostic criteria are neither necessary nor sufficient for membership in a given class, it is likely that no technique is an inevitable consequence of a given clinical strategy. Subtle variations in technique and the ingenuity of individual therapists to invent techniques ad hoc assure that there exists an almost infinite number of ways to operationalize or put into action a given clinical strategy.

Individuals should be viewed as system units that exist within larger ecological milieus, such as dyads, families, communities, and, ultimately, cultures. Like the personality system, these higher level systems contain homeostatic processes that tend to sustain and reinforce their own unique patterning of internal variables. The fact that the ecology of complex clinical syndromes and personality disorders is itself organizational and systemic argues for another principle of therapy: Pull as much of the surrounding interpersonal and social context into the therapeutic process as possible, or risk being defeated by them. Where ecological factors are operative, therapeutic gains may be minimized and the risk of relapse increased. In the best-case scenario, family members can be brought into therapy as a group or as needed; if no latent pathologies exist, the family will cooperate in discussing characteristics of the status quo that perpetuate pathology and explore alternatives that might promote change. In the worst-case scenario, family members will refuse to come into therapy under some thin rationale, probably because nonparticipation is one way to passively undermine a change they in fact fear. If family members are not motivated to assist in the therapeutic process, it is likely that the individual is in therapy either because he or she must be, as in cases of court referral, or because family members do not want the burden of guilt that would accrue from actively refusing assistance.

Procedural Caveats and Considerations

All personalized therapies must consider several factors following the implementation of the general plan. First, progress must be evaluated on a fairly regular basis; second, problems of resistance and risk should be analyzed and counteracted; and third, efforts should be made to anticipate and prevent relapsing.

In personalized therapies, where things hopefully will change rapidly, treatment review should be a continuous process, every few sessions or so. The purpose of evaluating the plan is to ensure that progress is directed to achieving its strategic goals. Part of the evaluation process is intended to give the therapist a rough sense of how long treatment will be. Should progress be delayed or fail to reach a reasonable level, then it is clear that some rethinking of goals and strategies is called for. Evaluating the progress of therapy is difficult when treatment is unstructured or when the time commitment is limited. Personalized therapy may begin with a series of explicit goals and modalities; however, these may change over time, especially if treatment is open-ended (Bergin & Lambert, 1978).

Originally planned strategies and modalities are periodically found lacking. Therapies start with a limited set of impressions and with only a rough notion of the more complex elements of the patient's makeup. As treatment proceeds and knowledge of the patient grows and becomes more thoroughly understood, this new information may strengthen the original plan and strategy; on the other hand, as the assessment process continues, so may the conception of the patient's psychic difficulties be altered. A fine-tuning process may be called for. The overall configuration of syndromes and disorders may require a significant shift toward the use of different domain-oriented modalities. Hence, both strategies and tactics may have to be modified to accord with this new information.

There are numerous issues that arise with patients as therapy progresses. Some patients are highly resistant to the probing and psychic dislodging they experience in treatment. Others feel they have become free from their original constraints, employing treatment as a rationale to engage in increasingly risky activities. Therapeutic resistance derives from the patient's defensive armor, usually indicating a reluctance to voice his or her feelings and thoughts to the therapist. Most *resistances* manifest themselves in a number of well-known ways: silence, lateness, becoming helpless, missed appointments, having significant memory lapses, or simply paying later and later each month. On the other hand, *risky* behaviors are likely to show themselves in a tendency to act out, to be open with regard to expressing resentments, proving the therapist is wrong, exhibiting parasuicidal behaviors, and engaging in irrational behaviors. As Messer (1992) has noted, however, resistances are not the enemy of therapy but an informative expression of the way patients feel, act, and think in everyday life.

There are several choices when resistances or risks present themselves. We can insist on continuing with the original plan; we can interpret the meaning of the resistance and point out the consequences of risky behaviors; or we can alter aspects of the overall treatment strategy. Whatever the choice will be, it should be formulated as a positive and active decision. Otherwise, the whole structure of the treatment plan may be seriously compromised.

Despite substantial progress over the treatment course, patients should leave therapy in a better state than when they entered. A worst-case scenario is when certain fundamental aspects of the patient's psychic makeup have remained unresolved at the point of treatment termination. Whether it is the patient's decision that he or she has had enough therapy, or the therapist believes that there will be diminishing returns for continuing further, it may be advisable at some point to terminate treatment.

It is the task of the good personalized therapist to help the patient anticipate potential setbacks, to avoid stressful situations in which the patient may be highly vulnerable, and to assist him or her to develop problem-solving skills, as well as to strengthen his or her more constructive potentials. It is not uncommon to have patients develop new psychic symptoms during the treatment process. More typically, many patients experience a reassertion of pathological thoughts and feelings following termination. We strongly encourage therapists to stretch the time between sessions as therapy progresses. This enables the therapist to determine which aspects of the treatment strategy have been resolved adequately and which remain vulnerable and potentially problematic. It is our general belief that adequate therapy should continue over these periodic sessions to ensure that substantial relapses will not occur. The reemergence of certain symptoms does not mean that the patient has deteriorated, but that the more complex elements of the patient's psyche have come together with life circumstances in an especially troublesome way. Such symptoms serve as clues to both the therapist and the patient, enabling them to learn and anticipate what will continue to be troublesome in the future.

The system we have termed personalized therapy has raised concerns by some as to whether any one therapist can be sufficiently skilled, not only in employing a wide variety of therapeutic approaches, but also to synthesize them and to plan their sequence. As the senior author was asked at a conference some years ago: "Can a highly competent behavioral therapist employ cognitive techniques with any measure of efficacy; and can he or she prove able, when necessary, to function as an insightful intrapsychic therapist? Can we find people who are strongly self-actualizing in their orientation who can, at other times, be cognitively confronting? Is there any wisdom in selecting different modalities in treating a patient if the therapist has not been trained diversely or is not particularly competent in more than one ore two therapeutic modalities?"

It is our belief that the majority of therapists have the ability to break out of their single-minded or loosely eclectic frameworks, to overcome their prior limitations, and to acquire a solid working knowledge of diverse treatment modalities. Developing a measure of expertise with the widest possible range of modalities is highly likely to increase treatment efficacy and the therapist's rate of success.

PART **TWO**

CHAPTER 2

Personalized Therapy for the Needy/ Dependent Personality Patterns

Recapitulation of the Personalized Therapy Idea

Each person is a synthesized and substantive system whose distinctive meaning derives from that old chestnut "The whole is greater than the sum of its parts." The problems of persons are an inextricably linked nexus of behaviors, cognitions, intrapsychic processes, and more. They flow through a tangle of feedback loops and serially unfolding concatenations that emerge at different times in dynamic and changing configurations. Behavioral acts, self-image cognitions, defense mechanisms—indeed, each functional and structural domain is contextualized by and interdigitated with all others as they take on the form of a single, cohesive organism. No one domain should be segregated out and made to stand on its own. Moreover, each component of these trait configurations has its role and significance altered by virtue of its place in these continually evolving constellations. In parallel form, so should personalized psychotherapy be conceived as a configuration of strategies and tactics in which each treatment modality is selected not only for its efficacy in resolving particular pathological features, but also for its contribution to the overall constellation of treatment procedures of which it is but one.

In our view, current debates regarding whether "technical eclecticism" (Lazarus, 1981) or "integrative therapy" (Arkowitz, 1992) is the more suitable designation for our approach are both mistaken. They have things backward, so to speak, because they start the task of intervention by focusing on methodology or theory first. Integration inheres in neither treatment techniques nor theories, be they eclectic or otherwise (Messer, 1986, 1992). *Natural integration exists in the person, not in theories or methodologies. It* stems from the interwoven character of the patient's traits and symptoms. Our task as therapists is *not* to see how we can blend discordant models of therapy, but to match the integrative pattern that is intrinsic in each patient, and then to select treatment goals and tactics that mirror this pattern optimally. It is for this reason, among others, that we have chosen to employ the label "personalized psychotherapy" to represent this model and approach to integrative treatment.

Many investigators have begun to combine two or three theories or modalities to see how well they may improve on the effectiveness of a single approach. But combinations of techniques are in themselves meaningless, in our judgment, because they are not designed to deal with the specific dysfunctions of a specific patient. Combining cognitive and interpersonal modalities, for example, may simply muddy the water, owing to the variety of traits and symptoms that inhere within each patient's pathology. This combination can be appropriate and useful if, and only if, the patients treated in this combinational fashion possess primary dysfunctions or deficiencies in both the cognitive and the interpersonal realms. In our view, it is not just the notion of modality combinations, nor any theoretical synthesis, that will work. We contend that *combinations will be effective if they are applied to the distinctive domain of dysfunctions of a specific patient.* Thus, in the psychopharmacologic area, a combination of certain medications (e.g., as when treating AIDS) can prove quite effective; however, other combinations, such as when two or three drugs are taken off the bathroom shelf, can result in dangerous consequences.

The Needy/Dependent Personality

Distinguished by their marked need for social approval and affection, and by their willingness to live in accord with the desires of others, needy personalities are among the most likely individuals to become distressed (Cogswell & Alloy, 2006). Characteristically, they are docile, noncompetitive, and passive. Apart from requiring signs of belonging and acceptance, dependents make few overt demands on others. Their own needs are subordinated and their individuality denied, as these individuals assume a submissive, self-sacrificing, and placating role in relation to others. Social tension and interpersonal conflicts are carefully avoided, and troubling events tend to be smoothed over or naively denied. Beneath their cooperative and affable presentation, however, may lie a plaintive and pessimistic quality. Dependents perceive themselves as weak, fragile, and ineffective. The recognition of their helplessness and utter reliance on others may result in public self-effacement and denigration. In addition, they may become conciliatory in relationships to the point of submitting themselves to intimidation and abuse (Millon, 1981, 1996b).

Given their susceptibility to separation anxiety, needy/dependent personalities are quite likely to experience any number of chronic syndromes. Frequently, the underlying characterological pessimism of these individuals lends itself to a chronic but mild depression or dysthymia. When faced with possible abandonment or the actual loss of a significant other, a major depression or panic attack may ensue. These individuals may react to notable stress with clinging helplessness and pleas for reassurance and support. Expressions of self-condemnation and guilt are also likely, as such verbalizations serve to deflect criticisms and evoke sympathetic reactions. Feelings of guilt can also act as a defensive maneuver to check outbursts of resentment or hostility. Fearful that their underlying feelings of anger might cause further alienation or retribution, dependents typically turn whatever aggressive impulses they possess inward, discharging them through despondency colored by self-derisive comments and expressions of contrition. On occasion, dependent personalities may make a desperate attempt to counter or deny emerging feelings of hopelessness and depression through a temporary reversal of their typical passive, subdued style into one of hypomanic activity, excitement, and optimism. Such dramatic shifts in affective expression may come to resemble a Bipolar Disorder.

The needy/dependent personality in our formulation corresponds to the psychoanalytic "oral character" type and, more specifically, to what has been termed in their literature the *oral sucking* or *oral receptive* character. For both Karl Abraham (1911/1968) and Freud (1916/1925), the orally fixated depressive or melancholic has great oral needs, manifested by sucking, eating, and insatiable demands for oral expressions of affection. Emphasis is also placed on affectional frustrations occurring during the pre-Oedipal period. In essence, the melancholic has experienced a pathological introjection, or identification, with the ambivalently regarded love object through the process of oral incorporation. Thus, an interpersonal conflict is transformed to an intrapsychic conflict, with the angry desire to devour the frustrating love object being turned inward and experienced as depression.

As psychoanalytic theory developed, the concept of orality was extended to include the general feelings of warmth, nourishment, and security. The dependent personality's reliance on external approval and support for maintenance of self-esteem made it particularly vulnerable to depression resulting from the loss of a significant other. Rado (1969) described melancholia as a "despairing cry for love"; Fenichel (1945) describes the orally dependent depressive as a "love addict."

A theory of depressive subtypes, based on attained level of object representation, has been developed by Blatt (1974, 2004; Blatt & Schichman, 1983). Of the two depressive subtypes offered, "anaclitic" and "introjective," the anaclitic depressive would correspond most closely to the dependent personality. Individuals with this form of depression have histories of impaired object relations at the primitive, oral level of development. Anaclitic depression is associated with intense dependency on others for support and gratification, vulnerability to feelings of deprivation, and considerable difficulties in managing anger expression for fear of alienating the love object.

This negative cognitive set of the dependent, that is, poor self-concept, disparaging view of the world, and the projection of continued hardships and frustrations in the future, is central to Beck's (1974) cognitive theory of personality. More recently, Beck, Freeman, and Davis (2003) have extended his cognitive formulation to include other predisposing and precipitating factors, including personality attributes that may lead to depression. They propose two basic personality modes, the "autonomous" and the "socially dependent," and describe the respective symptom patterns of each. Individuals in the socially dependent cluster depend on others for safety, help, and gratification and are characterized by passive receiving. Such individuals require stability, predictability, and constant reassurance in relationships. As rejection is considered worse than aloneness to the socially dependent, no risks are taken that might lead to alienation from sources of nurturance (e.g., asserting oneself with others). Similarly, socially dependent persons avoid making changes and exposing themselves to novel situations, as they feel ill-equipped to cope with the unexpected.

We next turn to the dependent personality as interpreted in Millon's polarity model; Figure 2.1 outlines the major motivational elements that undergird the ecologically adaptive style of this personality prototype. As with the majority of other personalities, the role of the enhancement (pleasure) and preservation (pain) polarities are of only

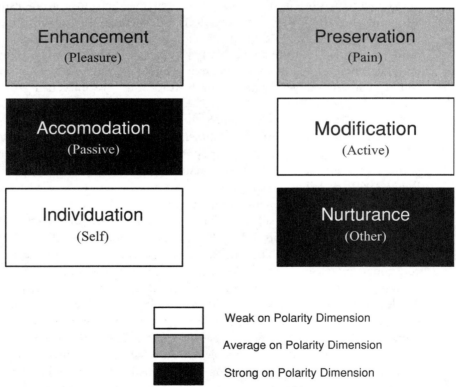

FIGURE 2.1 Status of the needy/dependent personality prototype in accord with the Millon polarity model.

modest significance. This minimal role is not found in the case of the schizoid, avoidant, and depressive personality patterns; there, the pleasure domain was notably deficient and the pain domain was prominent. In the needy/dependent personality, primary attention may be found in the other (nurturant) and the passive (accommodating) polarities. Dependents share with the histrionic personality style a major ecological commitment to an other-oriented direction; both seek support, attention, and protection from others. However, for the dependent personality pattern, there is also an adaptive style of searching for guidance and support from others, a need to have others not only provide nurturance and protection but also to guide and to show them how and when to achieve these security goals. This contrasts with the actively oriented ecological style of the histrionic personality, who arranges his or her life circumstances by making things happen. Histrionics may need others for attention and approval but are unwilling to accept the possibility that these might not be forthcoming; hence, they arrange and manipulate events rather than wait for others to do it for them. Histrionics take active steps to achieve their goals, effectively and reliably. By contrast, dependents entrust all to others, being passive, loyal, trustworthy, and dependable but lacking in initiative and competence.

Clinical Picture

In this section we draw on theory, clinical literature, and the *DSMs* to provide the structure and details of the dependent personality pattern (see Figure 2.2).

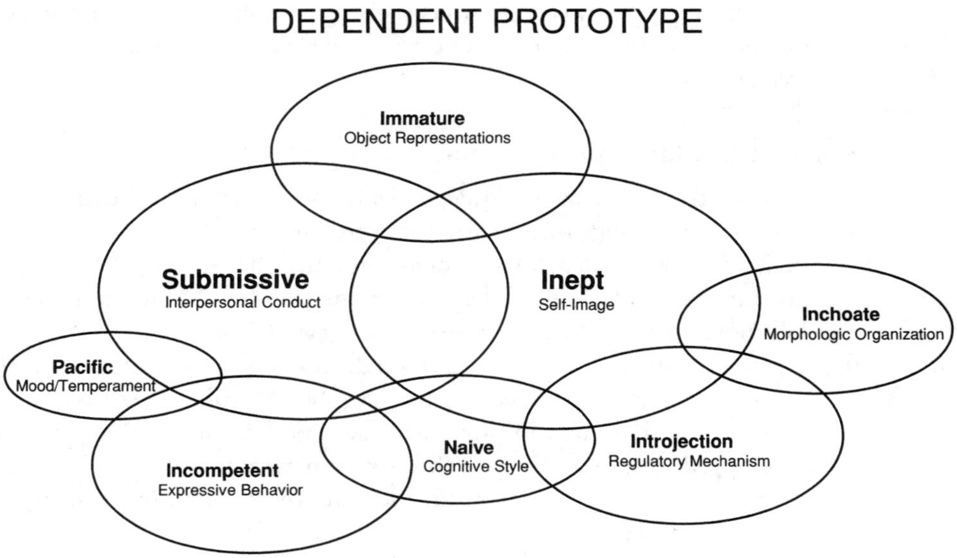

DEPENDENT PROTOTYPE

FIGURE 2.2   Salience of prototypal needy/dependent domains.

Although the following analysis is separated into eight domains, the traits described should be seen as forming a coherent picture. Congruity among the eight descriptive realms of behavior, phenomenological report, intrapsychic processes, and biophysical temperament should be expected because a distinguishing characteristic of a personality trait is its pervasiveness—that is, its tendency to operate in all spheres of psychological functioning (Gude, Hoffart, Hedley, & Ro, 2004). It should not be surprising, therefore, that each section provides a clinical impression similar to the others (see Table 2.1).

Incompetent Expressive Behavior

Among the most notable features of dependents is their lack of self-confidence, a characteristic apparent in their posture, voice, and mannerisms. They tend to be overly cooperative and acquiescent, preferring to yield and placate rather than be assertive. Large social groups and noisy events are abhorrent, and they go to great pains to avoid attention by underplaying both their attractiveness and their achievements. They are often viewed by friends as generous and thoughtful, and at times as unduly apologetic and obsequious. Neighbors may be impressed by their humility, cordiality, and graciousness and by the "softness" and gentility of their behavior.

Beneath their warmth and affability may lie a plaintive and solemn quality, a searching for assurances of acceptance and approval (Pincus & Wilson, 2001). These needs may be especially manifest under conditions of stress. At these times, needy/dependents are likely to exhibit overt signs of helplessness and clinging behaviors. They may actively solicit and plead for attention and encouragement. A depressive tone will often color their mood, and they may become overtly wistful or mournful. Maudlin and sentimental by disposition, they may also become excessively conciliatory and self-sacrificing in their relationships.

Submissive Interpersonal Conduct

What interpersonal behaviors do dependents use to manipulate their environment, and how do they arrange their relationships to achieve their aims?

A major problem for dependent individuals is that they not only find little reinforcement within themselves but feel that they are inept and stumbling, and thus lacking in the skills necessary to secure their needs elsewhere. As they see it, only others possess the requisite talents and experience to attain the rewards of life (Bolognini et al., 2003). Given these attitudes, they conclude that it is best to abdicate self-responsibility, to leave matters to others, and to place their fate in others' hands. Others are so much better equipped to shoulder responsibilities, to navigate the intricacies of a complex world, and to discover and achieve the pleasures to be found in the competitions of life (Loas et al., 2002).

To achieve their goals, needy/dependent personalities learn to attach themselves to others, to submerge their individuality, to deny points of difference, to avoid expressions

Table 2.1 Clinical Domains of the Needy/Dependent Personality Prototype

Behavioral Level:

(F) **Expressively Incompetent** (e.g., withdraws from adult responsibilities by acting helpless and seeking nurturance from others; is docile and passive, lacks functional competencies, and avoids self-assertion).

(F) **Interpersonally Dependent** (e.g., needs excessive advice and reassurance; subordinates self to stronger, nurturing figure, without whom may feel anxiously alone and helpless; is compliant, conciliatory, and placating, fearing being left to care for self).

Phenomenological Level:

(F) **Cognitively Naive** (e.g., rarely disagrees with others and is easily persuaded, unsuspicious, and gullible; reveals a Pollyanna attitude toward interpersonal difficulties, watering down objective problems and smoothing over troubling events).

(S) **Inept Self-Image** (e.g., views self as weak, fragile, and inadequate; exhibits lack of self-confidence by belittling own attitudes and competencies, and hence not capable of doing things independently).

(S) **Immature Objects** (e.g., internalized representations are composed of infantile impressions of others, unsophisticated ideas, incomplete recollections, rudimentary drives and childlike impulses, and minimal competencies to manage and resolve stressors).

Intrapsychic Level:

(F) **Introjection Mechanism** (e.g., is firmly devoted to another to strengthen the belief that an inseparable bond exists between them; jettisons independent views in favor of those of others to preclude conflicts and threats to relationship).

(S) **Inchoate Organization** (e.g., owing to entrusting others with the responsibility to fulfill needs and to cope with adult tasks, there is both a deficient morphologic structure and a lack of diversity in internal regulatory controls, leaving a miscellany of relatively undeveloped and undifferentiated adaptive abilities, as well as an elementary system for functioning independently).

Biophysical Level:

(S) **Pacific Mood** (e.g., is characteristically warm, tender, and noncompetitive; timidly avoids social tension and interpersonal conflicts).

Note: F = Functional Domains; S = Structural Domains.

of power, and to ask for little other than acceptance and support—in other words, to assume an attitude of helplessness, submission, and compliance (Berk & Rhodes, 2005). Moreover, by acting weak, expressing self-doubt, communicating a need for assurance, and displaying a willingness to comply and submit, dependents are likely to elicit the nurture and protection they seek (Straton, 2004).

Naive Cognitive Style

It is characteristic of dependents to limit awareness of self and others to a narrow sphere, well within comfortable boundaries (Beck et al., 2001). They constrict their world and are minimally introspective and Pollyanna-like with regard to difficulties that surround them (Tyrer, Morgan, & Cicchetti, 2004). From an introspective view, dependent personalities tend to be naive, unperceptive, and uncritical. They are inclined to see only the good in things, the pleasant side of even troubling events (Arntz, Dreessen, Schouten, & Weertman, 2004).

Inept Self-Image

Dependents view themselves as weak and inadequate individuals, fragile when feeling alone or abandoned, and generally incapable of doing things on their own without the support or guidance of another. Not only do they lack a sense of self-confidence, but for reasons noted previously, they have a tendency to belittle their own competencies, beliefs, and achievements. Needy/dependents not only believe they are of limited value to others, but prefer this image because few demands are made of inadequate persons, who are therefore often able to solicit the support and protection they desire.

From another perspective, dependents see themselves as considerate, thoughtful, and cooperative, disinclined to be ambitious, and modest in their aspirations. Closer probing, however, is likely to evoke marked feelings of personal inadequacy and insecurity. Dependents tend to downgrade themselves, claiming to lack abilities, virtues, and attractiveness. They are disposed to magnify their failures and defects. When comparing themselves to others they minimize their attainments, underplay their attributes, note their inferiorities, and assume personal blame for problems they feel they have brought on others. Of course, much of this self-belittling has little basis in reality. Clinically, this pattern of self-deprecation may best be conceived as a strategy by which dependents elicit assurances that they are not unworthy and unloved. Hence, it serves as an instrument for evoking praise and commendation.

Immature Object Representations

If one is able to examine the inner world of the dependents' representations of significant others, one is likely to see that these images are childlike, if not infantile, in character. The content of their intrapsychic world seems to be composed of unsophisticated ideas, incomplete recollections, and rudimentary aspirations. Others are seen as they may have been years before (e.g., as parents were when the patient was a child). Most other personality types hold mixed images of the past; although initially infantile or childlike, the overlays of subsequent experiences give them a completeness, such that later impressions become part of the overall picture. For the dependent, however, there is a fixation on the past, with prominence given to more youthful impressions.

Needy/dependents must be more than childlike if they are to secure and retain their hold on others. They must be admiring, loving, and willing to give their all. Only by internalizing the role of the totally submissive and loyal can they be assured of evoking consistent care and affection. Fortunately, most dependents have learned through parental models how to behave affectionately and admiringly. Most possess an ingrained capacity for expressing tenderness and consideration, essential elements in holding onto their protectors. Also important is that most dependents have learned the "inferior" role well. They are able, thereby, to provide their "superior" partners with the feeling of being useful, sympathetic, stronger, and competent—precisely those behaviors that dependents seek in their mates. From many sources, then, dependent personalities have learned interpersonal strategies that succeed well in achieving the goals they seek.

Introjection Regulatory Mechanism

The inadequacies that dependents see within themselves may provoke feelings of emptiness and the dread of being alone. These terrifying thoughts are often controlled by introjection, a process by which they internalize the beliefs and values of another, imagining themselves to be one with, or an integral part of, a more powerful and supporting figure. By allying themselves with the competencies of their partner, they can avoid the anxieties evoked by the thought of their own impotence. Not only are they uplifted by illusions of shared competence, but through incorporation they may find solace in the belief that the attachment they have constructed is firm and inseparable.

Denial mechanisms also characterize the dependent's defensive style. This is seen most clearly in the Pollyanna quality of dependents' thoughts. Dependents are ever-alert to soften the edges of interpersonal strain and discomfort. A syrupy sweetness may typify their speech, and they may persistently cover up or smooth over troublesome events. Especially threatening are their own hostile impulses; any inner feeling or thought that might endanger their security and acceptance is quickly staved off. A torrent of contrition and self-debasement may burst forth to expiate momentary transgressions.

Inchoate Morphologic Organization

The needy/dependent has entrusted to others the capabilities and responsibilities for dealing with life's tasks. As a consequence, the morphologic structure of the dependent's intrapsychic world has not developed an adequate diversity of regulatory controls (Bornstein, Hilsenroth, Padawer, & Fowler, 2000). What exists in this realm are either "borrowed" competencies through introjection, or a mélange of relatively underdeveloped and undifferentiated coping abilities. Although able to function adequately when allied or closely connected to others who can function for them, dependents are only weakly effective when coping on their own.

By acting in a weak and inferior manner, dependents effectively free themselves of the responsibilities they know they should assume but would rather not (Huprich, Clancy, Bornstein, & Nelson-Gray, 2004). In a similar manner, self-depreciation evokes sympathy and attention from others, for which dependents are bound to feel guilt. Maneuvers and conflicts such as these are difficult for dependents to tolerate consciously. To experience comfort with themselves, they are likely to deny the feelings they experience and the deceptive strategies they employ. Likewise, they may cover up their obvious need to be dependent by rationalizing their inadequacies—that is, by attributing them to some physical illness, unfortunate circumstance, or the like. To prevent social condemnation, they are careful to restrain assertive impulses and to deny feelings that might provoke criticism and rejection.

Dependents' social affability and good nature not only forestall social deprecation but reflect a gentility toward the self, a tender indulgence that *protects* them from being overly harsh with their own shortcomings. To maintain equilibrium, they must take care not to overplay their expressions of guilt, shame, and self-condemnation. They are able to maintain a balance between moderate and severe self-deprecation by a Pollyanna tolerance of the self, sweetening their own failures with the same saccharine attitude that they use to dilute the shortcomings of others.

Pacific Mood/Temperament

When matters are progressing well in their lives, needy/dependents tend to be warm, tender, and noncompetitive, timidly avoiding social tensions and interpersonal conflicts. However, this pacific mood gives way under conditions of rejection and abandonment, a time when dependents are likely to seek counseling or therapy (Massion et al., 2002). Underneath their initial Pollyanna veneer, these troubled dependents can no longer feel the joy of living. Once they begin to open up they will report deep feelings of insecurity, anxiety, discouragement, and dejection (Bienvenu & Brandes, 2005; Holmbeck & Durlak, 2005; McLaughlin & Mennin, 2005; Ng & Bornstein, 2005). Whatever their suffering may have been before, it is no longer done in silence, away from those for whom they had to appear pleased and content with life. Now that life has taken a turn for the worse, their underlying insecurities become evident in gloomy and tearful emotions (Fava et al., 2002).

Self-Perpetuation Processes

It may appear strange, even paradoxical, that the genuine affection and acceptance experienced in childhood by dependent personalities should dispose them to a needy pathology. For most of these individuals, childhood was a time of warmth and security, a period marked by few anxieties that were not quickly dispelled by parental attention and care. Too much of a good thing, however, can turn bad. Excessive parental shielding may establish habits and expectancies that are detrimental in the long run as they ill prepare the children to cope on their own with life. Accustomed to support from others and ill-equipped without them, dependents stand implanted, rooted to the deep attachments of their childhood. Unable to free themselves from their dependence, they face the constant danger of loss, dread desertion, and fear the abyss into which they will fall if left on their own. Beneath their pleasant and affable exterior, then, lies an extreme vulnerability, a sense of helplessness, and a fear of abandonment. Dependents'

Table 2.2   Self-Perpetuating Processes: Needy/Dependent Personality

Self-Depreciation
  Loses self-respect
  Deepens image of incompetence
  Senses futility of overcoming defects

Avoids Adult Activities
  Fears independence
  Self-restrictions diminish growth
  Becomes fixated in adolescence

Clinging Social Behaviors
  Exasperates those on whom they depend
  Reproaches self for dependence
  Continued inefficacy results in depression

lack of resources and their self-doubts compel them to seek safe partners, trustworthy figures "like mother" who can be depended on to assure them that they are loved and will not be deserted.

What does the future usually hold for needy/dependents? How and why do they remain fixed in their ways, and what approaches are best when intervening therapeutically? Questions such as these are addressed, albeit briefly, in this section of the chapter.

Needy/dependent personalities, despite claims to ineptness and inadequacy, employ an interpersonal coping strategy that recruits the nurture and support they need. Moreover, it is a style that forestalls their sinking into deeper levels of psychopathology. By soliciting attention and affection, dependents remain in close touch with the real world and are exposed constantly to social relationships that keep them from straying too far into the abyss of subjective distortion. Despite the fact that dependency behaviors protect against the pernicious and decompensating effects of social withdrawal and autistic distortion, the problem remains that the coping strategy persists far beyond its origins and ultimate utility. More important, it leads to self-defeating vicious circles (see Table 2.2). A brief review follows of some of the features that result in the aggravation of the dependent's characteristic inadequacies.

Self-Deprecation

Needy/dependents not only observe real deficits in their competence, but they deprecate what virtues and talents they may possess. This is done to prevent others from expecting them to assume responsibilities they would rather avoid. Successful as a shield against discomfort and in protecting their dependency needs, these actions are carried out at the cost of demeaning their own self-respect. Their rationalizations of inadequacy, offered for the benefit of others, have an impact on their own person.

Each time dependents announce their defects, they convince themselves as well as others and thereby deepen their self-image of incompetence. Trapped by their own persuasiveness, they further reinforce their belief in the futility of standing on their own, and they are thus likely to try less and less to overcome their inadequacies. Their strategy has fostered a vicious circle of increased helplessness and dependency.

Avoidance of Adult Activities

Dependents' sense of inadequacy, fear of failure, and hesitation about antagonizing others cause them to refrain from activities that may facilitate a more mature and independent lifestyle. For example, despite ample opportunities to learn skills and to assume more "manly" roles, some dependent men shy away from these "threats," fear they could never succeed, and prefer instead to remain inept but good-natured and easy to get along with. Self-imposed restrictions will diminish short-term embarrassments and anxieties associated with failure, but they also diminish the probability that the dependents will acquire competence and confidence that will enable them to function more maturely. By making themselves less accessible to growth opportunities, they effectively preclude further maturation, and thus become ever more needful of others.

Clinging Social Behaviors

Although dependents appease others and apologize for their incompetence, their need for affection and assurance that they will not be abandoned may become so persistent as to exasperate and alienate those on whom they lean most heavily. Of course, exasperation and alienation on the part of others only serve to increase the dependents' neediness. As the vicious circle persists, they may become more desperate, more ingratiating, and more urgently pleading and clinging, until they become millstones around their partner's neck. Wearying of demands to prove fealty and love, the stronger partner may come to openly express annoyance, disapproval, and, finally, rejection. When the dependent is seriously rebuffed, a cycle of decompensation may begin or increase in pace. Overt expressions of self-blame, self-criticism, and self-condemnation may come to the fore. Fearful of expressing hostility lest this result in further loss, dependents are likely to turn these feelings inward: first, to reproach themselves for their shortcomings and, second, to promise to be "different" and redeem themselves for their past mistakes. The new leaf they plan to turn over takes the form of promises of greater competence and less dependence—aspirations that run counter to their lifelong personality style. These goals rarely are achieved, and it is at this point that we often see the emergence of a serious symptom disorder such as a major depression.

Interventional Goals

Despite the possibilities of decompensation just noted, the prognosis for the needy/dependent pattern is relatively good. Needy/dependents are likely to have had a

Table 2.3   Therapeutic Strategies and Tactics for the Prototypal Needy/Dependent Personality

Strategic Goals
  Balance Polarities
    Stimulate active/modifying
    Encourage self-focus
  Counter Perpetuations
    Reduce self-depreciation
    Encourage adult skills
    Diminish clinging behaviors
  Tactical Modalities
    Correct submissive *interpersonal conduct*
    Enhance inept *self-image*
    Acquire competence *behaviors*

supporting relationship with at least one parent, and this provides them with a reservoir of security and a feeling of being loved and wanted. Each of these positive emotions will sustain a dependent through difficult periods. Additionally, affectionate parents serve as models for imitative learning, equipping dependents with reciprocal habits of affection and generosity. As noted earlier, dependency needs assure interpersonal contact, thereby forestalling the potentially decompensating effects of self-preoccupation and subjective distortion (Bender, 2005; see Table 2.3).

The needy/dependent's developmental history and early learning experiences have profoundly influenced his or her current personality pattern. The submissive dependence on others pervades all clinical domains and has resulted in an imbalance in the polarities. Because this personality style is so ingrained and others have learned to react to the dependent in a predetermined manner, the pattern perpetuates itself. Making the needy/dependent's life more balanced by targeting the weaker areas constitutes a major therapeutic goal for this disorder.

Reestablishing Polarity Balances

Dependents have learned that the source of pleasure and the way to avoid pain are found externally. They define themselves in terms of others and therefore seek nurturance from others. Given their often extreme reliance on their partner, alteration of the other-self polarity involves countering the belief that their fate is dependent on others and fostering self-focus as well as a diversification of coping strategies. To gain support and nurturance, dependents have learned to wait in a passive manner for others to take the lead. In the passive-active polarity, one of the main goals of therapy is to increase their active involvement in pursuing need satisfaction without excessive support from others.

Countering Perpetuating Tendencies

The needy/dependent's deep-seated feelings of incompetency must be addressed in therapy because they contribute to the failure to develop a more independent lifestyle. Increasing self-perceptions of adequacy will provide the dependent with the courage to engage in a wide variety of social experiences and hence will preclude the possibility of social withdrawal and isolation. A consequence of this improvement will be a lesser need for others to provide a more stable sense of security. A decrease in clinging behaviors will help interrupt the dependent perpetuating pattern because rejection by significant others and the internalization of failure becomes less likely. Additional perpetuating factors probably reflect childhood social stereotypes in which others have learned to selectively perceive only the person's dependent attributes and ignore efforts at independence. Changing the expectations of significant others leads to a broad range of social experiences that are essential for change.

Identifying Domain Dysfunctions

Most notable in the needy/dependent are his or her deficiencies in the self-image and interpersonal conduct domain. Targeting feelings of inadequacy and fostering the development of a more competent sense of self should be considered primary goals of therapy. This will be facilitated if a concurrent attempt is made to reduce the submissive behavior that characterizes dependents' interpersonal style. Expressively, dependents lack functional competencies, and their passivity diminishes opportunities for more diverse experiences that might promote feelings of adequacy. Therapy should further attempt to counter the needy/dependent's naive cognitive style that emerges when confronted with interpersonal difficulties and problematic events. Helping the dependent assess the validity of his or her beliefs about the consequences of assertive and autonomous behavior and engaging the patient in reality testing will clear the way for changes in this domain.

Intrapsychically, needy/dependents defend against stress by employing introjection as a primary mechanism. They deal with their feelings of ineptness by identifying with others. This gives them a false sense of security and protects them from exposing their own relatively undeveloped adaptive style. By promoting self-control, independent thinking, and a more active attempt at acquiring mature skills, the therapist can foster improvement. Helping dependents to establish an independent personal identity will also require replacing the internalized representations of others with more realistic, mature representations of their own.

Selecting Therapeutic Modalities

To facilitate improvements in the areas just noted, the therapist can opt to use a variety of techniques. These must be chosen and synchronized in such a manner as to allow for the optimal acquisition of independent and autonomous skills, while at the same time encouraging movement between self and others. Invariably, resistance will be encountered along the way, and an understanding of the nature of these obstacles and when they are likely to occur will assist in treatment planning.

Behavioral Techniques

Needy/dependents are rather passive and unsure of themselves, often waiting for others to provide support and guidance. *Behavioral* techniques can be employed after a functional analysis of behavior has been completed. This will bring to light the problem areas in the patient's life and target the avoidance behaviors that reinforce the maintenance of this pattern. A functional analysis of the dependent's style will reveal that although the immediate consequences of clinging behavior may be positive, long-term effects can run exactly counter to the desired effect and result in hostility from others.

With proper guidance, however, needy/dependents can start to recognize the patterns of their dependency, including the events and cognitions that prompt their behavior. Setting up an anxiety hierarchy of independent and assertive behaviors for gradual implementation is a good place to begin. Both role-playing and modeling can provide the patient with basic skills for a new repertoire of behaviors. Before attempting this, it is critical to assess whether the patient actually lacks functional competencies. If this appears to be the case, some remedial training of appropriate skills should be considered. In session, reinforcement and feedback can be provided immediately contingent on appropriate behavior. Gradual exposure can move from in-therapy situations to external settings, such as the home, social gatherings, and work, fostering generalization and maintenance of the newly acquired competencies. While the patient is working on the hierarchy, anxiety levels may temporarily rise. Teaching patients anxiety-reducing skills, such as breathing techniques and deep muscle relaxation, can help them feel more at ease and can additionally increase their tolerance for anxiety.

Needy/dependents' reluctance to stand up for themselves can be targeted with assertiveness training, and by specifically teaching skills that allow the expression of negative feelings in a constructive way. Complementary techniques include communication skills training and role-playing. Role-playing, as Klerman, Weissman, Rounsaville, and Chevron (1984) note, can accomplish two goals: It provides the therapist with a more adequate sense of the patient's relationships with others and can thus be quite revealing; additionally, it allows the patient to practice increasingly assertive behaviors.

Teaching self-management techniques and behavioral contracting can be most helpful with dependents in bolstering self-reliance. Initially the therapist will want to provide guidance when writing self-contracts to ensure that they are fair and manageable. The key to successful behavioral management here is appropriate reinforcement of the target goal, that is, increasingly independent behavior.

Interpersonal Techniques

Interpersonal techniques can be useful in treating needy/dependents (McCray & King, 2003), not only because they are receptive to treatment, but also because they are disposed to seek assistance wherever they can, especially in close interpersonal relationships. The strength and authority of the therapist comforts them with a feeling of assurance that an all-powerful person will come to their rescue when needed and provide them with the kindness and helpfulness they crave. Moreover, the task of unburdening their woes to a therapist calls for little effort on their part. Although they may lack accurate insight into their difficulties, dependents will provide ample data to lead the therapist to uncover the origins of their problems. Furthermore, dependents are disposed to trust others, especially therapists, to whom they are likely to attribute great powers and the highest of virtues. As therapy progresses, needy/dependent patients are likely to forget the primary complaint that brought them into treatment; in time, their only reason for continuing is to maintain their dependent attachment to their therapist. Many will attempt to seduce their clinician into their habits of avoiding decisions and asserting themselves. As should be evident, the clinician must resist the patient's wishes and, in a kindly way, insist that he or she give evidence of independent thoughts and actions.

It is very important that the relationship between the therapist and the dependent patient not reestablish the dominance-submission pattern that has characterized the dependent's history. Interpersonally, the needy/dependent needs to learn to separate and differentiate self from others, thereby becoming increasingly autonomous. A major challenge for the therapist is to draw these patients into a pattern of behaviors that are quite different for them, that is, to assist them to stop submitting to others and to learn the skills of being independent. This may prove difficult for dependents owing to their history of intense enmeshments with significant others and because they may lack an understanding of what it means to be separate and autonomous. From their viewpoint, they see relationships as consisting of two choices: either to dominate others or to submit to them. Because domination is considered a form of aggressive bullying, they reject it in favor of submission. The therapist can help the patient explore his or her long-standing patterns of interacting and how these have maintained his or her inadequate behaviors. Analysis of dependent behaviors displayed in session may shed further light on the dynamics of this mode of interacting. The therapist, at times, may wish to communicate personal reactions to provide the patient with valuable feedback. Benjamin (1993) points out that dependents have a restricted view of their interpersonal world and that they do not consider the possibility of being in charge or in control.

Group therapy may be particularly suitable as an arena for learning autonomous skills and as an aid to the needy/dependent's growth of social confidence. In this setting, patients can learn to assert themselves while receiving feedback that others will not abandon them when they display confidence and make independent decisions. Depending on the patient's level of motivation and potential for growth, either a supportive problem-solving group or a more insight-oriented group may be appropriate. Especially when the patient's difficulties are deeply ingrained, problem-solving groups may be particularly beneficial, such as those oriented to assertiveness training, decision making, and social skill acquisition. In the dyadic relationship between the therapist and the dependent, some regressive behaviors may be elicited as well as negative transferences, which may be counterproductive to therapeutic progress. In contrast, the group offers the advantage that when dysfunctional patterns are reactivated, feedback comes from equals. There is a good likelihood that constructive interactions will occur between the dependent and group members. Another advantage of the group setting is that abandonment issues may be less frequent because the dependent is not solely reliant on the therapist for nurturance.

Family or *couples* therapy may be helpful (Links, Stockwell, & MacFarlane, 2004b), especially in those cases where the family system is instrumental in maintaining the needy/dependent pattern. These patients can often function satisfactorily if their family consistently meets their needs; they become unsettled and symptomatic when such support decreases. The family can play an important role in facilitating behavior change by not excusing the dependent from assuming adult responsibilities. The role of societal and cultural factors, however, must be kept in mind when working with dependents and their families. Independent and assertive behavior may not be sanctioned by a large segment of the system. When work on interpersonal relationships is contraindicated because of these prohibitions, other options such as environmental change may be explored to maximize growth and minimize continued dependence. Encouraging the development of outside interests, for example, may open the door to myriad opportunities the dependent would never have considered for fear of endangering his or her relationships with significant others.

Cognitive Techniques

Beck et al. (2003) note that dependent persons show dichotomous thinking with respect to independence, believing either that one is completely dependent and in need of help or totally independent and alone; there do not appear to be gradations. This may contribute to a belief that the goal of therapy is independence and consequently isolation. The patient's unrealistic expectations about the consequences of displaying more independent behavior can be addressed cognitively by helping the patient place a variety of behaviors on a continuum from dependence to independence (Sochos, 2005).

Once needy/dependents develop a more realistic perception of their internal and external environment, there will be less need to suppress or minimize resentments and potential interpersonal conflicts (Bornstein, 2004). Successfully challenging automatic beliefs and maladaptive schemas is a primary part of this process. The therapist may initially need to provide direct assistance in identifying more rational responses and exploring alternative modes of interacting, but at some point in therapy, the patient must be encouraged to actively explore the consequences of alternative behaviors (Links et al., 2004b).

The dependent's automatic thoughts are likely to interfere with progress in therapy and will be evidenced by complaints of not being able to complete homework assignments or exercises. The therapist can use this resistance productively by asking the patient to test the validity of these thoughts through in-session reality testing. Emerging feelings of anxiety may produce resistance tactics, but a moderate degree of anxiety is necessary at times for change to occur. Time-limited approaches to cognitive treatment may also prove helpful in motivating increased patient activity. Knowing at the very outset that treatment will be limited to 10 or 15 sessions may lead patients to recognize that unlimited nurturance and dependence is not sustainable, hence, compelling them to confront their anxieties about abandonment and to undertake activities that may enable them to become autonomous.

Self-Image Techniques

Although there are a multitude of techniques the therapist may elect to use, the fundamental goal is to bolster the needy/dependent's self-image and encourage the use of a more active problem-solving approach in dealing with life's problems. In the course of therapy, these patients' distorted thoughts are identified, monitored, and subsequently challenged.

Initially, dependents will likely look to the therapist to provide them with answers and to tell them what to do. Guided discovery and Socratic questioning can help the patient arrive at a greater understanding of what is transpiring (Beck et al., 2003; Bornstein, 2004). The therapist can further this course by asking patients to record their perceptions and feelings about problematic events. In this manner, patients can monitor situations that occur during the week and start gaining more insight into their automatic thoughts and associated emotions. Particular attention should be paid to the sequence of events and their consequences, including reactions from significant others (Bornstein, 2004). This will highlight the sustaining nature of their dysfunctional style.

Working on identifying maladaptive and perpetuating patterns will soon bring to light the automatic and demeaning thoughts of the needy/dependent personality. Dependents are best described as naive and rather gullible. They tend to smooth over events that others would consider disturbing. Because they see themselves as unable to manage without the assistance of others, they may have developed this naive style and Pollyanna attitude to avoid interpersonal conflict and the expected repercussions that ensue. Therapy should assist patients to substitute passive cognitions with more active ones, and an improving self-image for an inept one. As Sperry (1995) has pointed out, a process of guided discovery and Socratic questioning may help these patients learn to form their own solutions and make their own decisions, reducing thereby their habitual reliance on others. Success in these techniques may become significant evidence to challenge the dependent's helplessness beliefs. Together with various behavioral experiments, for example, assertiveness and skill training, these Socratic tasks can facilitate a transition to greater independence.

The therapist may wish to use some gestalt techniques to facilitate schema changes at the emotional level, while simultaneously working on developing problem-solving skills. One such approach, the two-chair technique, allows for the expression of feeling without having to fear the consequences. The dependent can work on one part of the conflict while sitting on one chair and then switch chairs to play the role of his or her "adversary." The reversal technique may be especially suited to practice assertiveness skills, making the transition to facing the actual person less abrupt. The dependent can be instructed to act out the part of an uncompromising, obstinate person. A good deal of emphasis should be placed on the feelings experienced during these exercises. Suggesting that the patient write letters can further cultivate expression of emotion.

Intrapsychic Techniques

To rework deeper object attachments and to construct a base for competency strivings, it may be necessary to utilize *psychodynamic* approaches (Bender, 2005). The therapist-client relationship can be the basis for a corrective emotional experience. The patient can gradually start to internalize healthy components of this relationship, thereby replacing the immature representations currently existing. Gabbard (1994) comments on the importance of exploring unconscious factors that might contribute to dependence. He states that a submissive, clinging stance toward others may have different meanings for each dependent: For some it may be a defense against hostility; for others it is a way to avoid the reactivation of traumatic experiences. Exploring the dependent's past separations and their impact is recommended. A decreased but healthier intimacy with parents will ensue as a more realistic perception of the parents emerges. With more seriously impaired personalities, the goal of therapy may be to bypass total independence and instead gear therapy toward helping them substitute dependency on the original family with a less severe dependency on the marital partner (Stone, 1993). The therapist can serve as a temporary transitional object.

It is not unlikely that during the course of therapy, some relationships will come to an end; ultimately, so will the therapeutic relationship. As with other losses, some grief work may be necessary.

As patients' exposure to mature relationships starts to increase, the therapist's interventions may address their lack of diversity in internal controls and regulatory mechanisms. Dependents will often subordinate their own needs to those of others because they fear being deprived of a supporting relationship. Moreover, their low self-esteem leads them to place excessive value on others. As a result, the dependents' primary defense mechanism is introjection. Because they have always relied on others to take care of them and solve their problems, dependents have not pursued the development of independent skills. Their deficient morphologic structure can be targeted by focusing on gradually building skills and on self-management, thereby increasing coping abilities. As therapy progresses, the clinician should gradually increase his or her expectations of patients' self-initiated actions and autonomous decision making. These may be boosted with a variety of encouraging reinforcements for increased self-management.

Pharmacologic Techniques

Psychopharmacologic treatment, notably certain antidepressants and anxiolytic agents, may occasionally prove useful in treating dependents (O'Neil & Bornstein, 2001). Because dependents are often plagued by fatigue, lethargy, and diffuse anxieties, states that incline them to postpone efforts at independence, these agents may be used to promote vigor and alertness. Anxiety may temporarily increase when the patient is experimenting with increasingly autonomous behaviors because the threat of rejection or abandonment is perceived to be all too real. Restoring the patient's anxiety levels to normal limits may be facilitated by relaxation training. In those severe cases when extreme separation anxiety and possible panic attacks are present, SSRIs and tricyclic antidepressants, as well as monoamine oxidase inhibitors (MAOIs) may be considered, with appropriate consultation and follow-up. Special care should be taken *not* to allow the patient to become overreliant on medication, as well as to avoid medication with possible addictive properties. As Joseph (1997) has noted, the combination of pharmacologic agents in a broad-based psychotherapeutic model may have synergistic effects; medications may provide fairly rapid symptom relief, whereas other psychotherapies may furnish reassurance, understanding, and psychosocial coping skills.

Making Synergistic Arrangements

Needy/dependent personalities inevitably enter therapy soliciting active assistance from the therapist. As previously mentioned, the dependent is likely to feel positive about therapy and its prospects for providing nurturance, support, and guidance. Engaging the patient in therapy and establishing a long-term therapeutic alliance can be accomplished by initially giving the patient more directive feedback and engaging in acute problem solving. As Beck et al. (2003) note, it may be wise to allow some dependence in the treatment, as long as the therapist consistently works to wean the patient away from that dependence. According to these authors, progress in therapy from dependence to autonomy can be fostered by changing the structure of therapy itself. Sessions can move from the therapist's providing the structure and being more directive to the patient's dictating the agenda. Moving from individual to group therapy can additionally serve to reduce the patient's dependence on the therapist. When a trusting relationship has been formed, the therapist can make use of interpersonal reinforcement to encourage the patient to experiment with increasingly independent behaviors. If a significant degree of anxiety is present, therapy may be largely confined to more supportive methods until relief occurs. Psychopharmacologic intervention may then also be considered.

Cognitive and behavioral techniques are best used concurrently to deal with the almost inevitable resistance to giving up dependent behaviors. At the domain level, it will become evident that once they successfully start to build autonomous skills, dependents' view of themselves as capable, effective human beings will be enhanced. With the aid of behavioral techniques they should gradually acquire competencies to rectify their expressive and organizational deficits. Time will show the dependent, no longer incompetent, that abandonment and rejection are not imminent, thereby reducing the need for interpersonal clinging and introjection. Improvements in their self-image will in turn serve to increase the chances that they will attempt new behaviors and thereby acquire significant functional competencies.

Table 2.4 Needy/Dependent Personality Disorder Subtypes

Immature: Unsophisticated, half-grown, unversed, childlike; undeveloped, inexperienced, gullible, and unformed; incapable of assuming adult responsibilities. (Pure Subtypes)

Ineffectual: Unproductive, gainless, incompetent, useless, meritless; seeks untroubled life; refuses to deal with difficulties; untroubled by shortcomings. (Mixed Dependent/Schizoid Subtype)

Disquieted: Restlessly perturbed; disconcerted and fretful; feels dread and foreboding; apprehensively vulnerable to abandonment; lonely unless near supportive figures. (Mixed Dependent/Avoidant Subtype)

Accommodating: Gracious, neighborly, eager. benevolent, compliant, obliging, agreeable; denies disturbing feelings; adopts submissive and inferior role well. (Mixed Dependent/Histrionic Subtype)

Selfless: Merges with and is immersed in another; is engulfed, enshrouded, absorbed, incorporated, willingly giving up own identity; becomes one with or an extension of another. (Mixed Dependent/Masochistic-Depressive Subtype)

Illustrative Cases

Although all combinations are possible theoretically, experience and research show that only certain personality types tend to overlap or coexist with the needy/dependent personality pattern (Millon with Davis, 1996a; Millon, 1996b). This discussion draws on the evidence of several statistical cluster studies to supplement what theoretical deduction and observation suggest are the most prevalent personality mixtures. Also included are patterns that reflect differences in the pathogenic background of the various personality subtypes (see Table 2.4).

Case 2.1, Melissa K., 22

A Needy/Dependent Personality: Disquieted Type (Dependent with Avoidant Traits)

Presenting Picture

Melissa's mother brought her into therapy after she had an angry outburst that disrupted the household for 2 weeks. Melissa appeared quiet and pleasant on the surface, but she had a rather tight lip and stiff posture that belied this calmness. Underneath, fear and angry tension seemed to drive much of her behavior. Melissa lived with her mother, who structured her life for her, planned her meals, organized her recreation, and acted as her only companion. Melissa admitted to being very afraid of being left alone and tried to organize her life so that this was a rare occurrence. When she was alone in the house, she kept to her room, where she holed up with her romance novels and television. She held a part-time job as a clerk at a grocery store, where she had a coworker that mentored and supported her. Her mother generally provided her with the kind of constant attention and assurance that Melissa demanded, but on one occasion when on a business trip, she failed to telephone Melissa to inform her that she had safely arrived at her hotel. Melissa became enraged, screaming that she felt abandoned and forgotten. Her mother was becoming increasingly resentful of the demands Melissa was making on her and insisted that she seek therapy.

Melissa was not only apprehensive, but had acquired a pattern of withdrawing from social encounters. Further, she had built a tight armor to damp down and deaden excessive sensitivity to rejection. She frequently experienced loneliness and isolation. Although efforts were made to be pleasant and agreeable, she admitted underlying tension and emotional dysphoria, expressed in disturbing mixtures of anxious, sad, and guilt-ridden feelings. Despite past rebuffs and fears of isolation, she continued to evidence a clinging helplessness and a persistent search for support and reassurance. Her complaints of weakness and easy fatigability may have reflected an underlying mood of depression. Having experienced continuing rebuff from others, she may have succumbed to physical exhaustion and illness. Under these circumstances, simple responsibilities demanded more energy than she could muster. She expressed the feeling that life was empty but heavy, and she experienced a pervasive sense of anxiety and fatigue.

Clinical Assessment

As with other dependent varieties, Melissa's behavior could be characterized as submissively dependent, self-effacing, and noncompetitive. She leaned on others for guidance and security, virtually never taking her own initiative, and assumed a passive role in relationships. She also, however, gave evidence of intense apprehensiveness and fearfulness that overlay this sulking lack of initiative and an anxious avoidance of autonomy. Hence, as a *disquieted* dependent, she reflected a commingling of the passive *dependent* pattern, but with shades of the active–pain orientation of the *avoidant*. She was restlessly perturbed at times, seemed easily disconcerted and fretful, experienced a general sense of dread and foreboding, but, as with other dependents, she was apprehensively vulnerable to fears of abandonment and experienced a sense of loneliness unless she was near nurturing figures. With this anxiousness and fearfulness of loss, she ventilated her tensions through outbursts of anger directed toward others for having failed to appreciate her needs for security and nurturance. Although this did represent part of her attempt to more actively seek security, that very security that she so desperately needed was completely undone with these expressed resentments. Pivotal to timely significant change for Melissa was a focus on developing a more mature and resourceful sense of self, which would eventually allay both overdependence and self-uncertainties leading to fears of rejection or abandonment. To achieve the necessary receptivity and vigor for such measures, however, it was pragmatic to utilize an SSRI variant, paroxetine, which is effective in alleviating mixed anxious-dysphoric presentations revolving around social uncertainty. The therapeutic relationship was examined carefully so as not to reinforce the dominance-submission patterns that so aptly characterized Melissa's history. Early efforts in building the therapeutic relationship emphasized her strengths and interests, eliciting memories of when these interests fostered better social interaction. This laid the groundwork for Melissa to feel accepted and less threatened by the prospect of working with a professional whose job it would be to eventually help her dispute her own fears and self-doubts.

Domain Analysis

Melissa reluctantly completed an MCMI-III with Grossman Facet Scales, while her clinician also utilized the MG-PDC to ascertain confirmation of her dependent-avoidant patterns and to specify her most difficult and salient domains. Although she tended to self-efface to a high degree, the results were considered valid. Highlights from the domain assessment were as follows:

Inept Self-Image: Melissa viewed herself as incapable of carrying out even the simplest of tasks without involved supervision and direction. When not helped, she simply withdrew and sought solace in what she described as her "own little world" of her room, her books, and her television.

Temperamentally Anguished: Growing out of her disillusionment with herself as well as her longing to feel more socially adequate and personally efficacious was Melissa's tendency to feel an intense but concealed distress, which she was loath to admit, and which sometimes bred hostility and resentment.

Interpersonally Submissive: Entirely dependent on others and believing herself to be entirely ineffectual, Melissa regularly acquiesced to the wishes of others. This, too, appeared to stir some resentment in her dealings with family and those who mentored her.

Additionally, a constitutional conflict existed between her tendency to remain *passive* (protected, submissive, lethargic) in terms of autonomous functioning, and her tendency to *actively* withdraw from social settings and responsibilities, becoming defensive and even hostile when these conflicts became central.

Therapeutic Steps

Psychopharmacologic treatment was utilized as a short-term treatment geared toward promoting greater vigor and to counter dejection and anxiety states that predisposed Melissa to feelings of ineptness, unworthiness, and dependency, and that fostered her feelings of *anguish* that often preceded hostile outbursts. Both self-actualizing and directive cognitive approaches fostered the growth of autonomy and self-confidence. At first, owing to her anxious and morose outlook, she not only fixated on real deficits in her competence but also deprecated the virtues and talents she did possess. Trapped by her own persuasiveness, she tended to reinforce her belief in the futility of standing on her own and was therefore heavily disinclined to work at overcoming her inadequacies. As her pharmacologic treatment came to effective levels, cognitive methods (e.g., Ellis, Beck) were particularly helpful in reframing erroneous beliefs and assumptions about herself (i.e., *inept self-image*) as well as those she believed that others had of her.

Melissa's strategy had fostered a vicious circle of increased helplessness, depression, and dependency. By making herself inaccessible to growth opportunities, she effectively precluded further maturation and became more saddened and more dependent on others. Short-term techniques provided for the establishment and continuation of competence activities and the acquisition of skill-building behavior and assertive attitudes. To prevent Melissa from succumbing to further feelings of passive incompetence and feeling lost in fantasy preoccupations, interpersonal techniques such as those utilized by Benjamin and Kiesler were effective tools to combat *submissiveness,* especially after she had gained a modicum of confidence through cognitive tenets described earlier. Pressure on her to show marked increases in initiative and autonomy were gradual, however, because her capacities in this area were quite limited.

Brief and focused treatment created the misleading impression that progress would continue and be rapid. Despite initial indications of solid advances, Melissa resisted efforts to assume much autonomy for her future. Persuading her to forgo her long-standing habits proved to be extremely slow and arduous, but steps were undertaken to move forward in this regard and to provide support. Especially problematic was the feeling she had that an increase in the expectations of others would not be met and would thereby result in disapproval. Further efforts to help her build an image of competence and self-esteem were essential in forestalling later backsliding. Group therapy was pursued fruitfully as a means of learning autonomous skills and as an aid to the growth of social confidence. Circumscribed treatment efforts were directed at countering her dependency attitudes and behavior. A primary therapeutic task was to prevent Melissa from slipping into a totally ineffectual state as she sought to rely increasingly on a supportive environment. This program strengthened her attributes and dislodged her habit of leaning on others.

Case 2.2, Wayne M., 35

A Needy/Dependent Personality: Selfless Type (Dependent with Masochistic Traits)

Presenting Picture

Wayne, a mathematics teacher in a wealthy private school, described himself as "an easy grader." He liked all of his students, claiming that all were well-behaved, good kids. He got along exceedingly well with all of the administrators and other teachers on staff, but admitted to disliking the committee work that was required for his job. Wayne disliked taking sides if there was a disagreement among the teachers and claimed that in these scenarios, he couldn't even see that there *was* a real problem.

He lived with a roommate who paid all of the bills, called to get repairs made, and decorated and maintained the apartment. His girlfriend of 5 years seemed to make the rest of the decisions in Wayne's life, deciding what movie they would see and where to go to dinner. Wayne was invariably obliging to both his roommate and his girlfriend, seeming relieved that he didn't have to make such tough decisions. He always had a smile and a friendly word; he was responsive and agreeable, whatever it was that you could request; he was always willingly obliging. Difficulties arose in that Wayne always said yes, but rarely followed through in fulfilling what you wished of him. Unsure of himself and in many ways deficient in his competencies, he lacked the wherewithal to achieve what others expected of him. Adult activities called for more than good-natured agreeableness. They required concerted attention and a capacity to execute, not only difficult tasks, but even those that may be enjoyable and mutually rewarding.

One day, his girlfriend found the nerve to tell Wayne, in a fairly straightforward manner, that people liked him because he was so agreeable, but disrespected him because they felt he was entirely unreliable and simply a "yes-man." She suggested therapy; Wayne didn't really understand *why,* but also felt he should follow her directive. In the initial interview, when he felt safe enough to do so, Wayne did make mention of some anxious-depressive symptoms, not uncommon when dependency security is genuinely threatened.

Initial Impressions

As a *selfless dependent,* Wayne's behavior was best characterized by submissiveness, a high degree of agreeableness, and a leaning on others for affection, nurturance, and security to the point of marked self-denial. A central characterological feature with this man was a profound poverty in his *self-* orientation, as well as a rather heavy emphasis on *others,* perhaps even more so than other individuals fitting the criteria for Dependent Personality Disorder. This existed to such an extent that he seemed to effectively undo and defeat himself in the process. These patterns might aptly be identified as a basic amalgamation between the *dependent* and the *masochistic* personality styles. His fear of being abandoned led him to be overly compliant and obliging. He handled any fears by being socially gregarious and superficially charming, sometimes evident in attention-seeking and self-dramatizing behaviors. What differentiated Wayne's style of dependency from others, as well as from the more dependent variants of this histrionic feature, was his strong tendency to be self-sacrificing, his ability to adopt not only a submissive style, but to play the role well, sometimes even dramatically, of being inferior and subordinate. He also revealed a naive attitude toward interpersonal problems. Critical thinking was rarely evident, and most cognitive knowledge appeared to be almost entirely undeveloped and immature. Wayne always maintained an air of pleasantry and good spirits, a denial of all disturbing emotions, covering inner disharmonies by short-lived distractions. In part, this may have stemmed from a tendency to be genuinely docile, softhearted, and sensitive to the desires of others. Wayne was more than merely accommodating and docile in efforts to secure dependency needs. He was admiring and loving, giving all to those on whom he was dependent. He also learned to play the inferior role well, providing partners with the rewards of feeling useful, sympathetic, stronger, and more competent. He often actively solicited praise, willingly demeaned himself, and tended to be self-sacrificing and virtuous. All that really mattered to Wayne was that others liked him, were pleased by him, and were willing to accept his smiles and goodwill as sufficient. Fearing that he may fail to receive acceptance and approval by attempting any "real actions," that is, by seeking to execute adult responsibilities, he restrained himself from demonstrating his weaknesses and inefficiencies, reverting again and again to sociable pleasantries. Fearing conflict and rejection, stuck with his overpowering need to be liked and accepted, he was unable to follow through on any realistic commitments, lapsing once more into his friendly and ever-promising front.

The loss of significant sources of support or identification seemed to have prompted severe dejection in Wayne, although he avoided admitting this. Under such conditions of potential rejection or loss, he openly solicited signs of reassurance and approval. He admitted to engage in behaviors such as these (e.g., calling in sick, accepting too much responsibility for a social exchange) but did not recognize, consciously, these operational qualities or secondary gains. Guilt, illness, anxiety, and depression were frankly displayed as these tend to deflect criticism and transform threats of disapproval into support and sympathy. Interestingly, it was at this level that therapy began. Without an active challenge or passing judgment, the therapist skillfully examined and reflected these behaviors, highlighting possible discrepancies of action and desire (e.g., Wayne's emphasizing an occasional impression that someone may see his actions negatively). Wayne began voicing more troubled feelings at this, as he was shaken out of his complacency and denial, but felt secure enough in the therapy situation to tentatively explore these fears.

Domain Analysis

Eager to please, Wayne very agreeably participated in testing and was very inquisitive during feedback. The following domains were noted via the MG-PDC:

Interpersonally Submissive: Giving in to all requests and agreeing to any exchange, Wayne effectively set up situations that made it impossible to truly accommodate any. However, he believed he was giving himself "tokens," both socially and professionally, by such acquiescence.

Cognitively Naive: Somewhat Pollyannaish in his beliefs, Wayne believed that the best way to make his way in the world was to gloss over difficulties, "look on the bright side," and create an environment of overall agreement and consent.

Undeserving Self-Image: Although this was expressed as a more covert quality than if Wayne had presented with a more masochistic base pattern, this was a crucial aspect of his domain analysis, as it cloaked the fact that what he expressed as caring and willingness to do for others was really a preoccupation with his own sense of inadequacy and inability to achieve and express self-interests.

Therapeutic Steps

A baseline of rapport was established with a *humanistic* approach (in this case, motivational interviewing; Miller & Rollnick, 2002) involving genuineness and empathy in helping Wayne explore and begin to identify conflicts in his usual means of interacting (as noted in "Initial Impressions"). He was then able to withstand more directive *cognitive* and *interpersonal* methods designed to probe and modify his dysfunctional attitudes and ineffectual social habits. A cognitive reorientation approach assisted him in becoming more sensitive to and aware of objective reality and reinforced a less *naive* perspective that only lent itself to ineffective self-protectiveness. This proved especially helpful after taking steps to strengthen his capacity to confront his weaknesses and deficiencies. When he could deal with himself on a more realistic and insightful basis, he was less likely to develop illusory attitudes and dysfunctional behavior. Although he would protest this statement, Wayne was not truly inclined to seek therapy, and he covertly rejected what he feared was a "weak role" as patient. Nevertheless, the initial steps helped convince him that he could get along in his life appreciably better with guidance to eliminate shortcomings that proved demeaning to him. Although he sought to maintain a well-measured distance from the therapist, the empathic cognitive approach utilized from the outset minimized his resistance to the searching probes of personal exploration. Especially with the motivational interviewing approach, he became less perturbed over the implications of his deficiencies (i.e., his *undeserving self-image*) and was able to assume responsibility for his deficits. Reducing his evasiveness and unwillingness to face his difficulties significantly improved therapeutic progress.

Although he was concerned about appearances, such as being well thought of by a therapist, this supportive and cognitive reframing regimen was able to overcome Wayne's inclination to resist or deny psychological interpretations. His defensiveness in these matters was honored in this therapeutic approach, and probing and insight proceeded at a careful pace. Had he been asked to confront more than he could tolerate, emotional complications leading to a relapse may have resulted; it was important to aid him in narrowing the disparity between his public front and his inner deficiencies. Every effort was made to give substance to his intellectual insights, rather than have them merely serve as camouflage to deter probing by the therapist. At later stages, interpersonal techniques aimed at offering alternatives to his *submission needs* were incorporated, and insight-based changes were employed to modify some of his deeper ambivalences regarding important figures; these steps would help Wayne enhance conscious insights as well as less conscious roles of others as "dominant." His habitual evasiveness and discomfort with intimate issues was overcome with consistent direction and firmness. These were enhanced, following individual therapy, by focused (*group*) techniques to help him view himself in a more realistic social light and aided him in learning the skills of interpersonal relatedness without fearing disapproval and shame.

Case 2.3, Cindi S., 29

A Needy/Dependent Personality: Immature Type (Prototypal Dependent)

Presenting Picture

Cindi presented initially for couples therapy at the request of her boyfriend. Her couples therapist, after the initial interview, suggested to each that they also seek individual therapy, and Cindi was referred to another therapist for this portion of treatment.

Cindi was a teacher's aid working with young children, as well as a part-time college student seeking a degree in early childhood education. Her duties were limited to playing with the children and little else. She claimed to relate really well to the other children. With her sweet, round face, her baby voice and language, and ready giggles, it was not hard to imagine her playing blocks and sandbox with the 4-year-olds. She was relieved that she was "not the boss" and did not have more responsibilities. She lived with her mother, who often complained of Cindi's messy room, but overall Cindi seemed happy with the living arrangements. Her relationship with her boyfriend was more tumultuous. He complained regularly that Cindi was "acting like a baby" and he was tired of dealing with her "tantrums." Although she could see that the fighting needed to stop and was willing to "give therapy a try for all it's worth," she was pleased with how her life was progressing and saw little need to change or grow.

Initial Impressions

Some persons, like Cindi, remain childlike throughout their lives. She preferred childhood activities, found great satisfaction relating to children, and seemed either incapable of or to abhor activities and responsibility we assume are normal features of adult life. She was dependent not only because she was childlike in her outlook and competencies, but also because she seemed *satisfied* to remain childlike in her activities and orientation. It is individuals like Cindi whom we refer to as *immature dependent* personalities. In describing her as this nearly prototypal dependent (i.e., this subtype is most closely aligned with the evolutionary model's "passive–other" personality construction, without significant influence of other patterns), we might say that she was undeveloped, inexperienced, unsophisticated, unformed, and unversed. Pleased and satisfied with herself in not assuming adult roles and responsibilities, she was also incapable of doing so owing to her half-grown or childlike level of maturity. Whatever its origins, Cindi seemed to prefer, felt protected by, or found her greatest satisfactions in remaining oriented to the world of childhood and adolescence. To remain undeveloped was to find a more tranquil existence than found in adulthood, with its demands, strivings, competition, and responsibilities. For the most part, she was pleasant and sociable—as long as she was permitted to remain preadult in her preferences and activities. She became quite problematic to others when they expected more of her or demanded that she "mature" and get down to the business of life. Unfortunately, the business of life implies being and acting like an adult. To troubled parents or spouses these behaviors are often seen as signs of irresponsibility and neglectfulness.

Nonconfrontive, supportive measures would be the most efficacious plan to begin treatment with Cindi. As confrontive techniques would likely cause an emotional defensiveness, more *Rogerian* tenets were an appropriate beginning, allowing Cindi to voice her needs and her concerns. Effective and focused reflection helped her explore and illuminate troublesome interactions for herself at a pace in which she felt comfortable but did not become circuitous or defense-ridden.

Domain Analysis

Cindi enjoyed participating in filling out the MG-PDC; an unusual tactic, but one that helped her become more engaged, was for the clinician and Cindi to choose personality adjectives together.* As anticipated, the major domains were aligned with dependent patterns:

Inept Self-Image: Frightened of adult responsibilities and the often challenging situations brought on by autonomy, Cindi felt safest remaining with the perspective of helplessness and reliance. What was most notable, though, was that she seemed truly content to remain so.

Cognitively Naive: Limited in her sphere of knowledge about self and others, Cindi remained highly uncritical of herself and the world, preferring to keep matters simple and concrete. It seemed her occasional "tantrums" may have been fueled by this domain, as complexities of interrelationships were a poor fit for her template of how "things should be between people."

---

*It should be noted that this is not standardized use of the MG-PDC, and such approaches should be carefully considered for their clinical liabilities and potential gains. In this scenario, the clinician, one of the instrument's authors, chose to isolate the descriptive adjectives on a separate form and discussed their potential meaning and relevance with the patient in a clinically sensitive manner. Statements and descriptions on the original test form, if taken out of context by the patient, may have been potentially deleterious to progress.

Immature Objects (Intrapsychic Content): Cindi's representations of significant others were decidedly infantile, rudimentary, and incomplete. This served to reinforce her hold on others through her 20s, evoking consistent care from significant figures and feelings of guilt following any expressed upset on her part.

Therapeutic Steps

As noted, a supportive approach was the best initial vehicle for treating Cindi. Though pharmacologic agents were not employed in alleviating problematic periods, it should be noted that in those cases where they are used, the dosage should be restricted so that the patient does not experience significant decrements in efficiency. Methods of cognitive-behavioral treatment, introduced as Cindi became dissatisfied with her own insights into her conflicts with others, were designed to focus on dysfunctional self-statements regarding her view of herself as *inept*. These methods also proved effectual in countering her self-demeaning judgments as well as in providing structure to what she may have perceived as an ambiguous, elusive, and potentially threatening therapeutic relationship. It was most useful to help her reframe this tendency to observe deficits in her competence and to deprecate what virtues and talents she did possess. She did this to prevent others from expecting her to assume responsibilities she would rather avoid. Successful as a shield against discomfort and in protecting her dependency needs, these actions were carried out at the cost of forestalling the acquisition of mature abilities and self-respect. A short-term goal was one that focused and reoriented these tendencies into more constructive modes of thought.

This was an auspicious beginning to therapy, but it did not signify that future progress was to be rapid. Cindi sought a protective relationship with her therapist and was remarkably disinclined to acquire greater and healthier independence and autonomy. To reduce any backsliding, the therapist established the useful goal for her to relinquish her conforming and dependency habits. Efforts to assist her in building an image of true independence and self-esteem were facilitated by interpersonally focused programs (e.g., Klerman, Benjamin) geared toward strengthening her self-confidence and dislodging her habit of leaning on others. These were synergized in the framework of a brief psychodynamic structure stemming from the characteristics of the therapeutic relationship, aimed at helping her derive insight into her self-perceived role as submissive to the dominant, worldly, and capable character of others. In this manner, Cindi was able to make minor adjustments in her basic object dynamics (*immature objects*). Substantial growth in this regard would not be seen in treatment; it was possible only to introduce new perspectives and experiences and effectively "plant the seed."

Cindi viewed therapy as upsetting to her overly idealized view of herself as "perfect for what I've chosen to do with my life." Cognitive methods were employed to overcome her *naive thought content* and her inclination to resist probing and to deny psychological interpretations. Her defensiveness was honored, of course, and probing interpretations were oriented to short-term goals. Given her fear of humiliation and her reluctance to expose more than she could tolerate, actions that would have directly confronted Cindi would have invited emotional complications that potentially could have produced unnecessary setbacks. She sometimes voiced intellectual insights, but given her respectful, if not ingratiating, manner, this seemed to be camouflage to placate the therapist. Cindi's defenses were so well constructed that insight based on long-term techniques was likely to be of questionable value. Though paying lip service to treatment goals, she did not readily relinquish her defensive controls. Hence, brief and focused therapy proved to be the best option, although efforts were made to continue treatment as it was necessary to forestall probable recurrences.

Case 2.4, Thalya R., 23

A Needy/Dependent Personality: Ineffectual Type (Dependent with Schizoid Traits)

Presenting Picture

At the end of her first year as a kindergarten teacher, Thalya was referred to the Employment Assistance Program provider by a school administrator. Although her attendance was not a stipulation for future employment, Thalya obliged without question as to why this might be necessary, and was surprised to hear that it might be anything other than standard procedure for first-year teachers. She was reluctant to recognize any problems at school or with her job performance, as she felt that she got along quite well with the other teachers and staff; finally, however, she quietly agreed that there were several incidents that had happened over the course of the year. It appeared that she was not capable of handling even minor disagreements that went on between students. On quite a few occasions, she had to call in other teachers from the next room to handle routine disputes. Although she seemed undisturbed by, and even indifferent to, her lack of ability to handle these situations, it was clear that it was interfering with her job.

Thalya seemed almost possessed by a desperate need to lead a totally untroubled life and to be free of any and all responsibilities. She was willing to ignore difficulties by simply refusing to deal with them, to tune them out, or to let them be. She seemed resigned and not unhappy to accept her ineffectual fate—except for one thing: her need to be nurtured and protected by others. This extended to her home life as well, as Thalya shared an apartment with two other young teachers in her school. These women made all of the household decisions and Thalya was all too content to never have to make a choice or plan of action.

Initial Impressions

Other than seeking peace and amity with others at any price, Thalya was unwilling to face any of life's difficulties squarely. She had fallen to such a level as to be unable to deal with any complexity. If possible, she would have liked to turn her back on what she saw as a demanding world, or to bury her head as far as she could in the sand. Not wanting to deal with reality, she resisted all pressures that might intrude on her, sleepwalking through her life, increasingly disengaged and dependent. She clung to others in a childlike manner, even for the most basic requirements of everyday survival. Most prominent was her total malleability and lack of will.

As an *ineffectual dependent* type, Thalya showed a general lack of vitality, low energy level, fatigability, and a general weakness in expressiveness and spontaneity. Unlike the *schizoid* patterns, of which this subtype does show some facets, Thalya did not want to be isolated from close personal relationships. She wanted closeness and caring, but lacked drive and staying power, was deficient in her adult skills, and seemed simply unwilling to pursue solutions to the end of even minor problems. She needed reassurance that the therapeutic relationship and milieu would be secure, trusting, and sincere, as she had extreme characterologic anticipation of rejection, letdown, and hurt (burdensome orientation toward the importance of *others*). Therefore, a supportive approach was most influential in allowing Thalya enough comfort to begin focused work. It would be crucial to stimulate her *activity* orientation, having her assume adult activities and invest gradually in competent actions. With an increase in activity, Thalya's *pleasure* orientation would also be augmented through more meaningful experiences, which would eventually increase her motivation to develop her concept of *self*.

Domain Analysis

Ineffectual dependents like Thalya reflect the intermingling of both basic dependent and schizoid characteristics, as was seen on her MCMI-III Grossman Facet Scales, as follows:

> *Inept Self-Image:* Thinking herself entirely inadequate, Thalya readily belittled her opinions, attitudes, and competencies, leaving the door open for others to make decisions and orchestrate important aspects of her life; this extended to her willingness to be virtually walked on by important people in her life.

> *Expressively Impassive:* Possibly owing to her weakened self-image, Thalya routinely responded to environmental events from innocuous to threatening with a disengaged immobility, distancing herself from decisions and actions that could potentially affect any progression.

Interpersonally Submissive: Thalya followed directives of others verbatim, with virtually no self-derived input. She routinely subordinated herself to nurturing figures, believing she needed to be seen as entirely agreeable, submissive, placating, and compliant.

Therapeutic Course

As a first approach in a therapeutic program, an effort was made to assist Thalya in arranging for a more rewarding environment and in discovering opportunities that would modify feelings of *ineptness,* thus enhancing her self-worth. Supportive therapy was all she could tolerate in these very first sessions, that is, until she was comfortable dealing with her more painful feelings. Behavior modification was gradually introduced to enhance this modality, which began to introduce her to competent reactions to stressful situations that felt genuine to her. Through the synergy of these two modalities, she was able to learn that she did, in fact, have resources available that would not only dispute ingrained beliefs about her capability, but also allow her to feel that she did not have to simply disengage and sit idly by, leaving actions to others *(expressive impassivity).*

As trust in her therapist developed, Thalya became more amenable to methods of *cognitive reframing* to alter dysfunctional attitudes and depressogenic social expectations; particularly appropriate were methods such as those proposed by Beck and Meichenbaum. An important self-defeating belief that the cognitive approach sought to reframe was Thalya's assumption that she must appease others and apologize for her incompetence in order to ensure that she would not be abandoned. She began to see that this behavior tended to exasperate and alienate those on whom she leaned most heavily. This exasperation and alienation then served only to increase her fear and neediness. She came to recognize that a vicious circle was created, making her feel more desperate and more ingratiating. Not only did Thalya precipitate real difficulties through her self-demeaning attitudes, but she also perceived and anticipated difficulties where none existed. She believed that good things did not last and that the positive feelings and attitudes of those from whom she sought support would probably end capriciously and be followed by disappointment and rejection. This cognitive assumption had to be directly confronted by appropriate therapeutic techniques. What had to be undone was the fact that each time she announced her defects, she convinced herself as well as others and thereby deepened her discontent and her self-image of incompetence. Trapped by her own persuasiveness, she repeatedly reinforced her belief in the futility of standing on her own and was therefore likely to try less and less to overcome her inadequacies. A vigorous approach that illustrated her dysfunctional beliefs and expectations was used to break the circle and reorient her interactions with others to be less *submissive.* A combination of cognitive restructuring and the development of increasing interpersonal skills, particularly those proposed by Kiesler and Benjamin, proved an effective course by providing a means of learning autonomous skills and helping her grow in self-confidence.

Skillful attention was needed throughout treatment to alter Thalya's ambivalence about dependency and a discovery of her latent willingness to be used. Unless checked, she had difficulty sustaining a consistent therapeutic relationship and was prone to deteriorate or relapse. Maneuvers designed to test the dependability of the therapist were often evident. Empathic warmth needed to be evident throughout to help her overcome her fear of facing her own feelings of unworthiness. Similar support levels were necessary to undo her wish to retain her image of being a self-denying person. Thalya needed to be guided into recognizing the basis of her self-contempt and her ambivalence about dependency relationships. She was helped to see that not all nurturant figures would habitually become exploitive and even possibly abusive. Efforts to undo these self-sabotaging beliefs paid considerable dividends in short-term and possibly more substantial long-term progress.

Case 2.5, Kristine M., 38

A Needy/Dependent Personality: Selfless Type (Dependent with Depressive Traits)

Presenting Picture

Kristine was a student teacher in elementary education who showed little ambition or drive of her own. She relied on her husband to take her places because she never learned to drive a car, and she relied on her school's principal to include her in seminars and workshops to keep her busy and entertained. Kristine responded to almost every question she was asked with "Everything is okay," even when it was painfully clear that there were significant problems. She reported that she was nervous about some of her teaching responsibilities, especially having to shoulder the responsibility of being alone with the children. The first time she was put in charge, she had to call in the principal to take over. She also claimed to be scared when left alone in the house.

Kristine reported being more sad than usual in recent months. She had been thinking about her older sister, with whom she had been very close, who had died 2 years earlier. This sister had taken care of Kristine when they were younger, and Kristine revered her and wanted to be just like her. It seemed that Kristine not only subordinated herself to others, but merged herself totally with her husband and sister such that she lost herself in the process. She willingly gave up her own identity as an independent human being in order to acquire a more secure sense of significance, identity, emotional stability, and purpose in life. As the process of total identification with another became established and integrated, she failed increasingly to develop any of her own personally distinctive potentials. And as her own sense of self became a less significant part of her being, whatever she did was done almost entirely in the service of extending the status and significance of another.

Initial Impressions

As a *selfless dependent,* Kristine felt fulfilled by her associations. Not only did she willingly submit to the values and beliefs of her significant attachments, but her very sense of being depended on it. The more she fused with the idealized object, the more attached she was emotionally and the more she felt that she herself existed as a person that had significance in the world. What impulses and potentials that might have existed for Kristine as an independent person were denied or dissociated. She had become fully merged, as if she had no self, was a nonbeing, except for her coupling with another person. Her existence was *not* denied, but became an extension of the other person. So fused and entwined, she acted at times in ways quite divergent from what had been characteristic of her. Thus, she may have exhibited an air of confidence and self-assurance, but only as it reflected the achievements and powers of the person or institution to which she was united. In this way, she had not lost a sense of self-worth; rather, by virtue of her alliances, she had acquired and assumed that she herself now possessed many of the qualities that inhered in those with whom she identified.

Essential to a successful treatment process with this very unsure and self-diminished woman would be a supportive atmosphere, established from the outset, while trust and security were built within the therapeutic relationship. To facilitate more focused strivings, it would be prudent to address Kristine's depressive tendencies (losing further self-worth due to the threat of abandonment) with a pharmacologic regimen and gradually introduce tangible, innocuous behavior goals to build confidence and illustrate aspects of her own worthiness and reduce her despairing *pain* orientation. As her poise would improve, it would be possible to begin adjusting perpetuations that overemphasized her dependent role with *others*.

Domain Analysis

With the loss of her sister and consequent hopelessness, Kristine's basic dependent style became infused with elements of a depressive character. This was evident in her domain analysis, the highlights of which are as follows:

Interpersonally Defenseless: Beyond that of the "typical" dependent, this domain took on more of the depressive's character, with Kristine feeling unprotected and subject to abandonment. This drove her to seek solace, invariably in the nurturance of others, and at times this became the overriding quality seen in her clinical presentation.

Temperamentally Pacific: Kristine regularly was very warm, but timid, when life was in status quo, which spoke to her lack of ability to face any potential conflict or change. The content of her feelings changed, in something of an intellectualized way, when she was uncertain, and she spoke of pessimistic and dejected feelings when challenged.

Inchoate Organization (Intrapsychic Structure): Lacking in diversity of abilities and internal controls, Kristine's inner world seemed vague and ill-equipped to deal with the complexities of adult life, and she gave hints of a barrenness and weakness of inner structure that was effectively denied by what seemed to be a calm outer shell.

Therapeutic Steps

It was apparent that Kristine was immersed in a self-created environment that was at once comfortable but also bereft of interest, and this fostered a very marginal inner structure that succeeded only at masking deeper discontent. In this scenario, she was at first capable only of enduring a supportive milieu. A more demanding course of treatment at this early stage would have overwhelmed her and probably set the stage for premature termination. A psychopharmacologic regimen of paroxetine (an SSRI effective for feelings of inadequacy) was a beneficial catalyst for gradually allowing her to diminish her *pacific mood* and prepare to deal with more salient emotions. Kristine had an irrational fear of abandonment, more recently enhanced by a real loss (her sister), and she constantly felt she needed to placate others and habitually apologize for her perceived incompetence. Beyond inducing real problems with these dysfunctional habits, Kristine sensed and reacted to nonexistent difficulties. She seemed to live by the maxim "Good things don't last"; specifically, the people in her life who loved and respected her would inevitably let her down, and she would be abandoned. Simple behavioral modification exercises, combined with guided imagery aimed at relaxation, helped Kristine learn to respond more effectively to environmental stressors. The ensuing successes further enhanced her self-confidence, as well as trust and investment in the therapeutic relationship and her social environment.

Focused dynamic methods were utilized to explore ingrained object attachments and to enhance competency strivings, in an effort to give her otherwise *inchoate organization* needed reinforcements and maturity. Interpersonal methods, such as those of Benjamin and Klerman, as well as an adjunctive group milieu provided for further skill development and effectively combated feelings of social *defenselessness*. These methods were combined with some tenets of cognitive reframing aimed at helping her realize that her weak and inferior inner feelings may have actually helped cause isolation. Kristine learned that this alienation spurred further anxiety and dependency. From a cognitive perspective, each time Kristine proclaimed her imperfections, she added to a sense of discontent and unworthiness in herself as well as in others. She was capable of making a compelling argument for the uselessness of autonomy and subsequently rationalizing her failure to meaningfully pursue ambitions. As the therapist illustrated these dysfunctional beliefs, Kristine was able to break this vicious circle and reorient her behaviors more productively. This therapeutic strategy aimed at undoing this vicious circle of increased despondency and dependency. She made marked improvements with these combinatorial methods focused on breaking down these dependent habits and helping foster more autonomous, productive skills.

Resistances and Risks

The needy/dependent's receptiveness and the auspicious beginning of therapy may create a misleading impression that future progress will be rapid. These patients will quite naturally seek a dependent relationship with their therapist. Despite promises to the contrary, they will resist efforts to guide them into assuming independence and autonomy. Their goal is to elicit more nurturance and help from the therapist. All this is to be expected as their dependence is quite ego-syntonic. Assisting them in relinquishing their dependency habits will prove a slow and arduous process. Building an image of competence and self-esteem must proceed one step at a time through a program of strengthening attributes and dislodging the habit of leaning on others.

The therapist may get caught up in the patient's attempt to elicit support. After a while, excessive dependence can be exasperating. Resulting countertransference feelings of annoyance may lead to rejection once again, which in turn will intensify the dependency and clinging behaviors (Stone, 1993). Countertransference may also take the form of the therapist's allowing the patient to become emotionally dependent on him or her, resulting in reduced efforts at gaining independence. However, if attempts at autonomy are pushed too hard initially, the anxiety may result in premature dropout.

Another potential caveat concerns the dependent's search for approval. Observed behavior changes, such as enhanced assertiveness, may be confined to sessions with the therapist and not exhibited elsewhere. It is important to evaluate to what degree behavior change actually has occurred outside of the therapy setting. If the patient's environment continues to foster or maintain dependency, what appears to be progress in the therapy room may not have generalized to his or her dysfunctional world.

The therapist and patient should come to an understanding of the goals of therapy. Especially when resistance is encountered, reconceptualization of the dependent's therapeutic objectives may be useful. Progress in therapy may be impeded by the dependent's basic belief that he or she is inadequate. Dependents may feel incompetent to utilize treatment efficiently and may attribute progress made to the therapist rather than to the self (McCann, 1994). Reliance on medication may also strengthen the belief that success is attributable to external sources.

Neither the therapist nor the patient must forget that the ultimate goal is not necessarily complete independence, but rather the flexibility to move between self-reliance and a healthy mutual dependence.

CHAPTER 3

Personalized Therapy for the Sociable/ Histrionic Personality Patterns

S ociable/histrionic personalities, like needy/dependent personalities, are characterized by intense needs for attention and affection. Unlike the passive receptive stance of the dependent, however, the histrionic actively solicits the interest of others through seductive, immaturely exhibitionistic, or self-dramatizing behaviors. Toward assuring a constant receipt of the admiration and esteem that they require, histrionics develop an exquisite sensitivity to the desires and moods of those they wish to please. Some may perceive them as being rather disingenuous or shallow, yet they are typically viewed as gregarious, entertaining, and superficially charming (Flanagan & Blashfield, 2003). The histrionics extreme other-directedness and approval seeking results in a capricious and fickle pattern of personal relationships. Unlike the dependent's blind loyalty and attachment to one significant other, the histrionic is lacking in fidelity and dissatisfied with single attachments. The interpersonal relationships tend to be characterized by demandingness, manipulation, and, at times, childish dependency and helplessness. These behaviors are particularly pronounced in heterosexual relationships where the histrionic demonstrates a marked appetite for fleeting romantic encounters (Millon, 1981; Millon with Davis, 1996a).

Histrionics tend to be emotionally overreactive and labile. Frustration tolerance is quite low, and they are prone to immature stimulation seeking and impulsive responsiveness. Such individuals crave excitement, pleasure, and change and become easily bored with normal routines. A well-developed sense of inner identity is typically lacking in sociable/histrionics. Their perception of themselves is conceptualized in terms of their relationships and their effect on others (Morse, Robins, & Gittes-Fox, 2002). In contrast to their hypersensitivity to the thoughts and moods of others, such individuals are lacking insight into their own feelings. Their orientation is toward external stimuli, and only fleeting, impressionistic attention is paid to details. Their cognitive style is marked with difficulties in concentration and logical thinking. Experiences are poorly integrated and learned, and consequently, judgment is often lacking. In part, their cognitive flightiness results from their attempts to avoid potentially disrupting ideas and urges, for example, a recognition of their ravenous dependency needs and their resultant vulnerability to loss or rejection. Consequently, histrionic personalities will simply seal off, repress, or dissociate large segments of their memories and feelings (Crawford, Cohen, & Brook, 2001a, 2001b).

Histrionics' virtually insatiable needs for attention and approval make them quite prone to feelings of dejection and anxiety should they fail to evoke the recognition they desire (Bornstein, 1999). Signs of indifference or neutrality on the part of others are frequently interpreted as rejection and result in feelings of emptiness and unworthiness. Unlike the dependent's flat and somber symptom picture, Dysthymic Disorder in histrionic personalities is characteristically overplayed in dramatic and eye-catching gestures, characteristic of the histrionic's exhibitionistic display of mood (Bornstein, 1998). Episodes of the milder forms of depression are usually prompted less by fear of abandonment than by a sense of emptiness and inactivity. Such dysphoria is likely to occur when sociable/histrionics find themselves stranded between one fleeting attachment and another, or between one transitory excitement and the next. At such times of noninvolvement, histrionics sense their lack of inner substance and direction and begin to experience fears of an empty life and aloneness (Overholser, Stockmeier, Dilley, & Freiheit, 2002).

Complaints among histrionic personalities tend to be expressed in current, fashionable, or intellectualized terms (e.g., *existential anxiety* or *estrangement from the mass of society*). Expressing this distress through such popular jargon enables histrionics to rationalize their personal emptiness and confusion and, perhaps more important, provides them with a bridge to others at a time when they feel most isolated from the social life they so desperately seek (Sprock, 2000). Such pseudosophisticated expressions of disenchantment entertain and interest others and identifies the histrionic as being part of an "in" subgroup. Sociable/histrionics are also among the personality styles that may mask an underlying depression through physical disorders, hypochondriacal syndromes, or acting-out behaviors, such as drug abuse, overeating, and sexual promiscuity.

Depression and acute anxiety in histrionics are primarily precipitated by anticipated losses in dependency security and are more likely to be evidenced in an agitated rather than a retarded form. In the hope of soliciting support and nurturance, histrionics may wail aloud and make known their feelings of helplessness and abandonment. Suicidal threats or gestures are not uncommon at such times. Major depressions may also be colored with irritability and anger, although reproving reactions, especially from significant others, will cause histrionics to withdraw and substitute their anger with dramatic declarations of guilt and contrition.

Sociable/histrionic personalities may be particularly susceptible to Bipolar and Cyclothymic Disorders, as these syndromes are consistent with their characteristic socially gregarious and exuberant style. Severe separation anxieties or the fear of losing social approval may intensify histrionics' habitual behavior pattern until it reaches the forced and frantic congeniality of hypomania. To stave off the growing feeling of depressive hopelessness, tension may be released through hyperactivity and a frenetic search for attention.

Many of the psychoanalytic writings of the depressed oral dependent's pronounced affectional needs are equally applicable to depression in the histrionic personality. Freud (1932) wrote that a "dread of loss of love" governed the behavior of hysterics; Rado (1969) referred to the predepressive's strong cravings for narcissistic gratification and low tolerance of affectional frustration.

Liebowitz and Klein's (1979) "hysteroid dysphoria" portrays a chronic, repetitive, nonpsychotic depressed mood among these patients, a disturbance more frequent in women with pronounced needs for attention, approval, and praise, especially in a romantic relationship. Extreme intolerance of personal rejection is the hallmark of this disorder. Clinical syndromes in these individuals are usually of short duration and manifested symptomatically in overeating or craving for sweets, oversleeping, or extreme fatigue. Alcohol or drug abuse during brief episodes may also be common. Described as "attention junkies" with "addictions" to approval, hysteroid dysphorics possess many of the features characteristic of the sociable/histrionic personality. Hysteroid dysphorics also evidence considerably more unstable features (e.g., being prone to angry outbursts, impulsive acting-out, and physically self-damaging acts), which are suggestive of a more severe level of personality disorganization, such as the borderline personality.

We next review the evolutionary model and theory. The polarity schema to characterize the histrionic personality is presented in Table 3.1. The elements that stand out are a focus on others (nurturance) and on activity (modification). As is typical in most personality disorders, both pain and pleasure polarities are not notably significant.

In a manner similar to the dependent personality, the histrionic's psychic world is centered on relationships with other persons. However, the dependent and the histrionic differ markedly in their mode of adaptation; histrionics actively manipulate their environment to achieve their ends; by contrast, dependents are passive, not only accommodating to their environment, but looking to others to guide and nurture it. Histrionics engage in a variety of interpersonal maneuvers to ensure that others are attentive and approving, even desirous of and willingly offering tribute to them.

Dependents not only seek but need others to care and nurture them, as well as to provide them with guidance. By contrast, the histrionic is actively involved in giving to and even nurturing others. These latter behaviors are not altruistic, but a means of soliciting and ensuring reciprocal approval and esteem. It is the active-modifying stance that the histrionic takes to assure a continuous supply of admiration and fulfillment that distinguishes his or her style of behavior. Should this supply of reciprocal gratification fail to be forthcoming, the histrionic will quickly jettison the "defective" partner, turning without much ado to locate another who will supply these needs (see Figure 3.1).

Table 3.1   Clinical Domains of the Sociable/Histrionic Personality Prototype

Behavioral Level:

(F) **Expressively Dramatic** (e.g., is overreactive, volatile, provocative, and engaging, as well as intolerant of inactivity, resulting in impulsive, highly emotional, and theatrical responsiveness; describes penchant for momentary excitements, fleeting adventures, and short-sighted hedonism).

(F) **Interpersonally Attention-Seeking** (e.g., actively solicits praise and manipulates others to gain needed reassurance, attention, and approval; is demanding, flirtatious, vain, and seductively exhibitionistic, especially when wishing to be the center of attention).

Phenomenological Level:

(F) **Cognitively Flighty** (e.g., avoids introspective thought, is overly suggestible, attentive to fleeting external events, and speaks in impressionistic generalities; integrates experiences poorly, resulting in scattered learning and thoughtless judgments).

(S) **Gregarious Self-Image** (e.g., views self as sociable, stimulating, and charming; enjoys the image of attracting acquaintances by physical appearance and by pursuing a busy and pleasure-oriented life).

(S) **Shallow Objects** (e.g., internalized representations are composed largely of superficial memories of past relations, random collections of transient and segregated affects and conflicts, and insubstantial drives and mechanisms).

Intrapsychic Level:

(F) **Dissociation Mechanism** (e.g., regularly alters and recomposes self-presentations to create a succession of socially attractive but changing façades; engages in self-distracting activities to avoid reflecting on and integrating unpleasant thoughts and emotions).

(S) **Disjointed Organization** (e.g., there exists a loosely knit and carelessly united morphologic structure in which processes of internal regulation and control are scattered and unintegrated, with ad hoc methods for restraining impulses, coordinating defenses, and resolving conflicts, leading to mechanisms that must, of necessity, be broad and sweeping to maintain psychic cohesion and stability, but, when successful, only further isolate and disconnect thoughts, feelings, and actions).

Biophysical Level:

(S) **Fickle Mood** (e.g., displays rapidly shifting and shallow emotions; is vivacious, animated, and impetuous and exhibits tendencies to be easily enthused and as easily angered or bored).

Note: F = Functional Domains; S = Structural Domains.

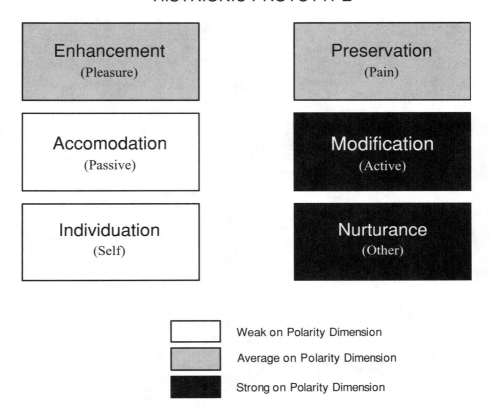

HISTRIONIC PROTOTYPE

Enhancement (Pleasure)	Preservation (Pain)
Accomodation (Passive)	Modification (Active)
Individuation (Self)	Nurturance (Other)

☐ Weak on Polarity Dimension

▨ Average on Polarity Dimension

■ Strong on Polarity Dimension

FIGURE 3.1 Status of the sociable/histrionic personality prototype in accord with the Millon polarity model.

Clinical Picture

This section should aid the reader in outlining a cognitive map, so to speak, of the prototypal sociable/histrionic personality (see Figure 3.2).

Histrionic personalities often demonstrate, albeit in caricature and mild pathological form, what our society tends to foster and admire in its members: to be well liked, successful, popular, extraverted, attractive, and sociable. Beneath this surface portrayal we often see a driven quality, a consuming need for approval, a desperate striving to be conspicuous and to evoke affection or attract attention at all costs. Despite the frequent rewards these behaviors produce, they stem from needs that are pathologically inflexible, repetitious, and persistent. In this section the histrionic picture is detailed in line with the four spheres of clinical observation and analysis employed in Chapter 2 for description of the dependent personality.

HISTRIONIC PROTOTYPE

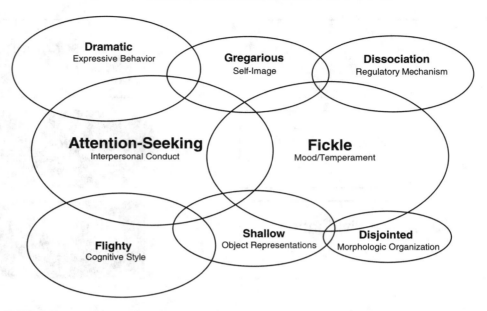

FIGURE 3.2   Salience of each personologic domain in the sociable/histrionic prototype.

Dramatic Expressive Behavior

Although not unique, there are distinctive aspects to the expressive behaviors of histrionics. They are overreactors, relating at times in a volatile and provocative manner, but usually displaying themselves in an engaging and theatrical manner. They show a tendency to be intolerant of inactivity, resulting in impulsive, capricious, and highly emotional behaviors. Similarly, there is a penchant for momentary excitements and hedonic ventures. Sociable/histrionic personalities often impress one at first meeting by the ease with which they express their thoughts and feelings, by their flair for the dramatic, and by their capacity to draw attention to themselves. These exhibitionistic and expressive talents are manifested, however, in a series of rapidly changing, short-lived, and superficial affects. Histrionic personalities tend to be capricious, easily excited, and intolerant of frustration, delay, and disappointment. Moreover, the words and feelings they express appear shallow and simulated rather than deep or real.

Attention-Seeking Interpersonal Conduct

Histrionics are more than merely friendly and helpful in their relationships; they are actively solicitous of praise, market their appeal, and are often entertaining and sexually provocative. Because affection and attention are primary goals, histrionics engage in a variety of maneuvers to elicit a favorable response (Brašic, 2002). Women may behave in a charming or coquettish manner; men are typically generous in praise and, on occasion, overtly seductive. Both men and women often display an interesting mixture of being carefree and sophisticated, on the one hand, and inhibited and naive, on the other. In the sphere of sexuality, for example, many histrionics are quite at ease while "playing the game" but become confused, immature, or apprehensive once matters get serious.

Characteristically, histrionics are unable to follow through and sustain the initial impression of goodwill and sophistication they convey. Their social life numbers many acquaintances but few friends. In most areas of personal activity they put up a good show at the start but often falter and withdraw when depth and durability in relationships are required.

It is toward the end of achieving these goals and avoiding these fears that histrionics have learned to manipulate others to suit them (Fossati et al., 2003). More than merely agreeable and friendly, they sell themselves by employing their talents and charm to elicit recognition and esteem. This is done by presenting an attractive front, by seductive pretensions, by a dilettantish sophistication, and by a show of postures and acts to impress and amuse others. Displays and exhibitions, dramatic gestures, attractive coiffures, frivolous comments, clever stories, and shocking clothes—all are designed not for self-expression but to draw interest, stimulation, and attention. In short, histrionics use themselves as a commodity with a bag of tricks, a conspicuous "personality" that corners all of the attention of those with whom they come into contact.

Histrionic personalities not only acquire skill in sensing what is salable or will get across to others, but they learn to be alert to signs of potential hostility and rejection. This hypervigilance enables them to quickly adapt their behaviors to minimize indifference and disapproval. Their interpersonal facility extends, therefore, not only to evoking praise but to avoiding rejection. By paying close attention to the signals that people transmit, histrionics can fashion their reactions to conform with the desires of others. Then they need not fear indifference or desertion as they are always ready to maneuver themselves to do things that correspond to the wishes and expectations of others.

Despite charm and talent for pleasing others, the histrionic fails to provide genuinely sustained affection. All that histrionic personalities offer in return for the approval they seek are fleeting and often superficial displays of affection.

Flighty Cognitive Style

Histrionics are inclined to avoid introspective thought. Lacking an integrated sense of self, owing to their exteroceptive orientation, they are overly suggestible, are excessively attentive to fleeting and superficial events, and integrate their experiences poorly (Cale & Lilienfeld, 2002; Klonsky, Jane, Turkheimer, & Oltmanns, 2002). This has resulted in a widely scattered but shallow pattern of learnings, as well as a tendency to speak in impressionistic generalities and to come to essentially thoughtless judgments (Sigmund, Barnett, & Mundt, 1998). The preoccupation of histrionic personalities with external rewards and approvals often leaves them bereft of an identity apart from others. They describe themselves not in terms of their own traits but in terms of their relationships and their effects on others. Histrionics behave like empty organisms who react more to external stimuli than to promptings from within. They show an extraordinary sensitivity to the thoughts and moods of those from whom they desire approval and affection. This well-developed radar system serves them well, for it not only alerts them to signs of impending rejection but enables them to manipulate the object of their designs with consummate skill.

This orientation toward external stimuli leads histrionics to pay fleeting, impressionistic, and scattered attention to details and accounts in part for their characteristic distractible and flighty behaviors. The susceptibility of histrionics to transient events parallels their superficial cognitive style, their lack of genuine curiosity, and their inability to think in a concentrated and logical fashion. Habits of superficiality and dilettantism may represent an intellectual evasiveness and a desire to eschew troublesome thoughts or emotionally charged feelings. Part of the flightiness of histrionic personalities derives from an avoidance of potentially disruptive ideas and urges, especially those that might bring to awareness their deeply hidden dependency needs. For these and other reasons they steer clear of self-knowledge and depth in personal relationships. In effect, histrionics dissociate themselves from thoughts, from people, and from activities that might upset their strategy of superficiality.

Gregarious Self-Image

Histrionic personalities view themselves as friendly and agreeable people. They consider themselves to be stimulating and charming, well liked by others, and able to be quite successful in terms of creating an exciting and interesting lifestyle. Important to them is the capacity to attract acquaintances, particularly by physical appearance, and by creating a busy and pleasure-oriented context for their social life. Many lack insight, however, failing to recognize, or admit to recognizing, their deeper insecurities, their desperate need to draw attention to themselves and to be well liked. Signs of inner turmoil, weakness, depression, or hostility are almost invariably denied, suppressed so as not to be part of their sense of self.

Shallow Object Representations

Most persons seek stimulation, attention, and approval, but it is only the histrionic personality who possesses an insatiable striving for these experiences, who feels devoid of an inner self and seeks constant nourishment to fill that void. Lacking a core identity apart from others, histrionics must draw nurture from those around them. It is others who supply the sustenance of life without which histrionics will feel a deep vacancy, a fear of collapse, and a falling apart in disarray or into the empty chasm that exists within them. The internalized objects of the histrionic's intrapsychic content are composed largely of superficial memories of past relationships. Owing to the facile manner in which histrionics attach themselves to others, their inner world comprises random collections of transient and unconnected affects, a template of insubstantial relationships, impulses, and memories. It is the scattering and incidental character of these inner templates that lead the histrionic to become ever more dependent on external stimulation and approval. How do histrionics manipulate their inner world to assure the stimulation and approval they require?

It may be useful before proceeding to note again that the interpersonal behaviors of most pathological personalities do not usually appear strikingly different from that seen among "normal" individuals. Their distinction lies not so much in their uniqueness or bizarreness but in their inflexibility and persistence.

Sociable/histrionics are often successful in accomplishing their aims of eliciting stimulation and captivating the attentions of others (Riesenberg-Malcolm, 1996). Their strategies are considered pathological because they fail to limit their manipulations to situations in which they are appropriate. Rather, they are applied indiscriminately and persistently, seeking to attract the attentions of insignificant persons in unsuitable circumstances. Histrionics' need for recognition and approval appears insatiable. As soon as they receive attention from one source, they turn their unquenchable thirst for approval to others. The histrionic is a bottomless pit into which esteem and tribute may be poured. Equally important is the observation that a failure to evoke attention and approval often results in dejection and anxiety. Signs of indifference or neutrality on the part of others often are interpreted as rejections and result in feelings of emptiness and unworthiness.

Having failed throughout life to develop the richness of inner feelings and lacking resources from which they can draw, histrionics have difficulty maintaining a full, meaningful, and stable relationship with another. At some level they also sense the disparity that exists between the favorable but superficial impression they give to others and their real lack of inner substance. As a result, they are likely to shy from prolonged contact with others for fear that their fraudulence will be uncovered.

In sum, the facile emotions of histrionics are shallow, fleeting, and illusory; not only are they unable to sustain close relationships, but they quickly abandon what few they may have had before the "truth" can be known.

Dissociative Regulatory Mechanism

As already noted, histrionics actively seek to avoid introspection and responsible thinking. Not only are they characteristically attuned to external rather than internal events, but their lifelong orientation to what others think and feel has prevented them from learning to deal with their own inner thoughts and feelings. As a consequence, they lack intrapsychic skills and must resort to gross mechanisms to handle unconscious emotions. What they have learned best is to simply seal off, repress, or dissociate entire segments of memory and feeling that may prompt discomfort. As a result, much of their past is a blank, devoid of the complex reservoir of attitudes and emotions they should have acquired through experience. Histrionics regularly alter and recompose their self-presentations to create a succession of socially attractive but changing façades. By disconnecting their true selves from the theatrical pose they present to the world, they can distract themselves sufficiently to avoid reflecting on and integrating the emptiness that inheres within them or the painful thoughts and emotions that otherwise surge up into consciousness.

To the degree that sociable/histrionics possess an inner world of thought, memory, and emotion, they try to repress it and to keep it from intruding into their conscious life. This they do for several reasons. First, their own sense of worth depends on the judgment of others; there is no reason to explore the inner self, for they cannot independently appraise their personal value or provide acceptance or approval. Second, by turning attention inward histrionics distract themselves from attending to the outer world. This divided attention can prove troublesome because they feel they must be ever alert to the desires and moods of others.

The contrast between their pretensions and objective reality leads histrionics to repress not only one or two deficiencies within themselves but all of their inner self; it is the triviality of their entire being, its pervasive emptiness and paucity of substance, that must be kept from awareness. Repression is therefore applied across the board; it is massive and absolute.

Disjointed Morphologic Organization

The morphologic structure and organization of the histrionic's inner world is loosely knit and carelessly united. Internal controls and regulations are scattered and unintegrated, with ad hoc methods used to restrain impulses, coordinate defenses, and resolve conflicts. Regulatory mechanisms must, of necessity, be broad and sweeping to maintain overall psychic stability and cohesion. Of course, when successful, these efforts only undermine psychic coherency by further disconnecting and isolating this personality's thoughts, feelings, and actions.

Having deprived themselves of past learnings, histrionics are less able to function on their own and thereby perpetuate their dependency on others. Moreover, to compensate for the void of their past, and for ignoring the guidance these learnings could provide, they remain locked into the present. In short, the intrapsychic world of the histrionic personality not only remains skimpy and insubstantial, but their preoccupation with external immediacies has led to a further impoverishment of what little richness and depth they may possess.

To preserve their exteroceptive vigilance, they must reduce inner distractions, especially those that may be potentially disturbing. Histrionics seek actively to blot out any awareness of the barrenness of their intrapsychic world. This inner emptiness is especially intolerable because it points to the fraudulence that exists between the impressions they seek to convey to others and their true cognitive sterility and emotional poverty.

Fickle Mood/Temperament

The biological underpinnings of the sociable/histrionic personality may not be too difficult to infer. Conceived in terms of temperament, histrionic behavior suggests both a high level of energy and activation and a low threshold for autonomic reactivity. Histrionics tend, in general, to be quick and responsive, especially with regard to the expression of emotions. Feelings of both a positive and a negative variety come forth with extreme ease, suggesting either an unusually high degree of sensory irritability, excessive sympathetic activity, or a lack of cortical inhibition. No single temperament label readily captures the highly fickle, intense, erratic, and wide range of emotions to which they are disposed.

It would seem reasonable that histrionic adults would have displayed a high degree of emotional responsiveness in infancy and early childhood. This inference derives from the facts that constitutional traits are essentially stable throughout life and that active and responsive children are likely to foster and intensify their initial responsiveness by evoking stimulating reactions from others.

Self-Perpetuation Processes

We all engage in automatic and persistent behaviors that are "senseless" if viewed in terms of their objective utility. The difference between the persistent behaviors we consider normal and those that are pathological lies in the fact that "normal" senseless and repetitive acts do not create problems or intensify existent ones. Pathological behaviors, no matter what their immediate utility, ultimately foster new difficulties and perpetuate old ones. This section considers aspects of histrionic behaviors that foster these consequences. Three characteristics of the histrionic pattern are discussed in this section, as each tends to set up vicious circles that promote new problems (see Table 3.2).

Table 3.2 Self-Perpetuating Processes: Sociable/Histrionic Personality

External Preoccupations
    Fleeting experiences resist internalization
    Impulsive behavior lacks connection to the past
    Few memory traces to evaluate future

Massive Repression
    Emotional insulation precludes emotional maturation
    Failure to merge new with old results in stagnation
    Retains values of childhood

Superficial Relationships
    Needs approval and stimulation
    Needed affection and support jeopardized
    Nothing exists to tide over empty times

External Preoccupations

This chapter has already recorded the observations that histrionics orient their attention to the external world and that their perceptions and cognitions tend to be fleeting, impressionistic, and undeveloped. This preoccupation with incidental and passing details prevents experiences from being digested and embedded within the individual's inner world. In effect, histrionics show little integration and few well-examined reflective processes that intervene between perception and action; behaviors are emitted before they have been connected and organized by the operation of memory and thought. The disadvantages of this hyperalertness to external stimuli may outweigh its advantages. Unless life events are digested and integrated, the individual gains little from them. Interpersonal transactions and learnings pass through the person as if he or she were a sieve. There is little opportunity to develop inner skills and few memory traces against which future experience can be evaluated. Indiscriminate and scattered responsiveness leaves the person devoid of an inner reservoir of articulated memories and a storehouse of examined ideas and thoughts. In short, an excessive preoccupation with external events perpetuates the histrionic's empty shell and further fosters dependence on others as the only source of guidance.

Massive Repression

The tendency of histrionics to seal off, repress, and make inaccessible substantial portions of their meager inner life further aggravates their dependence on others. By insulating their emotions and cognitions from the stream of everyday life, histrionics deny themselves opportunities to learn new alternatives for their behavior, to modify their self-image, or to become more genuinely skillful and knowledgeable persons. As long as they block the merger that should occur between new and old experiences they are likely to remain stagnant, unaltered, and impoverished. Deprived of opportunities to learn and grow, they will further perpetuate the vicious circle of dependency on others. As a consequence, the sociable/histrionic progresses little beyond childhood and retains the values and modes of behavior of an adolescent.

Superficial Social Relationships

The histrionic personality requires a retinue of changing events and people to replenish the need for stimulation and approval. Thus, as life progresses, histrionics move capriciously from one source to another. One consequence of these fleeting and erratic relationships is that sociable/histrionics can never be sure of securing the affection and support they crave. By moving constantly and by devouring the affections of one person and then another, they place themselves in jeopardy of having nothing to tide them over the times between. They may be left high and dry, alone and abandoned with nothing to do and no excitement with which to be preoccupied. Cut off from external supplies, histrionics are likely either to engage in a frantic search for stimulation and approval or to become dejected and forlorn. They may proceed through cyclical swings, alternating moments of simulated euphoria and excitement intermingled with longer periods of hopelessness, futility, and self-condemnation. Should deprivation be frequent or prolonged, the probability is high that these personalities will display the signs of a clear and serious affective disorder.

Despite their lack of well-developed inner resources, histrionics have a reasonably good prognosis because they possess motivation and skills for maintaining satisfactory interpersonal relationships. Given their desire to relate to others and their facility for eliciting attention and approval, the probability is slight that they will succumb to prolonged pathology.

Interventional Goals

Histrionics rarely seek therapy. When they do, it usually follows a period of social disapproval or deprivation, and with the hope that a therapist will help fill the void. Often, when the patient's social environment returns to its baseline level of reward, the patient will terminate therapy, regardless of whether any therapeutic shift in personality structure has taken place. For this reason it is a good idea for the patient and therapist to establish very specific treatment goals (Callaghan, Summers, & Weidman, 2003). This approach helps the patient remain motivated to stay in therapy despite rather vague presenting complaints such as boredom, restlessness, discontent, and loneliness. The histrionic personality also often reports a growing disaffection with his or her mate, a feeling that the vitality that supposedly characterized earlier years together has now palled. Sexual interest may have faded and the frequency of relations may have dropped due to impotence or frigidity. As disaffection intensifies, conflicts and tension rise, prompting the patient to feel a sense not only of loss but of rejection and hostility from his or her mate. Life feels as if it has taken on a purposeless and meaningless quality. The patient may begin to dramatize his or her plight, feeling that every recourse is hopeless and futile.

In planning a therapeutic intervention program, the ultimate goal is to correct the sociable/histrionic's tendency to fulfill all of his or her needs by focusing on others to the exclusion of self. This requires a shift not only on the self-other but on the active-passive polarities. Specific interventions aimed at reversing problem-perpetuating behavioral tendencies and at modifying personologic domain dysfunctions must be chosen according to the individual case (see Table 3.3).

Reestablishing Polarity Balances

Histrionic personalities operate from the basic premise that they are incapable of handling a large number of life's demands and that they need someone truly competent and powerful to do so for them. In their effort to ensure that someone with these attributes and power is in fact around and willing to take care of all those things they "cannot," the histrionic must spend his or her emotional and mental energy focusing on others. Attention to the "rescuer" must be vigilant so that at any sign of displeasure or potential rejection, the significant other can be placated, and thus the histrionic's survival secured. In addition, others must be charmed and impressed

Table 3.3   Therapeutic Strategies and Tactics for the Prototypal Sociable/Histrionic Personality

Strategic Goals

Balance Polarities

Diminish manipulative actions

Moderate focus on others

Counter Perpetuations

Reverse external preoccupations

Kindle genuine social relationships

Acquire in-depth knowledge

Tactical Modalities

Decrease *interpersonal* attention-seeking

Stabilize fickle *moods*

Reduce *dramatic* behaviors

Reorient Flighty *Cognitive* Style

enough to supply a generous dose of rewards, including praise and admiration, without which the histrionic becomes anxious and depressed. These efforts, despite coming naturally to the histrionic, are demanding enough that there are few resources left with which to examine his or her own internal state. Ironically, success at these goals obviates the need to develop instrumental competence.

To reestablish balance within the self-other polarity, histrionics must learn to turn to themselves and away from others as a means of gratification and to accomplish instrumental goals. In terms of overall adaptation, it would also serve histrionics well to shift away from their persistent attempts to ensure that the environment does indeed yield sought-for gratification and learn to channel time and energy in more profitable ways. As they become more passive in relation to their social environment and overcome the anxiety of giving up full control over the script of their social lives, sociable/histrionics may begin to enjoy the element of surprise that comes with not having to orchestrate every social interaction.

Countering Perpetuating Tendencies

In an attempt to evade the anxiety that accompanies internal exploration, histrionics engage in massive repression of their unsettled inner lives. Rather than face the existential anxiety that is an inevitable consequence of a deep appreciation of the nature of life, the histrionic adopts a protective superficiality. Whatever anxieties do penetrate the shallow surface from the repressed realm of deeper experience are kept at bay through a fantasy of fusion with a powerful other. These strategies, however, involve blocking those very cognitions and emotions that would allow histrionics to process stimuli in an adaptive way. In the case of the histrionic, the lack of fruitful mental processing does not generally involve any kind of thought disorder; distraction is the histrionic's dysphoria-avoiding secret. A constant stream of social excitement and engaging (if trivial) external preoccupations must be maintained to keep sociable/histrionics from facing the hollow inner turmoil they so dread. Such a strategy requires that the histrionic be adept at creating interpersonal drama and approval. When a relationship inevitably moves past the initial high and into the reality of interpersonal differences that need to be worked out, the histrionic must quickly secure approval and admiration to avoid falling prey to despair. Moving on to a new relationship provides another opportunity for a honeymoon period but ensures that relationships do not get past a superficial level of intimacy, leaving histrionics without solid relationships to provide support and understanding during inevitable lapses of high drama in their social lives.

In working with a histrionic, a therapist will probably find that the patient thwarts all attempts to examine thoughts and feelings. Patiently guiding the histrionic down the road to self-discovery can prove extremely helpful in reversing maladaptive patterns. If histrionics can bear to face their anxieties, they can also be convinced to give up the external preoccupations that distract them from the processing of stimuli. Allowing the mind to perform logical cognitive operations can begin to change their impressionistic and underdeveloped schemas about causal relationships among events, thoughts, and feelings. Focusing on such previously unexamined matters can result in the integration of past experiences. These, in turn, should lead to learning and the flexibility to engage in alternative and less adolescentlike forms of coping behavior as well as the development of a more mature level of personal independence. Self-examination can also help histrionics see the long-term futility of relationship hopping and how it serves to deprive them of the very security they crave. The value of making an effort to develop skills needed to deal with less gratifying aspects of relationships, and to tolerate times when the histrionic is not on center stage in exchange for long-term intimacy, can then be grasped.

Identifying Domain Dysfunctions

The most salient disturbances in the prototypical histrionic personality are in the mood, interpersonal conduct, expressive behavior, and cognitive domains. Histrionics exhibit fickle mood and temperament. They overreact to environmental events, displaying dramatic but shallow emotional reactions that often lead them to behave in a less than ideal way. Constantly on an emotional seesaw between enthusiasm and irritation (anything is better than boredom), they rarely have the emotional tranquillity necessary to encourage the development of adaptive behavior. Probably one of the most immediate ways to reduce their emotional hyperreactivity is to focus therapeutic sessions on their flighty cognitive style. Because avoiding introspection and obsessing about external events is their habit, cognitive approaches can help histrionics learn to integrate experiences and thus forge rational schemas with which to process stimuli more completely and meaningfully. Exploratory therapy, behavioral experiments, group therapy, and cognitive exercises all can help sociable/histrionics give up a lifestyle characterized by impulsive behavior and thoughtless judgment.

The flirtatious interpersonal behavior that is the hallmark of the histrionic personality inevitably produces long-term problems despite its short-term rewards. Although others are initially easily seduced and manipulated to do and say that which the histrionic wishes, ultimately the histrionic is perceived as shallow and flighty. Rarely do they experience the satisfaction of genuine intimacy and appreciation for the person they are. Once again, work in the cognitive domain can help histrionics see the advantages of limiting exhibitionistic and seductive behavior to only a few social contexts in which they are more appropriate. Behavior modification can be particularly helpful in teaching alternative behavior skills, such as more assertive communication. Because histrionics are resistant to giving up the colorful style of their demonstrative behavior that has gained them so much attention, they should be taught to discriminate when it is appropriate and when it will lead only to long-term complications and an unfavorable shallow impression. Similar interventions can prove invaluable in modifying the theatrical overresponsiveness the histrionic uses in an attempt to ward off boredom by creating momentary adventures.

The sociable/histrionic self-image is gregarious. The self is seen as charming and oriented toward a full and pleasurable social life. This would not be problematic in and of itself; the fact is that the histrionic does not know how to define himself or herself without reference to others. Lack of a personal identity leaves the histrionic open to despair when left alone. Defining a personal identity is a major therapeutic objective. Part of this work can involve examining the historical antecedents of the development of histrionics' shallow object representations schema and helping them see that human interactions, emotions, and conflicts can be integrated in logical, meaningful, and cohesive ways.

Intrapsychically, the histrionic tries to avoid stress by using dissociation as a regulatory mechanism, altering self-presentations to create a favorable response when one persona fails. Distraction is used to avoid painful internal experiences, even if personal identity and self-understanding must be sacrificed. Consequently, the morphologic organization of their mental coping and processing schemas and structures is weak and lacking cohesion. Without allowing themselves to think about stimuli, histrionics ensure that new behavioral strategies cannot be developed, and coping will be inflexible and lack logical cohesion, mirroring the morphological structure from which it stems. A therapeutic goal is to bring this fact to the histrionic's attention, so that he or she can make informed decisions about behavior patterns. Many histrionics would indeed like to develop a stronger and less reactive sense of self.

Selecting Therapeutic Modalities

Most histrionic patients tend to view the therapist as a magical and omniscient helper who has the power to solve all the patient's problems. Chances are good that the patient will try to charm the therapist with entertaining stories and good looks, or pull for attention and nurturing with a dramatic show of distress (Bender, 2005). Two main problems arise when the therapist gives in to the patient's dependency. First, the patient learns neither self-sufficient behaviors nor how to make decisions himself or herself, and second, the patient eventually discovers that the therapist's caretaking capacity is indeed not superhuman, and possibly terminates therapy prematurely due to anxiety and disappointment over this inevitable discovery (Horowitz, 1997). It is no easy task, however, for the therapist to consistently reinforce independent and assertive behaviors in the face of the histrionic's well-practiced emotionally seductive and compelling help-seeking style (Schwartz, 2001).

Behavioral Techniques

Behavioral interventions can initially be most useful in relieving symptoms of emotional distress in histrionic patients; relaxation training and problem-solving strategies are particularly helpful in this regard. More long-term objectives of changing coping styles involve an array of case-specific cognitive-behavioral experiments that allow patients to challenge their assumptions about their fundamental lack of capacity to care for themselves. Assertiveness training can provide histrionics with behavioral alternatives to the manipulative seductive ploys they use to procure what they want and need. Encouraging patients to do just what they most fear, in small and controlled steps while carefully monitoring their reactions, can lead to the acquisition of behavioral and coping skills that foster lasting changes in self-efficacy.

Behavior therapy might be sufficient to help overcome dysfunctional expressive maneuvers, yet the shallowness that histrionics adopt to avoid the deep existential aloneness that each individual experiences requires more searching therapeutic intervention. For therapy to be successful in the long run, histrionics must come to tolerate the very existential anxiety they so successfully, but superficially, have learned to defend against.

Interpersonal Techniques

The process of learning to tolerate existential anxiety necessitates that histrionics be able to tolerate the identity crisis that inevitably accompanies the examination of long-term core conflicts and deep-seated anxieties. In the outline of her *interpersonal* therapeutic approach, Benjamin (1990) suggests that histrionics can be supported through this process by warm sympathy toward their observing ego (the part of the patient that can rationally understand the ways certain behaviors can lead to problems), with whom the therapist can gang up against the "enemy": that part of the patient that feels compelled to keep acting out damaging histrionic patterns.

Interpersonal therapy also makes use of concrete problems and relationships as a springboard from which to examine dysfunctional patterns. Alternative behaviors are actively recommended. Benjamin (1990) summarizes the histrionic position as one in which interpersonal relationships are dominated by an overtly expressed friendly trust, accompanied by a disrespectful covert agenda of forcing nurturance and love from a powerful other. Seductive and manipulative behaviors are the means to the histrionic's coercive ends. Addressing transference issues directly through questions concerning the patient's feelings about the therapy and therapist are suggested. Revealed reactions can then be connected back to earlier history, and the self-perpetuating quality of these patterns can be explored. Delineating the differences between social and therapeutic relationships (differences in reciprocity, expectations) can be used to counter romantic transference reactions. A significant challenge in the early stages of treatment is transforming the patient's conception of therapy as a way of facilitating immature fantasies to a setting where independent skills can develop. A major issue in this regard stems from histrionics' belief that if they were to become autonomous, no one would care for them, in fact, that they would be abandoned.

Interpersonal therapists often suggest that *couples* therapy can be useful, particularly for pairs whose personality styles are complementary, as has been clinically noted to be commonly the case. Histrionics often become involved with overcontrolled compulsives; intervention that focuses on role reversal can lead to more balanced personality styles as new behaviors are integrated. Couples therapy may be extremely useful following a histrionic's emotional outbursts, such as threats of self-destructive behavior and/or engaging in seductive play with others in an effort to make his or her spouse jealous (Links, Stockwell, & MacFarlane, 2004a).

Group intervention approaches may be particularly efficacious with histrionic patients, although Slavson (1943) expressed concern that the capriciousness and unpredictability of these patients would engender unusual tensions within the group. By contrast, Gabbard (1994) finds that these patients tend to be useful group participants owing to their ability to express their feelings and thoughts openly and directly. A problematic consequence is that the group setting may frustrate the patient's desire for the exclusive attention of the therapist. On the other hand, having an opportunity to observe individuals with similar interpersonal patterns can provide the patient with a mirror that fosters better understanding of the impact of his or her own behavior on others. Multiple perspectives on the self afforded by group members can encourage patients to integrate diverse information and bolster object-representation schemas. As the group members' acquaintance with each other deepens through the process of mutual sharing and appraisal, it is doubtful that the group will continue to accept dramatic and flirtatious behavior as a substitution for genuine sharing. Group approval and encouragement of appropriate assertive behaviors and simultaneous disregard for sociable/histrionic displays can serve as powerful reinforcers that help bring about change, as long as the patient does not feel so threatened by being challenged that he or she drops out of the group.

Cognitive Techniques

The procedures of *cognitive* reorientation may also prove useful in helping histrionics gain insight into their patterns and in building a richer inner life that would decrease the patient's dependence on others for identity and reinforcements. Histrionics typically are motivated and cooperative. However, their rather diffuse cognitive style may not lend itself well to the highly structured nature of cognitive therapy. Hence, in the early stages of treatment, these patients may find the procedures of therapy somewhat difficult, especially when they are asked to focus their attention on one theme at a time. Also problematic is the tendency to wander about somewhat randomly, if not capriciously, crossing the boundaries set forth by the therapist. A firm and clear-cut set of agreements may usefully counter this tendency toward rather vague and diffuse goals. In time, histrionic patients may come to recognize the value of specific, if short-term, goals.

In the cognitive therapy approach outlined by Beck, Freeman, and Davis (2003) the initial challenge for the therapist is to be able to maintain the patience needed to help histrionics process and perceive environmental stimuli in ways that are largely characterologically unnatural to them. Persisting despite frustration is key to successful treatment. Learning the very process of cognitive therapy itself can ultimately prove to be the histrionic's greatest new tool, as new cognitive processing skills lead to novel interpretation of the environment that fosters increases in independent and competent behavior. As Beck et al., point out, it is especially important for the therapist to consistently reinforce assertive and competent responses so as not to encourage the dependent patterns that so often bring long-term distress despite immediate reinforcement. Because of the sociable/histrionic's lack of attention to detail, setting up specific goals can sometimes be difficult. However, insisting that histrionics establish very clear ideas about what their therapeutic objectives are (how their lives will be different) can help ensure that the goals are meaningful to them and that "termination by boredom" is less likely.

In terms of specific interventions, cognitive authors suggest that the first step is to help patients identify their dysfunctional automatic thoughts. Histrionics have trouble with this task, as they are not adept at processing environmental events, the thoughts they have, and the feelings conjured by them in logical and detailed ways. Learning this skill, however, allows patients to focus attention on their emotions and desires, identify cognitive distortions, and discover accurate causal relationships among environmental, cognitive, and emotional events. Another great advantage of focusing on learning to identify the relationship between automatic thoughts and behavior is that patients can learn to stop and try to figure out what thought they are having before reacting, thus learning to control their impulsivity. Learning to analyze these relationships in terms of a means-ends analysis can help make histrionics aware of behavioral consequences. These new insights can help persuade histrionics to undertake experiments in which they try on different behavioral styles for effect.

Self-Image Techniques

As difficult as it is to convince histrionics to engage in self-exploratory and logical cause-and-effect analysis, their need for approval can be taken advantage of in the initial stages of therapy by using approval and appreciation of strengths to reinforce their tentative efforts. Although direct advice giving is rarely profitable, helping the patient analyze the reasons for and consequences of life choices can be invaluable. Confrontation of the dependency wish and acceptance of the fact that it inevitably cannot be satisfactorily fulfilled represent a therapeutic milestone on the road to developing a more adaptive

personality structure. Once this goal is achieved, some sociable/histrionics can independently go on to make lasting changes in their lives. Others may need ongoing
support as they explore new avenues to developing an identity.

One of the major changes therapy aims to support is decreased manipulation. Helping histrionics identify their authentic wants is a necessary first step in facilitating
their genuine communication to others. Identifying desires can be seen as part of a
larger process of discovering a sense of identity; most histrionics spend so much time
focusing on others in an attempt to get their attention and approval, modifying their
behavior to impact on each particular individual, that they are hardly sure of who
the fundamental "I" in their personality is. Asking patients to make a list of things
they know about themselves, even as basic as favorite colors and foods, is a good way
to begin building a self-concept. Another important goal toward the end of increasing self-valuation is to decrease the histrionic's fear of rejection. Histrionics become
paralyzed by the possibility of a relationship's ending and often are convinced that
straightforward behavior (as opposed to the "irresistible" cute, coy, or dramatic ploys
they usually depend on) will be easier for others to turn their back on. The possibility
of a rejection can be cognitively handled in therapy by imagining what life was like
before a particular relationship, and how the patient could manage to survive in the
future if a particular relationship were to end.

Intrapsychic Techniques

Psychodynamic therapies tend to be the most common in treating histrionics
(G. Kraus & Reynolds, 2001). They are based on the premise that patients need
to grasp the familial origins of their desire to have all of their needs met by a significant
powerful other. The assumption is that excessive dependency is unresolved and often
unconscious, and that it needs to be brought to light. Techniques include analyzing
manipulative behavior and its subconscious as well as conscious goals. The futility of
the histrionic's efforts needs to be made clear: It is impossible to have all of one's needs
met by someone else without being prepared to tolerate loss of self-respect. These issues
can all be worked on within the framework of the inevitable transference reaction. Current psychodynamic thinking frames the patient's reactions toward the opposite-sex
therapist in terms of his or her goal of manipulating the therapist to satisfy all needs.
These goals spring from the patient's unconscious dependent fantasy relationship with
the opposite sex parent; nurturance—not sexual gratification—is considered the true
goal of even sexually provocative behavior.

Although the classic psychodynamic therapist stance of neutrality and refusal to
provide direct advice is successful with a large number of patients, those with very
pronounced ego weaknesses may suffer from this particular therapist style. Weaker
patients may decide that the therapist is withholding, not because of his or her desire
to communicate a lack of omniscience, but out of principle, and they may try to
extract these responses from the therapist at all costs. The ensuing transference drama
can be more disruptive to therapy than an interested and sympathetic, if noncommittal,
response to pleas for advice. Examination of such requests can in fact be used to point

out to the patient what one can reasonably expect from other people. No intervention plan is complete without providing the patient with alternative behavioral possibilities and an understanding of their possible advantages over current patterns.

Brief and short-term anxiety-provoking therapy (Hersoug, Bogwald, & Hoglend, 2004; Sifneos, 1972) may also prove of value for those patients who exhibit higher levels of functioning and good psychological-mindedness. Not all briefer approaches are likely to be effective; thus, Mann's (1973) time-limited approach may elicit transference relationships that may end too abruptly for many histrionic patients who develop intense bonds to their therapists.

Pharmacologic Techniques

Psychopharmacological intervention with histrionics is often limited to dealing with episodes of depression. When histrionics with depression come to the attention of a therapist, the comparative degree to which symptoms are biologically based versus the extent to which they are a means to secure therapist attention needs to be evaluated. The possible advantages of taking antidepressant medication as a complement to psychotherapy should be considered (Teusch, Böhme, Finke, & Gastpar, 2001). More specifically, and depending on the primary symptoms, either antidepressants or mood stabilizers may prove to be useful. If there is only a partial reduction of symptoms in response to the SSRIs, it may be useful to add a mood stabilizer, such as lithium, as an adjunctive medication. Taken in medically low dosages, mood stabilizers may decrease symptoms of emotional sensitivity and moodiness, with no likelihood of problematic side effects or addictive possibilities. As Joseph (1997) notes, these medications may very well improve confidence, impulse control, and frustration tolerance, thereby enabling the utility of psychosocial treatments to bring the patient to a higher level of mature functioning.

Making Synergistic Arrangements

A first therapeutic step might be to curtail the patient's tendency to overemotionalize and thereby aggravate his or her distraught feelings. Relaxation training and cause-and-effect thinking skills can be useful adjuncts to the initial phases of long-term exploratory therapies. If a histrionic presents with depression that is evaluated to be endogenous and interfering with adaptive functioning, antidepressant medication can be considered as a support to psychotherapy. However, the therapist must establish a solid alliance and specific goals before prescribing medication, as there is always the risk that as soon as the histrionic feels better, he or she will terminate therapy regardless of whether changes have been made.

Clients whose familial or couple environment encourages their patterns would do well to participate in specific family or couple interventions as an adjunct at some point in their individual therapy. Group therapy can also help histrionics by exposing them to others with similar behavior patterns, which they sometimes may resist seeing in

Table 3.4 Sociable/Histrionic Personality Disorder Subtypes

Theatrical: Affected, mannered, put on; postures are striking, eye-catching, graphic; markets self-appearance; is synthesized, stagy; simulates desirable/dramatic poses. (Pure Subtype)

Appeasing: Seeks to placate, mend, patch up, smooth over troubles; knack for settling differences, moderating tempers by yielding, compromising, conceding; sacrifices self for commendation; fruitlessly placates the implacable. (Mixed Histrionic/Dependent Subtype)

Vivacious: Vigorous, charming, bubbly, brisk, spirited, flippant, impulsive; seeks momentary cheerfulness and playful adventures; animated, energetic, ebullient. (Mixed Histrionic/Narcissistic Subtype)

Disingenuous: Underhanded, double-dealing, scheming, contriving, plotting, crafty, false-hearted; egocentric, insincere, deceitful, calculating, guileful. (Mixed Histrionic/Antisocial Subtype)

Tempestuous: Impulsive, out of control; moody complaints, sulking, precipitous emotion, stormy, impassioned, easily wrought-up, periodically inflamed, turbulent. (Mixed Histrionic/Negativistic Subtype)

Infantile: Labile, high-strung, volatile emotions; childlike hysteria and nascent pouting; demanding, overwrought, fastens onto and clutches another; is overly attached, hangs on, stays fused to and clinging. (Mixed Histrionic/Borderline Subtype)

themselves, and gives them the opportunity to be rewarded for appropriate behavior from a group of people. Because others are the most powerful reinforcers for histrionics, this forum can potentially show rapid results.

Illustrative Cases

As noted in previous chapters, this section draws on extensive clinical observations as well as research on cluster and factor analysis that provides an empirical base for determining variants and coexisting personality disorders. Table 3.4 illustrates clinical synthesis of these personality subtypes.

Case 3.1, Joey S., 36

A Sociable/Histrionic Personality: Theatrical Type (Histrionic Prototype)

Presenting Picture

Joey was a comedy writer who seemed to always be performing. As a matter of fact, he was a former stand-up comic and, by his own admission, was quite good at it. He decided to forgo this original career choice owing to his distaste for other performers in the business. He complained that the others "never seem to have an offstage mode to their personalities"; this made for some rather shallow characters and meaningless friendships, and Joey viewed himself as "above" all that. However, on meeting Joey, it was obvious that most of what he complained about in others was present in himself! From outward behaviors such as his preoccupation with fixing his hair or his description of his chameleonlike wardrobe, to his discussion, which alluded to the transient nature of his interpersonal context, it was obvious that Joey was aware of something in himself that did not allow others to see his off-stage or true personality.

Problems had arisen as a consequence of this overly flexible image of self. Despite the charm and adaptiveness of these maneuvers, the ability to simulate all types of roles and characters, Joey complained of a vague sense of inner emptiness. He was stunned one morning when he woke up and could not think of even one intrinsic substantial self-quality; rather, he merely saw a "set of mirrors" that reflected what would be pleasing and attractive to others. Everything was simulated and expedient, all was pragmatic and marketable. Joey was a superb manipulator of symbols that mimic reality but felt destitute in terms of what he described as "my nonsymbolic self." Since that day, which was several months back by the time he sought help, Joey had felt apathetically depressed and found himself entirely unable to write.

Initial Impressions

Joey, a *theatrical histrionic,* could be seen as the dramatic, romantic, and attention-seeking caricature of the basic histrionic. Reminiscent of Fromm's (1941) description of the "marketing orientation," Joey lived life as if he were a commodity, an object for sale. No personal characteristic was seen as intrinsic, that is, a stable and fundamental aspect of who he was. It was the appearance of things that was everything. Joey was adept at transforming himself into something synthesized, something that appeared in ways other than it really was. It is this readily devised image that was projected on the world, shifting from time to time as the occasion called for. He packaged himself to meet the expectations of others as closely as possible. He was a chameleon of sorts, changing his colors and shadows to fit whatever environment he found himself in.

We might describe Joey as affected and mannered, one who puts on striking and eye-catching postures and clothes, one who markets his appearance to others and who simulates desirable and dramatic poses that are fabricated or synthesized to create an appealing image of himself. As was obvious from the start, much of Joey's characteristic operations were depleted; it would be important, first, to reacclimate him to his more familiar self. Thus, the initial milieu allowed him to focus on *self* and encouraged him to "first, touch base with the smoke and mirrors, then look behind them." This early supportive approach allowed him to relive a bit of his gratifying past and invest in his rather befuddled self-image. Joey quickly regained an *active* orientation in this process, as he was quite willing to share past triumphs with the therapist, and this renewed vigor primed him for deeper, more challenging explorations.

Domain Analysis

Joey was disclosing, but not forthright, in the clinical interview. Clarification came via a series of testing measures inclusive of the MCMI-III, Grossman Facet Scales, and the MG-PDC. Highlights of Joey's domain analysis were as follows:

Interpersonally Attention-Seeking: Masking fears of invalidation from important figures in his life, Joey made it a point to "refuse to be invisible" in his interactions. He regularly solicited laughs, praise, and accolades through a veneer of sophisticated wit.

Expressively Dramatic: Never one to be "shown up" in his crowd of entertainers, Joey would go to great lengths in melodramatic and caricatured behaviors to flaunt his thespian acumen, as well as to demonstrate hyperreactivity to the responses of others.

Temperamentally Fickle: Unrestrained in his autonomic reactivity, Joey showed a tendency to be swayed quickly and easily through a smorgasbord of fleeting and momentary feelings, governed largely by the most immediate and transparent stimuli in his environment.

Therapeutic Steps

The empathic and encouraging atmosphere fostered from the outset helped Joey realize that he could, in fact, secure approval and love from significant people in his life without resorting to "the façade." Following early *supportive* measures geared toward engaging Joey with the therapeutic process, it was necessary to work with him to reorient his tendencies toward more grounded, and less constant, patterns of garnering attention. Likewise, it was beneficial to address interpersonal difficulties by working toward a more empathic stance in relationships, that is, to assist him in acquiring a more genuine, honest, give-and-take style of socialization, rather than simply vying for self-serving *attention*. This was begun with behavior skills development, which would serve to ingrain healthier and more germane social skills, rather than relying only on his flair for the *dramatic*. From here, a combination of cognitive reframing (e.g., Beck) and interpersonal training (e.g., Klerman, Kiesler) proved useful to two specific therapy goals, which were largely social in nature. It was important for Joey to build his capacity for empathy and impulse control, which would augment his ability to sustain attachments without exploitation, as well as for him to learn to focus on the present environment as opposed to past events. It was largely unnecessary to help him find means of self-expression or insight, as he showed little difficulty in these areas.

Joey originally felt that he could work matters out on his own; as a result, it was some time before he actually sought help. Such a stance frequently leads to diminished investment in the process of treatment and perhaps more self-diagnosing or resistance. For Joey it led to apathy, repetitive social aberrations (as he repeatedly "forced" himself into more positive moods), and then resultant discontent. Not surprisingly, he resisted being frank and open with a therapeutic authority figure, instead masking deeper feelings of ambivalence and pessimism with a jovial façade; he had to be confronted cognitively to foster more serious disclosures and discussions leading to more direct connections with genuine feelings and concerns. Joey's tendencies included avoiding more substantial issues by wandering randomly among superficialities, and these trends needed to be stifled. This was accomplished by employing cognitive-behavioral techniques to cut through his more *fickle temperamental* tendencies. Also, it was helpful to maintain contact with family members, as they often had a different take on current matters, and sometimes an utterly contradictory viewpoint. Overall, treatment was most efficacious when it was focused on short-term goals, such as confronting his problematic behaviors and attitudes, restoring balance to his self-image, and bolstering those effective coping strategies that he did possess.

In this regard, efforts were directed at countering Joey's self-indulgent and exploitive presentation, which produced disapprobation and censure from others. Through the use of cognitive techniques, he was guided to see that this demeanor led to negative outcomes, such as estrangement, and the inability to elicit anything positive from others. As he gained interpersonal awareness (e.g., Benjamin), he became more successful at assessing situations objectively, learned how to be more clear and forthright rather than exploitive, and was able to put forth a more attractive and respected personality.

Case 3.2, Suzie P., 29

A Sociable/Histrionic Personality: Infantile Type (Histrionic with Borderline Traits)

Presenting Picture

Suzie had recently been reprimanded at work due to customer complaints and erratic work habits, which subsequently resulted in her demotion from full-time to part-time status at her job at a department store. This change prompted a rather severe and sudden anxiety (though her erratic emotionality seemed more characterological than immediate), as she now did not know if she would be able to save enough money to enroll in art school, and she really felt she needed this job to have a consistent reference on her resume. She explained that she had had many previous jobs, and something would always happen to cause her to walk out. She described significant relationships in her life that were of a similarly fragmented nature. Although she was currently involved with a new person, Suzie spoke frequently of her ex-boyfriend, who was "responsible" for her decision to go into art. He eventually moved out because he felt she was erratic in affect from moment to moment and regarded decisions as important one day, but discarded the next (e.g., marriage). Suzie's feeling, though, was that he said he'd always be there, but "as men do, he lied."

As the initial interview went on, she gradually revealed a troublesome relationship with her father, who had abandoned the family in her early adolescence only to return when Suzie was in high school with a whole new demanding attitude toward her. She, of course, rejected him and his new demeanor and viewed her ex-boyfriend as "the first healthy relationship I've ever had with a man, and he even let me down." Suzie often complained bitterly about the lack of care expressed by others and of being treated unfairly. These behaviors kept others constantly on edge, never knowing if they would be reacted to in a cooperative or a sulky manner. Although occasionally making efforts to be obliging, Suzie frequently precipitated interpersonal difficulties by constantly doubting the genuineness of interest others expressed. These irritable and childlike testing maneuvers frequently exasperated and alienated those on whom she depended. Her social network grew increasingly weary of these behaviors, leading her to react by vacillating erratically between expressions of gloomy self-deprecation, behaving in a sexually provocative manner, and being petulant and bitter.

Initial Impressions

Suzie demonstrated a compounding of histrionic and borderline personality features akin to what Kernberg (1967) has referred to as the "infantile personality." She evidenced labile and diffuse emotions, childlike pouting, and demanding-clinging behaviors, as well as a crude and direct sexual provocativeness. She displayed a childlike hysteria, often fastening onto and clutching significant others, seemingly fused to them. Her behavior was typified by deep and varying recurring moods, prolonged periods of self-deprecation, and episodes of high energy and impulsive, angry outbursts. There was an anxious seeking for reassurance from others to maintain equanimity. An intense fear of being abandoned led her to be overly compliant at one time, profoundly gloomy the next, behave with negativistic outbursts and tantrums, and then engage in sexually provocative behaviors. Some saw Suzie as submissive and childlike, and others as unpredictable, irritable, and irrational. There appeared to be an affective-activity equilibrium that was in constant jeopardy. As a consequence, Suzie vacillated between being high-strung, manipulative, and moody, and was particularly sensitive to the pressures and demands of others. In evolutionary terms, Suzie's overall polarity structure was in a constant state of unrest, and it would be of primary importance to start by easing these highly volatile conflicts. More specifically, emphasis continually changed between being fully *self*-oriented (expressing and declaring her autonomy and her adult status, albeit in a naive, resentful manner) and *other*-oriented (dependent, provocative, attention seeking, submissive). In an empathic milieu, it would be necessary first to resolve these tendencies via interpersonal means designed to establish more genuine and less manipulative relationships, beginning with her relationship with the therapist. Throughout the course, it would be necessary to work at reducing her constitutional proclivity toward highly *active,* anxious patterns, which continually fed the conflicts between polarities.

Domain Analysis

The struggle between childlike acquiescence and adult self-assertion constantly intruded into Suzie's life, as was seen in her pattern of MCMI-III Facet Scale scores, as well as her MG-PDC results:

Dissociation Mechanism: By incorporating defenses that served to create an ever-changing but momentarily self-pleasing mélange of characteristics, and remaining removed from constancy in her self-concept, Suzie effectively denied herself introspective vulnerabilities.

Shallow Objects (Intrapsychic Content): Suzie's views of significant figures incorporated only their momentary impulse qualities and served almost exclusively to allow her some immediate sense of self through superficial meanings ascribed to the person and the relationship.

Interpersonally Paradoxical: Unpredictably contrary, Suzie's actions with significant people in her life often provoked her alienation, despite the intention of these acts to pull people closer and to develop stronger bonds.

Therapeutic Steps

A primary short-term goal of treatment with Suzie was to aid her in reducing her intense ambivalence and growing resentment of others. With an empathic and brief focus, it was possible to initiate a productive therapeutic relationship. With a therapist who could convey genuine caring and firmness, she started to overcome her tendency to employ maneuvers to test the sincerity and motives of the therapist. Although she would be slow to reveal her resentment because she disliked being viewed as an angry person, these feelings were brought into the open and dealt with in a kind and understanding way. She was disinclined to face her ambivalence, but her mixed feelings and attitudes were a major focus of treatment. To prevent her from trying to terminate treatment before improvement occurred and to forestall relapses, the therapist employed techniques to counter Suzie's expectation that supportive figures would ultimately prove disillusioning. Circumscribed interpersonal approaches (e.g., Benjamin, Kiesler) were used to deal with the seesaw struggle Suzie enacted in her relationship with her therapist. She would alternately exhibit ingratiating submissiveness and a taunting and demanding attitude. Similarly, she solicited the therapist's affections, but when these were expressed, she rejected them, voicing doubt about the genuineness of the therapist's feelings. The therapist used *cognitive* procedures to point out these contradictory attitudes. It was important to keep these inconsistencies in focus or Suzie would have appreciated the therapist's perceptiveness verbally but not altered her attitudes. Involved in an unconscious repetition-compulsion in which she re-created disillusioning experiences that paralleled those of the past, she started to recognize her *dissociative* mechanisms cognitively and also was taught to deal with the enactment of *paradoxical* interactions interpersonally.

Despite her ambivalence and pessimistic outlook, there was good reason to operate on the premise that Suzie could overcome past disappointments. To capture the love and attention only modestly gained in childhood could not be achieved, but habits that provided only partial satisfaction could be altered in the here and now. Toward that end, the therapist helped her disentangle the *shallow object representations* that produced only momentary gains while setting herself up for eventual disappointment. For example, she both wanted and did not want the love of those on whom she depended. Despite this ambivalence, she entered new relationships, such as in therapy, as if an idyllic state could be achieved. She went through the act of seeking a consistent and true source of love, one that would not betray her as she believed others did in the past. Despite this optimism, she remained unsure of the trust she could place in others. Mindful of past betrayals and disappointments, she began to test her new relationships to see if they were loyal and faithful. In a parallel manner, she attempted to irritate and frustrate the therapist to check whether he would prove to be as "fickle" and "insubstantial" as others had in the past. It was here that the therapist's warm support and firmness played a significant short-term role in reframing Suzie's erroneous expectations and in exhibiting consistency in relationship behavior.

Although the rooted character of these attitudes and behaviors complicated the ease with which these therapeutic procedures could progress, short-term and circumscribed cognitive and interpersonal therapy techniques were quite successful. A thorough reconstruction of personality was not necessary to alter Suzie's problematic pattern. In other words, the therapist did not set goals too high because Suzie may not have been able to tolerate demands or expectations well. Brief therapeutic efforts were directed to build her trust, to focus on positive traits, and to enhance her confidence and self-esteem.

Case 3.3, Allison S., 25

A Sociable/Histrionic Personality: Vivacious Type (Histrionic with Narcissistic Features)

Presenting Picture

Allie was a flight attendant who was seemingly very satisfied with her work, as she had the opportunity to meet and interact with virtually "everybody." She was very comfortable with the brief interactions she had with a very wide audience, and even commented that one of her favorite tasks was the "performance" aspect of the emergency procedure presentation at the outset of each flight. She had recently been suspended due to several customer complaints that she had "snapped" at them, and counseling was suggested by her supervisor. She willingly agreed to do anything to salvage her job but mused that an alternative career might be modeling. Although quite upbeat and pert throughout the interview, it is rather interesting to note how quickly (albeit *briefly*) she shifted her affect back and forth from lively and happy to perturbed and tense at the mere mention of an unpleasant subject. She spoke of a series of men she has dated, and in the same breath mentioned that she was married approximately 2 years prior to the interview, for a very short time. Allie quickly changed the subject by stating that this was a brief, unpleasant period of her life, but that it was so insignificant that she felt even mentioning it was "a waste of breath."

For the most part, Allie's tendency was to be overly cheerful, of a lively and spirited nature, disposed to live life to the fullest in a brisk and vigorous way. She was distinguished by the animated nature of her movements, by her lack of disposition to sit still and relax for any period of time. She always seemed to be on the go, gesticulating freely and in a highly expressive manner, enjoying conversations, and producing ideas in a quick tempo. She raced her physical and psychic engines, exhibiting vigor in her movements, as in all other aspects of her behaviors and thoughts. For the most part, she was quite cheerful, although inclined to be rather superficial in the topics she discussed. She moved from one thing to another, often in a joyous and joking manner. She was notably thrill seeking, easily infatuated, and overly, but transiently, attached to one thing or person following another. She was restlessly energetic, ebullient, seeking momentary playful and joyful adventures, without imposing constraints on where and when these were to be pursued. She almost always viewed things from an optimistic and cheerful perspective; serious and problematic matters tended to be glossed over or overlooked entirely.

Initial Impressions

A frequent association has been found between histrionic and hypomanic features. In addition to the high level of energy and vigor that typifies hypomanic types, *vivacious histrionic* personalities such as Allie tend to be clever, charming, flippant, and capable of weaving fanciful images that intrigue, seduce, and exploit the naive.

Given these latter characteristics, it should not be surprising that she also exhibited a variety of narcissistic personality traits. Allie was driven by a need for excitement and stimulation; this energetic and driven young lady acted impulsively, was unable to delay gratification, and evidenced a penchant for momentary excitements and fleeting adventures, with minimal regard for later consequences. She lacked social dependability, exhibiting a disdain for the effects of her behaviors, as she pursued one restless chase or satisfying one whim after another. There was a capricious disregard for agreements hastily assumed, and she easily may have left a trail of broken promises and contracts, squandered funds, and distraught employers. Lacking inner substance and self-discipline, tempted by new and exciting stimuli, and skilled in attracting and cheerfully seducing others, Allie may have traveled an erratic course of flagrant irresponsibility and left in her wake the scattered debris of seductive and once promising hopes. She needed to be engaged and invested in the process of therapy, as she was prone to only be half-hearted. A humanistic/Rogerian milieu would serve to first focus her on objective aspects of herself that would serve to lay a foundation for a more genuine, less compensatory sense of *self*. Her interest needed to be held initially, and this was achieved by implementing a short-term approach from the outset. Occasionally encouraging her indulgence in reliving past achievements, the therapist enabled Allie to rebuild her previously synthetic self-esteem. Allie quickly became an active partner in restoring her self-confidence by recalling and elaborating on her attributes and competencies in front of the therapist. Her comfort and regained confidence also served to set the stage for more integrated, less exploitive interactions with and perspectives regarding *others*. It would not be until a later point that she could tolerate adjustments in her interactions and her constitutional tendency to be overly *active*.

Domain Analysis

Allie's MG-PDC highlighted facets of both histrionic and narcissistic patterns, as follows:

Interpersonally Exploitive: Allie tended to devalue and hurt others, mainly through irresponsible, discourteous, and socially unmindful acts as opposed to malevolent intentions; she felt entitled, lacked empathy, and routinely took others for granted, whether they were significant figures, casual associates, or strangers.

Cognitively Flighty: Taking her cues almost exclusively from the environment and the actions of others from whom she sought approval, Allie paid little attention to nuances or details, especially those orienting her to her own actions that may have served to create fleeting or disjointed relationships or situations.

Gregarious Self-Image: Allie synthesized a self-view that was unquestionably charming, stimulating, and effervescent, and disallowed any impressions that may have served to contradict this.

Therapeutic Steps

Allie's life situation became increasingly discouraging during the early period of treatment when she was not working. A positive and encouraging therapeutic approach focusing on her prior achievements enabled her to regain the feeling that she was genuinely worthy of affection from those who mattered to her, and she did not have to rely on the more fleeting interactions of customers, coworkers, or other, more random people who crossed her path. As the therapist evidenced empathy and genuineness in the therapeutic relationship while providing opportunities for Allie to reflect on her positive attributes without "performing," Allie began feeling less compensatory and synthetic, and more legitimately confident. *Gregariousness,* to Allie, changed meaning; her *self-image* gradually shifted from one who could not be anything less than perfectly charming and bubbly, to one who accepted both her sparkle and her blemishes. Gaining a more realistic, accepting, and diversified sense of self provided a sturdier platform on which to incorporate more challenging therapeutic matters. As she evidenced a more stable and accepting sense of self, short-term efforts were made to counter her characteristic self-indulgence, as well as her *interpersonal exploitiveness* that evoked condemnation and disparagement from others. She was guided, first through cognitive techniques, to see that these acts created negative consequences and that the ensuing alienation only added to the difficulties she was facing, as well as her ability to elicit positive attitudes and actions from others. As treatment continued, the therapist directed efforts primarily toward building greater empathy and impulse control rather than seeking to achieve expressive and insight-oriented goals, toward focusing on here-and-now behavior rather than actions in the past, and toward helping Allie learn how to sustain attachments through nonexploitive behavior. This was best achieved by a combination of cognitive reframing (e.g., Beck, Ellis) and interpersonal (e.g., Klerman, Kiesler) training, enhancing her attractiveness and success in her relationships with others.

As the precipitant for her treatment was situational rather than internal, it is important to note that Allie did not seek therapy voluntarily. She was fully convinced that if she were just left alone, she could work out any difficulty she might have with others. This would have led to backsliding and recurrences of her less than socially acceptable behavior. If treatment had been self-motivated, however, it may have been due to upsetting family problems, legal entanglements, social humiliation, or achievement failures. Allie's complaints took the form of vague feelings of boredom, restlessness, and discontent, all of which were expressions of her *cognitive flightiness.* Her tendency was to avoid major problems by wandering from one superficial topic to another, and this would inevitably lead to relapses. Hence, this had to be monitored and prevented. Interpersonal treatment methods that focused on her irresponsibility and impulsivity were particularly helpful, especially those that highlighted relationships with family members and important coworkers, who frequently reported matters quite differently than did Allie. Again, treatment was best geared to short-term goals, such as countering her problematic stances, extinguishing questionable behavior, reestablishing psychic balance, and strengthening previously socially acceptable coping patterns.

Case 3.4, Milton D., 41

A Sociable/Histrionic Personality: Appeasing Type (with Dependent/ Compulsive Features)

Presenting Picture

What Milton was doing in a therapy office was something of a mystery to him. He had initially seen a physician due to vague somatic complaints (mostly digestive in nature) and inability to sleep through the night. His physician also noted Milton's rather diffuse anxiety, which appeared more troublesome when he was outside of work and finding himself with no one to interact with. As a result, his physician recommended therapy.

Milton's personality might have been described by his work role: the "right-hand man." He seemed to be in a constant state of inertia, always searching for not only the best way, but *every fathomable* way he might please those around him. The most conspicuous example of this behavior was Milton's constant accommodation of his employer. From having a cup of coffee waiting at her fingertips at the precise moment she desired one, to picking up her children at their school, to wearing a pager so that she could reach him literally any time she desired, *nothing* was ever too much should it serve to gain her favor. When asked about the need for such pacification, Milton remarked that it *was* well above and beyond the call of duty, but perhaps this would make him look most favorable in his boss's eyes. He also alluded to the fact that although there had historically been no association between the two of them outside of work, "perhaps some day there would be." When asked about life outside of work, Milton immediately began speaking of his relationship with his mother. Though he did not go into much detail, it was apparent that this relationship, too, was one geared solely toward winning approval. As a youngster, Milton admitted, he experienced never-satisfied parents who found nothing about him that pleased them and nothing that was seen as appealing or attractive or right. His late father, especially, goaded Milton to *prove* that he was virtuous, competent, attractive, and worthy. Milton's reaction, of course, was to strive fruitlessly to appease the unappeasable, to placate the implacable, and now he found himself investing much of his life zealously searching for ways to elicit admiration and respect from others.

Initial Impressions

The desire to please others, to make them like him, to approve of him, to tell him that what he was doing was good, was the major driving force that motivated Milton, an *appeasing histrionic* subtype. Approval from others was his supreme goal. Not only did Milton want to show everyone that he loved them and would do anything for them, but he wanted everyone to praise and commend him in return. The search for reciprocal recognition and approval compelled and justified everything he did, as was seen in the pattern of his MCMI scores. He showed an unusual knack for pleasing people, for being thoughtful about their wishes, for making them friends rather than mere acquaintances. What is most distinctive about histrionics such as Milton is the need to placate others, to try to mend schisms that have taken place, and to patch up or smooth over troubling matters. He would moderate conflicts by yielding, compromising, and conceding to the wishes of others and was ready to sacrifice himself for approval and commendation. The configuration of characteristics that typify this appeasing type often encompasses an admixture of histrionic, dependent, and compulsive features. Alert to every sign of potential indifference, Milton quickly anticipated and avoided what might have been seen as unfavorable; he appraised matters and then enacted what would make him most appealing in the eyes of others. He wished to be a faultless pleaser, invariably seen as well-intentioned, not only in a superficial and momentarily obliging way, but through acts of genuine goodwill that others could not help but appreciate. He was a magnificent flatterer, willing to sacrifice any and all signs of integrity to evoke praise and goodwill. Beneath his surface affability, however, Milton felt himself to be a worthless person, marked early in life as inferior or troublesome, consigned to a self-image of being profoundly inadequate, unloved, and unlovable. He desperately tried to compensate for his deficiencies, invariably looking for ways he could gain some measure of appreciation. He kept this hidden hostility at bay, deeply suppressed, while his yearning for favorable signs of affection continued to gnaw painfully within him. Initial efforts with Milton would require that his dependent, *other*-oriented pattern remain at least somewhat intact while he began exploring his difficulties, as too soon a break from this strategy would likely stifle growth and cause undue emotional stress. A humanistic, empathic milieu would be needed to set the stage for more focused interventions.

Domain Analysis

Milton was eager to find out what his MCMI-III scales would say about him and how the facets of his personality might add up to the whole. He was intrigued by how these facets, measured by the Grossman Facet Scales, contained both characteristics of strength and potential liabilities:

Interpersonally Attention-Seeking: While he felt it a positive attribute to be able to attract appropriate attention from others, Milton frequently made it a point to be the "apple of everyone's eye," which paradoxically left him somewhat alienated and invariably quietly disappointed.

Reliable Self-Image: Conscientious and caring to a fault, Milton was mercurially dependable to others, but found himself hard-pressed to tend to his own needs or issues, which were frequently and regularly falling by the wayside.

Immature Objects (Intrapsychic Content): Models of interrelationships remained childlike and only primitively developed, as Milton seemed to approach all others as parental figures who needed to be appeased and pleased by "what a good little boy" he was.

Therapeutic Steps

It was expected that as more self-sufficient skills and thoughts would be clarified and enacted by Milton, a validation of his self-image would emerge, allowing for a more permanent, characterologic shift toward autonomy. Following the establishment of therapeutic rapport, it was important to work toward more genuine social skills (a more autonomous, self-driven stance) and correcting the faulty self-perpetuation regarding the all-importance of winning constant approval (gradual work toward diminishing other-orientation). To achieve significant goals employing short-term methods, some environmental changes were introduced early to maximize Milton's growth and to minimize his continued dependency. Clonazepam, an antianxiety agent that works at a moderate pace, was useful in increasing his confidence and vigor without overemphasizing the role of the medication as "the magic pill that takes care of everything." Although Milton was disinclined at the outset to share intimate feelings, wanting instead to simply be told what to do and be "fixed" by the professional, he responded well to the therapist under a treatment regimen that was strong in empathic caring. This empathic stance would begin a process of therapeutic transference in a brief psychodynamic framework, serving to realign and more fully develop *mature object relations.* Rather than a focused technique aimed at a specific goal, the nature of this relationship served, throughout this short-term intervention, to encourage Milton to gradually forgo persistent dependency maneuvers for more confident and parallel interrelations.

As noted, Milton welcomed the opportunity to depend on the strength, authority, and helpfulness of the therapist. This auspicious beginning was most fortunate, but it gave a misleading impression of significant progress. Despite initial successes, Milton resisted genuine moves to gain independence. This was a delicate balancing act: Without undermining his erroneous beliefs and the behavior they engendered, Milton may have become inactive or withdrawn from treatment, relapsing or regressing to his pretreatment level of adjustment. But had the therapist moved too quickly and broken the entire dependency bond prematurely, or had he tried to accomplish too much too soon, therapy may have precipitated unwarranted emotions or erratic behavior. The therapist began challenging Milton with well-timed cognitive and interpersonal confrontations, but only as Milton brought matters up as "unsolvable" for himself. Examples of this included setting up a therapeutic double-bind to explore possible outcomes of Milton not immediately appeasing his supervisor (*reliable self-image*) and creating realistic interpersonal role-play to examine differential responses to Milton's *seeking versus nonseeking of attention*. Dependency as a concept in the therapeutic relationship was challenged at a later point, as a more egalitarian therapeutic bond was created, as part of a move toward a more existential milieu to foster growth and the prevention of setbacks.

Case 3.5, Annmaria M. 38

A Sociable/Histrionic Personality: Tempestuous Type (Histrionic with Negativistic Features)

Presenting Picture

Annmaria was referred for therapy by her general practitioner after experiencing discomfort with unusually intense cramps, muscular pains, and irregularities in her menstrual cycle. Being a dancer, she did not expect her monthly cycle to be regular, but the symptoms she was experiencing seemed to have no clear physical etiology.

In the initial interview, Annmaria constantly sought approval, soliciting it from the therapist by both overtly flirtatious behaviors and direct questioning. This behavior, notably, had a very guarded edge to it, as it was apparent that *no one* was allowed past her persona. Annmaria also evidenced a brooding resentfulness and anger, very swiftly showing hostile underpinnings whenever she was reminded of anyone who might have behaved less than "perfectly," from her perspective. These brief outbursts would be followed immediately by a noticeable effort to regain control and the reassumption of her previous characteristic front. Her behavior was typified by a high degree of emotional lability and short periods of impulsive acting-out, alternating with depressive complaints, moodiness, and sulking. Her hypersensitivity to criticism, low frustration tolerance, immature behaviors, short-sighted hedonism, and excitement and stimulation seeking were also most salient. Emotions surged readily to the surface, evident in a distractible, flighty, and erratic style of behavior. Her sense of guilt, anger, and desire rose quickly but intermittently to the surface in pure and direct form. She admitted feeling frequently out of control, overly reactive to minor provocations, but she would not acknowledge her turbulent acting-out. When not overly wrought up, she exhibited moody complaints and sulky behaviors, but quickly reverted to an angry and inflamed response to minor events.

Initial Impressions

In Annmaria, a *tempestuous histrionic,* we see many features of the negativistic personality and, as she presented more acutely, some characteristics of the borderline as well. Annmaria behaved by fits and starts, shifting capriciously down paths that led only to interpersonal strife, often precipitating wrangles with others and disappointments for herself. Her moods were brittle and variable, with periods of high excitement and affability alternating with a leaden paralysis, fatigue, oversleeping, or overeating, all of which she tried to control. She displayed short-lived, dramatic, and superficial affects and reported a tendency to be easily excited and then quickly bored. Her mood levels were highly reactive to external stimulation. Feelings of desperation or euphoria were expressed dramatically and more intensely than justified by the situation. Despite her desire to be liked, her personality generated chronic and repeated conflicts with others. She often behaved like a child: demanding, self-centered, and uncontrolled. She seemed unable to put effective limits on her emotionally impulsive and irritable behaviors, often flying off the handle and succumbing to temper tantrums. When cut off from needed external attentions, Annmaria engaged either in a frantic search for approval, became easily nettled and contentious, or became dejected and forlorn. Untreated, she might have become less and less histrionic in her behaviors and more and more disgruntled, critical, and envious of others, grudging their good fortune with a jealous, quarrelsome, and irritable reaction to minor slights. She might have come to be preoccupied with bodily functions and health, overreacting to illness and voicing unreasonable complaints about minor ailments. These symptoms would probably have been displayed exhibitionistically to regain lost attention and support.

Annmaria's self-perpetuating patterns included a strong tendency to attempt to manipulate her environment (*active–other*-orientation), but also a deep-seated hostility stemming from a rather pervasive, disenchanted *self*-image; this was a breeding ground for an internal-external conflict. It would be most useful for the therapist to establish a firm but empathic therapeutic stance, maintaining openness and understanding but remaining impervious to her provocations. The therapist needed to readily see things from her point of view and to convey a sense of trust and a feeling of alliance. Brief treatment required a balance of professional firmness and authority, mixed with tolerance. By building an image of a fair-minded and strong authority figure, the therapist successfully encouraged Annmaria to change her expectations, providing a model for her to learn the mix of power, logic, and fairness. At later stages of treatment, it would be appropriate to work toward interpersonal improvements, establishing goals that would help her gain more effective and satisfying social skills.

Domain Analysis

Annmaria initially resisted psychological testing, noting, "I get pushed and prodded enough at work; I don't need to do that here, too." When she was informed that the measures were not intrusive and would provide a lot of good material for reflection, she reluctantly acquiesced. Highlights from the MCMI-III Grossman Facet Scale scores and MG-PDC results were as follows:

Cognitively Skeptical/Capricious: Annmaria's thought process revolved heavily around trust versus mistrust, with most of her beliefs leaning toward the cynical negativistic quality; however, the volatility and changeability of her perceptions also resembled the borderline's changeable perceptions as she hoped for better and precipitated letdown after letdown.

Interpersonally Attention-Seeking: Although Annmaria insisted that her attention-getting job "was always left at work," much of her motivation appeared to stem from her constant solicitation of approval from others, as well as her manipulation of events to put herself in the spotlight.

Gregarious Self-Image: Annmaria relied heavily on sex appeal to foster attention; however, this also fueled the fire for hostilities toward those who responded to this aspect of her personality.

Therapeutic Steps

Beginning with the tolerant but professional demeanor demonstrated by her therapist, Annmaria began to experience a new model for adult relationships. Although many psychodynamic/object-relations possibilities could have been selected, these were not explored in this treatment, as it was thought best to concentrate on skill development rather than insight, and much supportive work would first be needed before skill development could take place. For this intervention, simply having a model for more mature object representations served to plant a seed in Annmaria's development. Less confrontive humanistic approaches provided her with opportunities to vent anger, but more important, she began to voice conflicts regarding her feelings for people and actively questioned whether her typical conviviality should be a one-size-fits-all approach to her interactions. Once drained of hostile feelings and more aware of how different people respond to this persona (her *gregarious self-image*), she was led to examine other habitual behaviors and cognitive attitudes and was guided into less destructive perceptions and outlets.

A useful goal for Annmaria was to tolerate the experience of responsibility for the turmoil she sometimes caused. Beckian-oriented cognitive methods, using a measure of confrontation, helped undermine her tendency to always trace problems to another person's stupidity, laziness, or hostility (her *skepticism*), as well as her tendency to impulsively interpret events at face value, subject to extreme volatility due to blaming others (her *capriciousness*). She did begin to accept responsibility for some of her difficulties, but it was important, during these cognitive exercises, that her therapist was prepared to deal with Annmaria's inclination to resent him for supposedly tricking her into admitting it. Similarly, the therapist needed to be ready to tolerate challenges and avoid efforts to outwit him. Annmaria tried to set up situations to test the therapist's skills, to catch inconsistencies, to arouse ire, and, if possible, to belittle and humiliate him. Restraining impulses to express condemning attitudes was an important task for the therapist, but one that was used for positive gains. Annmaria also attempted to entice the therapist using more flirtatious and sexually provocative behaviors; this *attention-getting* interpersonal strategy, like the others, did not elicit the response she was used to. Frustrated, and depleted of her usual defenses, she began self-confrontation regarding her characteristic behaviors; this led to an opportunity to explore a greater spectrum of interpersonal dynamics utilizing methods described by Benjamin and Kiesler to help discover more socially acceptable behaviors that would seem germane to Annmaria. In the remaining sessions, Annmaria built on these new interpersonal skills, looking to her therapist for feedback regarding efficacy and appropriateness, and began to self-monitor her perceptions and responses to both innocuous and challenging situations.

Resistances and Risks

A therapist whose own sense of identity and self-worth are largely satisfied by being very helpful to others may easily be manipulated into playing the savior role and actually repeat the patient's maladaptive experiences of significant others. Other therapists may find the flighty sociable/histrionic style annoying; hypervigilant histrionics are apt to sense the disapproval and in fact regress further into their manipulative, theatrical ways. It is important for therapists to make a real effort at empathy lest their intervention efforts be jeopardized. On the other hand, empathy should not imply playing the histrionic's game. Despite the entertaining and charming communication style, it is very important for the therapist to maintain sober and respectful attention. The playful banter that is often therapeutically helpful with other personality styles can serve in the case of the histrionic to reinforce the belief that one is always on display and must charm those around one to get attention and approval. A more serious attention, particularly a stance of respect toward the patient, helps provide the histrionic with alternative interaction schemas.

Some sociable/histrionics fear the possibility of becoming drab and dull even as they see the advantages of becoming deeper and adopting a more premeditated behavioral style. It is a good idea to encourage more constructive expression of the histrionic's natural dramatic flair (often it can be used to advantage by enlisting the dramatic persona to work with the therapist against maladaptive cognitions and behaviors) rather than a complete suppression of such tendencies, which may lead to termination.

One of the frustrations a therapist might feel when working with histrionics is their tendency to have pseudo-insights. Just when the therapist is sure that the therapy has come to a breakthrough, the vague and forgetful style of the histrionic leads to rapid disintegration of apparent gains. The tendency of the patient to want to make the therapist feel important in the hopes of thereby securing special treatment also often leads to enthusiastic agreement with the therapist, despite the lack of real internalization of the issues. Patience on the part of the therapist is a must if his or her disappointment in pseudo progress is not itself to become disruptive.

CHAPTER 4

Personalized Therapy for the Confident/ Narcissistic Personality Patterns

The essential feature of these personality patterns is an overvaluation of self-worth and a grandiose sense of self-importance and uniqueness (Britton, 2004; Perry & Perry, 1996). In seeming contradiction to the inflated self-concept is an inordinate need to be loved and admired by others (Imbesi, 2000). Unlike the ravenous affectional needs of histrionic and dependent personalities, however, narcissists believe that they are entitled to tribute and praise by virtue of their "specialness." These personalities also share the antisocial's features of egocentricity, interpersonal exploitation, and exaggerated needs for power and success (Plakun, 1990). Unlike the anger and vindictiveness of antisocials, however, narcissists are characterized by a benign arrogance and a sense that they are "above" the conventions and reciprocity of societal living (Miliora, 1998). There is little real empathy for others, but rather, a tendency to use people for self-enhancement and for indulging their own desires. Those who satisfy their needs are idealized, whereas those who serve no immediate purpose are devalued and even treated contemptuously (Muscatello & Scudellari, 2000). This shifting of overvaluation and denigration may occur frequently within the same relationship. There is an expectation of preferential treatment and special favors, without assuming reciprocal responsibilities.

Confident/narcissistic personalities are cognitively expansive, enjoying fantasies of unrealistic goals, with a tendency to overestimate their abilities and achievements (Ronningstam, 1998). However, these exaggerated feelings of personal importance can leave the narcissist quite vulnerable to injuries of self-esteem and pronounced feelings of unworthiness should their grandiose self-expectations not be met (Fernando, 1998). Although characteristically imperturbable and insouciant, repeated failure and social humiliations may result in uncertainty and a loss of self-confidence (Geiser & Lieberz, 2000). Over time, with the growing recognition of inconsistencies between their self-perception and their actual performance, comes self-disillusionment, feelings of fraudulence, and, in some cases, a chronic state of dysthymia (West, 2004). In other instances, a psychic blow generated from a single event (e.g., a humiliating defeat or a public criticism) may precipitate a brief but severe depressive episode. Such states rarely endure for extended periods, as depression is not experienced as consonant with the narcissist's self-image. The symptomatology of the narcissistic depression may be quite variable, shifting from dramatic expressions of worthlessness and self-deprecation to irritable demandingness and criticism of others. These perceptions tend to be attributed to external, "universal" causes rather than to personal, inner inadequacies (Abramson, Seligman, & Teasdale, 1978). Consistent with this formulation, narcissists may subtly accuse others of not supporting or caring for them enough. At other times, hostility may be directly expressed, as the narcissist becomes enraged at others being witness to his or her shame and humiliation.

Klerman (1974, p. 139) described narcissistic depression as a response to fallen self-esteem, a signal of discrepancies within the self-system between "ideal expectations and practical reality." Depression in such individuals follows the inability to maintain the unreasonable expectations set for themselves and others. Kernberg (1975, 1986) provides perhaps the most eloquent description of the process of self-disillusionment in the narcissist:

> For them, to accept the breakdown of the illusion of grandiosity, means to accept the dangerous, lingering awareness of the depreciated self-the hungry, empty, and lonely primitive self surrounded by a world of dangerous sadistically frustrating and revengeful objects. (1975, p. 311)

According to Millon (1969/1985, 1996b), both the confident/narcissistic and the nonconforming/antisocial patterns (described in this and the next chapter) turn inward for gratification, having learned to rely on themselves rather than others for safety and self-esteem (Glickauf-Hughes, 1997). Weakness and dependency are threatening. Because both narcissists and antisocials are preoccupied with matters of personal adequacy, power, and prestige, status and superiority must always be in their favor (Kernberg, 2001). They fear the loss of self-determination, proudly display their achievements, and strive to enhance themselves and to be ascendant, stronger, more beautiful, wealthier, and more important than others (Witte, Callahan, & Perez-Lopez, 2002). In some, it is what they think of themselves, not what others say or can provide for them, that serves as the touchstone for their security and contentment (Rivas, 2001).

These two independent personality patterns have been conceived of as two major subtypes in earlier writings (Millon, 1969/1985): the passive-independent, or narcissistic personalities, who are confident of their self-worth and who feel they need be merely themselves to justify being content and secure; and the active-independent, or antisocial personalities, who struggle to prove themselves, who insist on their rights and will be harsh and ruthless when necessary to retaliate or gain power over others

(Gunderson & Ronningstam, 2001). For the narcissistic type, self-esteem is based on a blind and naive assumption of personal worth and superiority. For the antisocial type, it stems from distrust, an assumption that others will be humiliating and exploitive (Fernando, 2000).

The confident/narcissistic personality, in accord with Millon's ecological framework and its evolutionary model of polarities, is portrayed in Figure 4.1. What is most notable in this chart is the primacy of both passive/accommodation and self-individuation in the narcissist's adaptive style (Imbesi, 1999). This translates into the narcissist's focus on self as the center of one's existence, with a comparable indifference to others (nurturance). Owing to an unusual developmental background, in which others overvalued the narcissist's self-worth by providing attention and tribute unconditionally, these patients fail to develop the motivation and skills ordinarily necessary to elicit these tributes (Aizawa, 2002). To them, merely being who they are is sufficient; they

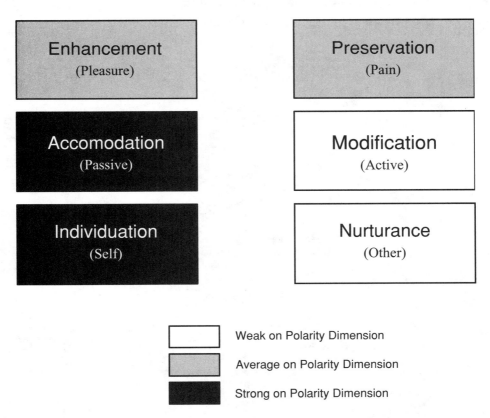

FIGURE 4.1 Status of the confident/narcissistic personality prototype in accord with the Millon.

do not have to do anything, much less achieve, to elicit signs of admiration and high self-esteem. Narcissists are passive, therefore, because they expect the rest of the world to do their bidding without reciprocal efforts.

Whereas narcissists assume that others will favor them without efforts on their part, antisocial personalities make no such assumptions at all. The active–modifying polarity is preeminent in antisocials because they feel they have been mistreated and undervalued. They must actively usurp and take from others that which they assume will never be given them; nothing is voluntarily supplied by others. Whereas narcissists expect others to be freely forthcoming, antisocials expect nothing and hence must take what they can.

Clinical Picture

As in previous chapters, we provide a wide range of perspectives for observing and conceptualizing the traits of the confident/narcissistic personality patterns (see Figure 4.2).

This discussion turns first to the typical characteristics of the narcissistic personality as organized in the eight clinical domains format (see Table 4.1).

NARCISSISTIC PROTOTYPE

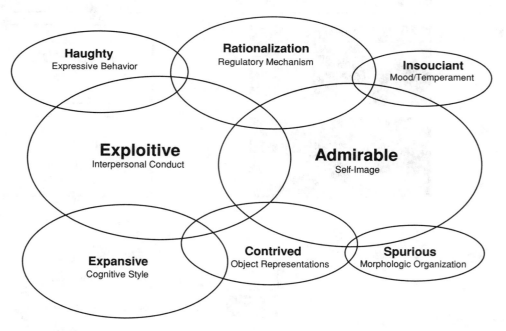

FIGURE 4.2 Salience of prototypal confident/narcissistic domains.

Table 4.1 Clinical Domains of the Confident/Narcissistic Personality Prototype

Behavioral Level:

(F) **Expressively Haughty** (e.g., acts in an arrogant, supercilious, pompous, and disdainful manner, flouting conventional rules of shared social living, viewing them as naive or inapplicable to self; reveals a careless disregard for personal integrity and a self-important indifference to the rights of others).

(F) **Interpersonally Exploitive** (e.g., feels entitled, is unempathic, and expects special favors without assuming reciprocal responsibilities; shamelessly takes others for granted and uses them to enhance self and indulge desires).

Phenomenological Level:

(F) **Cognitively Expansive** (e.g., has an undisciplined imagination and exhibits a preoccupation with immature and self-glorifying fantasies of success, beauty, or love; is minimally constrained by objective reality; takes liberties with facts and often lies to redeem self-illusions).

(S) **Admirable Self-Image** (e.g., believes self to be meritorious, special, if not unique, deserving of great admiration; acts in a grandiose or self-assured manner, often without commensurate achievements; has a sense of high self-worth, despite being seen by others as egotistic, inconsiderate, and arrogant).

(S) **Contrived Objects** (e.g., internalized representations are composed far more than usual of illusory and changing memories of past relationships; unacceptable drives and conflicts are readily refashioned as the need arises, and others are often simulated and pretentious).

Intrapsychic Level:

(F) **Rationalization Mechanism** (e.g., is self-deceptive and facile in devising plausible reasons to justify self-centered and socially inconsiderate behaviors; offers alibis to place self in the best possible light, despite evident shortcomings or failures).

(S) **Spurious Organization** (e.g., morphologic structures underlying coping and defensive strategies tend to be flimsy and transparent, appearing more substantial and dynamically orchestrated than they are in fact, regulating impulses only marginally, channeling needs with minimal restraint, and creating an inner world in which conflicts are dismissed, failures are quickly redeemed, and self-pride is effortlessly reasserted).

Biophysical Level:

(S) **Insouciant Mood** (e.g., manifests a general air of nonchalance, imperturbability, and feigned tranquillity; appears coolly unimpressionable or buoyantly optimistic, except when narcissistic confidence is shaken, at which time either rage, shame, or emptiness is briefly displayed).

Note: F = Functional Domains; S = Structural Domains.

Haughty Expressive Behavior

It is not uncommon for narcissists to act in an arrogant, supercilious, and disdainful manner. There is also a tendency for them to flout conventional rules of shared social living. Viewing reciprocal social responsibilities as being inapplicable to themselves, they act in a manner that indicates a disregard for matters of personal integrity and an indifference to the rights of others. When not faced with humiliating or stressful situations, narcissists convey a calm and self-assured quality in their social behavior. Their seemingly untroubled and self-satisfied air is viewed, by some, as a sign of confident equanimity. Others respond to it much less favorably; to them, these behaviors reflect immodesty, presumptuousness, pretentiousness, and a haughty, snobbish, cocksure, and arrogant way of relating to people.

Narcissists appear to lack humility and are overly self-centered and ungenerous. They characteristically, but usually unwittingly, exploit others, take them for granted, and expect others to serve them, without giving much in return. Their self-conceit is viewed by most as unwarranted; it smacks of being "uppity" and superior, without the requisite substance to justify it.

Exploitive Interpersonal Conduct

As noted, confident/narcissists feel entitled, expecting special favors without assuming reciprocal responsibilities. Not only are they unempathic, but they take others for granted, are often shameless in the process, and use others to enhance their own personal desires. Unfortunately for them, narcissists must come to terms with the fact that they live in a world comprising others. No matter how preferred their fantasies may be, they must relate and deal with all the complications and frustrations that real relationships entail (Dickinson & Pincus, 2003). Furthermore, and no matter how satisfying it may be to reinforce oneself, it is all the more gratifying if one can arrange one's environment so that others will contribute their applause as well. Of course, true to their fashion, narcissists will seek to accomplish this with minimal effort and reciprocity on their part. In contrast to the dependent personality, who must submit and acquiesce to evoke favorable rewards, or the histrionic, who must perform and be attractive to win praise from others, narcissists are likely to contribute little or nothing in return for the gratifications they seek. In fact, some narcissists assume that others feel honored in having a relationship with them, and that others receive as much pleasure in providing them with favors and attention as the narcissist experiences in accepting these tributes.

It should not be surprising that the sheer presumptuousness and confidence exuded by the narcissist often elicits admiration and obedience from others (Dickinson & Pincus, 2003). Furthermore, narcissists typically size up those around them and quickly train those who are so disposed to honor them; for example, narcissists frequently select a dependent mate who will be obeisant, solicitous, and subservient, without expecting anything in return except strength and assurances of fidelity. It is central to narcissists' interpersonal style that good fortune will come to them without reciprocity. Because they feel entitled to get what they wish and have been successful in having others provide them with comforts they have not deserved, narcissists have little reason to discontinue their habitual presumptuous and exploitive behaviors.

Expansive Cognitive Style

For the most part, narcissists exhibit an undisciplined imagination and seem preoccupied with immature and self-glorifying fantasies of success, beauty, or romance. Although nondelusional, they are minimally constrained by reality. They also take liberties with facts, embellishing them, even lying, to redeem their illusions about their self-worth. Narcissists are cognitively expansive. They place few limits on either their fantasies or their rationalizations, and their imagination is left to run free of the constraints of reality or the views of others. They are inclined to exaggerate their powers, to freely transform failures into successes, to construct lengthy and intricate rationalizations that inflate their self-worth or justify what they feel is their due, quickly depreciating those who refuse to accept or enhance their self-image.

Admirable Self-Image

Narcissists feel justified in their claim for special status, and they have little conception that their behaviors may be objectionable, even irrational. Narcissists believe that they are special, if not unique, persons that deserve great admiration from others. Quite frequently they act in a grandiose and self-assured manner, often without commensurate achievements. Although they expect to be seen as meritorious, most narcissists are viewed by others as egotistic, inconsiderate, and arrogant. Their self-image is that they are superior persons, "extra-special" individuals who are entitled to unusual rights and privileges. This view of their self-worth is fixed so firmly in their minds that they rarely question whether it is valid. Moreover, anyone who fails to respect them is viewed with contempt and scorn (Patton & Meara, 1996).

It is not difficult to see why the behaviors of narcissists are so gratifying to them. By treating themselves kindly; by imagining their own prowess, beauty, and intelligence; and by reveling in their "obvious" superiorities and talents, they gain, through self-reinforcement, the rewards that most people must struggle to achieve through genuine attainments. Narcissists need depend on no one else to provide gratification; they always have themselves to "keep them warm."

Contrived Object Representations

The internalized representations of past experiences are deeply embedded and serve as a template for evaluating new life experiences (Kernberg, 1998). For the narcissist, these object representations are composed far more than usual of illusory and changing memories. Problematic past relationships are readily refashioned so as to appear entirely consonant with the narcissist's high sense of self-worth. Unacceptable impulses and deprecatory evaluations are quickly transformed to enable these persons to maintain their preferred and contrived image of both themselves and their past. Fortunately for most narcissists, they were led by their parents to believe that they were invariably lovable and perfect, regardless of what they did and what they thought. Such an idyllic existence could not long endure; the world beyond home is not likely to have been so benign and accepting. As a consequence, narcissists must transform the less palatable aspects of their past to be consistent with what they wish the past was rather than what it was in fact.

Rationalization Regulatory Mechanism

What happens if confident/narcissistics are not successful—if they face personal failures and social humiliations? What if realistic events topple them from their illusory world of eminence and superiority? What behaviors do they show, and what mechanisms do they employ to salve their wounds?

Still confident and self-assured, narcissists deceive themselves with great facility, devising plausible reasons to justify their self-centered and socially inconsiderate behaviors (Glasser, 1997). With an air of arrogance, narcissists are excellent at rationalizing their difficulties, offering alibis to put themselves in the best possible light, despite evident shortcomings or failures on their part.

If rationalizations fail, they will likely become dejected and shamed and feel a sense of emptiness. Narcissists will have little recourse other than to turn for solace to their fantasies. In contrast to the antisocial personality (described in the next chapter), most narcissists have not learned to be ruthless, to be competitively assertive and aggressive when frustrated. Neither have most acquired the seductive strategies of the histrionic to solicit rewards and protections. Failing to achieve their aims and at a loss as to what they can do next, they are likely to revert to themselves to provide comfort and consolation. It is at these times that their lifelong talent for imagination takes over. These facile processes enable them to create a fanciful world in which they can redeem themselves and reassert their pride and status. Because narcissists are unaccustomed to self-control and objective reality testing, their powers of imagination have free rein to weave intricate resolutions to their difficulties.

What the narcissist is unable to work out through fantasy is simply repressed, put out of mind and kept from awareness. As noted previously, narcissists invent alibis, excuses, and "proofs" that seem plausible and consistent and convince them of their continued stature and perfection. Flimsily substantiated rationalizations are offered, but with a diminished air of confidence and authority. However, narcissists may never have learned to be skillful at public deception; they usually said and did what they liked without a care for what others thought. Their poorly conceived rationalizations may, therefore, fail to bring relief and, more seriously, may evoke scrutiny and deprecating comments from others. At these times, narcissists may be pushed to the point of employing projection as a defense, as well as to begin to construct what may become rather primitive delusions.

Spurious Morphologic Organization

Narcissists suffer few conflicts; their past has supplied them, perhaps too well, with high expectations and encouragement. As a result, they are inclined to trust others and to feel confident that matters will work out well for them. As will be detailed in a later section, this sanguine outlook on life is founded on an unusual set of early experiences that only rarely are duplicated in later life.

The structural organization of the narcissist's inner world for dealing with life tends to be quite flimsy and transparent to the discerning observer. From a surface view, one would assume that narcissists' personality organization is more substantial and dynamically orchestrated than it is in fact. Owing to the misleading nature of their early experiences, that is, that they really did not have to do much to make the world work for them, these people have never developed the inner skills necessary to regulate their impulses adequately, to channel their needs skillfully, or to acquire a strategy in which conflicts are resolved, failures are overcome, and a genuine sense of competence is regained following problematic experiences.

Reality bears down heavily at times. Even the routine demands of everyday life may be viewed as annoying incursions by narcissists. Such responsibilities are experienced as demeaning, for they intrude on the narcissist's cherished illusion of self as almost godlike. Alibis to avoid "pedestrian" tasks are easily mustered because narcissistics are convinced that what they believe must be true and what they wish must be right. Not only do they display considerable talent in rationalizing their social inconsiderateness, but they utilize a variety of other intrapsychic mechanisms with equal facility. However, because they reflect minimally on what others think, their defensive maneuvers are transparent, a poor camouflage to a discerning eye. This failure to bother dissembling more thoroughly also contributes to their being seen as cocksure and arrogant.

Unable to disentangle themselves from lies and inconsistencies, and driven by their need to maintain their illusion of superiority, they may begin to turn against others, accusing others of their own deceptions, their own selfishness, and their own irrationalities. It is at these not very typical times that the fragility and pathology of the narcissist become clearly evident. Breakdowns in the defensive structure of this personality, however, are not too common. More typically, the exploitive behaviors and intrapsychic maneuvers of narcissists prove highly adaptive and provide them with the means of thwarting serious or prolonged periods of dejection or decompensation.

Insouciant Mood/Temperament

Roused by the facile workings of their imagination, confident/narcissists experience a pervasive sense of well-being in their everyday life, a buoyancy of mood, and an optimism of outlook—*except* when their sense of superiority has been punctured. Normally, however, their affect, though based often on their semigrandiose distortions of reality, is generally relaxed, if not cheerful and carefree. There is a general air of nonchalance, an imperturbability, a feigned tranquillity. Should the balloon be burst, however, there is a rapid turn to either an edgy irritability and annoyance with others or to repeated bouts of dejection characterized by feeling humiliated and empty. Shaken by these circumstances, one is likely to see briefly displayed a vacillation between rage, shame, and feelings of emptiness.

Table 4.2   Self-Perpetuating Processes: Confident/Narcissistic Personality

Illusion of Superiority
    Sees no reason to develop skills
    Views striving with contempt
    False self-image leads to feelings of fraudulence

Lack of Self-Control
    Takes unjust liberties with social rules
    Prevaricates and fantasizes freely
    Fantasies recede from objective realities

Social Alienation
    Unable to join in social give-and-take
    Selfishness evokes condemnation
    Misinterprets others' intentions and actions

Self-Perpetuation Processes

A major factor in the perniciousness of personality pathology is that its characterological behaviors are themselves pathogenic. Pathological personality patterns perpetuate themselves by setting into motion new and frequently more troublesome experiences than existed in the past. This section turns to a number of these self-perpetuating features (see Table 4.2).

As with all personalities, narcissists exhibit their style with persistence and inflexibility. They cannot alter their strategy because these patterns are deeply ingrained (Soyer, Rovenpor, Kopelman, Mullins, & Watson, 2001). Rather than modifying their behavior when faced with failure, they may revert more intractably to their characteristic style; this is likely to intensify and foster new difficulties. In their attempts to cope with shame and defeat, they set up vicious circles that only perpetuate their problems. Three of these are elaborated next.

Illusion of Competence

Narcissists assume that the presumption of superiority will suffice as its proof. Conditioned to think of themselves as able and admirable, they see little reason to waste the effort needed to acquire these virtues. Why bother engaging in such demeaning labors as systematic and disciplined study if one already possesses talent and aptitude? Moreover, it is beneath one's dignity to struggle as others do. Because they believe that they are well endowed from the start, there is no need to exert their energies to achieve what they already have. They simply assume that what they wish will come to them with little or no effort on their part.

Many confident/narcissists begin to recognize in time that they cannot live up to their self-made publicity and fear trying themselves out in the real world. Rather than face genuine challenges, they may temporize and boast, but they never venture to test their adequacy. By acting in this way they can retain their illusion of superiority without fear of disproof. As a consequence, however, narcissists paralyze themselves. Their unfounded sense of confidence and their omnipotent belief in their perfection inhibit them from developing whatever aptitudes they may in fact possess. Unwilling or fearful of expending the effort, they may slip increasingly behind others in actual attainments. Their deficits may become pronounced over time, making them, as well as others, increasingly aware of their shortcomings. Because their belief in their superiority is the bedrock of their existence, the disparity between their genuine and their illusory competence becomes extraordinarily painful. The strain of maintaining their false self-image may cause them to feel fraudulent, empty, and disconsolate. They may succumb to periodic depressions or may slip slowly into paranoid irritabilities and delusions.

Lack of Self-Controls

The narcissist's illusion of superiority and entitlement is but one facet of a more generalized disdain for reality. Narcissists are neither disposed to stick to objective facts nor to restrict their actions within the boundaries of social custom or cooperative living. Unrestrained by childhood discipline and confident of their worth and prowess, they may take liberties with rules and reality, and prevaricate and fantasize at will. Free to wander in their private world of fiction, narcissists may lose touch with reality, lose their sense of proportion, and begin to think along peculiar and deviant lines. Their facile imagination may ultimately evoke comments from others concerning their arrogance and conceit. Not disposed to accept critical comments about their "creativity" and needing to retain their admirable self-image, narcissists are likely to turn further to their habit of self-glorification. Lacking social or self-controls, however, their fantasies may take flight and recede increasingly from objective reality.

Social Alienations

Were narcissists able to respect others, allow themselves to value others' opinions, or see the world through others' eyes, their tendencies toward illusion and unreality might be checked or curtailed (Links & Stockwell, 2002). Unfortunately, narcissists have learned to devalue others, not to trust their judgments, and to think of others as naive and simpleminded. Thus, rather than question the correctness of their own beliefs, they assume that it is the views of others that are at fault (Alarcon, 1996). Hence, the more disagreement they have with others, the more convinced they are of their own superiority and the more isolated and alienated they are likely to become. These ideational difficulties are magnified further by their inability to participate skillfully in the give-and-take of shared social life. Their characteristic selfishness and lack of generosity often evoke condemnation and disparagement from others. These reactions drive narcissists further into their world of fantasy and only strengthen their alienation.

And this isolation further prevents them from understanding the intentions and actions of others. They are increasingly unable to assess situations objectively, thereby failing further to grasp why they have been rebuffed and misunderstood. Distressed by these repeated and perplexing social failures, they are likely, at first, to become depressed and morose. However, true to their fashion, they will begin to elaborate new and fantastic rationales to account for their fate. But the more they conjecture and ruminate, the more they will lose touch, distort, and perceive things that are not there. They may begin to be suspicious of others, to question others' intentions, and to criticize others for ostensive deceptions. In time, narcissists' actions will drive away potential well-wishers, a reaction that will only serve to "prove" their suspicions.

Deficient in social controls and self-discipline, the confident/narcissist's tendency to fantasize and distort may speed up. The air of grandiosity may become more flagrant. They may find hidden and deprecatory meanings in the incidental behavior of others, becoming convinced of others' malicious motives, claims on them, and attempts to undo them. As their behaviors and thoughts transgress the line of reality, their alienation will mount, and they may seek to protect their phantom image of superiority more vigorously and vigilantly than ever. Trapped by the consequences of their own actions, they may become bewildered and frightened as the downward spiral progresses through its inexorable course. No longer in touch with reality, they begin to accuse others and hold them responsible for their own shame and failures. They may build a "logic" based on irrelevant and entirely circumstantial "evidence" and ultimately construct a delusional system to protect themselves from unbearable reality.

Interventional Goals

Despite the potential for serious decompensation, as just described, most narcissists function successfully in society if they possess even a modicum of substance and talent to back their confidence (M. P. Warren & Capponi, 1996). Difficulties arise only when a marked disparity exists between their presumptions and their actual competence (Stewart, 1997). Narcissists' bountiful reservoir of faith in themselves can withstand considerable draining before it runs dry. A particularly painful blow to their pride, however, may precipitate a depressive disorder that causes "intolerable" and unaccustomed discomfort. Such an event may entail a severe occupational failure, an embarrassing loss of public esteem, or a sudden change of attitude on the part of a previously idolizing partner. The suffering endured as a result of the crisis is often perceived as exceptional in itself and as deserving of professional attention.

Once involved in treatment, however, narcissistic patients present resistances that make personality restructuring a difficult goal to realize. They persist in blaming others for all of their difficulties, adopt a position of superiority over the therapist, and perceive any attempt at constructive confrontation as humiliating criticism. If comfort and regained confidence are the goals, however, these can often be achieved in only a few sessions. The therapist can hold narcissists' initial interest by allowing

**Table 4.3 Therapeutic Strategies and Tactics for the Prototypal Confident/
Narcissistic Personality**

Strategic Goals
   Balance Polarities
      Stimulate active-modifying
      Encourage other-focus

   Counter Perpetuations
      Undo insubstantial illusions
      Acquire discipline and self-controls
      Reduce social inconsideration

   Tactical Modalities
      Moderate admirable *self-image*
      Dismantle *interpersonal* exploitation
      Control haughty *behavior*
      Diminish expansive *cognitions*

them to focus attention on themselves, and by further encouraging discussions of their past achievements the therapist may enable them to rebuild their recently depleted self-esteem. Not infrequently, self-confidence in narcissists is restored by talking about themselves, by recalling and elaborating their attributes and competencies in front of a knowing and accepting person.

Merely reestablishing former levels of functioning, however, especially rebuilding the narcissist's illusions of superiority, may prove over the long run to be a disservice to the narcissistic patient. Until more realistic self-evaluation is achieved, it is not likely that narcissists will be motivated to develop competencies and socially cooperative attitudes and behaviors that would lead to more gratifying and adaptive lives. If their capacity to confront their weaknesses and deficiencies is strengthened, patients may be able to acquire greater self-control, become more sensitive and aware of reality, and learn to accept the constraints and responsibilities of shared social living (see Table 4.3).

Reestablishing Polarity Balances

Characteristic narcissistic confidence, arrogance, and exploitive egocentricity is based on a deeply ingrained, if sometimes fragile, self-image of superior self-worth (Slavinska-Holy, 1988). Achievements and manifest talents are often not proportional to the narcissist's presumptions of "specialness." The alternative to maintaining unsustainable beliefs of personal infallibility, that is, recognition of imperfections, limitations, and flaws, however, is tantamount to reconciliation with failure and utter worthlessness. For some narcissists such unreal expectations for themselves stem from experiences in which otherwise doting parents became unsupportive or even abusive at the manifestation of "imperfection" in their child; others simply cannot conceive of life among the "masses." As those around narcissists "dare" not to notice their special uniqueness and then behave appropriately, narcissists turn away from attempting to secure comfort from "simpleminded" others whose place it is to tend them (S. M. Johnson, 1987). Instead, they increasingly rely on themselves as a source of rewards. Turning inward provides the opportunity to pamper and ponder themselves and to fantasize about the great recognition that will come to shine on them one day. Thus narcissists, who start out high on the self polarity, become increasingly less other-oriented with the passage of time.

In the mind of the narcissist, others are the source of all his or her troubles and difficulties and are responsible for any failures to achieve fantasized goals. Not only do others have to make this up to the narcissist, but their natural inferiority dictates that they should attend to all the narcissist's whims and needs. The narcissist's exploitive egocentricity is not the two-faced, contract-breaking, means-to-an-end exploitiveness of the antisocial. Rather than actively planning, narcissists' arrogance and snobbish sense of superiority lead them to believe that others "owe" them something, and their self-centered convictions of genuine entitlement result in the "passive" exploitation of others. The sense of superiority often results in a lack of goal-oriented behavior in general; narcissists simply believe that good things are their due, a natural by-product of their intrinsic "specialness." This nonadaptive bias toward the passive end of the active-passive dimension often results in personal, social, and professional stagnation.

A main therapeutic goal in trying to increase a narcissist's other-orientation and active goal-directed behaviors is to help him or her accept that although human imperfections are inevitable, they are not necessarily a sign of failure or worthlessness (Waska, 1996). If narcissists can appreciate the benefits (lack of pressure, decreased fear of criticism) of not needing to be infallible, they may be able to consider their part of the responsibility for any difficulties they may be having. Active problem solving and improved interpersonal interaction is a worthy goal.

Countering Perpetuating Tendencies

Narcissists' characteristic difficulties almost all stem from their lack of solid contact with reality. The same disdain for objectivity prevents effective coping with subsequent troubles. The problem-perpetuating cycle begins with early experiences that provide noncontingent praise that teach narcissists to value themselves regardless of lack of accomplishment. Their inflated sense of self-worth causes them to conclude that there is little reason to apply any systematic effort toward acquiring skills and competencies when "it is so clear that" they already possess such obvious and valuable talents and aptitudes (Kurtz, 1997). Their natural gifts, they believe, are reason enough for them to achieve their goals and earn others' respect.

In time, confident/narcissists come to realize that others, who are expending considerable effort to achieve goals, are moving ahead and receiving more recognition. Envious and resentful that the acknowledgment that is "rightfully theirs" is being bestowed on others, narcissists intensify their boasting and air of superiority (Ornstein, 1998).

Eventually, the prospect of actually going out in the world and risking humiliating failure for all to witness becomes untenable in the face of the grand illusions of personal competence narcissists feed to themselves and others.

The problems posed by narcissistic illusions of competence feed into and are exacerbated by social alienation and lack of self-controls (Cartwright, 2002). The conviction that they are "entitled" leads narcissists to harbor disdain for social customs and cooperative living. A lack of respect for others' opinions and feelings leads to a failure to integrate normative feedback about their behaviors and illusions. In fact, the conviction that others are simpleminded and naive causes narcissists to retreat further into their illusory and isolated world of fantasy at every hint of disapproval. Self-serving rationalizations of others' lack of adulation can escalate till complementary paranoid delusions of persecution and grandiose illusions become firmly entrenched. Were narcissists to possess some self-controls, their social isolation may not have such dire consequences. Internal reality testing, however, is as neglected as are external inputs. Rather than working to realize ambitions, threat of failure and conceit push narcissists to retain their admirable self-image through fantasy. The regard for reality that would prevent narcissists from perpetuating their psychological and coping difficulties are notably absent.

Therapeutic intervention offers an inroad into the pathological cycle through the modification of the overblown self-image. As the self is appraised more realistically, as perfection is seen as unattainable, and as the need to employ self-discipline to achieve goals is understood, the narcissistic patient may come to recognize and accept his or her similarity to others. As the patient begins to make genuine efforts to improve the genuine quality of life, an appreciation for others' hard work and achievements may develop and replace chronic envy and resentment. Intervention aimed directly at increasing empathic understanding can lead to a sensitivity to other's feelings that fosters motivation to adopt cooperative interpersonal behaviors. Toward this end, the narcissist can choose to learn to tolerate and make use of constructive social feedback. Day-to-day successes can eventually provide the gratification that can bolster the patient's resolve not to perpetuate nonadaptive cognitive and behavioral strategies and help control the impulse to escape into unproductive flights of fantasy. If social isolation is thus decreased, therapeutic work has led to hard-won modifications in the patient's deeply entrenched lifestyle.

Identifying Domain Dysfunctions

The most salient narcissistic dysfunctions are manifested in the self-image and interpersonal conduct domains and are expressed in the form of an admirable self-concept and unempathic, even exploitive, treatment of others. At best, the narcissist confidently displays achievements and behaves in an entitled, and occasionally grating manner. Facts are twisted and the line between fantasy and reality becomes blurred as narcissists boast of unsupportable personal successes and talent; at the same time, interpersonal behavior moves toward the inconsiderate, arrogant, and exploitive. Others may express irritation at the unsubstantiated grandiosity of the narcissist's fantasies and at the inequitable nature of his or her social interactions. However, owing to their sense of self-importance, narcissists feel justified when taking advantage of others to indulge their desires and enhance their situation with no consideration of reciprocal responsibilities. As long as this self-schema is maintained, the narcissist has little chance of finding motivation to effect changes in other areas. Thus, a first therapeutic intervention needs to focus on accepting a realistic self-image. As the cognitive foundation on which exploitive behavior is justified is weakened, interventions that increase empathic understanding and cooperative interactions can become the clinical focus. The possible advantages of these cognitive and behavioral modifications—warmer receptions from others and a more solid personal sense of efficacy—can then be integrated to encourage further development.

Successful intervention in the primary domains can lead to beneficial advances in secondary domains. Furthermore, resolving secondary domain dysfunctions therapeutically can also bolster progress in the more salient areas. Behavioral interventions, including role-playing, techniques of behavioral inhibition, modeling, and systematic desensitization, that elicit nonadulating therapeutic feedback can help extinguish haughty expressive behavior as well as exploitive interpersonal conduct. These in turn can result in more genuine interpersonal events that subsequently serve as useful counterexamples to unrealistic or contrived object representations. Such exercises and the results they generate may set the groundwork for a more searching exploration of the patient's internalized schemas and their negative consequences. Illusory ideas and memories and pretentious attitudes can eventually be replaced with reality-based experiences and object representations.

As the patient comes to grasp the nonadaptive nature of the expansive narcissistic cognitive style, preoccupation with immature fantasies may be decreased. As cognitive and behavioral dysfunctions come to be regulated, the narcissist's insouciant mood is also likely to be naturally tempered. Baseline nonchalance and buoyancy can be replaced with more context-appropriate feelings. The rages, shame, and emptiness that resulted from undeniable discrepancies between self-image and reality are often modified along with the patient's self-concept. In some cases, psychopharmacological intervention may be indicated if a resistant depression appears to be interfering with therapeutic progress.

Ultimately, therapeutic interventions in these domains can have a beneficial effect on this personality's spurious morphologic organization. Flimsy defensive strategies can be replaced by stronger coping mechanisms, and the stress-reducing regulatory mechanism of rationalization can be given up for more realistic and growth-fostering inner and outer self-representations.

Selecting Therapeutic Modalities

Working with narcissists is difficult for therapists who seek change in a patient's personality. Benjamin (1993) notes that the patient's presumptions of entitlement and admiration may encourage the therapist to join the patient in mutual applause, while criticizing the rest of the world. Alternatively, the patient may maintain a stance of superiority. Neither kind of therapeutic alliance helps the patient achieve more adaptive functioning. Any confrontation of the confident/narcissist's patterns will be experienced as criticism, however, and chances are high that the patient will choose to terminate therapy. Benjamin suggests that narcissists may consider changing their interpersonal habits if they are convinced that it will lead to a more favorable response from others. Overall, best therapeutic outcomes may come from honest interpretations presented in a tone of approval and acceptance (Callaghan et al., 2003). Good therapeutic gain will result when the patient internalizes the therapist's empathic acceptance of the patient's faults and deficits. As children, most narcissists were noncontingently praised for their "perfection," and may have been led to feel like utter failures when their inevitable lack of perfection was too apparent to be ignored. The therapist's attitude that faults are inevitable and perfectly human provides an opportunity for realistic self-evaluation of self-worth that was rarely provided in the typical narcissist's early learning history. Carefully timed self-disclosures of the therapist's reactions toward the patient can also potentially lead to substantial therapeutic gain. Such information can encourage the patient's insight into the negative impact of his or her habitual behaviors on others, and, if revealed with supportive skill, can foster motivation to modify these habits.

Behavioral Techniques

Behavioral approaches to treating narcissistic behaviors (e.g., sexual exploitation) and destructive habits (e.g., overspending, not working) include contingency management and behavioral response prevention. Systematic desensitization of evaluation distress and role-play reversals that increase empathic understanding of others can also be useful adjuncts to individual therapy (Turkat, 1990). Sperry (1995) notes that the process of disclosing personal shortcomings and social weaknesses are alien to narcissists; hence, they believe that behavioral interventions are easier to implement earlier in treatment than later because they call for less self-disclosure than do other techniques or become more frequent over time.

Interpersonal Techniques

Benjamin's (1993, 2005) *interpersonal* approach suggests that achieving the first crucial therapeutic objective, the patient's recognition of problematic interpersonal patterns, is particularly challenging with narcissistic patients. While the therapist's empathic understanding is necessary in facilitating this process, the form of therapist statements needs to be carefully considered to prevent encouraging narcissistic tendencies inadvertently. Benjamin provides examples of more and less therapeutically effective statements in discussing a narcissistic patient and his dissatisfied wife. An example of a response that probably encourages a narcissistic schema is "You have been trying so hard to make things go well, and here she (your wife) just comes back with complaints." Benjamin notes that such a therapist response would probably enhance the patient's pattern of externalizing and blaming. A preferred alternative would be "You have been trying so hard to make things work well, and you feel just devastated to hear that they aren't going as perfectly as you thought." The advantage of this response is that it encourages the patient to examine internal processes and reaction patterns.

Many theorists believe that accurate and consistent empathic mirroring is central to effective treatment. Empathy provides a foundation for learning self-control. Similarly, patients may be able to internalize the therapist's empathic affirmation of their value. Also valuable is helping narcissistics patient to learn to tolerate their realistic faults and weaknesses. This can be achieved when the therapist models behavior in which his or her own mistakes or errors are overtly acknowledged. On occasion therapists may wish to confront, albeit gently, patients' attitudes of grandiosity and entitlement. Care should be taken, however, not to undo the therapeutic relationship.

Present habits become clearer when their functional significance is grasped. To this end, the patient's pattern of emotional reactions such as envy and feelings of entitlement can be traced to early interactions with significant others. Internalized representations of these early figures continue to guide present functioning. As the patient comes to recognize which attitudes and behaviors are motivated by earlier internalizations, he or she may become freer to modify them. An example provided by Benjamin is a patient who expressed anger and envy about a friend's receipt of public acknowledgment of success. The therapist shifted the patient's focus to issues underlying the envy by asking him how his mother would react to such news. Further discussion helped clarify to the patient that his concern about her reaction of disappointment (real or internalized) supports his unpleasant envious feelings. Such insight can help the patient resolve to detach from internalized representations of such figures. Finally, it is noted that once the patient accepts that unattainable ambitions and maladaptive behaviors need to be given up in favor of more realistic and fruitful cognitive and interactive habits, the bulk of the therapeutic challenge may be well on its way; new learning may be a relatively easy undertaking thereafter.

Couples and *family* interventions can be a very effective way for the narcissist to learn to relate to another person in an empathic way (Kurtz, 1997; Links & Stockwell, 2002). Benjamin points out that encouraging simple expressions of affect may serve to perpetuate rather than modify problems when working with a narcissist and his or her spouse, particularly if the spouse exhibits dependent or masochistic traits (often found to be the case). Spouses with these characteristics are prone to accept the narcissist's blame for the couple's difficulties. Instead, the complementarity of the partners' patterns needs to be confronted and collaboration from both parties secured. Agreements about reallocation of household duties and funds can help the narcissist give up the "entitled" role. Role-plays and role-reversals can help teach the narcissist empathic understanding that would make such transitions more palatable. Benjamin points out that for role-playing techniques to be successful, the narcissist's exact words and inflections must be used by the spouse; failure in exact mirroring can lead to rage and withdrawal. Properly done, however, this technique can also bring home the fact that the patient is not always at the center of the spouse's experiential field, which serves not only to decrease feelings of grandiosity and entitlement, but also to reduce the perception that every instance of the spouse's failure to notice the narcissist is necessarily an insult. In broader based family treatment settings, the therapist should function to constrain untoward affects and acted-out impulses. Moreover, every effort should be made to redirect such troublesome responses and to restore disturbed family communications to their best former levels, most notably with increased mutual support.

Group approaches can be problematic, as the patient often experiences rage and counters with withdrawal at any hint of empathic failure from other group members or from the therapist. On the other hand, sharing therapy with others provides an opportunity for patients to constrain their self-indulgences and to practice empathy. To the degree that a constructive and encouraging working relationship can be established, it may be possible to set limits on the patient's less desirable characteristics and his or her desires for special treatment. Systematically examining the patient's reactions can help provide the patient with insight, given that the therapist-patient relationship is strong enough for the patient to tolerate the stresses of the group setting. If the group can offer unanimous strong support, the patient is more likely to consider feedback about his or her unappealing behavior patterns. A variety of divergent factors may contribute to group effectiveness with confident/narcissists. For the most part, feedback from peers is likely to be more acceptable than feedback from the authoritative therapist. Similarly, the intense emotion associated with personal deficits is diluted within the group, as opposed to individual treatment. As Grotjahn (1984) has noted, there are several unique elements for narcissists in group settings: an increase in the capacity to empathize with others, experiencing the mirroring of one's personal needs, and the availability of new objects for idealization.

Cognitive Techniques

The *cognitive* approach to treating narcissistic personality disorder outlined by Beck et al. (2003, p. 248) suggests that although long-term treatment goals vary with each patient, they are likely to include "adjustment of the patient's grandiose view of self, limiting cognitive focus on evaluation by others, better management of affective reactions to evaluation, enhancing awareness about the feelings of others, activating more empathic affect, and eliminating exploitive behavior." Beck et al. suggest that general interventions should be tailored to what they refer to as the three narcissistic hallmarks of dysfunction: grandiosity, hypersensitivity to evaluation, and lack of empathy.

From a cognitive perspective, confident/narcissists' tendency to overvalue themselves is based on faulty comparisons with others, whose differences from themselves are overestimated (Beck et al., 2001). When the comparison obviously favors another, however, narcissists tend to undervalue themselves to a disproportionate extent. Much of these extremes in thinking can be attributed to an all-or-nothing categorical style. The therapist aims to temper extreme dualistic thinking by endorsing more realistic middle-ground positions. Another useful technique is to encourage patients to make comparisons intrapersonally rather than using others as reference points so that progress can be internally and more honestly gauged. Searching for personal similarities with others is another cognitive exercise that can lead to improved attitudes and empathic social behavior. Beck et al. (2003) also note that pervasive cognitive orientations can be modified by encouraging patients to provide evidence for case-appropriate "alternative beliefs," which, if integrated, help reverse narcissistic tendencies. Examples of such therapeutic positions include "One can be human, like everyone else, and still be unique"; "Colleagues can be resources, not just competitors"; "Everyone has flaws"; "Feedback can be valid and helpful. It's only devastating if I take it that way"; and "Ordinary things can be very pleasurable."

Another recommendation is to encourage the confident/narcissistic to modify his or her fantasies. Rather than attempting to eliminate a deeply entrenched fantasizing habit, however, the typically unrealistic and unadaptive contents can be replaced with attainable gratifications and pleasures. For example, fantasizing about singing a hit song in front of an audience of thousands can be replaced by imagining singing with a community choir. By focusing on the potential gratification of engaging in the activity itself, rather than on others' positive evaluation of the performance, more realistic fantasizing can serve as a covert rehearsal of adaptive and esteem-building behavior.

Self-Image Techniques

The flip side of narcissistics' craving for recognition and adulation is their hypersensitivity to criticism and their defensive grandiosity. Systematic desensitization through exposure to a hierarchy of negative feedback can be effective in reducing troublesome responses. The therapist can utilize the visualization of coping strategies that enable the narcissist to deal effectively with constructive criticism (Affsprung, 1998). Additional exercises toward this end include learning how to decide whether a particular evaluative situation is important, and how to request specific feedback from others. This can reduce the time and energy needed for more important tasks that narcissists use up anxiously pondering the opinions of others, even in situations of no consequence. Thought stopping can be used to intervene with this form of obsessive rumination.

In working toward the end of increasing the confident/narcissist's empathy, two general stages of intervention may be recommended (Lacroix, Peterson, & Verrier, 2001). First, the empathic deficit needs to be brought to light. The therapist can often be helpful by drawing attention to others' feelings. If necessary, instances of inconsiderateness or exploitation should be pointed out, albeit gently. In the second stage, the patient can actively imagine how others feel; this is often effectively accomplished by engaging in emotion-focused role-plays and role-reversals. Specific new beliefs regarding the significance of others' feelings can be explored and verbalized. Behaviors that are consistent with these beliefs can be devised and rehearsed, both in therapy and outside.

Intrapsychic Techniques

Psychodynamic approaches to restructuring the narcissistic personality are generally based on one of two approaches, the first proposed by Kernberg (1975), the second by Kohut (1971). Kernberg formulates narcissistic grandiosity to be a result of the child's rage at mother's indifference or rejections. Kohut sees the disorder as a developmental arrest caused by a maternal failure to validate her child's developing self-worth. Kernberg's clinical recommendations include confronting the patient's conscious and subconscious anger, examining negative transference toward the therapist, and addressing the patient's use of defenses such as splitting, projection, and projective identification (Romano, 2004). According to Kernberg, symptomatic improvement is more likely to be rapid with supportive rather then expressive methods. Kohut's model encourages the therapist to assume a sympathetic and accepting stance while addressing the objective need for the patient to accept personal limitations (Ivey, 1999). Short-term methods may be especially useful for crisis intervention and to establish a bridge to more long-term treatment procedures (Rovik, 2001). Binder (1979, 2004) reports on the use of a brief treatment method for increasing self-esteem, also in preparation for a longer term program. The hope here is to increase the patient's awareness of his or her vulnerability to shame and disappointment, as well as to increase the capacity to moderate intense affects, such as irritability and rage (Hingley, 2001).

Pharmacologic Techniques

It is unclear whether the narcissistic arrogance and sense of grandeur seen among narcissists lend themselves to any of the pharmacologic agents that are currently available (Teusch et al., 2001). Of course, should the narcissist succumb to feelings of depression, consideration must be given to the use of antidepressant medications (SSRIs). Similarly, signs of hypomania or grandiosity may call for one or another of the mood stabilizers (e.g., lithium). Should the symptomatology become more severe, perhaps approaching a mild level of paranoia, low doses of several antipsychotics may prove useful (e.g., risperidone, olanzapine).

Making Synergistic Arrangements

The initial phase of therapy with a narcissistic patient needs to focus almost exclusively on building a supportive working alliance. Confronting the patient's maladaptive behaviors before his or her trust and respect for the therapist are established is likely to lead to premature termination (Goldberg, 2003). Once this foundation has been laid, intervention focus can turn to increasing the patient's insight into his or her behavior. The developmental history and functional significance of patterns can be explored, and undesirable consequences can be clarified. Working toward helping the patient integrate more adaptive behavioral and cognitive alternatives can then begin.

At this point the therapist can consider several adjunct interventions (Agass, 2000). If resistant depression is judged to be interfering with functioning, and the therapist judges that alleviation of acute dysphoria will not lead to abandonment of more long-term reconstructive goals, pharmacological treatment should be carefully considered. If appropriate, group, couple, and/or family therapy may be useful concomitant approaches. Group intervention is more likely to lead to therapeutic gains if the group can provide strong support to offset the patient's tendency to withdraw at the first hint of

Table 4.4   Confident/Narcissistic Personality Disorder Subtypes

Elitist: Feels privileged and empowered by virtue of special childhood status and pseudo-achievements; entitled façade bears little relation to reality; seeks favored and good life; is upwardly mobile; cultivates special status and advantages by association. (Pure Narcissistic Subtypes)

Amorous: Sexually seductive, enticing, beguiling, tantalizing; glib and clever; declines real intimacy; indulges hedonistic desires; bewitches and inveigles the needy and naive; pathologically lying and swindling. (Mixed Narcissistic/Histrionic Subtypes)

Unprincipled: Deficient conscience; unscrupulous, amoral, disloyal, fraudulent, deceptive, arrogant, exploitive; a con man and charlatan; dominating, contemptuous, vindictive. (Mixed Narcissistic/Antisocial Subtype)

Compensatory: Seeks to counteract or cancel out deep feelings of inferiority and lack of self-esteem; offsets deficits by creating illusions of being superior, exceptional, admirable, noteworthy; self-worth results from self-enhancement. (Mixed Narcissistic/Avoidant-Negativistic Subtype)

illusion-shattering confrontation. Couple and family therapy provide an opportunity for behavioral exercises such as role-plays that increase empathy and sharpen insight into the problem-perpetuating nature of cognitive and behavioral habits specific to the patient's personal life. Guided negotiation with significant others can help break complementary patterns that support narcissistic behavior and lead to new interactions that provide gratification and bolster the patient's motivation to continue working toward adaptive change.

Illustrative Cases

Clinical experience and research employing the MCMI-III (Millon, Millon, Davis, & Grossman, 2006) suggest several personality blends that incorporate distinct narcissistic features (Millon with Davis, 1996a). A review of the developmental background of other narcissistic personalities contributed further to the variants described in these case studies (see also Table 4.4).

Case 4.1, Eddie F., 44

A Confident/Narcissistic Personality: Unprincipled Type (Narcissistic with Antisocial Traits)

Presenting Picture

Eddie was a hydraulics equipment salesman who had come up from the production line, first to significant success in the sales field, then to a reprimand and employee assistance program counseling mandate from his manager who had received "one too many complaints." Initially, Eddie simply seemed self-assured, but this veneer quickly gave way to a more realistic picture of an intimidating, manipulative man. He explained that his success was a result of the use of various special techniques that others were afraid to employ. He saw himself as separate and apart from the crowd of salesmen, as he was one who would not get "pushed" by a customer. He also explained with a knowing grin that it was possible to butter up any deal with fraudulent use of the expense account. Eddie saw himself as an entirely "free agent," meaning that neither the rules of employment nor of society applied to him, and that this freedom allowed him to successfully pursue virtually anything he wanted. He went so far as to suggest that his therapist was merely a "clock puncher" and a prisoner chained to his desk; in the same breath, he muttered, "Yeah, okay for you, not for me." Perhaps one of the most striking moments of the interview came when Eddie was describing his parents. He saw his mother, a quiet, dutiful woman, as "nothing really special"; he saw his father, on the other hand, by virtue of his beer consumption and the ability to make his point clear (with a "whipping"), as an impressive, revered figure. Eddie saw no problems with his on-the-job performance, but went along with what he called "the counseling drill" to get past this "belabored point."

Initial Impressions

Unprincipled narcissists such as Eddie, that is, those narcissists who more *actively* exploit (sharing this polarity dimension with antisocials), often are successful in society, keeping their activities just within the boundaries of the law; they enter into clinical treatment rather infrequently, and then, generally not without some directive or mandate from others. Eddie's behavior was characterized by an arrogant sense of self-worth, an indifference to the welfare of others, and a fraudulent and intimidating social manner. There was a desire to exploit others, as well as an expectation of special recognition and consideration without assuming reciprocal responsibilities. He appeared devoid of a superego; that is, he evidenced an unscrupulous, amoral, and deceptive approach to his relationships with others. More than merely disloyal and exploitive, he was similar to society's con men, bearing vindictiveness and contempt of his victims. Unlike with other personality patterns exhibiting similar behaviors (e.g., other base patterns exhibiting antisocial domains, such as the histrionic), it would have been ill-advised to indulge in *self-image* techniques, which could have guided the process into digressions rather than real process about his perceived grandeur. Although it would be important to garner understanding of Eddie's point of view and express accurate empathy, it would be equally crucial for the therapist to maintain a steadfast posture that remained focused on tangible interventions. Of primary importance would be enhancement of Eddie's alertness to the needs of *others*, while diminishing his *self*-important illusion. Equally necessary were adjustments to Eddie's social outlook, which would include some clarification along *active versus passive* motivations: One of Eddie's primary perpetuations was his tendency to actively exploit others, yet to maintain a laid-back, uncaring attitude regarding anyone or anything that didn't immediately affect him. A major focus of therapy would be to introduce steps to overcome these deficient controls, while instilling a greater sense of empathy for others. While it was very important to avoid emphasizing Eddie's negative attributes, the therapeutic relationship also depended on not allowing him to assert dominance in treatment in his usual way.

Domain Analysis

The features that were clearly seen in Eddie's MCMI-III data, inclusive of the Grossman Facet Scales, as well as the MG-PDC, support the conclusion that he presented an admixture of both narcissistic and antisocial personality characteristics. Salient domains included the following:

Interpersonally Exploitive: Clearly lacking in empathy, and more active in this regard than most narcissists, Eddie maintained, in thoughts and actions, the notion that he was the only person in his world who mattered and that others existed merely to fulfill his agenda.

Acting-Out Mechanism: Beyond an ingrained understanding that "buttering up" is often more effective than overt hostility, Eddie was unconstrained by social responsibility or remorse. Instead, direct manipulations and malice emanated from him, albeit through a façade of charisma and wit.

Cognitively Deviant/Expansive: Both narcissistic and antisocial aspects of Eddie's mind-set were highly important here; this combination of deceitfulness and self-illusory qualities gave him permission to be entirely "exempt" from any social constraint.

Therapeutic Steps

Eddie evidenced a rash willingness to risk harm and was notably fearless in the face of threats and punitive action. Malicious tendencies were projected outward, precipitating, from the report of family members, frequent personal and family difficulties, occasional legal entanglements, and, of course, the current vocational difficulty. Vengeful gratification was often obtained by slyly humiliating and dominating others. Lacking a genuine sense of guilt, Eddie enjoyed the process of swindling others, outwitting them in a game he enjoyed playing in which others were held in contempt owing to the ease with which they could be seduced. Relationships survived only as long as he had something to gain. People were dropped with no thought to the anguish they may have experienced as a consequence of his careless and irresponsible behaviors. Throughout the early treatment sessions, he maintained a careful distance from the therapist and would attempt to thwart any exploration of personal issues that may have implied any deficiency on his part.

This particularly defensive stance called for the therapist's direct, firm confrontation, while maintaining a safe but honest therapeutic environment through an empathic attitude. Eddie's acceptance of this environment was questionable, and his attitude toward the process ambivalent, until he came to respect the therapist as being forthright and not easily intimidated. The most effective course to begin changing some of his troubling attitudes and behavior was a reality therapy (e.g., Glasser) framework infused with focused *cognitive reorientation* techniques. As the therapeutic relationship began to develop and a modicum of comfort was established, the therapist was able to begin confronting Eddie's *expansive thoughts;* those of a more *deviant* nature, because they were given permission by the expansive cognitions, were more naturally undermined owing to this progressive, bimodal catalytic sequence. With this consistently honest and confrontive stance, the treatment setting transformed from an environment that at the outset frequently witnessed attempts at dominance, to one of relative cooperation and efficacious collaboration, within approximately five sessions.

Eddie was skilled in the ways of social influence, was capable of feigning an air of justified innocence, and was adept in deceiving others with charm and glibness. Lacking any deep feelings of loyalty, he successfully schemed beneath a veneer of politeness and civility. His principal orientation was that of outwitting others, getting power, and exploiting them "before they do it to you." To prove his courage, he may have even invited danger and punishment that only verified his unconscious recognition that he deserved to be punished. Rather than having a deterrent effect, it reinforced his *exploitive interactions* and *intrapsychic acting-out.* Group therapy was most beneficial after setting the groundwork with individual *interpersonal* methods (e.g., Kiesler, 1986; Klerman, 1984) aimed at exploring and adjusting his social skills and demeanor, as the members provided a means for Eddie to express himself without his usual arrogant front in a benevolent and noncritical environment.

It is important to reemphasize a general tone that pervaded this treatment. Eddie had not sought therapy voluntarily and was convinced from the outset that there really was no problem. According to his "scorecard," he was coming out ahead, after all, and others, according to him, were merely "stooges too stupid to figure out how to get ahead in this world." It was quite transparent that entering therapy put his pride on the line, and that was not a position he was inclined to take lightly. Although Eddie's self-esteem needed to be augmented as a result of his being placed in the role of patient, the therapist needed to maintain his authoritative therapeutic posture. Self-confidence was intermittently restored, as necessary, by brief visitations to his accomplishments, a process that took minimal therapeutic time. It was more pressing, however, to work with Eddie to instill a sense of empathy for others and to understand and accept the unspoken contract of restraint and responsibility in society. This measure, aimed at preventing recurrences, required that no deceptions were made by Eddie and that his compliance was sincere.

Case 4.2, Mitch E., 24

A Confident/Narcissistic Personality: Amorous Type (Narcissistic with Histrionic Traits)

Presenting Picture

Mitch was a bartender who seemed enamored with his recently redefined life and line of work. He had recently moved to an urban area, given up his public relations post at a nonprofit agency, and "come out of the closet" to his devout Christian family, an event, Mitch joked, "that rivaled the drama surrounding Richard the Third's beheading." Tending bar in a nightclub allowed Mitch to perform, he explained, thereby garnering much attention and attracting many sexual partners. He was proud of his social life and conquests, evidenced by his detailed recounting of a "heavy night" the preceding evening, followed by his comment, "I'm going to hook up again tonight with someone else, it's almost guaranteed." His recent experiences had been with very short-term partners, but he had previously been married. He described this relationship in very nonchalant terms, seeming to bestow as much importance to the arc of this 6-year relationship as he would to a Saturday afternoon's activities. "We were together through college," he explained, "but she knew as well as I, maybe even better," noting that she used to become "almost violently jealous" of his male friends. He admitted that he had had a "one-time" fling with two friends, but he wrote it off as college experimentation. "That wasn't significant, in any way, I don't think," he explained, noting that it wasn't until 3 years later that he came out after his ex-wife's confrontation.

Mitch seemed content with new developments, and he was rather unclear in his reasons for seeking therapy, stating, "I'm fine with being gay; it's just that everyone I know has a shrink and I probably should, too." It was inferred that he sensed some inadequacy in himself (though not overt) that could not be fulfilled by his exploits, along with a vague tinge of guilt over some of his less honest manipulations.

Initial Impressions

The distinctive feature of Mitch, an *amorous narcissist,* was an erotic and seductive orientation and a building up of his self-worth by engaging others in the games of sexual temptation. He had an indifferent conscience, that is, an aloofness to truth and social responsibility that, if brought to his attention, elicited an attitude of nonchalant innocence. Almost invariably *self*-oriented, he was facile in the ways of seduction, often feigning an air of dignity and confidence, and was rather skilled in deceiving others with his clever glibness. Although indulging his hedonistic desires, as well as pursuing numerous beguiling objects at the same time, he was strongly disinclined to become involved in a genuine intimacy. Rather than investing his efforts in one appealing person, he sought to acquire a coterie of amorous objects. Initial tactics needed to focus on altering his perpetuating belief of his own importance and the devaluation of (but reliance on) *others*; this approach would thereby serve to establish improved social skills and more genuine relationships.

Also, Mitch displayed a highly *passive* affective stance, presenting as entirely nonchalant and superficial when it came to intimacy; concurrently, he was rather *active* in his pursuit of a style of life that provided adequate stimulation and reinforcement of his image as a dominant and expansive sexual being. This inconsistency was one of the cornerstones of initial therapy.

Mitch did attempt to manipulate and monopolize the process of therapy, relying on his well-practiced and suave seductive tactics; an interpersonally respectful but firm and focused attitude on the part of the therapist helped engage and control his wandering conquest tales, braggadocio, and attempts to glibly and affably seduce the therapist into the role of an audience member. A greater modicum of structure than can be found with traditional humanist/existential (e.g., Rogerian) or insight-oriented approaches was necessary to begin this process. While tenets of humanistic and supportive approaches were necessary and appropriate to address his uncertainty regarding his purpose in treatment, and would become more prominent in later stages, focused and carefully worded challenges to his basic motivations (e.g., the aforementioned *active*-stimulus-seeking versus *passive*-affective demeanor) were necessary to engage Mitch more genuinely in the therapeutic process. It was possible, in essence, to create a *therapeutic double bind* through cognitive challenges to help Mitch focus on some of these very basic motivational conflicts.

Domain Analysis

The qualities outlined in the previous section strongly suggest that narcissistic personality types such as Mitch possess numerous characteristics that are primary among histrionic personalities. These tendencies were supported by his domain analysis, as measured through the MCMI-III's Grossman Facet Scales:

Interpersonally Exploitive/Attention-Seeking: At the heart of Mitch's conflict lay the inconsistent aspects of wanting greater intimacy and attention, while devaluing and manipulating others without regard to their needs.

Cognitively Expansive: Mitch had developed a fairly resilient, yet still shallow, veneer of considering himself dominant, embodying sexual prowess, and able to seduce anyone with minimal effort on his part.

Gregarious Self-Image: Considering himself affable and alluring and able to attract and maneuver through a friendly and likeable persona, Mitch effectively glossed over any feelings of insecurity and was able to sustain his vanity through avoiding more complex interaction.

Therapeutic Steps

For Mitch, the more expressive and longer term techniques would not have been useful, as he was prone to self-illusions too easily reinforced by the imaginative freedom these methods foster. As indicated earlier, *cognitive confrontation* and *reorientation* were the most effective catalysts for Mitch to modify some of his *expansive attitudes* about himself and his actions. Untroubled by conscience and needing nourishment for his overinflated self-image, he fabricated stories that enhanced his worth and thereby succeeded in seducing others into supporting his excesses. During this early stage, he navigated his way around any investigations into personal issues by using his charm and jumping from one superficiality to the next, as well as casting responsibility for himself onto others. Delicate but honest reflection and confrontation were necessary; any overemphasizing of shortcomings might have led to regression in establishing rapport. As his more affable but trite veneer gave way through these cognitive measures to increasingly more meaningful exchanges with the therapist, Mitch was able to begin working on his erroneous assumptions regarding himself and his social context (e.g., Beck, Ellis). Cognitively based methods were also effective at undermining faulty beliefs that prompted Mitch's tendency to devalue and *exploit others*. It was, at first, unfathomable to him that his assumptions were askew, as he had consistently assured himself that everyone else's views were inane. That is, he simply couldn't be wrong, as his modus operandi seemed to work well for him, yet so many others seemed to be discontent. As the therapist gradually introduced new cognitive understanding and empathic reflection, Mitch began to understand the basic tenet that disparity between himself and those more sensitive (or perhaps, more accurately expressive) did not necessarily mean that his views were superior.

Until these basic erroneous thoughts and interpersonal attitudes were adequately addressed, Mitch cared little to shoulder genuine social responsibilities and was resistant to change his seductive ways. He wouldn't "buckle down" in a serious relationship and expend effort as a more genuine pathway to self-worth. Never having learned to control his fantasies or be concerned with matters of social integrity, he maintained his bewitching ways, by deception, fraud, lying, and charming others through craft and wit as necessary. These methods were neither hostile nor malicious in intent. Instead, they served to foster his amorous narcissism. Rather than applying his talents to the goal of tangible achievements or genuine relationships, he devoted his energies to constructing intricate lies, to cleverly exploiting others, and to slyly contriving ways to extract from others what he believed was his due. *Interpersonal* methods (e.g., Benjamin, Klerman) were fruitfully employed following the aforementioned cognitive measures to examine these assumptions and reevaluate his *attention-seeking* relational manner. These focused interpersonal methods, along with a concurrent assignment to a *group therapy* milieu, helped him reassess himself more realistically and effectively and provided a forum for him to experiment with more cooperative and sociable behaviors.

Generally, an illusion that calls for brief confrontive therapy with amorous narcissists is based on the fact that these patients are unlikely to seek therapy on their own. They typically believe that they will solve everything for themselves by simply being left alone. In Mitch's case, where treatment was self-motivated, it was later discovered that it was prompted by a covert inner feeling of failure. As those focused confrontations and interpersonal realignments gained a modicum of success, and Mitch felt more at ease with the therapeutic relationship, he finally admitted that he was fearful of sex, afraid that his pretensions and ambitions would be exposed and found wanting, especially given the relative freshness of his alternative lifestyle. His sexual banter and seductive pursuits were merely empty maneuvers to overcome deeper feelings of inadequacy, possibly linked to fears of rejection, and masked behind an air of *gregariousness*. Although he seemed to desire the affections of a warm and intimate relationship, when he found it he felt restless, unsatisfied, and ill at ease. Having won someone over, he needed to continue his pursuit. It was the act of exhibitionistically being seductive, and hence gaining in narcissistic stature, that compelled him and masked his insecurity. The achievement of ego gratification would terminate for a moment, but then it had to be pursued again and again.

Regardless of what his promptings were, seeking professional help harmed his pride. Though he gave lip service to accepting therapy, this attitude was rather tentative and delicate at the outset of the therapeutic relationship. Personalized psychotherapy for Mitch took an arc from the more focused to the more open-ended. A more *existential/humanistic* approach gradually replaced confrontation as he was more spontaneously able to self-challenge and reconstruct his self-image from *gregarious* to a more germane self-quality, rather than utilize it to cover up self-doubt. Self-acceptance became the overarching theme of the final few sessions. Although it was appropriate to help Mitch rebuild his guarded, deflated self-image, the therapist could not appear submissive lest Mitch revert rapidly to many of his older, problematic tactics. An objective geared more at preventing recurrences was that of helping Mitch become more empathic with others and to understand the effects of his behavior in social interactions. This required enhancing his ability to honestly scrutinize any self-deficiency. The therapist was alert in this regard not to be deceived by mere perfunctory acquiescence.

Case 4.3, Royson H., 49

A Confident/Narcissistic Personality: Compensatory Type (Narcissistic with Avoidant and Negativistic Traits)

Presenting Picture

Royson's employer insisted that he seek therapy "for everyone's sake, not just for you." As Royson put it, however, he certainly was *not* one who needed any help. He dismissed his employer's intentions as "hatred of a visionary," which was to be expected from "feeble minds" such as those of his supervisors, coworkers, "or anyone else, for that matter." He insisted that he was the very best in his field of toy design, that the company was lucky to have him, but that tensions arose because none of the "higher-ups" recognized his genius. Moreover, those who worked under him had become frustrated at his "inability to communicate" his ideas, intentions, and instructions, but Royson refused to "spell every little thing out for them," as they were all adults capable of understanding. Recently, Royson had been passed over for a promotion, which he emphatically stated that he deserved. Most interesting, however, is that the therapist suggested the possibility of becoming his own boss, yet this seemed to cause a clear yet unspoken trepidation, hardly an attribute of a self-confident expert in a field. In fact, it was rather transparent that Royson sought others to fulfill his strivings for prestige. His motive was to enhance his self-esteem, to obtain and to store up within himself all forms of recognition that would "glorify" his public persona.

Much to the annoyance of others, he "acted drunk" as he recounted his successes and record for others to acknowledge all forms of even minor public recognition. In effect, he actively worshipped himself, becoming "a legend in his own mind." As this inflated and overvalued sense of self rose ever higher, he increasingly looked down on others as devalued plebeians. It was this haughty and disrespectful attitude, his supervisor had noted, that drove him to request that Royson seek treatment. More and more, he had acquired a deprecatory attitude in which the achievements of others, not excluding his superiors, were ridiculed and degraded.

Initial Impressions

Deviating in a fundamental way from other narcissistic subtypes, Royson's motivations were *compensatory* in their nature. The origins that undergirded his overtly narcissistic behaviors derived from an underlying sense of insecurity and weakness rather than from more overvalued feelings of self-confidence and high self-esteem. Beneath his surface pseudoconfidence, the posture he exhibited publicly, Royson was driven by forces similar to those of negativistic and avoidant personalities. Like others labeled "narcissistic" by those in the psychoanalytic community, Royson was likely to have suffered wounds in early life, and, in essence, he sought to make up or compensate for these early life deprivations. For Royson, life was a search for pseudostatus, an empty series of aspirations that served no purpose other than *self*-enhancement. This search for these vacuous goals, a search with a hazy sense of self-value that had but little contact with tangible achievements, began to run wild. Instead of living his own life, Royson pursued the leading role in a false and imaginary theater. Nothing he achieved in this pursuit related much to reality; in other words, he remained quite *passive,* as does the prototypal narcissist, when it comes to actual achievement orientation, yet was very *active* in awareness of others' responses to him, akin to negativistic and avoidant patterns. Owing to the insecure foundations on which his narcissistic displays were grounded, he was hypervigilant, exquisitely sensitive to how others reacted to him, watching and listening carefully for any critical judgment, and feeling slighted by every sign of disapproval. On some level, he recognized his fraudulence and feared discovery that he routinely conveyed impressions of being in higher standing than he knew was truly the case. Despite this awareness, he did not act shy and hesitant, as one might expect. Instead, he submerged and covered up his deep sense of inadequacy and deficiency by pseudo-arrogance and superficial grandiosity.

Because Royson was prone to be agitated in his general demeanor, and unlikely to take kindly to *insight-oriented* therapy, a first-order tactic would be to dissipate some of his anger and agitation via pharmacologic treatment in order to refocus on changing perpetuating perceptions that rejection and humiliation are always one mistake away. This would alleviate the need to be *actively* scanning the environment for disapproval and constantly seeking to overcompensate for perceived inner inadequacies by establishing his narcissistic illusion of grandeur and perfection. He could then generate more productive energies toward real accomplishment. Also vital would be clarification and alteration of a rather difficult, constitutional *self-other* conflict. Important in achieving these goals was to restrain the impulse to react to Royson with disapproval and criticism. An important step beyond building rapport with him was to see things from his viewpoint. To achieve the circumscribed goals of therapy required that the therapist convey a sense of trust and willingness to develop a constructive treatment alliance. A balance of professional authority and tolerance diminished the probability that he would impulsively withdraw from treatment or shortly regress to prior problematic states.

Domain Analysis

Many problematic domains were apparent in Royson's clinical assessment, running the gamut, as expected, from narcissistic to negativistic to avoidant domains. The most prominent and significant were the following:

Expressively Haughty/Resentful: Royson not only maintained a pompous air of being above others, and of being disdainful of societal expectations, but his behavioral quality extended into a hostile and defensive view toward everyday annoyances and "common" people.

Cognitively Expansive: Preoccupied by his grandiose self-view and belief in his incomparable genius, Royson actively praised his so-called accomplishments and sought similar accolades from others.

Temperamentally Irritable/Anguished: Highly reactive to slights, evidencing extreme discomfort (nearly emulating physical pain) at the mention of differing needs or opinions, and always seeming at the brink of explosion, Royson's sympathetic nervous system always felt taxed by any stimuli.

Therapeutic Steps

Multiple modalities needed to be coordinated in this intervention. Among those chosen at the outset, as indicated before, was a *pharmacologic* treatment (the SSRI paroxetine), which could assist in modulating the threshold and intensity of Royson's reactivity, lessening *irritability* and *anguish* brought about by discomforting environmental stimuli (e.g., others' opinions). Pharmacologic agents are not notably effective in dealing with individuals such as Royson, but it was worthwhile to evaluate and subsequently implement this treatment in terms of its efficacy in minimizing the frequency and depth of his hostile feelings, thereby decreasing some of the self-perpetuating consequences of his aggressive behavior. Also of note, the therapist was cognizant of Royson's inclination to be spoiling for a fight, almost enjoying tangling with the therapist to prove his strength and test his powers. A mixed *cognitive* and *emotion-oriented* technique (e.g., Beck, 1974; Greenberg & Safran, 1987) was employed to counter his omnipresent undertone of defensiveness that gave rise to his *expansive thought pattern,* that is, the expectation that the therapist would prove to be devious and hostile and needed to be met with one-upmanship. By confronting and then venting these feelings, Royson was able to dilute his inclination to repeatedly distort the incidental remarks and actions of the therapist so that they appeared to deprecate and vilify him. Similarly, a worthy brief therapeutic goal was to undo his habit of misinterpreting what he saw and heard and magnifying minor slights into major insults and slanders.

Well-directed *behavioral* approaches provided Royson the opportunity to vent *resentfulness* in a more productive manner that did not encourage rehearsing the symptom. Once his hostility was more benignly channeled, he was led to explore his habitual expectations and attitudes and was guided through various *behavior-change* techniques that helped to modify his *haughty expression,* which was generally a reaction to rather destructive perceptions. *Insight-oriented* procedures were not indicated as they were not likely to be of short-term utility, nor were techniques oriented to a thorough reworking of Royson's aggressive strategies. Rather, more behaviorally directed methods geared to increase restraint and control were usefully pursued. *Interpersonal* techniques (e.g., Klerman, Benjamin) may also have been fruitful in teaching him more acceptable social behavior. *Group* methods were attempted, but Royson ended up intruding on and disrupting therapeutic functions. This modality was attempted because it was thought that he would become a useful catalyst for group interaction and possibly improve his social skills and attitudes.

Effective brief techniques were called for because Royson was not likely to be a willing participant in therapy. Specifically, he had agreed to therapy under the pressure of vocational difficulties (e.g., as a consequence of aggressive behavior on the job). One task of a cognitive approach was to get him to tolerate guilt or to accept a measure of blame for the turmoil he caused. Reframing his perceptions to ones that were more realistic countered his belief that a problem could always be traced to another person's stupidity, laziness, or hostility. Even when he accepted some measure of responsibility, he did not feel defiance and resentment toward the therapist for trying to point this out. Although he sought to challenge, test, bluff, and outwit the therapist, a strong, consistent, but fair-minded cognitive approach was successful in reducing these actions and aided him in assuming a more calm and reasoned attitude.

Case 4.4, Camillo R., 39

A Confident/Narcissistic Personality: Elitist Type (Prototypal Narcissist)

Presenting Picture

Camillo had been a graduate student since his early 20s and was on his fourth master's degree, having studied ancient literature, physics, psychology, and now theology. He had initiated therapy at the request of his girlfriend, who complained that Camillo had become verbally abusive and highly demanding in recent months, but also emotionally distant.

Camillo described himself as a Renaissance man and projected that his future employment would be as an expert in his chosen field; this would be, according to him, the best and only possible use of his time. He stated, with no hesitancy, that as an only child, he was not required to take on any family responsibility and that he had all the time he could ever want to pursue and develop his own interests. He was always received as one of the brightest children in school, and he had had no difficulty throughout his extensive academic career.

Camillo viewed his relationship with his girlfriend thus: "She's pleasant and yes, satisfactory." With further questioning, however, it was apparent that he seemed to value her only in terms of what she could do for him. When asked about the verbal abuse, he replied, "That would be true if I called her names or belittled her; it's not abuse to expect her to listen and obey and fill her role around the house and not talk so much. Also, she could use a little shaping up physically and socially; she needs to look right next to me." If there was any real life dissatisfaction present, from Camillo's point of view it was that he had a hard time finding things to do that would be worth his very precious time, and that left much time for boredom and lethargy.

Initial Impressions

Reich (1933) captured the essential qualities of what we are terming the *elitist narcissist* when he described the "phallic-narcissist" character as a self-assured, arrogant, and energetic person "often impressive in his bearing . . . and . . . ill-suited to subordinate positions among the rank and file." Taken with his inflated sense of self more so than with his actual self, Camillo, representing the purest variant of the narcissistic style, was deeply convinced of his superior self-image, albeit one that was grounded on few realistic achievements. To Camillo, it was the appearance of things that was perceived as objective reality; his inflated self-image was his intrinsic substance. Only if these illusory elements to his self-worth were seriously undermined would he begin to acknowledge his deeper shortcomings. Ironically, almost everything he did was done to persuade others of his specialness rather than to put his efforts into acquiring genuine qualifications and attainments. Clearly *passive-self* in terms of evolutionary motivation, he believed the grounds for fulfillment were not determined by genuine accomplishments, but by the degree to which he could convince others of their reality, false though their substance may be.

To be celebrated, even famous, is what drove him, rather than to achieve substantive accomplishments. In whatever sphere of activity mattered to him, Camillo only invested efforts to advertise himself, to brag about achievements, substantive or fraudulent, to make anything he had done appear to be "wonderful," better than what others may have done, and better than it may actually have been. Clinically notable, by making excessive claims about himself, Camillo exposed a great divide between his actual self and his self-presentation. In contrast to many narcissists who recognize this disparity, he was convinced and absolute in his belief in himself. Rather than backing off, withdrawing, or feeling shame when slighted or responded to with indifference, Camillo redoubled his efforts, acting increasingly and somewhat erratically to exhibit deeds and awards worthy of high esteem.

As Camillo was shrouded in illusion in almost every sense, it would be expected that treatment would be complicated by his deep-seated beliefs. It would be essential to establish a relationship marked by candor and honesty. To establish a solid working alliance, the therapist approached Camillo very directly, though without disapproval, skillfully thwarting his evasiveness and unwillingness, which otherwise would have seriously interfered with rapport building. With a firm but consistently honest and confrontive approach, the therapist avoided giving witness to struggles in which Camillo sought to outwit the therapist and assert his dominance. The therapist needed to maintain great patience and equanimity to establish a spirit of genuine confidence and respect. Throughout therapy, it was helpful to frame interventions in terms of improved, more genuine accomplishments and interactions, rather than "corrections," or other terminology that implied deficiencies, as Camillo was guarded and resentful of such insinuations.

Domain Analysis

As Camillo was ill-disposed to treatment and wished to make therapy as brief and nonintrusive as possible, he declined to participate in assessment measures. The clinician was, however, able to identify some preliminary target domains through the MG-PDC, as follows:

Admirable Self-Image: Believing fully in his specialness, whether or not merited, Camillo was self-assured and replete with admirable qualities, despite a lack of commensurate achievements.

Cognitively Expansive: Camillo's perception was that he was almost magically beyond others by nature and immune to measures based in reality that may have differed with this view. Self-glorified and taking liberties with reality in supporting his illusion, he was preoccupied with this fantasy of specialness.

Interpersonally Exploitive: Along with his view of specialness and immunity from rules of interpersonal respect, Camillo was unknowingly threatening his primary relationship via exploitive and incidental abusive interactions.

Therapeutic Steps

As the therapeutic relationship was rather fragile and at risk of being jeopardized by certain types of confrontations, care was taken not to stress Camillo's deficiencies. Efforts were made, however, to not afford him a dominant position in treatment after his initial discomfort had receded. Early on, and perhaps too early, the therapist began addressing Camillo's belief that he did not need to consider changing his views because he believed he was already almost perfect. This made him loath, initially, to accede to therapy, but he did acquiesce to a short-term regimen, maintaining a well-measured distance from the therapist, trying to resist the searching probes of personal exploration, especially those that implied any deficiencies on his part. After this brief setback in rapport building, Camillo became more able to tolerate measures aimed at bringing conflicting motivations to light. An effective cognitive confrontation method countered his tendency to exaggerate his abilities and prowess, bringing awareness of his *expansiveness* into the therapy dynamic. Gradually, he started to recognize that indeed, he was gifted and, in fact, more than many others, but that he had relatively little to point to in terms of tangible accomplishments. This also affected his *admirable self-image,* calling into question his status as a visionary and self-proclaimed Renaissance man. Although efforts needed to be made to rebuild Camillo's recently depleted self-esteem, the therapist took measures not to appear subservient in the process. Camillo's self-confidence was rapidly restored by allowing him to revisit specific achievements and successes, such as his previously earned degrees and accolades gained as a result of these accomplishments. Having experienced a modicum of guilt in reflecting on prior disparaging remarks he had made over the years for faults he had within himself, he was better able to understand and integrate a sense of empathy for the next stage of treatment.

Moving on to *interpersonal* techniques with a strong cognitive component, Camillo was challenged to undo distorted expectations focused on extinguishing his tendency to think of others as naive and simpleminded and therefore "less than." Rather than question the correctness of his own beliefs, he was habituated to assume that others' views and ways were always to blame. The therapist called into question his habit of assuming that the more disagreements he had with others, the more evident was his own superiority and the more presumptuous and *exploitive* this allowed him to be. On his own, Camillo began to connect this tendency to his relationship with his girlfriend. A useful adjunctive therapy evolved from here; his girlfriend had wanted to seek *couples counseling,* and Camillo, after gaining a modicum of empathy, acquiesced to this request. Unfortunately, shortly thereafter he prematurely terminated individual treatment. The outcome of this couples treatment is not known, but it may likely have included a goal that would help prevent recurrences: that of guiding him into becoming more sensitive to the needs of others and accepting the constraints and responsibilities of shared social living. This would require strengthening Camillo's capacity to face his shortcomings frankly. Care would need to be taken in this regard not to be deceived by mere superficial compliance with these efforts.

Resistances and Risks

Narcissists are not inclined to seek therapy. Their pride disposes them to reject the imperfection-confirming "weak" role of patient. Most are convinced they can get along quite well on their own (McCown & Carlson, 2004). Often, if a narcissist does accept voluntary treatment, he or she will try to enlist the therapist to support the opinion that the patient's problems are largely the result of the imperfections and weaknesses of others. Alternatively, the narcissist may adopt a stance of superiority and discredit the therapist, or terminate treatment prematurely. In sum, narcissists will not accede to therapy willingly. Moreover, once involved, they will maintain a well-measured distance from the therapist, resist the searching probes of personal exploration, become indignant over implications of deficiencies on their part, and seek to shift responsibility for these lacks to others. The treatment setting may witness struggles in which narcissists seek to outwit the therapist and assert their dominance. Stone (1993) notes that much of the narcissistic patient's sarcasm, devaluation, and domination toward the therapist can be seen as a test of whether the therapist will respond in kind and therefore, like the patient's parents (who may have modeled the offensive behavior), is not to be trusted. Setting limits without resorting to an accusatory or attacking stance can prove to be invaluable in working with these patients. Great patience and equanimity are required to establish the spirit of genuine confidence and respect without which the chances of achieving reconstructive personality change become even slimmer.

CHAPTER 5

Personalized Therapy for the Nonconforming/Antisocial Personality Patterns

The *DSM-IV* provides a rather detailed listing of the delinquent, criminal, and socially undesirable behaviors that may be found among nonconforming/antisocial personalities, but fails, in our opinion, to deal with the personality characteristics from which such antisocial behaviors stem (Blackburn, Logan, Renwick, & Donnelly, 2005; Edens, 2006; Edens, Marcus, Lilienfeld, & Poythress, 2006; Ogloff, 2006; Vasey, Kotov, Frick, & Loney, 2005; Vien & Beech, 2006). In adopting a focus on the "criminal personality," insufficient attention is paid to individuals with similar propensities and basic traits who have managed to avoid criminal involvement (Millon, 1981, 1996b). It is our contention that antisocial personalities are best characterized by hostile affectivity, excessive self-reliance, interpersonal assertiveness, callousness, and a lack of humanistic concern or sentimentality (Millon, Simonsen, Birket-Smith, & Davis, 1998). Such individuals exhibit rebelliousness and social vindictiveness, with particular contempt being directed toward authority figures. Other notable features in the antisocial personality include a low tolerance for frustration, impulsivity, and an inability to delay gratification (Cooke, Michie, Hart, & Clark, 2005). Consistent with this is a tendency to become easily bored and restless with day-to-day responsibilities and social demands (DeMatteo, Heilbrun, & Marczyk, 2006). Not only are such individuals seemingly undaunted by danger and punishment, but they appear attracted to it and may actually seek it out or provoke it. Our portrayal of the nonconforming/antisocial personality is more consistent with the concept of the sociopathic or psychopathic personalities as depicted in the early writings of Cleckley (1941). These individuals are most notable for their lack of shame, incapacity for object love, impulsivity, emotional shallowness, superficial social charm, and an inability to profit from experience (Millon et al., 1998).

An argument may also be made for a "nonantisocial" variant of the antisocial personality. Such individuals may view themselves as assertive, energetic, self-reliant, and hard-boiled, but also realistic, strong, and honest (Rutter, 2005). In competitive societies, these traits tend to be commended and reinforced. Consequently, such individuals may achieve business authority or political power, which provide socially sanctioned avenues for expressing their underlying self-interest and/or mean-spirited temperament.

Nonconforming/antisocials often are finely attuned to the feelings, moods, and vulnerabilities of others, taking advantage of this sensitivity, however, to manipulate and control. On the other hand, they typically evidence a notable deficit in self-insight and rarely exhibit foresight (Patrick, Hicks, Krueger, & Lang, 2005). Inner tensions, frustrations, and dysphoria inevitably occur, but such discomforts are not tolerated for very long, being discharged through acting-out rather than intrapsychic mechanisms. Frequent references are made to the antisocial's active avoidance of and inability to tolerate awareness of depression (Reid, 1978). In this framework, they do not often demonstrate clinical syndromes.

Although the antisocial's active independence, internal locus of control, and appetite for stimulating change may militate against the impact of life stressors, these same characteristics can also make the antisocial vulnerable to infrequent clinical episodes. Precipitants for depression, for example, might include situations of forced interpersonal submissiveness or curtailed personal freedom (e.g., incarceration or required military service), as well as internal conditions (e.g., medical illness or age-related physical decline) that result in incapacitation, passivity, or immobility. It has also been suggested (Reid, 1978) that depression may ensue when antisocials are forced to confront their inner emptiness, emotional void, and tenuous object relations. Again, this forced recognition is most likely to occur when antisocials are made to feel inadequate or weakened in a way that strips from them their resilient shell of narcissism.

Describing the antisocial, Beck and Freeman (1990) proposes an "autonomous mode" characterized by a great investment in preserving and increasing his independence, mobility and personal rights. For such action-oriented individuals, their well-being is dependent on their ability to maintain their autonomy and direct their own activities without external constraint or interference. There is little care regarding the needs of others, with a corresponding lack of responsiveness to external feedback and corrective influences. It should be noted that the autonomous individuals described by Beck are also characterized by excessively highly internalized standards and criteria for achievement, features that may be more indicative of the compulsive character structure or the noncriminal variant of the antisocial personality. Such individuals tend to experience a hostile depression, characterized by social withdrawal, rejection of help, self-criticism, resistance to change, and active violent forms of suicide attempts.

Several major theorists have recognized the strong similarity between the antisocial and the narcissistic personality (e.g., Kernberg, 1992). Many studies have investigated the attributes of both of these patterns, yet clarity regarding their central features is often lacking in the analytic literature. The evolutionary model, with its polarity schema, may provide us with insights that other approaches have only hinted at faintly but have not established firmly. Reviewing Figure 5.1, we can see the prominence assigned to both the self (individuating) and active (modifying) polarities. This suggests that antisocials are driven, first, to benefit themselves and, second, to take vigorous action to see that these benefits accrue to themselves (Blair, Peschardt, Budhani, Mitchell, & Pine, 2006; Vincent, 2006). This pattern is similar to yet different from that seen in narcissists, where an unjustified self-confidence assumes that all that is desired will come to them

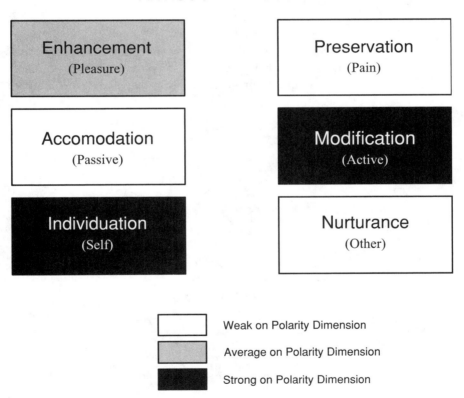

ANTISOCIAL PROTOTYPE

Enhancement (Pleasure)	Preservation (Pain)
Accomodation (Passive)	Modification (Active)
Individuation (Self)	Nurturance (Other)

☐ Weak on Polarity Dimension

▨ Average on Polarity Dimension

■ Strong on Polarity Dimension

FIGURE 5.1 Status of the nonconforming/antisocial personality prototype in accord with the Millon polarity model.

with minimal effort on their part. The antisocial assumes the contrary (Timmerman & Emmelkamp, 2005). Recognizing by virtue of past experience that little will be achieved without considerable effort, cunning, and deception, the antisocial knows that desired ends must be achieved through his or her own actions (Kotler & McMahon, 2005). Moreover, these actions serve to fend off the malice that one anticipates from others and to undo the power possessed by those who wish to exploit one.

Clinical Picture

This section provides the reader with a systematic analysis of the prototypal domains and personality variants of the antisocial disorder (see Figure 5.2).

The major features of this personality pattern are approached in line with the domain levels used in previous chapters. Here we identify characteristics that are relatively specific to the prototypal antisocial disorder (Chabrol & Leichsenring, 2006). Unless noted, the domains described should be generally applicable to most of the adult subtypes (see Table 5.1).

Impulsive Expressive Behavior

Many of these personalities evidence a low tolerance for frustration, seem to act impetuously, and cannot delay, let alone forgo, prospects for immediate pleasure. They are precipitous and irrepressible, acting hastily and spontaneously in a restless,

ANTISOCIAL PROTOTYPE

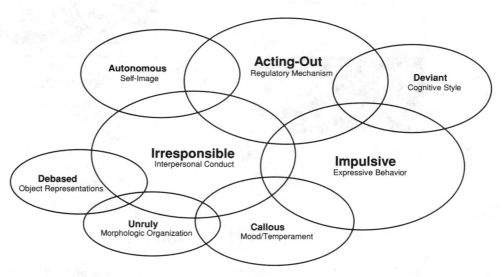

FIGURE 5.2 Salience of prototypal nonconforming/antisocial domains.

Table 5.1   Clinical Domains of the Nonconforming/Antisocial Personality Prototype

Behavioral Level:

(F) Expressively Impulsive (e.g., is impetuous and irrepressible, acting hastily and spontaneously in a restless, spur-of-the-moment manner; is short-sighted, incautious, and imprudent, failing to plan ahead or consider alternatives, much less heed consequences).

(F) Interpersonally Irresponsible (e.g., is untrustworthy and unreliable, failing to meet or intentionally disregarding personal obligations of a marital, parental, employment, or financial nature; actively intrudes on and violates the rights of others, as well as transgresses established social codes through deceitful or illegal behaviors).

Phenomenological Level:

(F) Cognitively Deviant (e.g., construes events and relationships in accord with socially unorthodox beliefs and morals; is disdainful of traditional ideals, fails to conform to social norms, and is contemptuous of conventional values).

(S) Autonomous Self-Image (e.g., sees self as unfettered by the restrictions of social customs and the constraints of personal loyalties; values the image and enjoys the sense of being free, unencumbered, and unconfined by persons, places, obligations, or routines).

(S) Debased Objects (e.g., internalized representations comprise degraded and corrupt relationships that spur revengeful attitudes and restive impulses; are driven to subvert established cultural ideals and mores, as well as to devalue personal sentiments and to sully, but intensely covet, denied material attainments of society).

Intrapsychic Level:

(F) Acting-Out Mechanism (e.g., inner tensions that might accrue by postponing the expression of offensive thoughts and malevolent actions are rarely constrained; socially repugnant impulses are not refashioned in sublimated forms, but are discharged directly in precipitous ways, usually without guilt or remorse).

(S) Unruly Organization (e.g., inner morphologic structures to contain drive and impulse are noted by their paucity, as are efforts to curb refractory energies and attitudes, leading to easily transgressed controls, low thresholds for hostile or erotic discharge, few subliminatory channels, unfettered self-expression, and a marked intolerance of delay or frustration).

Biophysical Level:

(S) Callous Mood (e.g., is insensitive, irritable, and aggressive, as expressed in a wide-ranging deficit in social charitableness, human compassion, or personal remorse; exhibits a coarse incivility, as well as an offensive, if not reckless, disregard for the safety of self or others).

Note: F = Functional Domains; S = Structural Domains.

spur-of-the-moment manner. Their impulsive behaviors are short-sighted, incautious, and imprudent. There is minimal planning and limited consideration of alternative actions, and consequences are rarely examined or heeded. Antisocial types appear easily bored and restless, unable to endure the tedium of routine or to persist at the day-to-day responsibilities of marriage or a job (Blair et al., 2006; Sharp, van Goozen, & Goodyer, 2006). Others of this variant are characteristically prone to taking chances and seeking thrills, acting as if they were immune from danger. There is a tendency to jump from one exciting and momentarily gratifying escapade to another, with little or no care for potentially detrimental consequences (Lynam & Gudonis, 2005). When matters go their way, these antisocial variants often act in a gracious, cheerful, saucy, and clever manner. More characteristically, their behavior is brash, arrogant, and resentful.

Although the preceding relates to the prototypical antisocial, it does suggest a type-casting that is somewhat misleading (Lahey, Loeber, Burke, & Applegate, 2005). There are many individuals who are intrinsically antisocial in the broad sense but who appear quite conventional in their appearance, manners, and styles of behavior. These nonstereotypical antisocials portray themselves in a manner consistent with their often rather conventional occupations. Hence, an aggrandizing and self-seeking physician will look and act like a physician, not like some riffraff gang member. The point to be made is that one should not be misled into assuming that antisocials advertise their inclinations by superficial appearances (Benning, Patrick, Blonigen, Hicks, & Iacono, 2005).

Irresponsible Interpersonal Conduct

It can be safely assumed that most nonconforming/antisocials are untrustworthy and unreliable in their personal relationships. They frequently fail to meet or to intentionally disregard obligations of a marital, parental, employment, or financial nature. Not only do these personalities intrude on and violate the rights of others, but they seem to experience a degree of pleasure in transgressing established social codes by engaging in deceitful or illegal behaviors (Martens, 2005). Not only do they covet both power and possessions, but they gain special joy in usurping and taking from others. For some, what can be plagiarized, swindled, and extorted are fruits far sweeter than those earned through honest labor. Once having drained all one can from one source, others are sought to exploit, bleed, and then cast aside. Pleasure in the misfortunes of those in power or of means is particularly gratifying among most antisocial types (Forouzan & Cooke, 2005).

Having learned to place their trust only in themselves, these personalities have few feelings of loyalty and may be treacherous and scheming beneath a veneer of politeness and civility (Salekin, Leistico, Trobst, Schrum, & Lochman, 2005). People are used as a means to an end, often subordinated and demeaned so that they can vindicate themselves for the grievances, misery, and humiliations they experienced in the past. By provoking fear and intimidating others, they seek to climb out of the lowly caste into which they feel they were thrust in childhood (Blonigen, Hicks, Krueger, Patrick,

& Iacono, 2005). Their search for power and material gains, therefore, is not benign; it springs from a deep well of resentment and the desire for retribution and vindication.

The most distinctive characteristic of nonconforming/antisocials is their tendency to flout conventional authority and rules. They act as if established social customs and guidelines for self-discipline and cooperative behavior do not apply to them. In some, this disdain is evidenced in petty adolescent disobedience or in the adoption of unconventional values, dress, and demeanor (Dadds, Fraser, Frost, & Hawes, 2005; Lahey et al., 2005). Many express their arrogance and social rebelliousness in illegal acts and deceits, coming into frequent difficulty with educational and law enforcement authorities.

Despite the disrespect they show for the rights of others, many antisocial types present a social mask, not only of civility but of sincerity and maturity (Marmorstein & Iacono, 2005). Untroubled by guilt and loyalty, they develop a talent for pathological lying. Unconstrained by honesty and truth, they weave impressive tales of competency and reliability. Many are disarmingly charming in initial encounters and become skillful swindlers and impostors. Alert to weaknesses in others, they play their games of deception with considerable skill. However, the pleasure they gain from their ruse often flags once the rewards of deceit have been achieved. Before long their true unreliability may be revealed as they stop working at their deception or as their need grows to let others know how clever and cunning they have been.

Deviant Cognitive Style

Many nonconforming/antisocials construe events and interpret human relationships in accord with socially unorthodox beliefs and morals. In the main, they are disdainful of traditional ideals, fail to conform to acceptable social norms, and are often contemptuous of conventional ethics and values (Blair, 2005). It should be noted that these personalities exhibit both clarity and logic in their cognitive capacities, an observation traceable to Pinel's (1798) earliest writings. Yet they actively disavow social conventions, show a marked deficit in self-insight, and rarely exhibit the foresight that one would expect, given their capacity to understand (at least intellectually) the implications of their behavior. Thus, despite the fact that they have a clear grasp of why they should alter their less attractive behaviors, they fail repeatedly to make such modifications. To them, right and wrong are irrelevant abstractions. It is not their judgment that is defective, but their ethics. Whereas most youngsters learn to put themselves in the shoes of others in a responsible and thoughtful way, antisocials use that awareness to their own purposes. To them, every opportunity pits their personal desires against those of others, resulting in the decision that it is they alone who deserve every break and every advantage (Frick & Morris, 2004).

It should be evident that many of these personalities are unable to change because they possess deeply rooted habits that are largely resistant to conscious reasoning (Pietrzak & Petry, 2005). To make their more repugnant behaviors more palatable to others, antisocial types are likely to concoct plausible explanations and excuses, often those of "poor upbringing" and past "misfortunes." By feigning innocent victimization, they seek to absolve themselves of blame and remain guiltless and justified in continuing their irresponsible behaviors (Farrington, 2005). Should their rationalizations fail to convince others, as when they are caught in obvious and repeated lies and dishonesties, many will affect an air of total innocence, claiming without a trace of shame that they have been unfairly accused.

Autonomous Self-Image

There are two aspects to the image of self that are found among nonconforming/ antisocials. The first and more obvious one is the sense of being unconventional and disdainful of the customs that most persons in society admire and seek to abide by. The more antisocials reject societal values and goals and the more dissimilar they can be from "ordinary" people, the more gratified they will be with themselves. Hence, to be clever and cunning or disrespectful and deviant are both valued self-images.

Underlying these public presentations is a more fundamental desire, that of being unfettered by the constraints of personal attachments, that is, being free and unencumbered by connections and responsibilities to others. The sense of autonomy that drives this image of self is one in which the antisocial feels unconfined by persons, places, obligations, and routines. It is also important to antisocials to arrogate to themselves a sense of magisterial self-sufficiency. This independence from others often makes them too proud to ask for anything, unwilling to be on the receiving end of the kindness and care others may express. It is not only humiliating to be the recipient of the goodwill of others, but antisocials can never trust others to act out of genuine concern and interest. They must remain inviolable so that they will never be humiliated or hurt again. It is the antisocial who must be the one to intimidate and reject others.

Antisocials do what they believe is right for them, disregarding the fact that it is patently dishonest or deceptively manipulative. Rarely would they apply the term "antisocial" to themselves; rather, in their view, that term is suitable to those whose actions they disdain. Should they acknowledge being involved in behaviors that skirt the spirit of the law, perhaps even exaggerating the extent of these deviations, antisocials will defend themselves by saying "Others not only do it, but get away with it," or "Everything in society is rotten to the core." White-collar antisocials have contempt for violent antisocials who possess the same basic personality; similarly, violent antisocials will scorn the white-collar type for being slyly devious and cowardly.

Debased Object Representations

If we look at the world through the eyes of antisocials—a place fraught with frustration and danger, a place where they must be on guard against the malevolence and cruelty of others—we can better understand why they behave as they do. They have no choice. You cannot trust what others will do (Murrie, Cornell, & McCoy, 2005). They will abuse, exploit, and dispossess you, strip you of all gratifications, and dominate and brutalize you, if they can. To avoid a fate such as this, one must arrogate all the power one can to oneself; one must block others from possessing the means to be belittling, exploitive, and harmful. Only by an alert vigilance and vigorous counteraction can one withstand and obstruct others' malice. Displaying weakness or being willing to appease and compromise are fatal concessions to be avoided at all costs. Only by acquiring personal and material power can one be assured of gaining control of one's life. Further, only by usurping the powers that others command can one thwart them from misusing it. Given these fears and attitudes, we can readily see why these personalities have taken the course they have. It is only through self-sufficiency and decisive action that they can forestall the dangers in the environment and maximize the bounties of life.

Partly a result of their past experiences and partly a result of their current opportunities, the internalized objects of the antisocial comprise memories and images of a degraded and corrupt nature. It is these debased objects that spur the antisocial's restive impulses and vengeful attitudes. Not only are these personalities driven to subvert established cultural ideals, but they seek to devalue personal sentiments and to sully, though they intensely covet, the material wealth that society has denied them.

Acting-Out Regulatory Mechanism

The inner tensions that normally accrue by postponing the overt expression of manipulative thoughts and malicious feelings are *not* constrained by most antisocials (Hale, Goldstein, Abramowitz, Calamari, & Kosson, 2004). Rather, these exploitive and resentful dispositions are discharged directly and precipitously, enacted without guilt or remorse. In contrast to most other personalities, where socially repugnant impulses and feelings are either refashioned or repressed, the antisocial permits them open exposure, acts them out, so to speak, despite their disingenuous and socially offensive character (Westermeyer & Thuras, 2005).

Projection is another mechanism employed by antisocials. Accustomed throughout life to anticipate indifference or hostility from others and exquisitely attuned to the subtlest signs of contempt and derision, they are ever ready to interpret the incidental behaviors and remarks of others as fresh attacks on them. Given their perception of the environment, they need not rationalize their outbursts. These are fully "justified" as a response to the malevolence of others. The antisocial is the victim, an indignant bystander subjected to unjust persecution and hostility. Through this projection maneuver, they not only disown their malicious impulses but attribute the evil to others. As persecuted victims, they feel free to counterattack and gain restitution and vindication.

Unruly Morphologic Organization

Constraints that help form a structure for personality organization are both few and undeveloped among antisocials. Their psychic system is poorly constructed to achieve the purposes for which the components of the intrapsychic mind are designed. As a consequence of this unruly organization, efforts to curb refractory energies and pernicious attitudes are weak or ineffectual (Birbaumer et al., 2005; Frick & Dantagnan, 2005; Montagne et al., 2005). Controls are easily transgressed, and there is a consequential low threshold for both deviousness and irresponsible actions, as well as for hostile and erotic discharge. There is also an intolerance for delaying frustrations, unfettered self-expression, and few subliminatory channels developed to orient impulses of a problematic nature.

Acts that devalue their past leave a deep emptiness in antisocials (Johansson, Kerr, & Andershed, 2005). Having been jettisoned by their own actions, there is now an inner scarcity of internalized objects. And it is this inner emptiness, at least in part, that drives the antisocial to his or her aggrandizing behaviors. This is done with surface appearances, covering up or filling inner deficiencies by exploiting and usurping what others possess. Aggrandizing actions serve to make up for internal scarcities as much as for external deprivations.

The morphologic organization of antisocials is an open system possessing few valued components and few mechanisms for dynamic processing. It is the unruly and empty character of their intrapsychic world that necessitates aggrandizing themselves through superficial materialistic attainments: the big ring, the expensive and colorful car, fancy clothes and shoes. Having ousted their past life from their inner world, antisocials are alienated from themselves, unable to feel any form of experiential depth. And because nothing and no one can be trusted, neither possesses value to the antisocial, other than momentarily (Hicks & Patrick, 2006). Hence, we see a hedonistic need to experience things that provide only immediate pleasure or momentary recognition and significance. These, too, will be quickly jettisoned lest they take over and control the antisocial's life (Burnette & Newman, 2005). Nothing is permitted permanence, be it a person or a once-appealing material object.

Callous Mood/Temperament

As noted, most of these personalities act out their impulses rather than reworking them through intrapsychic mechanisms. Although showing restraint under certain conditions, antisocials have a tendency to blurt out feelings and vent urges directly (Cale & Lilienfeld, 2006). Rather than inhibit or reshape thoughts, this personality is inclined to express them precipitously and forcibly. This directness may be viewed by some as commendable, an indication of frankness and forthrightness (Blair et al., 2004). Such an appraisal may be valid at times, but this personality manifests these behaviors, not as an expression of honesty and integrity, but from a desire to shock or put off others. Hence, among antisocials, we see an emotional disposition to be irritable and aggressive (Fung et al., 2005).

Among many antisocials, there is a wide-ranging deficit in social charitableness, in human compassion, and in personal remorse and sensitivity (Kiehl, Bates, Laurens, Hare, & Liddle, 2006; Larsson, Andershed, & Lichtenstein, 2006; Llanes & Kosson, 2006; Mitchell, Avny, & Blair, 2006). Beyond their lack of deeper sensitivity, many antisocials possess a lust for life, a passion with which they are willing to pursue excitement and hedonistic pleasures. There appears also to be an impulse to explore the forbidden, an enjoyment in testing the limits of one's tolerance of pain and one's assertive powers. Thus, their passion appears to be for intensity and excitement, not just pleasure.

Related to their expansive and risky inclination is their seeming disdain for human compassion and sensitivity. Callousness thrives on adventure and risk, rather than on concern and empathy (Kiehl et al., 2004; Raine et al., 2004). From these deeper temperamental sources, if we can speak of them in this manner, we see the emergence of cynicism and skepticism, distrust of the ostensive goodwill and kindness of others (Strand & Belfrage, 2005). Not uncommon among the less socially advantaged antisocial is a coarse incivility, as well as an offensive, if not reckless disregard for the safety or welfare of both self and others.

Self-Perpetuation Processes

An essential element of individuals with personality disorders is that their efforts to cope with their world are themselves pathogenic, that is, create self-defeating actions (see Table 5.2).

Distrustful Anticipations

The antisocial's strategy is clear: Only by vigilant disinterest and vigorous counteraction can one withstand and obstruct the insensitivity and hostility of others (Stuart, Moore, Gordon, Ramsey, & Kahler, 2006; J. I. Warren & South, 2006). Getting close, displaying weakness, and being willing to appease and compromise are fatal concessions to be avoided at all costs. Only by acquiring power for oneself can one be assured of gaining the rewards of life; only by usurping the powers that others command can one thwart them from misusing it. Given these fears and attitudes, we can readily see why antisocials have taken their course of action and independence. Only through self-sufficiency and decisiveness can they forestall the indifference or dangers of their environment and thereby maximize achieving the bounties of life.

Table 5.2   Self-Perpetuating Processes: Nonconforming/Antisocial Personality

Anticipates Distrust
   Expects belittlement and exploitation
   Self-sufficiency used to forestall threat
   Provokes others to react hostilely

Vindictive Interpersonal Behavior
   Pleasure gained in usurping from others
   Scheming beneath a veneer of civility
   Elicits resentful reactions

Weak Intrapsychic Controls
   Angry feelings vented directly
   Impulsive rashness and temptation
   Sees self as victim or innocent bystander

Unfortunately, these self-protective attitudes set into motion a vicious circle of suspiciousness and distrust, provoking others to react in a similarly cool and rejecting fashion. Potential sources of warmth and affection become wary, creating the indifference and rejection that prompted the antisocial's distrust in the first place. Hence, nonconforming/antisocials have activated a repetition of their past, further intensifying their sense of isolation, their resentments, and their need for autonomy.

Vindictive Interpersonal Behavior

The defensive actions of the antisocial serve more than the function of counteracting exploitation and indifference (Lobbestael, Arntz, & Sieswerda, 2005; Pfiffner, McBurnett, Rathouz, & Judice, 2005). Antisocials are driven by a need to vindicate themselves, a desire to dominate and humiliate others, to wreak vengeance upon anyone who has mistreated them. Not only do they covet possessions and powers, but they gain special pleasure in usurping and taking from others (a symbolic sib, for example).

Not only does the strategy of autonomy and domination gain a measure of release from past injustices but, as with most coping maneuvers, it proves helpful in achieving rewards in the present. Most people find themselves intimidated by the antisocial's calculated pose of resentment and provocative look, as well as the overt threat of an emotional outburst, if not physical violence. In using these terrorizing behaviors, antisocials have at their disposal a powerful instrumentality for coercing others, for frightening them into fearful respect and passive submission.

Although many persons with the basic antisocial personality style find a niche for themselves in society where their exploitive and intimidating behaviors are sanctioned, even admired, they are ultimately self-defeating, no less so than occurs among more socially troublesome antisocials (Cooke, Michie, Hart, & Clark, 2004). The cleverly conniving businessman, the physically brutal army sergeant, the stern and punitive school principal set into motion angry and resentful reactions from others, re-creating what they had experienced in earlier life: a menacing and rejecting environment of persons who learn neither to trust them nor to care for them.

Weak Intrapsychic Control

Threats and sarcasm are not endearing traits. How does one justify them to others, and by what means does the antisocial handle the fact that these behaviors may be unjust and irrational?

As noted earlier, the antisocial personality has usually rebelled against the controls that parents and society have proposed to manage and guide his or her impulses. Rarely do these youngsters substitute adequate controls in their stead; as a consequence, they fail to restrain or channel the emotions that well up within them. As feelings surge forth, they are vented more or less directly; thus, we see the low tolerance, the impulsive rashness, the susceptibility to temptation, and the acting out of emotions so characteristic of this pattern.

Obvious and persistent acting-out and rebelliousness cannot be overlooked. To make it acceptable, antisocial individuals fabricate rather transparent rationalizations. They espouse such philosophical balderdash as "Might is right"; "This is a dog-eat-dog world"; "I'm being honest, not hypocritical like the rest of you"; "It's better to get these kids used to tough handling now before it's too late"; and "You've got to be a realist in this world. Most people are either foolish idealists, appeasers, commies, or atheists." Seeing the world in this way, antisocials feel fully justified in their actions and need not be restrained; if anything, they consider them more valid than ever.

Accustomed throughout life to indifference and hostility from others, and exquisitely attuned to the subtlest sign of contempt and derision, the well-entrenched nonconforming/antisocial begins to interpret the incidental behaviors and innocent remarks of others as signifying fresh attacks on him or her (Simonoff et al., 2004). Increasingly, antisocials find evidence that now, as before, others are ready to persecute, to slander, and to vilify them. Given this perception of their environment, they need not rationalize their outbursts; these are "justified" reactions to the disinterest and malevolence of others. It is others who are contemptible, slanderous, and belligerent and who hate and wish to destroy them. Antisocials see themselves as victims, as innocent and indignant bystanders subject to unjust persecution and hostility. Through this intrapsychic maneuver, they not only disown and purge their own exploitive and malicious impulses but attribute this evil to others. They have absolved themselves of the irrationality of their resentful outbursts; moreover, as persecuted victims, they are free to counterattack and to gain restitution and vindication. As expected, antisocials have now created a world, composed in their own imagination, that continues to haunt and denigrate them, an inescapably malicious environment of rejection and deprecation—yet one of their own making.

Interventional Goals

Antisocials usually present for treatment as a result of an ultimatum. Therapy is often the choice made between losing a job, being expelled from school, ending a marriage or relationship with children, or giving up a chance at probation and psychological treatment. Under other circumstances treatment is usually forced upon them; most prisons and other correctional facilities require inmates to attend psychotherapy sessions. In either case, a therapist working with an antisocial personality is likely to experience frustration and exasperation regarding the patient's clear lack of insight and/or motivation to change (Martens, 2004). Antisocials do not regard their behavior as problematic for themselves, and its consequences for others, who are judged to be potentially unreliable and disloyal, is not a concern of theirs (Paris, 2004).

The patient's attitude toward the therapist will typically take one of two forms. The antisocial will try either to enlist the therapist as an ally against those individuals who forced the antisocial to enter therapy or to con the therapist into being impressed with his or her "insight" and reform in an effort to secure advantage with some legal institution. The therapist's most effective recourse is to try to impress upon antisocial patients how their behavior is in fact disadvantageous to them in the long run. The therapist can only hope that this insight will lead to behavior that is also advantageous to those who deal with antisocials, that is to say, behavior that is less abusive, exploitative, and criminal. The chances of the antisocial changing his or her duplicitous patterns owing to the development of a real concern for others is slim.

Some clinicians believe that the chances for real gains increase with the patient's age. Although the incidence of nonconforming/antisocial personality does decline in middle age, it is likely that this statistic reflects two factors entirely incidental to the intrinsic character of the disorder. First, those whose antisocial behaviors persist are ultimately imprisoned for prolonged periods; they are, in effect, out of commission by 25 or 30 years of age. Second, those who survive in the mainstream of society are likely to have learned to channel their abusive and impulsive tendencies more skillfully or into more socially acceptable endeavors. It is not probable that their basic personality has been altered, only that it expresses itself in a less obviously flagrant and public way.

Ideally, therapeutic intervention would help reestablish a reasonable equivalence between the imbalanced polarities of the antisocial personality. The goal is to help these patients increase their other-orientation and decrease their use of active exploitation as a means of securing rewards. This would reflect an increased sensitivity to the needs and feelings of others. More realistically, the antisocials' problem-perpetuating tendencies are usually curbed only by convincing them that it is in their immediate best interests to do so (see Table 5.3).

Table 5.3   Therapeutic Strategies and Tactics for the Prototypal Nonconforming/ Antisocial Personality

Strategic Goals

Balance Polarities
    Shift focus more to needs of others
    Reduce impulsive acting-out

Counter Perpetuations
    Reduce tendency to be provocative
    View affection and cooperation positively
    Reverse expectancy of danger

Tactical Modalities
    Offset heedless, shortsighted *behavior*
    Motivate *interpersonally* responsible *conduct*
    Alter deviant *cognitions*

Reestablishing Polarity Balances

Antisocials' underlying motive is to exploit before being exploited. As children, antisocials typically learn that the world will treat them unfairly, if not harshly; others are perceived, not as a source of rewards, but as potential exploiters or degraders. Antisocials defensively turn to themselves not only to protect themselves against potential harm, but to secure gratification. When rewards do involve other persons, it is not in the sense that the antisocial derives pleasure from sharing and intimacy. Others are essentially treated like objects; even highly personal interactions such as friendships and sexual relations are essentially instances of simple self-gratification. Retribution for past and present injustices is sought indiscriminately, whether or not the antisocial's victims are among the original offenders. Compensation for past deprivations is ruthlessly sought out and taken wherever it can be obtained. This active quest for self-gain, combined with a lack of other-orientation, leads to the manipulative, exploitive, and often criminal behavior so characteristic of the antisocial personality.

Ideally, therapeutic intervention would lead to increased balance on the self–other polarity, where others would be perceived as relatively benign and as having the potential to meet the antisocial personality's needs without exploitation. An appreciation and respect for the feelings and desires of others might result. The active stance toward securing rewards (at the expense of others) would ideally shift to a more socially and personally adaptive stance.

Countering Perpetuating Tendencies

Antisocials learn early that they do best by anticipating and reacting to an indifferent and unreliable environment with defensive autonomy, if not suspicion and hostility. The protective shell of anger and resentment that develops also acts as a perceptual and cognitive filter well past childhood. In their effort not to overlook any signs of threat, they persistently misinterpret incidental events as evidence of the devious and untrustworthy impulses of others. Often overlooked or suspiciously dismissed, on the other hand, are signs of objective goodwill. Expressions of affection and cooperative prosocial tendencies that do not escape antisocials' awareness are demeaned so as to ensure that they do not put themselves in a "dangerously" vulnerable position. This also ensures that they do not experience their environment in a way that would encourage them to bring their defenses down. In fact, antisocials feel the need to demonstrate their invulnerability, both to themselves and to potentially threatening others, by provoking them, both physically and verbally. Alternatively, the antisocial may engage in illegal "beat the system" schemes that lead to run-ins with the law and aggressive, mean-spirited, and punitive officials. The defensive counterhostility on the part of others helps maintain the antisocial's conviction that the world is a denigrating place.

In working with an antisocial patient, the therapist would probably do well to try to impress upon the patient the possible advantages (for the patient) of altering his or her socially repugnant behaviors (Skeem, Edens, Camp, & Colwell, 2004). Despite self-interest being the primary motivator in increasing prosocial acts, the consequent decrease in abrasive social encounters may over time alter the antisocial's belief about the degree of intrinsic threat in the environment. Attempts at altering such beliefs directly would be likely to elicit disdain for the therapist that can lead to an increased desire to con, manipulate, or teach a lesson to the "sappy and naive wimp."

Identifying Domain Dysfunctions

The primary domain dysfunctions of the antisocial personality are seen in the socially evident irresponsible interpersonal conduct, impulsive expressive behavior, and acting-out regulatory mechanism. The antisocial is constantly calculating how to maximize personal benefits in any given situation; broken promises, failed obligations, and illegal behaviors are the inevitable consequences of always putting one's desires before marital, parental, employment, or financial responsibilities. Expressive behavior is impulsive, incautious, and shortsighted. Consequences do not play a role in the antisocial's behavioral decisions. Intrapsychic tensions are coped with by using acting-out as a regulatory mechanism; offensive thoughts and malevolent actions are neither constrained for any length of time, nor are they sublimated into more adaptive forms. Instead, impulses are directly expressed with no concern for the damaging effects they will have on others. Once again, teaching antisocials to consider the consequences of their actions and to see personal advantages in behaving in prosocial ways and in accordance with others' wishes is a first step in altering their dysfunctional personality style.

Changes in behavior that prove to be beneficial to the antisocial's lifestyle may have some positive effects on other dysfunctional domains. The antisocial has an autonomous self-image and enjoys seeing his or her personal freedom as unrestrained by the loyalties or social customs that "bog down" most individuals. Once again, the personal advantages in adhering to the norms can help shift this image somewhat to a more adaptive interdependent one (Hicks, Markon, Patrick, Krueger, & Newman, 2004). Such interventions as wilderness therapy (discussed in the following section) can also be useful in this regard. Morphologic organization of the few weak inner defensive operations antisocials possess is unruly; impulses are rarely restrained or modulated. Learning cognitive and behavioral strategies for acting as a result of consequences can help provide guidelines for some personally and societally adaptive personality traits. Antisocials' debased inner object representations are a juxtaposition of impulses to seek revenge and subvert established mores, as well as to demean personal sentiments and material attainments that were denied them in early life. Increased personal satisfaction and stability may lead to a decreased drive to actively rebel against "the system" and an increased motivation to work with it to their advantage.

Other dysfunctional domains are more difficult to influence. The antisocial's deviant cognitive style consists of socially unorthodox beliefs and morals, disdain for traditional ideals, and contempt of conventional rules. The characteristic callous temperament is marked by an insensitive and unempathic, even ruthless indifference to the welfare of others. These features are more likely to be masked than changed in a majority of cases.

Selecting Therapeutic Modalities

Developing rapport with the patient is a real challenge for the therapist working with an antisocial individual (D'Silva, Duggan, & McCarthy, 2004). Benjamin (1993) suggests that it is virtually impossible to achieve collaboration with an antisocial patient in ordinary dyadic therapy without adjunct intervention geared toward that very aim (discussed in the following section). Power struggles need to be avoided at all costs (Reid & Gacono, 2000). Frances et al. (1984) suggest that the therapist openly acknowledge the vulnerability of the therapy setting to the patient's manipulative talents. The goal is to decrease the chances that the patient will feel challenged by the therapist and thus become oppositional and counteract. Toward this end, it is also crucial that the therapist does not assume the role of an evaluator. This is easiest to achieve in therapeutic settings that involve a team of therapists, usually inpatient settings, where a clinician other than the primary therapist provides access to privileges.

The personality style of the therapist is even more important when working with Antisocial Personality Disorder than with most other patients. Beck et al. (2003) suggest that the following therapist characteristics are particularly helpful when working with an antisocial patient: self-assurance, a reliable but not infallible objectivity, a relaxed and nondefensive interpersonal style, clear sense of personal limits, and a strong sense of humor.

Behavioral Techniques

Although the frequency of certain repugnant actions may be reduced using behavioral techniques such as aversive conditioning, gains rarely extend beyond the treatment setting and do not generalize to other, equally offensive habits, much less correct the underlying causative dysfunctions. Because the vast majority of antisocial personalities have good social skills and are not impaired in their functioning by anxiety, most behavioral techniques prove of minimal value in a treatment program (Valliant, Hawkins, & Pottier, 1998).

Interpersonal Techniques

The *interpersonal* approach to therapy outlined by Benjamin (1993, 2005) is based on the assumption that antisocials have not had a learning history with warm and caring figures that could lead to normal attachment and bonding experiences. Instead, the antisocial maintains an interpersonal position of cool detachment and autonomy that is masked by a friendly charm that gives the antisocial a good measure of interpersonal control. This superficial social ease may lead some therapists to believe that a therapeutic alliance can be achieved with this patient. Benjamin emphasizes, however, that the antisocial cannot be expected to genuinely collaborate with the therapist, and thus initial interventions cannot take the typical dyadic form of interpersonal therapy. Treatment interventions aim at providing these patients with consistent and well-modulated warmth needed to overcome their marked socialization deficits.

Benjamin suggests several methods that may facilitate this objective. One is based on a milieu treatment program. This program does not try to bring antisocial patients from their suspicious and cynical baseline position with likely futile efforts of friendliness and helpfulness. Instead, the staff is advised to adopt the patient's baseline position and to ignore him or her. After the patient is familiarized with the milieu program, punishment would ensue from noncompliance. As the patient exhibits behaviors in accordance with the treatment plan, progressively greater autonomy and friendly interaction is granted by the staff.

Interventions that provide opportunities for interdependence are encouraged. The need for cooperation and deference to the group (to ensure one's ultimate welfare) can be taught in *wilderness* programs. Here, difficult and often dangerous group tasks require individual and group commitment. Inappropriate behavior carries with it the risk of rapid, unpleasant consequences from either hard-to-con nature or fellow antisocial participants. Exercises that require cooperation, such as getting everybody over a 14-foot sheer wall and "blind trust walks," also necessitate that participants gain trust and yield control. Benjamin reports that a group of male incest perpetrators manifested increases in self-perceived self-control after a 1-day intervention of this type, whereas controls from the same population who engaged in a day-long hike exhibited no such changes. Benjamin states that once the processes of bonding and interdependence have begun, antisocials should now have the capacity to collaborate with the therapist. At this point self-destructive features of their lifestyle can be recognized and understood, and skills such as self-care, delay of gratification, and empathy for others can be discussed and perhaps acquired.

Family approaches are often attempted in inpatient settings. Depending on the degree of antisocial tendencies of family members, intervention can range from supportive (of baffled and often despairing relatives) to active system change (in cases where the family inadvertently or knowingly supports or encourages antisocial habits). Success depends largely on the situation; working with families of several antisocial personalities is likely to be doomed to failure. Evidence suggests that antisocials are disinclined to become involved in family treatment. Nevertheless, the possibilities of constructive change will be enhanced to the extent that family members become engaged (Martens, 2004). Typically one finds that spouses and other close relations have either ignored or reacted inconsistently to the antisocial's problematic behaviors. Once the family has learned to act consistently and to set clear limits, there is a possibility that the patient's pathological behaviors may be diminished.

Group situations allow antisocials to learn long-term problem-solving techniques by aiding others in similar situations, and successes in the lives of other group members can serve as positive models for antisocial patients. In general, well-structured arrangements for group treatment have been shown to be reasonably effective with these patients. Exploratory and nondirective groups, composed of heterogeneous personality styles, do not work nearly as well as those that are put together by the therapist and are homogeneous with regard to their antisocial characteristics. Here, the therapist should be in charge of both the content and the interactional process. It is advisable, where feasible, that two therapists work together with these patients. This model should help preclude the possibility that a single group leader will become an easy target for isolation or attack. As Walker (1992) has noted, having two group leaders not only enables a second source of identification for patients to emulate, but permits the therapists to adopt a "good guy/bad guy" approach.

Cognitive Techniques

Cognitive techniques are outlined in Beck et al. (2003) and are based on the assumption that changes in affect and behavior can be brought about by the patient's reevaluation of basic assumptions regarding key problem areas in his or her life (Davidson & Tyrer, 1996). Beck et al. note that this model tries to improve moral and social behavior not through the induction of shame or anxiety, but through enhancement of cognitive functioning. They suggest that the treatment plan be based on a cognitive-growth-fostering strategy: helping the patient move from concrete operations and self-determination to abstract thinking and interpersonal thoughtfulness (formal operations).

A thoroughgoing review of the patient's life needs to be undertaken to identify special problem areas. The patient's significant others can be particularly helpful in this regard. Cognitive distortions related to each problem area need to be identified; these frequently include the following:

Justifications: "Wanting something (or wanting to avoid something) justifies my actions."

Thinking is believing: "My thoughts and feelings are completely accurate, simply because they occur to me."

Personal infallibility: "I always make good choices."

Feelings make facts: "I know I am right because I feel right about what I do."

The impotence of others: "The views of others are irrelevant to my decisions, unless they directly control my immediate consequences."

Such assumptions are self-serving and minimize future consequences. The goal of therapy is for the patient to recognize the implications of his or her behavior and how it affects others, and for long-range consequences to be considered. This does not represent real "moral" development, but rather constitutes a change from not caring what others think or feel to caring what they think or feel because their reactions can be advantageous or disadvantageous for the antisocial. The chances of an antisocial patient truly caring about others' welfare is very slim.

Beck et al. (2003) offer suggestions about how to overcome antisocials' resistance to enter and stay with therapy. Antisocial behavior should be described as a "disorder"; the chances of the patient feeling accused thereby diminishes, thus increasing the probability of cooperation. The so-called disorder can further be framed as causing long-term negative consequences for the afflicted individual, such as incarceration, physical harm from others, and loss of contact with friends and family. An initial experimental trial can be suggested, in which therapy can be explained as "a series of meetings that take place with an interested observer for the purpose of evaluating situations that might be interfering with the patient's independence and success in getting what he or she wants" (p. 156). Noncompliance with therapy guidelines, such as missing sessions, not doing homework, or being hostile or noncommunicative despite the therapist's stance as a helper, warrants discussion about the patient's feelings about therapy.

Therapeutic intervention includes helping the patient set clear priorities and examine a full range of possibilities and consequences before drawing a conclusion about appropriate behavior. The choice-review exercise is very useful in this regard. A problem situation is rated on a scale of 1 to 100 to represent the patient's satisfaction. A series of behavioral responses to the problem are then listed, each with a rating of 1 to 100 in terms of its effectiveness in solving the problem. Advantages and disadvantages of all the alternatives are listed, and a final decision is made on the basis of the overall attractiveness of the consequences of each choice. Persistent choice of ineffective alternatives indicates a need to examine particular skill deficits or undetected dysfunctional beliefs.

Patients who have demonstrated appreciable progress may still be susceptible to later relapse. In the very late stages of treatment, every effort should be made to alert these antisocials to those life situations that are prone to trigger their misbehaviors and poor thinking. The therapist will thereby have an opportunity to strengthen the patient's coping when facing life's inevitable and unpredictable pressures.

Self-Image Techniques

The troublesome nature of the antisocial's characteristic behaviors suggests that self-actualizing techniques should be dealt with primarily through methods proposed by Glasser (1961, 1965, 1990). In contrast to the majority of other self-enhancing procedures, Glasser's reality therapy/choice theory is well suited to counteract the patient's irresponsibility, self-centeredness, and social insensitivity. The confrontational and strong-willed posture of the therapist may be necessary to make the patient aware that his or her actions have more negative than positive consequences. Similarly, various gestalt methods may be employed to help the patient recognize that others are not as positively reinforcing as he or she may be inclined to think they are. Both Glasser's and gestalt procedures can also be employed to guide patients to a more realistic appraisal of themselves, as well as how others react to their behavior.

Intrapsychic Techniques

There is a widespread pessimism as to whether intrapsychic therapy can produce significant changes in the antisocial. The problem is stated well by Gabbard (1990, 1994), who raises the question of whether such patients, with their uncertain outcomes, are worth expending the time and money required by this approach to therapy. Meloy (1988) notes several contraindications to any form of therapy with these patients: violence toward others, absence of remorse, inability to develop emotional attachments, and intense countertransference fears on the part of the therapist. The last of these also relates to the difficulties associated in forming a therapeutic alliance.

Moreover, *psychodynamic* approaches tend to be difficult to undertake because antisocials are not apt to internalize therapeutic insights without external controls or interventions, even if they do stay in treatment for more than a few sessions. If severe limits are put on the antisocial personality (such as in highly controlled incarceration settings), anxiety and depression may lead some patients to be more amenable to change. Almost any other treatment orientation would have a greater (if limited) chance at success given the antisocial's lack of insight and low tolerance for boredom or slowly progressive changes.

Pharmacologic Techniques

No definitive pharmacologic techniques appear to be available to counteract the difficulties and emotions spurring the antisocial's behaviors (Mulder, 1996). However, some studies suggest that the use of either SSRIs, antipsychotics (risperidone), or mood stabilizers may reduce both impulsive behavior and outbursts of aggressiveness (Hirose, 2001; Mulder, 1996).

Making Synergistic Arrangements

If the resources are available, a therapist working with an antisocial would do well to involve the patient in an adjunct intervention that explores the diversity of human interdependence. Wilderness therapy or supervised nurturant role exposure (working with children or animals) can activate cooperative schemas that may increase the chances of a real relationship's developing between patient and therapist. In the case of aggressive antisocial patients, the therapist can consider evaluating the appropriateness of psychopharmacological intervention to help control physically abusive behavior. Group therapy with other antisocial patients can provide the patient with an opportunity to come in contact with credible role models. Potential benefits of changing the antisocial behavioral style can be observed in others' positive experiences. Helping people with similar life difficulties come up with solutions can also encourage insight about behavioral consequences in the patient's own life. Another adjunct that may prove to be a helpful addition to dyadic therapy is family intervention, particularly in cases where family dynamics inadvertently support antisocial behavior.

Illustrative Cases

The combinations described in this section appear to constitute the great majority of so-called antisocial personality types. Although the focus here is on those features that distinguish the various antisocial amalgams, it should be noted that all combinations exhibit certain commonalities, most notably a marked self-centeredness and disdain for others. Security and gratification are achieved primarily by attending to oneself; the interests and needs of others are given incidental consideration, if attended to at all. Each of these personality mixtures views the world at large as composed of opportunities for exploitation and self-aggrandizement.

Table 5.4   Nonconforming/Antisocial Personality Disorder Subtypes

Covetous: Feels intentionally denied and deprived; rapacious, begrudging, discontentedly yearning; envious, seeks retribution, is avariciously greedy; pleasure mostly in taking rather than in having. (Pure Antisocial Subtype)

Nomadic: Feels jinxed, ill-fated, doomed, and cast aside; peripheral drifters; gypsylike roamers, vagrants; dropouts and misfits; itinerant vagabonds, tramps, wanderers; impulsively not benign. (Mixed Antisocial/Schizoid-Avoidant Subtype)

Risk Taking: Dauntless, venturesome, intrepid, bold, audacious, daring; is reckless, foolhardy, impulsive, heedless; unblanched by hazard; pursues perilous ventures. (Mixed Antisocial/Histrionic Subtype)

Reputation Defending: Needs to be thought of as unflawed, unbreakable, invincible, indomitable; formidable, inviolable; intransigent when status is questioned; overreactive to slights. (Mixed Antisocial/Narcissistic Subtype)

Malevolent: Belligerent, mordant, rancorous, vicious, malignant, brutal, resentful; anticipates betrayal and punishment; desires revenge; truculent, callous, fearless; shameless. (Mixed Antisocial/Sadistic-Paranoid Subtype)

Psychopaths, sociopaths, sadists, and antisocial personalities have been lumped together in various ways in the past century. Each has been described by a parade of both common and contradictory characteristics. Some clinicians have described them as sharing a number of features, such as being impulsive, immature, naive, aimless, and flighty. No less frequently, it has been said that they are sly, cunning, and well-educated sorts who are capable of making clever long-range plans to deceive and exploit others. To complicate the clinical picture further, they have been noted for their cruel aggressiveness and for the keen pleasures they derive in disrupting and intimidating others. At still other times, they are pictured as lacking true hostility and are believed to feel considerable discomfort when their actions prove harmful to others. This confusion stems in part from a failure to recognize that these repugnant behaviors may spring from appreciably different personality combinations or mixtures. In this section, we limit ourselves to variants that have at their core the aggrandizing elements that we believe are central to the antisocial personality pattern (see Table 5.4).

Case 5.1, Randall M., 37

A Nonconforming/Antisocial Personality: Covetous Type (Antisocial with Narcissistic Features)

Presenting Picture

Randall chose counseling as an alternative to incarceration after his fourth recorded infraction involving petty theft. Entirely unapologetic for his actions, he explained that his philosophy of life was simply to "make things happen," meaning that he would do anything necessary, without barriers or boundaries, to get the material possessions, status, and money he wanted.

Randall grew up poor in an affluent community; his father abandoned the family without means when Randall was 5 years old. Being the "oddball" among what he called "a haven for trust-fund babies," he was frequently the brunt of his peers' jokes. To Randall, it was therefore simply "poetic justice" when he began selling them drugs in late high school (he quipped, "Personally, I think it's funny that they paid me to put that shit in their systems just to die early"). Randall felt that the world was a hard place, and one had to be deceitful in manipulating the system to get one's fair due. Throughout the years since high school, he had held a number of simple "cover" jobs and always supplemented his income and fulfilled his needs through dishonest schemes and practices associated with these jobs. He once went into business for himself, running a cleaning service in which he contracted with wealthy families, earned their trust, and later burglarized their homes.

Randall liked to present himself as a "big spender," always quick to pick up the tab for dinners or social gatherings, mainly as a way of flaunting his attainments. He also mentioned that his girlfriend, who was a "decent enough and loyal person," was someone who "needed some training" in order to fulfill his needs.

Initial Impressions

Randall is an example of what we are terming the *covetous antisocial*. He is an individual who feels that life has not given him his due, that he has been deprived of his rightful level of emotional support and material rewards, that others have received more than their share, and that he personally was never given the bounties of the good life. Therefore, Randall was motivated both by envy and a desire for retribution. These goals could be achieved by the assumption of power, best expressed through avaricious greed and voracity. To usurp that which others possessed was the highest reward he could attain. Not only could Randall then gain retribution, but he could fill the emptiness within himself. More pleasure came from taking than in merely having.

Though sharing some of the narcissist's quest for status, Randall differed in that he did not manifest a benign attitude of entitlement, but rather, an active exploitiveness stemming from a deep and pervasive sense of emptiness, a powerful hunger for the love and recognition he did not receive early in life. No matter how successful, no matter how many possessions he may have acquired, he still felt empty and forlorn. Owing to the belief that he would continue to be deprived, he showed minimal empathy for those whom he exploited and deceived. Although Randall's chief goal was aggrandizement through the possession of goods usurped from others, it should not be forgotten that insecurity had been central to the construction of his strategy and to the avaricious character of his pathology. His most salient characterologic features revolved around this retribution, driven by an inner emptiness and overemphasis on his earlier unfair lot in life; therefore, an extremely *self*-driven style (completely forsaking *others*) emerged.

This extremely angry man expends an enormous amount of energy (*active*-orientation) scheming and manipulating, reaping as much (if not more) satisfaction from the chase as the catch. It would first be necessary to dispel anger before concentrating on such perpetuating tendencies as the aforementioned deviant thoughts, short-sighted social conduct, and destructive actions. Additionally, a strong focus on developing more *empathic* and responsible thoughts and actions, increasing this focus as therapy progressed, would be most beneficial in establishing a more appropriate interpersonal style.

Domain Analysis

Randall agreed to take the MCMI-III, but, not unexpectedly, his profile was of questionable validity due to an extremely low disclosure pattern and the endorsement of a validity item. However, it was possible to identify the following problematic domains via the MG-PDC:

Cognitively Deviant: Contemptuous of widely held ethical standards, Randall was well aware of acceptable norms and actions but consistently sought ways to "beat the system," even getting a thrill from getting away with some aspect of social norms.

Interpersonally Irresponsible: Although he showed a social mask of civility and charm and made promises and solicited trust, Randall actively sought to undermine others as a swindler and an impostor. When caught, he would take a great deal of pride in describing his dishonest and irresponsible conduct.

Admirable Self-Image: Randall acted in a self-aggrandizing manner, considering himself to be "above" others who "simply don't have the capacity to get what they deserve," and was quick to flaunt his so-called accomplishments, measured in money and material goods.

Therapeutic Steps

Effective brief techniques were called for because Randall was not a willing participant in the process of therapy. He agreed to treatment only under the pressure of legal difficulties, and, as noted in his assessment, he was resistant to engage in the process. "What do I have to do, and how long do I have to do it?" was the explicit question he asked of the therapist. Understanding that a reflective attitude, typical of a humanistic approach, would likely invite game playing and undermining, the therapist took on a more direct, nuts-and-bolts approach: "I can't tell you exactly how long, but what I will do is tell you, the first stage will be assignment to an anger management group, and then come back between sessions and talk to me about what you picked up. Then we'll get an idea of how long." This well-directed behaviorally based intervention allowed Randall an opportunity to marginally participate in the group procedure, but then return and tell the therapist what they *weren't* getting at, for him. After two sessions, Randall was beginning to vent and drain his pent-up anger in session and began to be self-motivated for the group.

As he became drained of his excess anger, Randall was better able to handle specific, fairly worded, and honest *cognitive confrontations* that would set the stage for unearthing his usual *devious thought* process. Less destructive perceptions grew from this intervention as he learned, first, that some of the content of the anger management group had some merit (e.g., sources of anger such as the belief that everyone's out to get *you*) and, second, that alternative outlets for his resentments and interpersonal frustrations existed, some of which provided more fulfillment than the perpetual need to "get the best" of someone. An additional task of this cognitive approach was to get Randall to tolerate guilt or to accept a measure of responsibility for the turmoil he caused, which required instilling some flexibility in his otherwise impermeable *admirable self-image*. Reframing his perceptions to ones that were more realistic countered his belief that a problem could always be traced to other people's circumstances. Even when he accepted some measure of responsibility, he did not need to feel defiance and resentment toward the therapist for trying to point this out. Although he sought to challenge, test, bluff, and outwit the therapist, a strong, consistent, but fair-minded cognitive approach reduced these actions and aided him in assuming a more calm and reasoned attitude.

Insight-oriented procedures were attempted, but were not of short-term utility, nor were techniques oriented to a thorough reworking of his aggressive strategies. More behaviorally directed methods geared to increase restraint and control were most effective. *Interpersonal* techniques (e.g., Klerman, Benjamin) were also fruitful in teaching him more *responsible* social behaviors. The groundwork for this interpersonal component to Randall's treatment had actually occurred in the earlier anger management group. At the time, Randall intruded on and disrupted therapeutic functions; at this later stage, and in conjunction with interpersonal approaches conducted in individual sessions, he became a useful catalyst for group interaction and was able to gain some constructive social skills and attitudes.

Case 5.2, Gustavo R., 44

A Nonconforming/Antisocial Personality: Malevolent Type (Antisocial with Sadistic Traits)

Presenting Picture

Gustavo was seen for therapy following a dispute at work that turned physical. The chief dispatcher for the local franchise of a national moving company, "Gus" enjoyed most aspects of his work, but especially its concomitant authority. In his position, nearly 200 drivers and associate dispatchers had to follow his directives. There had been several fistfights and more than a dozen shouting matches recorded in Gus's employee file, and he brazenly joked, "That's probably not even half, not even a quarter!" The particular incident that brought him into treatment involved a physical altercation which, according to the company's record of the incident, was, in fact, provoked by the other party. However, this followed years of Gus's provocations, and the other party, a senior driver, was nearly killed as Gus struck him with a hard steel tube. Gus remarked, "I should've just killed him; he's looking to retire, what's he got to live for? It would have been a favor."

Gus maintained an affable façade during the interview, but it was apparent that he was defensive and more than a bit agitated by having to submit to treatment. When asked about home life, he explained that he generally had a good marital relationship, but occasionally his wife would be disrespectful and he would have to respond physically. He defined mutual respect as a quid pro quo, whereby if someone earned his approval, he would "take care of them," but he was not to be trifled with. He made it clear that honor was central to having a healthy life, citing his "no-good, alcoholic, cheating" father he wasn't going to emulate. However, he could recall as a child defending his father against neighborhood derogation and disrespect, regardless of what he really thought. "It wasn't my opinion that was important," he explained, "it was the family's honor."

Initial Impressions

Not all antisocials desire to fill their sense of emptiness by pursuing material acquisitions. It is their reputation and status that they wish to defend or enlarge. For Gus, a *malevolent antisocial,* these malicious acts were primarily defensive, designed to ensure that others recognized him as a tough and potent person, that no one would get away with anything that would slight his status, and that he could not be pushed around. He needed to be thought of as an invincible and formidable individual, and others should be aware that he possessed strength to invulnerability. In these features, we see a strong amalgamation with the characteristics of the sadistic personality. He reacted with great intensity when his status and capabilities were questioned. He was perpetually on guard against the possibility that others would denigrate or belittle him. Although Gus would respond instantaneously to slights, some reputation-defending antisocials are known to brood and work themselves up until the proper moment arises to act defensively and assertively.

As with the other antisocials, a major aspect of therapeutic intervention would be renegotiating a balance on the subject–object polarity more in favor of *other* and less of *self*. Perhaps nowhere else is this more true than in this subtype. The central issue in Gustavo's life was dominance directly over others, not muddled by representations such as material possession. A first order of intervention would be to establish an empathic yet firm therapeutic relationship not characterized by defensiveness or disapproval, where his hostilities could be explored experientially. Gus would be able to explore and gain a clearer sense of the implications of his chronically competitive proclivity, hopefully with a reorientation toward cooperation. It would also be important to diminish provocations, thereby encouraging a more balanced *active/passive* approach to interactions with his environment and establishing a basis for more genuine and balanced social relationships.

Domain Analysis

Gus agreed to assessment, although the MCMI-III modifying indices detected a strong bias toward *desirability;* that is, his response tendency leaned toward presenting himself in an unrealistically favorable manner. Given his guardedness and active attempts to prove himself invulnerable, this was not a surprising tendency. Although scores appeared partially deflated and had to be corrected for underreporting, Gus's profile report did indicate some problematic domains on the Grossman Facet Scales, also reflected on the MG-PDC, as follows:

Acting-Out Mechanism: Gus showed little constraint or subsequent remorse when frequently airing his hostile and forceful disposition. Usually without provocation, he flaunted an attitude, followed by a threatening tone and, as necessary, physical force, projecting an impression of "tough guy."

Cognitively Dogmatic: Unbending and closed off to the feelings and opinions of others, Gus adopted an inflexible belief system valuing only strength and invulnerability, as well as a keen awareness of others' weaknesses, and thereby rationalized his contempt for "lesser others."

Expressively Impulsive: Showing no tolerance for frustration, Gus acted precipitously, imprudently, and with no more than a short-sighted perspective. He was often able to steer clear of consequences through his ability to persuade and, when necessary, enforce in his dogmatic style, but recent events proved to be more than others were willing to tolerate.

Therapeutic Steps

With a brief therapeutic focus, care was taken not to stress Gus's deficiencies because this might have endangered the therapeutic relationship. Efforts were made, however, not to allow him to assume a dominant posture in treatment after his initial discomfort had receded. He maintained a well-measured distance from the therapist, trying to resist the searching probes of personal exploration, especially those that may have held implicit suggestions of deficiencies on his part. Although short-term methods were suited to Gus, the techniques of *environmental management, psychopharmacologic treatment,* and *classical behavior modification* would be of limited value in effecting change. Altering his attitudes toward himself and his less than socially acceptable behavior was best brought about through procedures of *cognitive reorientation.* Once a baseline of rapport has been established, Gus was able to withstand methods that confronted his *dogmatic views.* His belief that he need not consider changing his views because he was already perfect needed to be confronted early on (e.g., Beck, Ellis). An effective cognitive confrontation method countered his efforts to shift responsibility for his own deficiencies to others. It was also important to infuse elements of *interpersonal methods* in this approach, as Gus's cognitive content featured very strong social habits and attitudes. Unless dealt with directly, yet without disapproval on the part of the therapist, his evasiveness and unwillingness may have seriously interfered with short-term progress. With a firm but consistently honest and confrontive technique, the therapist averted struggles in which Gus sought to outwit the therapist and assert his dominance. The therapist maintained great patience and equanimity in establishing a spirit of genuine confidence and respect. Further focused interpersonal methods, such as *family therapy,* would be of value following this personalized intervention to continue to advance his less inflexible and more realistic self-view, as well as to learn sharing and cooperation skills.

Prior to involving other family members, however, it was necessary to put some effort into Gus's *impulsivity* in his actions, as well as, on a deeper level, his lack of controls, represented by his *acting-out mechanism.* Longer-term efforts, such as *insight-oriented* treatments, would not likely be of use here, as Gus would accede to only minimal interventions and would likely reject efforts he perceived to be too probing. However, it does help illuminate, contextualize, and orient *behaviorally based* interventions to understand the background of these domains. Gus's reputation defending, especially during adolescence, reflected his social position and group status. He needed to overcome past deficits that made him particularly sensitive to signs of indifference and disinterest, as well as criticism. Expressing both his internal needs and his public reputation, Gus did things that demonstrated to his peers that he was a "contender," a person of potential significance. This also required acts of aggressive leadership or risk-taking behaviors, potentially of a violent nature. For Gus, what was initially intended as a defensive step to protect his standing had become a major drive and aim in itself.

Case 5.3, Shawn M., 39

A Nonconforming/Antisocial Personality: Risk-Taking Type (Antisocial with Histrionic Features)

Presenting Picture

Shawn was always testing the limits of his existence and, as his friends said, "he has a death wish he tries to sell as a quest for the ultimate life." Originally from a small town in the Midwest, he moved to New York City at the age of 16 to join the "independent-minded." Most recently, Shawn was arrested for jumping into a swimming pool from a hotel balcony, and his significant other, whom he called his "girlfriend du jour," let him know in no uncertain terms that he had problems she wouldn't tolerate any more. "She went mental, totally ballistic," Shawn said with a laugh, "but she's got a point. I'm getting old and sloppy and one day I'm gonna end up buying the farm over bad form or something idiotic. Maybe she's right and I should come in here and shrink my head a little bit." Shawn showed nothing but contempt for people living the "quieter life," stating directly that those people were rotting, living only vicariously through the television set. His preferred activities included sky diving and drag racing, and he always tended to be the most intemperate character among other risk takers. Most sponsors of these events, as a matter of fact, eventually removed him from events for this reason. To hear Shawn explain it, this was all reasonably normal, and he felt "sorry" for those who couldn't push their human limits. As he said, "You have to have a hint of death in your life for existence to be truly savory." At first, Shawn might have seemed simply adventurous and healthy, but it quickly became apparent that his routine flirtations with death via life-endangering stunts, as well as his preference to die "in pieces on a runway" rather than by a meaningless heart attack, were manifestations of something more maladaptive.

Initial Impressions

Beyond his inability to exert controls on impulsive behaviors and feelings, Shawn, a *risk-taking antisocial,* was unblanched by events that most people experience as dangerous or frightening. He gave evidence of a venturesomeness that appeared blind to the potential of serious consequences, persisting in a hyperactive search for hazardous challenges and for gambling with life's dangers. In fact, he was recklessly foolhardy, scoffing at genuine hazards, and disposed to pursue truly perilous ventures. In essence, his commingling of both antisocial and histrionic features carried a motivation aimed at finding excitement and stimulation via intrinsically perilous, fleeting adventures. Shawn's actions were driven by the feeling of being trapped and burdened by responsibilities, by feeling suffocated and constrained, by routine and boredom. He was unflinching in his need for autonomy and independence but lacking the habits of self-discipline required for genuine autonomy.

It was absolutely essential for the therapist to be open to see things from Shawn's point of view and to convey a sense of trust. To achieve reasonable short-term goals, this relationship building could not be interpreted as a sign of the therapist's capitulation to his bluff and arrogance; rather, it needed to be very clear that this was to be a therapeutic establishment of rapport and alliance. This required a balance of professional firmness and authority, mixed with tolerance for his less attractive traits. Early treatment would need to be focused on establishing a more grounded belief system that would allow Shawn to view choices on more than just a superficial level, as well as establish a solid, empathic (although not submissive) working alliance with the therapist. It would be necessary to stimulate a more mature *other* orientation, one that would appreciate the experience of the people around him.

Shawn's perpetuations included a highly *active* orientation that refused to allow him to assume any sort of laid-back stance (meager *passive* orientation); a personalized treatment would need to focus from the outset on working toward a more balanced activity polarity. These measures would also be geared toward instilling a greater sense of trust, reducing his vindictive inclinations, and bolstering his responsible actions and thoughts through adjustments in his *self*-orientation.

Domain Analysis

Shawn's domain analysis from the MG-PDC and MCMI-III Grossman Facet Scales revealed the following tendencies:

Autonomous Self-Image: Shawn enjoyed a self-view that he needed nobody, that his thoughts and actions were entirely his own, and that he needn't concern himself with others. This, of course, was tantamount to lack of empathy.

Cognitively Flighty: Never one to focus on one nuance at a time, Shawn moved through thought processes as whims struck, usually influenced by his perpetual novelty seeking.

Interpersonally Irresponsible: Shawn did not necessarily act vindictively toward others, but his interpersonal style could be thought of as neglectful, as he often hurt others by virtue of his intrepid but destructive acts.

Therapeutic Steps

Through reasoned and convincing comments, the therapist provided a learning model for Shawn in terms of the mix of power and logic. Less confrontive cognitive approaches provided Shawn with opportunities to address his contempt for others in a rational and focused manner, effectively slowing down his rapid and *flighty* thought process which perpetuated, in essence, his habit of snap judgments about non-thrill-seekers. Almost a dissociative strategy, this superficial and flighty style was really a means of keeping others in the role of observer of his antics. If they weren't close, and if they were relegated to passive props in his life, he did not feel at all controlled by them. Once this hostile belief structure was examined, Shawn began noticing a major fault in his logic; in essence, he was on a path toward becoming the very thing he was hostile toward: a caricature. Sure enough, he would not be the caricature of a couch potato, but rather, that of a daredevil who had become disengaged from all others. Simply put, he left others with no choice but to *stop caring* about his stunts. This examination of his habitual behavior and cognitive attitudes helped Shawn find less destructive outlets than before. *Interpersonal* methods, such as those of Benjamin and Kiesler, provided a means to explore more *responsible* interpersonal transactions. A *group* modality was also utilized during this early stage which dealt rather uniquely with anger management from a short-term, focused interpersonal perspective. At first, Shawn intruded and disrupted therapeutic functions, but as he incorporated changed cognitions and actions, he became a useful catalyst for short-term group interaction and gained some useful insights, as well as a few constructive social skills.

It should be noted that more nondirective and insight-oriented modalities were not appropriate at the earlier stage, as is the case with most antisocial patterns, but especially given the fact that the precipitant for Shawn's treatment was situational rather than internal. Hence, he did not seek therapy voluntarily, and he was convinced that if he were just left alone, there wouldn't be a problem. Such beliefs had to be confronted expediently, though with caution. Similarly, if treatment had been self-motivated, it would probably have been inspired by a series of legal entanglements or achievement failures. Whatever Shawn's reasons for therapy, a structured cognitive and interpersonal-change approach was required at the outset. Shawn's disinclination to be candid with authority figures led to his meandering from one trivial subject to the next. This inclination had to be monitored and prevented. To ensure that he took discussions seriously, he had to see evidence of his contribution to his troubles, yet he would not accept a directly confrontive manner. The therapist, wisely, tied into Shawn's self-deprecating humor as a means to bridge this difficulty. In so doing, he was able to disengage Shawn's usual defensiveness toward authority figures and establish a more meaningful dialogue from an early stage. Of course, there were resistances (as noted in the following paragraph), but this engagement not only relaxed Shawn, but also kept him focused on his role in this process. It also set the stage for a gradual loosening of the tightly focused and structured intervention that initiated the process, allowing Shawn to begin exploring implications of his *autonomous self-view* from a more existential perspective. Treatment was still best geared to short-term goals, such as building controls rather than insights, toward the here and now rather than the past, and toward teaching him ways to sustain relationships cooperatively rather than with dominance and attention seeking. However, with the early structure set as comfortable but form-fitting, Shawn's later musings regarding self-image remained more relevant and focused than they would have had the therapist allowed more open-ended discussions in the earlier stages.

A potential roadblock for Shawn throughout therapy, especially during the early stages, was his intolerance of guilt and his reticence to accept blame for the turmoil he frequently caused. When he did accept responsibility for some of his difficulties, it was important that the therapist was primed to deal with Shawn's inclination to resent the therapist for supposedly tricking him into admitting it. Similarly, Shawn frequently attempted to outwit the therapist, and the therapist had to be ready to be challenged and to avoid these efforts. On a few occasions, Shawn set up situations to test the therapist's abilities, to catch inconsistencies, to arouse his ire, and to belittle and denigrate him. Restraining impulses to express condemning attitudes was a major task for the therapist, but one that was used for positive gains, especially when tied into the application of combined cognitive (e.g., Beck, Ellis) and interpersonal interventions.

Case 5.4, Matt S., 31

A Nonconforming/Antisocial Personality: Nomadic Type (Antisocial with Avoidant and Schizoid Features)

Presenting Picture

Matt was an involuntary patient, seeking treatment after being convicted of a minor drug possession charge. "It's kind of stupid if you ask me; I mean, who the hell am I hurting, that anyone would care about, anyway, smoking a little dope." He seemed entirely uninterested in the fact that he had been arrested while driving under the influence, and a sympathetic judge, realizing he needed his driver's license for work, kept a DUI off his record. "Who cares? I didn't kill anyone; it was a deserted back road. Besides, I pulled one over there: I'm not working anyway." He described himself as a person who makes his own rules and does what he wants. At the time of this interview, he was living with a woman whom he had met several weeks prior and whom he described as "nice" and "not really demanding." Usually, he said, the women he meets will become more and more "impossible," insisting that he get a job, help around the house, or not sleep with other women. For the time being, it appeared as though Matt would be able to live off this woman's salary and not have to make any immediate changes. Historically, the longest such arrangement had lasted 9 months, and he could "never do that again."

As indicated, Matt was unemployed at the time of the initial interview and had no direct plans to pursue employment. Apparently, he was fired from his body work job for taking days off without notice and coming in late, but he saw this as unfair because he *did* his work when he was there.

Late in the initial interview, after some prompting, Matt begrudgingly began describing his upbringing, which included an alcoholic mother and a rule-following father. He seemed to hold contempt especially for his father, as, in Matt's view, his strict adherence to society's norms and expectations got him "absolutely nowhere."

Initial Impressions

Generally speaking, antisocials are characterized by overtly oppositional, hostile, and negativistic behaviors that are actively enacted to undermine societal values. Matt, however, a *nomadic antisocial,* sought to run away from a society in which he felt unwanted, cast aside, and abandoned. In certain respects, Matt's antisocial characteristics melded with both the schizoid and avoidant personalities, although other nomadic antisocials may possess traits only of one or the other. Instead of reacting antagonistically to this rejection by seeking retribution for having been denied the normal benefits of social life, Matt drifted to the periphery of society, scavenging what little remains he could find of what he could not achieve through acceptable social means. Gypsylike in his roaming, Matt was comparatively harmless, owing to his general indifference and disengagement from life. However, in contrast to those of a more schizoid or avoidant orientation, he was deeply angry and resentful and had needs for life's pleasures, such as sex. His impulses were more malevolent, despite his peripheral and nomadic existence. When stirred by inner needs or environmental circumstances, his pent-up hostility could be discharged against those who seemed weaker than himself. Furthermore, with little regard for his personal safety, and with minimal planning, Matt viewed the vagabond lifestyle as an optimal life strategy. He exhibited what may be described as a "passive asociality," and despite its drawbacks, he chose to drift aimlessly, to show little serious forethought, and to possess few, if any, inclinations toward serious endeavors. His sense of "being no place" is both similar to and different from the experience of depersonalization; Matt appeared vaguely disconnected from reality, possessed no clear sense of self, and seemed to be a transient both within himself and his environment. He was hypersensitive to disapproval, and his primary coping strategy was to *actively* detach; therefore, it was necessary to begin building the therapeutic relationship by trust and reassurance that he was not subject to "harsh" societal criticisms (*pain* orientation typical of the avoidant). As he acceded to this unfamiliar sort of relationship, some of the sources of his hostility were revealed, setting the stage for more effective relational attitudes (adjustment toward greater *other* orientation, clarification of a somewhat befuddled sense of *self*).

Domain Analysis

As indicated previously, Matt's MCMI-III revealed a 3-point elevation, with his most salient domains heavily represented by schizoid, avoidant, and antisocial facets. Further analysis of his MG-PDC revealed the following significant traits:

Interpersonally Irresponsible/Unengaged: Clearly, Matt lacked empathy and interpersonal connection; this combination created a distancing from affective involvement with others (a protective stance) and also an apparent callousness to those interpersonal difficulties he created via his uninvolvement.

Cognitively Deviant: Skeptical of the motives of even benevolent others largely due to a long-standing track record of rejection and disappointment, Matt schemed dispassionately to meet his own needs despite the obvious cost to others, and felt his were the only ones that mattered.

Alienated Self-Image: This avoidant characteristic spoke to Matt's tendency to push himself toward the periphery of society under the guise of *autonomy,* but truly was a coping style to normalize feelings of inadequacy, inferiority, and of being a "throwaway" or "misfit."

Therapeutic Steps

Primary goals in brief therapy included the facilitation of more genuine autonomy, the building of confidence, and the overcoming of fears of self-determination. As was to be expected, there was a period of initial resistance. At first, it was important to counter Matt's feeling that the therapist's efforts to encourage him to assume responsibility and self-control were a sign of rejection, rather than an approach aimed at correcting his introspections of *alienation*. A warm and empathic building of trust helped prevent disappointment, dejection, and even rage. These potential reactions were anticipated, given his characteristic style, and they needed to be responded to with equanimity if fundamental changes were to be explored and relapses prevented. As a sound and secure therapeutic alliance was established, Matt learned to tolerate these often befuddling feelings that generated autonomy/interdependence conflicts and to begin to accept that the two were not mutually exclusive. Defenses became more fluid with a release of this extremism, and Matt gradually became more tolerant to focused interventions to follow.

Learning how to face and handle his unstable emotions was coordinated with the strengthening of healthier attitudes through *cognitive* (e.g., Meichenbaum, 1977; Beck et al., 2003) and *social learning* (e.g., Bandura, 1959) methods. More specifically, core assumptions regarding the motivations of other people, as well as his own negative and inferior self-view, were examined and disputed. These were the fodder for coping strategies such as *deviant* schemes for attaining needs regardless of the potential damage to others or to himself. The therapist served as a social learning model to demonstrate how feelings, conflicts, and uncertainties could be approached with reasonable foresight and resolved with equanimity.

As implied by his affective instability and self-deprecation, Matt avoided confronting and resolving his real interpersonal difficulties. His *irresponsible interpersonal* acts were, in essence, a double-edged sword. Although he relieved passing discomfort and strains through reckless and thoughtless interactions, he perpetuated faulty attitudes and strategies. In truth, his attempts to depersonalize (i.e., his *unengaged* demeanor) by inherently shutting down interpersonal caring or consciousness perpetuated feelings of emptiness and boredom that he was, at first, loath to admit. These distorted attitudes and faulty behavior were the main targets of cognitive and interpersonal therapeutic interventions (e.g., Benjamin, Kiesler).

Special care was called for in this focused treatment regimen to counteract the possibility that Matt's hold on reality would disintegrate and his capacity to function wither. Similar care was necessary when his strategies proved wearisome and exasperating to others, precipitating their anger. Had he begun to succumb to depression or to an erratic surge of hostility, pharmacologic agents would have been considered. It also would have been necessary to anticipate and quell the danger of suicide during these episodes. Although this did not manifest, a major concern during the early periods with Matt was the forestalling of a likely decompensatory process. Among the early signs of such a breakdown would have been marked discouragement and melancholic dejection. At this phase, supportive therapy and cognitive reorientation methods would have been actively implemented. Efforts would have been made to boost Matt's sagging morale, to encourage him to continue in his usual sphere of activities, to build his self-confidence, and to deter him from being preoccupied with his melancholy feelings. He would not be pressed beyond his capabilities, however, for any failure to achieve goals would only have strengthened his conviction of his incompetence and unworthiness. Properly executed cognitive methods oriented to correcting erroneous assumptions and beliefs would have been especially helpful in this scenario.

Resistances and Risks

Despite the therapeutic focus on the disadvantages of the antisocial lifestyle, many emotional and material advantages militate against possible therapeutic headway. Feelings of control, power, and even rage can produce a high that the patient is understandably not willing to give up. Unlike other personality types who experience considerable discomfort in association with their symptoms, the antisocial's dysfunctional behaviors are rewarded more often than punished, and consequences are contingent on reactions of others and tend not to be immediate. Because neither antisocial symptoms nor their consequences generate immediate and internally generated discomfort, they do not serve to directly extinguish antisocial behavior. A cooperative and congenial attitude often is a mask for evasive behavior that is adopted to gain advantage with the therapist and legal authorities. Some antisocial patients who come to therapy as an alternative to jail may clearly not be participating in therapy. Therapists may feel compelled to continue with the intervention process to "rescue" the patient from incarceration, but in fact unwittingly reward antisocial behavior and support the lifestyle by helping the patient avoid the legal consequences of his or her choices. It can also undermine the very purpose of the legal system: to protect innocent society members from harm.

A different kind of countertransference reaction can lead to animosity that can interfere with potential therapeutic gains: Therapist suspiciousness and anger about being lied to and manipulated, feelings of frustration and helplessness about apparent lack of intervention success, and disdain and disgust for the antisocial patient and his or her lifestyle are common. Therapy with this group can prove to be highly frustrating and nongratifying and, in the opinion of many therapists, generally unsuccessful. As antisocials are very sensitive to negative evaluation, power struggles and evaluation of the patient by the therapist should be avoided if at all possible. In in-inpatient settings this is easier to achieve as a clinician other than the therapist can be responsible for providing access to privileges; the primary therapist should not be viewed by the patient as an evaluator, but rather as a strategic helper. However, the therapist should resist intervening on the patient's behalf.

Many therapists are discouraged by the conviction that even when some behavioral changes are secured, it is highly unlikely that they reflect any change in moral character. Rather, they represent an accommodation to the constraints of society to yield a more profitable lifestyle for the antisocial individual. Some therapists try to keep in mind that circumscribed goals that decrease problems for those around the patient as well as for the patient himself or herself are valid; others worry that a veneer of socialization may lead to disastrous personal consequences for people who would have been less likely to be duped by these antisocials had therapy not been undertaken and the patients not learned to present themselves well in the short term.

CHAPTER 6

Personalized Therapy for the Assertive/Sadistic Personality Patterns

A t the most fundamental level, the primary motives that guide the lives of discordant types conflict directly with one another (Hare, Cooke, & Hart, 1999; Murphy & Vess, 2003; Stone, 1998). No matter what their other inclinations may be, their internal orientations move in opposing ways; to remain at war with oneself is intrinsic to their psychic makeup. Not only do these contrasting perspectives fail to resolve internal conflicts, but they are likely to intensify them. Thus, if the defendant wins the case, the prosecutor must lose, and vice versa. In the masochistic personality, for example, these individuals consciously hold high expectations of others, who, of course, almost invariably fail to meet them. As a consequence, masochists unconsciously wish retribution and to derogate others but, if they were to do so, they would assault the very persons they desire will love and care for them. As the saying goes, these personalities can't win for losing, nor can they lose for winning.

More specifically, in both the sadistic and masochistic types, the conflict between the pain–pleasure polarities of Millon's evolutionary theory represents a transposition such that normally pleasurable experiences are viewed as painful, and normally painful experiences are felt as pleasurable (Blizard, 2001). In the compulsive and negativistic personalities, it is the *self* and *other* polarities that are in conflict; that is, the more they are disposed toward one component of the polarity pair, the more they are inclined to reverse themselves and turn toward the second. In sum, in the sadistic and masochistic types we find a psychic *discordance* between the survival functions of pain and pleasure.

The notion of an abusive, explosive, and violent character type (individuals who are destructive to life) long preceded the decision of the *DSM* to introduce the Sadistic Personality Disorder in 1987. The official proposals at that time coalesced viewpoints of numerous theorists and clinicians. As is well-known, the introduction in the *DSM-III-R* was shortly followed by the deletion of the disorder in *DSM-IV*. It should be self-evident that our society has become increasingly preoccupied with matters of public violence and private abuse (Millon et al., 1998). Some commentators have characterized our times as a period when incivility and crudeness have come to the fore not only as inevitable products of a declining society, but also as sanctioned, encouraged, and even admired qualities of life. One need not look very far to see the pervasive nature of this plague of murder and mayhem in our daily news, our films and TV, as well as in the lyrics of our popular songs. And yet, at this point in time, the *DSM-IV* Task Force saw fit to delete the characterization of a violence-prone personality. Offering rationalizations galore, the Task Force sought to justify the decision to delete the sadistic disorder from the nomenclature. Having been privy to these justifications, the senior author of this text cannot help but conclude that the true motive for this decision was essentially a political one, a decision to sweep under the rug what was difficult to sustain in the face of unrelenting criticisms by a small minority of mental health professionals. How ludicrous it will appear to clinicians in the next decade when they reflect on a course of action that essentially ran away from perhaps the most significant personality problem of the twenty-first century.

It should be noted that sadistic behaviors are not limited to the actions of violent psychopaths who are seen only in the back wards of state prisons, those crudely vicious and brutalizing members in society's periphery (Craig, 2003; Kaminer & Stein, 2001; Myers, Burket, & Husted, 2006). Through sublimation, if nothing else, many such individuals may be found at the center of everyday society. They are seen, for example, in the harsh moralism of congressmen whose truculence is "justified" by the "arrogant demands" of "alien" immigrant groups. Such behavior is evident in the machinations of politicians whose façade of so-called good intentions cloaks a lust for power that leads to repressive wars and socially demeaning legislation. Less dramatically, and more frequently, these individuals participate in the ordinary affairs of life: the harshly punitive and abusive father; the puritanical fear-inducing minister; the vengeful dean; and the irritable, guilt-producing mother.

We turn our attention to the evolutionary model, specifically viewing the polarity schema as presented in Figure 6.1. As can be seen, the primary focus for the aggressive/sadistic centers in the pain (preservation) and active (modifying) polarities. At first glance, one might be inclined to note that the polarity focus is essentially the same as seen in the avoidant personality, where both pain and active polarities are preeminent as well. However, the avoidant actively anticipates and escapes from abuse, whereas the sadistic actively assaults and degrades others. Both are active, but one imposes pain, whereas the other avoids pain. The reversal sign in the sadistic/aggressive figure signifies that sadists engage in behaviors that are discordant, given evolution's progression through life enhancement, that is, seeking joy, optimism, and pleasure in relating to one's environment. In their stead, the sadistic acts in a hostile and malevolent manner, actively working toward harmful and ruinous ends. Rather than uplifting and

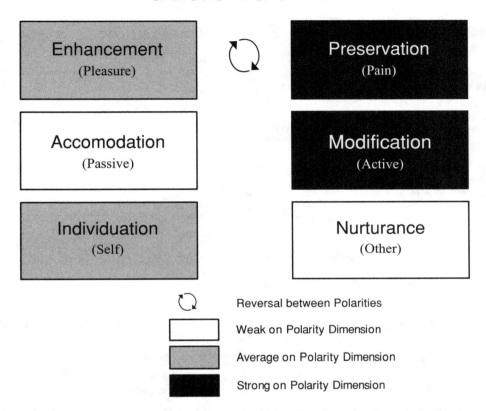

SADISTIC PROTOTYPE

FIGURE 6.1   Status of the assertive/sadistic personality prototype in accord with the Millon polarity model.

preserving life, the sadist is actively evil, violent, and deadly, assaulting and demeaning others instead of encouraging and enhancing them.

Clinical Picture

As in prior chapters, we furnish the reader with a variety of sources to assist in the appraisal of the assertive/sadistic personality, first noting how their features show up in eight clinical domains and then describing the several subtypes in which they express themselves (see Figure 6.2).

The major features of this personality pattern are approached in line with the domain levels used in previous chapters. Identifying characteristics often are similar to those of the antisocial personality inasmuch as they frequently covary as personality mixtures (see Table 6.1).

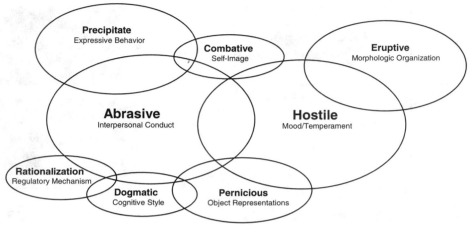

FIGURE 6.2   Salience of prototypal assertive/sadistic domains.

Precipitate Expressive Behavior

Many people shy away from these personalities, feeling intimidated by their brusque and belligerent manner. They sense them to be cold and callous, insensitive to the feelings of others, gaining what pleasure they can competing with and humiliating everyone and anyone. These aggressively oriented personalities tend to be argumentative and contentious. Not infrequently, they are abrasive, cruel, and malicious (Porter & Woodworth, 2006; Wise, 2001). They often insist on being seen as faultless, invariably are dogmatic in their opinions, and rarely concede on any issue despite clear evidence negating the validity of their argument. Most behave as if the "softer" emotions were tinged with poison. They avoid expressions of warmth and intimacy and are suspicious of gentility, compassion, and kindness, often seeming to doubt the genuineness of these feelings.

They have a low tolerance for frustration and are especially sensitive to reproachful or deprecating comments. When pushed on personal matters or faced with belittlement, they are likely to respond quickly and to become furious and vindictive; easily provoked to attack, their first inclination is to demean and to dominate. In sum, sadists are disposed to react suddenly and abruptly, evidencing outbursts of an unexpected and unwarranted nature. Although it is not true of all sadists, there is a tendency to be recklessly reactive and daring, to be unflinching and undeterred by pain, as well as undaunted by danger and punishment.

Abrasive Interpersonal Style

Sadistic personalities, by definition, reveal satisfaction in intimidating, coercing, and humiliating others. Some are experts in expressing verbally abusive and derisive social

Table 6.1   Clinical Domains of the Assertive/Sadistic Personality Prototype

Behavioral Level:

(F) Expressively Precipitate (e.g., is disposed to react in sudden abrupt outbursts of an unexpected and unwarranted nature; recklessly reactive and daring, attracted to challenge, risk, and harm; unflinching, undeterred by pain, and undaunted by danger and punishment).

(F) Interpersonally Abrasive (e.g., reveals satisfaction in intimidating, coercing, and humiliating others; regularly expresses verbally abusive and derisive social commentary, as well as exhibiting vicious, if not physically brutal, behavior).

Phenomenological Level:

(F) Cognitively Dogmatic (e.g., is strongly opinionated and closed-minded, as well as unbending and obstinate in holding to own preconceptions; exhibits a broad-ranging authoritarianism, social intolerance, and prejudice).

(S) Combative Self-Image (e.g., is proud to characterize self as assertively competitive, as well as vigorously energetic and militantly hardheaded; values aspects of self that present pugnacious, domineering, and power-oriented image).

(S) Pernicious Objects (e.g., internalized representations of the past are distinguished by early relationships that have generated strongly driven aggressive energies and malicious attitudes, as well as by a contrasting paucity of sentimental memories, tender affects, internal conflicts, shame, or guilt feelings).

Intrapsychic Level:

(F) Isolation Mechanism (e.g., can be cold-blooded and remarkably detached from an awareness of the impact of own destructive acts; views objects of violation impersonally, as symbols of devalued groups devoid of human sensibilities).

(S) Eruptive Organization (e.g., despite a generally cohesive morphologic structure composed of routinely adequate modulating controls, defenses and expressive channels, surging powerful and explosive energies of an aggressive and sexual nature threaten to produce precipitous outbursts that periodically overwhelm and overrun otherwise competent restraints).

Biophysical Level:

(S) Hostile Mood (e.g., has an excitable and irritable temper that flares readily into contentious argument and physical belligerence; is cruel, mean-spirited, and fractious, willing to do harm, even persecute others to gets own way).

Note: F = Functional Domains; S = Structural Domains.

comments. Others exhibit physically vicious and brutal behaviors (Geberth & Turco, 1997; Holt, Meloy, & Strack, 1999; Tweed & Dutton, 1998). Still others are sexually abusive, enjoying the process of demeaning members of their own or opposite sex.

Not only does the strategy of assertion and domination gain release from past injustices, but, as with most coping maneuvers, it often proves successful in achieving current psychological rewards. Because most persons are intimidated by hostility, sarcasm, criticism, and threats of physical violence, the aggressive demeanor of these personalities is a powerful instrumentality for coercing others and for frightening them into fearful respect and submission. Moreover, some sadistic/aggressive personalities frequently find a successful niche for themselves in roles where their hostile and belligerent behaviors are not only sanctioned but admired. The ruthless and cleverly conniving businessman, the intimidating and brutalizing sergeant, the self-righteous and punitive headmistress, the demanding and dominating surgical chief—all illustrate roles that provide outlets for vengeful hostility cloaked in the guise of a socially responsible and admirable function.

Dogmatic Cognitive Style

Despite their seemingly crude and callous actions, many sadists are finely attuned to the subtle elements of human interaction. A minor segment within this group may be constitutionally gross and insensitive, but the great majority, though appearing to be coarse and unperceptive, are in fact quite keenly aware of the moods and feelings of others. Their ostensive insensitivity stems from their tendency to use what weaknesses they see in others for purposes of upsetting the latter's equilibrium. In short, they take advantage of their perception of the foibles and sensitivities of others to manipulate and be intentionally callous.

It would not be inconsistent to find that most assertive/sadists are strongly opinionated and closed-minded with regard to their beliefs and values. Once they have a point of view, they will not change it. Hence, they tend to be unbending and obstinate in holding to their preconceptions. Of additional interest is the disposition of these personalities to a broad-ranging social intolerance and prejudice, especially toward envied or derogated social groups, ethnic, racial, or otherwise.

Of special note is the sadist's unusual sensitivity to signs of derision and derogation from others. Owing to their expectation of disparagement and belittlement, sadists are likely to see these qualities in the most neutral and incidental of remarks or looks. Should they be unable to vent the rage that such derision and denigration evoke in them, it is probable that their fury will be discharged toward the first person they can find—most typically, after a few drinks, toward members of their immediate family.

Combative Self-Image

The majority of sadistic personalities are likely to view themselves as assertive, energetic, self-reliant, and perhaps hardboiled, but honest, strong, and realistic (Holt et al., 1999; May & Bos, 2000). If we accept their premise that ours is a dog-eat-dog world, we can understand why they would prefer a self-image of being tough, forthright, and unsentimental rather than malicious and vindictive. Hence, these personalities seem proud to characterize themselves as competitive, vigorous, and militantly hard-headed. Some value aspects of themselves that present a pugnacious, domineering, and power-oriented image, all of which enhance their sense of self and gives a favorable interpretation to their malevolent, even warlike behaviors.

Pernicious Object Representations

The inner templates that guide the perceptions and behaviors of the sadistic personality are composed of aggressive feelings and memories and images comprising harsh relationships and malicious attitudes. Hence, whatever they experience in life is immediately recast to reflect the expectancy of hostility and the need to preempt it. Not to be overlooked is the fact that there is a marked paucity of tender and sentimental objects and an underdevelopment of images that activate feelings of shame or guilt. In their deeply imbued jungle philosophy of life, where "might makes right," the only course to which they are disposed is to act in a bold, critical, assertive, and ruthless manner.

The harsh and antihumanistic dispositions of the assertive/sadistic personality are manifested in a number of ways. Some are adept at pointing out the hypocrisy and ineffectuality of so-called do-gooders. They rail against the devastating consequences of international appeasement. They justify their toughness and cunning by pointing to the hostile and exploitive behavior of others. Contemptuous of the weak and the underprivileged, they do not care one iota if they themselves are looked on with disfavor. They claim that "good guys come in last." To them, the only way to survive in this world is to dominate and control it.

Isolation Regulatory Mechanism

Intrapsychically and dynamically, the most distinctive transformations of the sadist's inner world are those processed by the isolation mechanism. Many of these personalities are remarkably and cold-bloodedly detached from an awareness of the impact of their destructive acts. For example, their spouse and children are perceived as objects devoid of human feeling and sensibility. The painful consequences of their cruel behaviors are kept from mind. In the same manner, sadists who engage in group scapegoating view the objects of their violations impersonally, merely as despised symbols of a devalued people, devoid of human sensibilities and feelings.

Despite the relative openness with which assertive/sadists voice their thoughts and feelings, they have learned that there are times when it is best to restrain and transmute them. One cannot function effectively in society if one constantly bursts forth with hostility. To soften and redirect these urges, these individuals depend primarily on three mechanisms: rationalization, sublimation, and projection. The simplest means of justifying one's aggressive urges is to find a plausible and socially acceptable excuse for them. Thus, the blunt directness that characterizes the sadist's social behavior is rationalized as signifying frankness and honesty, a lack of hypocrisy, and a willingness to face issues head-on—as being realistic and not mealy-mouthed and soft-headed. More long-range and socially sanctioned resolutions of hostile urges are seen in the occupations to which these aggressive personalities gravitate. Many sublimate their impulses in highly competitive business enterprises, in military careers, and the legal profession. Disposed to ward off threat by aggressive counteraction, sadists accentuate the disapproval they anticipate from others by projecting their own hostility onto them. This act enables these personalities to justify their aggressive actions because they perceive themselves to be the object of unjust persecution.

Eruptive Morphologic Organization

In the main, the morphologic structure of the sadist's inner world is composed of routinely adequate modulating controls, reasonable defensive operations, and numerous expressive channels. Nevertheless, there are powerful and explosive energies of an aggressive and sexual nature that are so forceful as to periodically overwhelm and overrun these otherwise competent restraints. As a consequence, periodic eruptions are manifested, resulting in the harsh and cruel behaviors we see among these personalities.

Similarly, the psychic organization of sadists possesses intense and explosive emotions derived from the nature of their early life experiences. Rather than backing off and restraining these internalized experiences and objects, they become quickly or persistently manifested in overt actions. Furthermore, these personalities dread the thought of being vulnerable, of being deceived, and of being humiliated (Schoenewolf, 1997). They assume they will receive no greater kindness from others than they have in the past. Others are seen as potentially threatening, and sadists claim they must be aggressive to defend themselves. Their principal task is to gain power over them before others can outfox and dominate them. People are seen as ruthless. It is this "fact" that makes sadists act as they do. They must outmaneuver others at their own game. Personal feelings are a sign of weakness and of maudlin and sloppy sentimentality. No one can make it in this life if he or she lets feelings get in the way.

Hostile Mood/Temperament

Many sadists have an excitable and irritable temper that flares readily into contentious arguments and physical belligerence. Others are notably mean-spirited and fractious, willing to do harm, perhaps even to persecute others as a means of getting their own way. Beyond their callous disdain for the rights of others, these personalities may be deficient in the capacity to share tender feelings, to experience genuine affection and love for another or to empathize with their needs. Among the more vicious types, pleasure is gained in both the thought and process of hurting others and in seeing others downtrodden and suffering pain. Thus, many sadistic personalities are not only devoid of shame or remorse for their malicious acts, but they may obtain a perverse and cruel satisfaction thereby. To achieve these malevolent ends, sadists may go out of their way to intimidate and harm others, enjoying not only the tangible fruits of their abuse and deceit but the distress and misery they leave in their wake.

Self-Perpetuation Processes

Despite the fact that sadists learn behavioral strategies to optimize positive experiences, they produce, as do all pathological strategies, certain self-defeating actions. They are not only adaptively inflexible and thereby ineffective in dealing with novel challenges, but they rest upon a rather tenuous and easily upset psychic balance. Perhaps their most destructive consequence is that they foster rather than resolve problems (see Table 6.2).

Perceptual and Cognitive Distortions

Most of what is communicated and experienced in life is fragmentary in nature—a few words, an intonation, a gesture. On the basis of these suggestive but incomplete messages we come to some conclusion or inference as to what others seek to convey. We constantly read between the lines on the basis of past experiences, enabling us thereby to give these incidental cues their coherence and meaning. Among the determinants of what we fill in are our moods and anticipations. If we expect someone to be cruel and abusive, we are likely to piece together the hazy elements of the communication in line with this expectancy. If we feel downhearted, it appears that the whole world is downcast and gloomy with us. Because the outlook and moods of most of us are episodic and temporary, these intrusions tend to be counterbalanced. That is, we may be suspicious of certain persons but overly naive with others; we may feel blue some days but cheerful and optimistic on others.

This pattern of variability and balancing of mood and attitude is less typical of pathological than "normal" personalities. In the assertive/sadistic individual, for example,

Table 6.2   Self-Perpetuating Processes: Assertive/Sadistic Personality

Perceptual-Cognitive Distortions
   Others seen as devious and derogatory
   Unable to recognize objective goodwill
   Creates imagined dangers

Contempt for Warmth and Affection
   Empathy seen as repugnant
   Tender feelings subvert hardheaded realism
   Abusive manner blocks others' affections

Creates Realistic Antagonisms
   Intentionally provokes conflict
   Seeks challenges and dangers
   Imagined humiliations become reality

there is an ever-present undertone of anger and resentment, a persistent expectation that others will be deviously denigrating, if not openly hostile. Because these moods and expectancies endure, these personalities are likely to repeatedly distort the incidental remarks and actions of others so that they appear to deprecate and vilify them. They persist in misinterpreting what they see and hear and magnify minor slights into major insults and slanders.

Despite the fact that this personality's aggressive reaction to external threat is understandable given past experience, it promotes repetitive, self-defeating consequences. For example, by perceiving derogation from others where none exists, these individuals prevent themselves from recognizing and appreciating the objective goodwill of others when it is there. Their reality is what they perceive, not what objectively exists. Thus, their vulnerability to deprecation blocks them from recognizing the presence of experiences that might prove gratifying and thereby change the course of their outlook and attitudes. Moreover, their distortion aggravates their misfortunes by creating, through anticipation, fictitious dangers and humiliations that duplicate those of the past. Rather than avoiding further pain and abuse, the sadist's hypersensitivity to derogation uncovers them where they do not exist. In essence, sadists' moods and defenses have fabricated dangers from which they cannot escape because they derive from within themselves.

Demeaning of Affection and Cooperative Behavior

This personality is not only suspicious of, but tends to depreciate sentimentality, intimate feelings, tenderness, and social cooperativeness. These individuals lack sympathy for the weak and oppressed and are often contemptuous of those who express compassion and concern for the underdog. Given their past, there is little reason to expect that the sadistic personality would be empathic and sentimental. What affection and consideration did they enjoy in childhood? They learned too well that it is best to trust no one. Why be sympathetic and kindly? Should they chance again the rebuffs they believe they suffered at the hands of their parents and, later, in the case of the several subtypes, from society as a whole? Will not others undo them and infringe upon the fragile self-esteem that they so desperately seek to uplift, and that is so vital to them?

By denying tender feelings, they protect themselves against the memory of painful parental rejections. Furthermore, feelings of sympathy would be antithetical to the credo they have carved for themselves as a philosophy of life. To express the softer emotions would only undermine the foundations of their coping strategy and reactivate feelings that they have rigidly denied for years. Why upset things and be abused and exploited again? Sympathy and tender feelings only get in the way, distract and divert one from being the hardheaded realist one must be. Of course, this very attitude creates a vicious circle. By restraining positive feelings and repudiating intimacy and cooperative behaviors, these personalities provoke others to withdraw from them. Their cold and abusive manner intimidates others and blocks them from expressing warmth and affection. Once again, by their own action, they create experiences that only perpetuate the frosty, condemning, and rejecting environment of their childhood.

Creating Realistic Antagonisms

The assertive/sadistic personality evokes counterhostility, not only as an incidental consequence of his or her behaviors and attitudes but because he or she intentionally provokes others into conflict. These persons carry a chip on their shoulder, often seem to be spoiling for a fight, and appear to enjoy tangling with others to prove their strength and test their competencies and powers. Having been periodically successful in past aggressive ventures, they feel confident of their prowess. They may seek out dangers and challenges. Not only are they unconcerned and reckless, but they appear poised and bristling, ready to vent resentments, demonstrate their invulnerability, and restore their pride.

Unfortunately, as with their perceptions and attitudes, these aggressive, conflict-seeking behaviors only perpetuate their fears and misery. More than merely fostering distance and rejection, they have now provoked others into justified counterhostility. By spoiling for a fight and by precipitous and irrational arrogance, they create not only a distant reserve on the part of others but intense and well-justified animosity. Now they must face real aggression, and now they have a real basis for anticipating retaliation. Objective threats and resentments do exist in the environment now, and the *vicious* circle is perpetuated anew. Their vigilant state cannot be relaxed; they must ready themselves, no longer for suspected threat and imagined hostility, but for the real thing.

Interventional Goals

The prognostic picture for this personality cannot be viewed as promising (Stone, 2005), unless the person has found a socially sanctioned sphere in which to channel his or her energies and hostilities. Even though a large majority of these individuals are able to disguise their pathological character by selecting vocations and hobbies that provide a socially acceptable outlet for their aggressive impulses, the persistent nature of their condition will eventually get them into trouble. At work, such individuals may have misused their status, and at home, domestic violence may have escalated. The strain on coworkers and family members has become so great that, as a last resort, these personalities are "forced" to seek help.

In other cases, the criminal justice system may have caught up with the transgressor. Violent and controlling behaviors that earlier were sanctioned are likely to have deteriorated into vengeful actions against arbitrary victims. These acts may no longer be tolerated, because the transgressions have become so blatant that the public can no longer claim ignorance and societal pressures force law enforcers to take an active stance.

Not uncommonly, sadists lack insight into the nature of their interpersonal difficulties and the emotional distress they cause. More often, they simply do not care. Capacity for insight, however, is not a guarantee that treatment will succeed. Because it is impossible to force collaboration and coerce these patients to truly engage in treatment, it is unlikely that much of the underlying personality structure will be altered by the therapeutic process.

Table 6.3 Therapeutic Strategies and Tactics for the Prototypal Assertive/Sadistic Personality

Strategic Goals

Balance Polarities
Reverse discordance of pain–pleasure
Reduce active-self focus

Counter Perpetuations
Control abusive behaviors
Identify precipitants of acting-out
Modify macho/truculent image

Tactical Modalities
Moderate hostile *moods*
Undo *interpersonal* abrasiveness
Control precipitous *behaviors*

Cardinal aims of personologic therapy with the sadistic personality are to balance the polarities by reversing the discordance of pain–pleasure and reducing the active self-focus. Other important goals of treatment are to increase interpersonal sensitivity and reduce the sadist's hostile and, at times, volatile moods. Improvements in these and other domains are central to reversing the perpetuation of the maladaptive pattern (see Table 6.3).

Reestablishing Polarity Balances

The sadistic personality's primary mode of relating to others is by inflicting pain. The humiliation and victimization of others allows sadists to discharge pent up anger and their own psychic pain. For some, this is experienced as pleasurable, even though it objectively runs counter to life enhancement. Sadists actively engage in behaviors that will allow them to control and display dominance over others. Ideally, therapeutic intervention would assist these personalities in recognizing that rewards can be obtained from interpersonal relationships devoid of destructive elements, and thereby remediate the reversal in the pain–pleasure polarity.

The active approach these personalities take is in the form of manipulative schemes, venomous acts of cruelty, and, at times, reckless outbursts of hostility without control. The therapist must work with these patients to move them toward the passive end of the continuum and facilitate the acquisition of greater restraint and compassion. Sadists are generally unmoved by the hurtful consequences of their malicious intentions. Balancing the self–other polarity can be promoted by augmenting their ability not only to empathize with others, but to encourage them to engage in acts that lead to the preservation rather than the destruction of life.

Countering Perpetuating Tendencies

Given their early hurtful experiences, it is not surprising that sadists have come to expect abuse from others. However, this expectancy is often unrealistic in their current environment. These personalities have learned to selectively attend to stimuli from their surroundings that tend to support their distorted beliefs. Most of their current experiences are malevolently colored, and the benign motives of others are misconstrued. It is therefore important that therapeutic strategies focus on increasing accurate perceptual judgments and reducing cognitive distortions. Gradually, aiding the assertive/sadistic personality to interpret his or her environment in a more realistic manner will be an important step in exposing the person to potentially gratifying experiences and reversing the maladaptive pattern.

Sadists have further learned to be wary and distrustful of others. Displaying sentiments and responding sympathetically to others are interactional styles they carefully avoid to protect themselves from anticipated humiliation and abuse. Although this rigid coping style allows these individuals to practice great restraint in displaying emotions, others tend to be intimidated by this "macho" image and are likely to withdraw as a result. To prevent the re-creation of earlier unloving and hostile experiences, sadistic personalities must learn to be more emotionally involved in their relationships with others. This will be facilitated if they allow their softer side to emerge. Intervention must stress further social cooperation rather then personal individuation.

A vital component of the vicious circle that sadists have created for themselves is their hostile and belligerent mode of interacting. One of the rewards of this interactional style is the feeling of self-importance. Not surprisingly, their aggressive and reckless ventures provoke counterhostility, and what once was an imagined foe may now be an actual adversary. Sadists must learn to put down their weapons and let down their guard. Assisting these individuals in finding alternative avenues for self-enhancement, without attacking others, may provide a link to a new chain of positive reactions. Their image will gradually improve once the acting-out behaviors are under control.

Identifying Domain Dysfunctions

The most salient dysfunctions in the sadistic personality are in the mood and interpersonal conduct domains. Hostile moods and an abrasive interpersonal style are central characteristics of this cruel and abusive personality. To these individuals, coercion and intimidation are instrumental in providing rewards and a sense of personal control. Teaching sadists alternative styles of interacting that will enhance their self-efficacy, as well as encouraging them to sublimate their aggression more appropriately, may have important therapeutic implications.

Other prominent dysfunctions are observed in the expressive behavior and morphological organization domains. Uncontrolled outbursts of aggressive impulses will sporadically wipe out otherwise adequate control mechanisms. Sadists, however, are undeterred by the consequences of their explosive reactions. This lack of regard for possible negative repercussions is one of the reasons these domains are so difficult to influence. One of the goals of personologic therapy with this disorder is to facilitate the acquisition of more prosocial behaviors. This includes teaching sadists to display greater restraint when impulses threaten to overwhelm them. Helping these individuals gain control over their eruptive behavior will facilitate work in other domains.

Sadists will be hard-pressed to give up those behaviors that have been instrumental for so long. Not only do their internalized representations of the past contain mainly destructive elements, but sadists also lack those sentiments that would allow them to show compassion for others and feel remorse for any harm done. Instead, they regard others merely as impersonal objects not worthy of respect. In contrast, most sadists view themselves as strong, hardheaded, and competitive. These personality features will be difficult to alter because their dogmatic and rigid cognitive style is likely to interfere with efforts to modify other domain dysfunctions. Cognitive restructuring can aid these individuals to broaden their perspective and enable them to make more accurate attributions.

Therapeutic efforts to improve cognitive as well as other areas of functioning should draw on the self-serving motives that underlie the sadist's behavior. Although it is unlikely that treatment will transform such individuals into compassionate, self-sacrificing human beings, if they perceive that displaying such behaviors is in their best interest, progress can be made.

Selecting Therapeutic Modalities

The treatment of the sadistic personality presents quite a challenge for the therapist. Oftentimes, these individuals enter the therapeutic arena involuntarily and will comply only superficially to satisfy others' demands. The therapist will have to be careful not to be conned into believing that actual therapeutic gains have been achieved when they have not. Sadistic patients will be hard-pressed to recognize and admit their contribution to the presenting problem; instead, they will blame their victims.

Of therapeutic relevance are the resources available to the therapist and the patient's level of motivation. For example, a setting such as an institution allows the therapist to exercise greater control over the patient's immediate environment (Murphy & Vess, 2003). Similarly, if family members or significant others can be targeted for intervention as well, the chances of maintaining progress are greater. It is unlikely that interventions that target only specific symptoms will have long-range effects if the context or source of the sadist's problems remains as before.

Behavioral Techniques

Behavioral intervention may be employed to target both aggressive and impulsive symptomatology. Appropriate methods should be selected depending on the function these behaviors serve (Glancy & Saini, 2005). For some, explosive outbursts of violence signify a release of pent-up anger. Teaching these individuals impulse management techniques may enhance their ability to keep their anger under control. Relaxation training can help reduce the frustration that tends to escalate and overwhelm them. Once the therapist has gained a greater understanding of the situations that tend to elicit anger, a hierarchy of anger-arousing stimuli can be set up as part of systematic desensitization. Anger management efforts may also involve social skills training, with an emphasis on improving less hostile forms of assertiveness, as well as making environmental modifications to help the patient avoid upsetting stimuli.

For other assertive/sadistic patients, aggression serves an instrumental purpose. The therapist may have to deal more directly with the calculated nature of their maliciousness by impressing on these patients that adverse consequences will be imminent. These individuals are, however, unlikely to benefit solely from aversive conditioning. Teaching them self-management techniques may be beneficial if the rationale is presented that they exert more control this way.

It is clear that sadistic personalities represent a rather heterogeneous group; interventions will have to be carefully selected to reflect the therapist's conceptualization of each patient's problems. A behavioral formulation based on a detailed functional analysis will aid the therapist in gaining a more accurate understanding of the contextual determinants that are instrumental to the maintenance and perpetuation of aggressive behaviors.

Unfortunately, the effectiveness of behavioral methods is questionable (Glancy & Saini, 2005). Some methods, such as contingency management programs, are best utilized in institutional settings where more control can be exercised over the distribution of reinforcers. Unfortunately, treatment gains rarely extend far beyond the therapy setting. The problems with behavior generalization and maintenance may be due to the lack of environmental consistency. Working with the patient's spouse or family whenever possible may enhance treatment efficacy.

Interpersonal Techniques

Interpersonal techniques, such as those recommended by Benjamin (1993, 2003) for the treatment of the antisocial personality, can also be utilized with sadistic patients. Unfortunately, collaboration, a vital component of the interpersonal approach, is hard to achieve. Benjamin suggests several alternative methods for eliciting collaboration and fostering bonding. One example is placing the patient in an institutional setting where more control can be exercised over the interpersonal messages from staff members. As a result, one of the links in the perpetuating chain, that is, others reinforcing aggressive-sadistic acts, is broken. Another goal of these interventions is to set up alternative bonding experiences as well as situations that promote collaboration. Exposing the sadistic patient to a variety of life-enhancing experiences may fuel his or her desire to give up controlling and exploitive behaviors. Benjamin stresses, however, that unless the link between violent acts and the consequent highs that they may generate has been broken, sadistic individuals will see little reason to end their practices.

Group therapy may be indicated in that for many sadists this setting may present a less emotionally threatening environment than does individual therapy. The most effective groups are probably those in institutional settings where more control can be exerted over stable attendance, an important factor in the development of a cohesive group (Pica, Engel, & Welches, 2003). Members in the group can exert pressure on the patient to express resentments and anger verbally, thereby reducing acting-out behavior. Gabbard (1994) notes that in some specialized settings, such as in Patuxtent, Maryland, treatment is enhanced by the homogeneous compositions of the residents. This program uses group confrontation by peers who may be more effective in engaging the sadistic patient owing to their considerable familiarity with the manipulative and cunning schemes he or she employs.

Family and *couples* therapy may be indicated when those individuals in the sadist's immediate surroundings are experiencing extreme discomfort. The family may inadvertently support the sadist's maladaptive patterns. Fostering growth of the family unit as a whole may depend on the cooperation of the other members. When working with families and couples, the therapist must take care to investigate both partners' history of abuse. A wife who has been abused in the past may have come to expect revictimization. As Stone (1993) notes, unhappy marriages often consist of a victimizer-victim pairing. He further points out that the therapist may have difficulty empathizing with the more openly abusive partner. If these countertransference feelings persist, it may be wise to use a cotherapist. The therapist can help family members communicate more clearly with each other without criticism and derisive commentary.

Cognitive Techniques

Cognitive techniques, such as those proposed by Beck (1990, 2003) for the treatment of the antisocial personality, may also prove useful with sadistic patients. Cognitive therapy can help them shift their thinking from a rigid closed-mindedness to a broader range of cognitions that may generate greater tolerance for the beliefs and values of others.

The assertive/sadist's dysfunctional belief system includes the assumption that because he or she has been hurt in the past, similar treatment can be expected in the future; therefore, it is best not to trust anyone. If others are out to get you, why not beat them first? Maladaptive schemas also include the belief that one should feel pleased with venting one's "powers," regardless of the damage done to others. When exploring these faulty assumptions, the therapist must take care not to attack the patient, yet must be sure to communicate that his or her harmful actions are not acceptable. One of the goals of cognitive therapy is to assist the patient in reevaluating the consequences of his or her aggressive behavior and how it adversely impacts everyone in the long run.

Utilizing a cognitive-behavioral approach may be especially helpful with sadists who lack impulse control or act out in a harsh manner with others (Glancy & Saini, 2005). Thus, behavioral anger management techniques may be employed to control these patients' impulses and to fully recognize the awful consequences of their behaviors. Patients may also acquire a measure of comfort when the former triggers for such action are present. As a consequence, they may become less inclined to act out problematic thoughts and feelings, acquiring thereby a less intense and hostile inner world.

Furthermore, by learning to engage in prosocial behaviors, the patient will avoid the adverse consequences of hostility and, most important, he or she may be able to obtain constructive rewards from more agreeable behaviors. The therapist can aid the patient in evaluating the advantages and disadvantages of various options that are available. Beck et al. (2003) have suggested using a structured format when reviewing different problem areas in the patient's life and evaluating the risk-benefit ratio of various choices. Ideally, cognitive interventions with the sadistic patient will result in a higher level of thinking and moral reasoning, one characterized by tolerance for others, capacity for shame, and open-mindedness.

Self-Image Techniques

The deep ambivalence that characterizes sadists results in a conflicting set of self-images. On the one hand, sadists express intense hostility by abusing and destroying others; they know this to be a true element of themselves. On the other hand, most sadists feel a considerable measure of shame and guilt for the havoc they wreak. Although these contradictory images of self coexist, the patient may try, albeit unsuccessfully, to bring them together into a synthetic oneness. Several self-actualizing procedures may prove helpful; for example, a Rogerian method may assist patients to express their contradictory feelings, enabling the therapist to point out how their sense of self is conflictful; these procedures may also be productive in providing opportunities for imaginal ventilation and, hence, reducing to some degree the actuality of their feelings of anger. Similarly, a dialogue of an existential/humanistic nature may provide patients with an opportunity to recognize that their sadistic urges are not as reprehensible as they may feel them to be. Along another line, Glasser's (1965) reality/control methods may be employed to teach the patient to face the destructive consequences of his or her behaviors, as well as to develop constructive attitudes to replace those of a more destructive nature. Also of potential use are experiential techniques that may help patients to become aware of the prodromal cues that signify a desire to discharge anger before they reach an explosive extreme.

Intrapsychic Techniques

Psychodynamic approaches may prove useful if the patient is sincerely engaged in the therapeutic process. One of the goals of analytically oriented intervention is to help patients recognize their own contribution to their difficulties and to minimize the use of defenses such as isolation, rationalization, and projection. Sadistic patients must relinquish claims that they deserve rewards for their behavior. There may be times that countertransference feelings such as impatience, annoyance, hatred, and riddance-wishes will be elicited (Stone, 1993). If perceived as such by the patient, this recreates the atmosphere of his or her early home life. Therapists must contain their feelings instead of acting on them, thereby providing the patient with a new object relationship.

Stone notes that, in time, patients may come to understand how the attack mode elicits defensiveness and counterattack from others. Eventually, they may be able to recognize that their preconceptions about others may be partially incorrect. These benevolent experiences may overpower the internal images of significant figures from the past as being malevolent.

Blackburn (1993) notes that it is unlikely that therapy will have favorable results unless the patient is able to express emotions. Strong affect will appear only after he or she has been in treatment for a prolonged period of time. These new feelings are bound to be alien to the sadistic patient and may induce anxiety. The therapist must therefore continually provide encouragement.

Pharmacologic Techniques

Pharmacotherapy plays a minor role in the treatment of the sadistic personality. To these personalities, the use of medications may be viewed as a threat to self-control and may further signify weakness. The use of typical or atypical antipsychotic medication may be evaluated when aggressive and impulsive behaviors predominate or when violent mood swings occur (J. Kraus & Sheitman, 2005; Rocca, Villari, & Bogetto, 2006). To gain collaboration, the therapist must emphasize to the patient how the medication can increase self-control.

Making Synergistic Arrangements

Although each of the approaches discussed previously has its own merits, those programs that rely on a combination of techniques are more likely to influence the different domain dysfunctions. Interventions where the therapist has more control over the patient's environment should be considered if the resources are available. In these controlled settings, the patient will experience less difficulty in gaining control over his or her hostile impulses. Anger-arousing stimuli can also be kept to a minimum. Growth in this area can then facilitate work in other domains.

If sadistic individuals become involved in individual psychotherapy first, it is imperative that they perceive possible gains from treatment. Otherwise, they are likely to drop out. Once again, the therapist will have to emphasize that the techniques employed are in their best interest. For example, gaining control over their volatile nature will reduce others' tendency to withdraw or react with counterhostility. Adjuncts such as group and family methods should be considered from the outset, because they promote system change rather than individual change. Family therapy may increase empathy and emotional involvement with the other members of the system, thereby promoting the development of trust and tolerance for others. Over time, interpersonal and psychodynamic approaches may aid the patient in developing more secure object relations.

Table 6.4 Assertive/Sadistic Personality Disorder Subtypes

Explosive: Unpredictably precipitous outbursts and fury; uncontrollable rage and fearsome attacks; feelings of humiliation are pent-up and discharged; subsequently contrite. (Pure Sadistic Subtype)

Spineless: Basically insecure, bogus, and cowardly; venomous dominance and cruelty is counter-phobic; weakness counteracted by group support; public swaggering; selects powerless scapegoats. (Mixed Sadistic/Avoidant Subtype)

Enforcing: Hostility sublimated in the public interest; cops, "bossy" supervisors, deans, judges; possesses the "right" to be pitiless, merciless, coarse, and barbarous; task is to control and punish, to search out rule breakers. (Mixed Sadistic/Compulsive Subtype)

Tyrannical: Relishes menacing and brutalizing others, forcing them to cower and submit; verbally cutting and scathing, accusatory and destructive; intentionally surly, abusive, inhumane, unmerciful. (Mixed Sadistic/Negativistic-Paranoid Subtype)

Illustrative Cases

It may seem strange in this text to discuss subtypes of the sadistic personality, given the fact that the broader construct of a sadistic personality type has itself been deleted from the official *DSM-IV* classification system. One might ask, "Why bother describing multiple variants of a personality disorder that is no longer part of the *DSM*?" As noted, it the belief of the senior author that the sadistic personality prototype should have remained as part of the official classification. Hence, the recognition that several varieties of the disorder are likely to exist seems to be a reasonable position. In the following, we have sought to describe some of the central features that may differentiate the major subtypes of this disorder (see Table 6.4).

Case 6.1, Gerardo H., 29

An Assertive/Sadistic Personality: Explosive Type (Sadistic with Borderline Features)

Presenting Picture

Gerardo, according to his girlfriend, would routinely "go ballistic" and lose all sense of control without warning or foresight. Although he sought therapy mainly at of the insistence of his girlfriend, he did express a faint interest in understanding and changing his outbursts, though it was unclear how genuine this motivation was. Upon further inquiry, he did say, "I don't know what the big deal is; most men I know need to get a little rough once in a while." What typically would happen, he stated, was that he would be involved in a nonphysical, seemingly unemotional argument with his girlfriend, and very suddenly and without much warning, he would be overcome with a "blind rage" and would hit her. "You know, I'm all calm, cool, collected for a little while, but she keeps on pushing and it's like the switch gets turned. Then I'm all about ending the argument, even if I have to get, you know, physical." Gerardo described the sensation as his entire body getting hot, although this would only occur a few seconds before the explosion. He stated that he did not like anyone telling him what to do or what he can or cannot do, and described a long history of anger, dating back to childhood. His parents frequently slapped him, and when he grew older, he eventually slapped them back. By the age of 15 he had run away from home. He stated that fighting with his girlfriend was not the first time he had been physically hostile in a relationship, but it was the first time he saw any reason to change this pattern.

Clinical Assessment

It is the unpredictability and sudden emergence of hostility that differentiates Gerardo, an *explosive sadist,* from other variants of this personality type. When feeling thwarted or threatened, Gerardo manifested childlike tantrums, uncontrollable rage, and fearsome attacks on others, most frequently against members of his family or his girlfriend. Others would be taken off-guard, bewildered by the change, and generally silenced or rendered passive by the magnitude of his outburst. Before its intensive nature could be identified and constrained, there was a rapid escalation of fury in which unforgivable things were said and unforgettable blows were struck. As with children, tantrums were instantaneous reactions to cope with frustration or fear. Despite his assertions to the contrary, this explosive behavior was not primarily an instrumentality, but rather an outburst that served to discharge pent-up feelings of humiliation and degradation. Gerardo was disappointed and feeling frustrated in life and sought revenge for the mistreatment and deprecation to which he felt subjected. In contrast to other sadists, he was not typically surly and truculent.

From the preceding descriptions, it would not be unreasonable to hypothesize that Gerardo possessed beneath his surface controls a wide-ranging pattern akin to what we describe as *borderline*. Often precariously under control, but lacking the cohesion of psychic structure to maintain these controls, Gerardo periodically erupted with the precipitous and vindictive behaviors that signify his sadistic personality style. Whether justified or not, certain persons came to symbolize for him the sense of frustration and hopelessness he felt and that sparked his explosive reactions. These symbolic figures had to be "obliterated," in his eyes, lest they block all avenues of escape. Feeling trapped and impotent, Gerardo would be provoked into a panic and blind rage. His violence was a desperate, lashing-out act against symbols rather than reality. Not surprisingly, he established "safe partners" for abuse; currently it was his girlfriend who came to symbolize his failures and frustrations, someone who "knows" of his inadequacies, and someone who was realizing considerable success and autonomy in her life (she was currently finishing an MBA degree). With minimal prompting, Gerardo's full rush of hostile feelings were directed at her. Sometimes, the mere presence of the symbol stirred his deep feelings of failure and reminded him of the violations to his hopes and his integrity that he had experienced throughout his life. Although insidious in its development, once another person represented his frustrations and life's impossibilities, little was required to prompt an explosive reaction.

Whether or not Gerardo's self-motivated reasons for seeking treatment were genuine, it was most beneficial that he agreed to therapy, as this aided in rapport and trust building, which is often very difficult with this subtype. In the context of this therapeutic relationship building, Gerardo became oriented to more logical modes of interaction. The possibility of becoming sensitive to cues that portend an explosive outburst allowed for supportive approaches to begin treatment. A limitation, however, was the lack of structure and time focus. Infusing this initial approach with tangible goals such as identification and reevaluation of precipitants to his "explosions" was effective in keeping Gerardo on-task and motivated. These precipitants included his characteristic disillusionment, hopelessness, and sense of failure; it was also important to examine his perceived satisfaction with "obliterating" those people close to him (adjusting the discordance between *pain* and *pleasure*). Rather than regressing into a more primitive stance as a reaction to stress, Gerardo would be encouraged to begin exploring better options for more satisfying relationships and conflict resolution through a reduction in his ingrained *active-self* focus.

Domain Analysis

Gerardo was reticent regarding testing, which was apparent on his MCMI-III; a flat profile was produced from that sitting. He noted, "I don't like to put so much out there on paper; that's a permanent record." Following assertions regarding confidentiality, a reasonably valid profile was obtained. The clinician's checklist, the MG-PDC, was utilized to augment the domain analysis; not surprisingly, the most salient domains were more implicit than explicit (i.e., more in the experiential/intrapsychic realms than in more obvious cognitive, interpersonal, or behavioral domains):

Pernicious Objects (Intrapsychic Content): Early memories lingered just around the level of consciousness for Gerardo, which spoke of harsh consequences for minor infractions, hostility in place of understanding, and punishment for "stepping out of line"; behavioral sequelae arose from this undergirding, including sharp and vicious responses to minimal provocation.

Eruptive Organization (Intrapsychic Structure): Gerardo generally "kept it together" with self-imposed and learned controls that stultified more troublesome and radical impulses that stood by, waiting for expression.

Uncertain Self-Image: Always prone to interpret the mildest slight as a reflection of his feelings of inadequacy, Gerardo evidenced a wavering sense of identity replete with feelings of emptiness, poor self-definition, and uncertainty in regard to ambition or motivation; to cover this feeling, he clung tenaciously to rationalizations of his eruptive style as "my definition of a man."

Therapeutic Steps

As might be evident from the foregoing, much of Gerardo's immediately apparent qualities seemed to be simple attempts to cope with much more complex issues; the conundrum, then, became how to maintain a focused, forward-moving paradigm, without allowing him to put up roadblocks to progress with rationalizations, or to attempt to manipulate the therapist with irrelevancies. *Motivational interviewing* (e.g., Miller & Rollnick, 2002) provided this bridge to begin treatment in a manner that led Gerardo to gain fuller self-expression in an experiential and supportive mode that, owing to its directiveness, kept goals and underlying motivations in view. In this manner, he felt less threatened while making increasingly vulnerable admissions. In a matter of two or three sessions, Gerardo was comfortable talking about his feelings of inadequacy, identity difficulties, and trepidation about his self-worth (i.e., his *uncertain self-image*). Equally essential to the success of this approach was the therapist's readiness to see things from his point of view and to convey a sense of trust and to create a feeling of alliance. Focused treatment with Gerardo required a balance of professional firmness and authority, mixed with tolerance for his more volatile tendencies. By building an image of a fair-minded and strong authority figure, the therapist was able to gradually introduce *cognitive* methods that further encouraged Gerardo to change his expectations that people were inevitably going to slight, denigrate, or otherwise attack his sense of identity. These less confrontive cognitive approaches provided ample opportunities for him to vent his anger, even in short-term therapy.

Once drained of his more hostile feelings, Gerardo was led to examine his habitual behavior and attitudes and was guided into less destructive perceptions and outlets. A brief dynamic approach (e.g., Strupp & Binder, 1984), which included elements of behavioral and relational techniques, began the process of realigning and reintegrating many historical and experiential ambivalences by providing, first, a new experience, and then, greater insight. Trying on new behaviors, both socially and personally, gave rise to Gerardo's greater insight into his *pernicious intrapsychic content,* thus creating a better explanatory context for him to employ in place of more immediate, impulsive action. In essence, he became retrained to experientially notice the cues to rising anger and hostility, and then to immediately put into place more logical, measured templates for what he was feeling. Combined in this approach were attempts to address Gerardo's *eruptive internal organization.* Although not addressed directly by any one modality, this aspect was kept in place and was implicit in many of the therapeutic progressions that took place. Further, *interpersonal* methods, such as those of Benjamin and Kiesler, provided a means to examine relational transactions and discover wherein tensions arose. Through reasoned and convincing comments, the therapist provided a model for Gerardo to learn the mix of power, logic, and fairness and to find resources for his coping skills and mechanisms.

Case 6.2, Ron R., 44

An Assertive/Sadistic Personality: Tyrannical Type (Sadistic with Negativistic and Paranoid Features)

Presenting Picture

Ron was seen as part of an incident-debriefing and screening program for municipal workers following an on-the-job accident. The head of a fire station, Ron was proud that while other stations resembled "fraternity houses," his was consistently awarded for top-level discipline, a standard he would do anything to maintain. A former military sergeant, he admitted getting a sort of "high" from pushing his crew's limits in training, often going far beyond protocol. When they would reach the point of no further tolerance, Ron mused, he would push them further in order to, as he put it, "break their spirit entirely so I can rebuild it in *my* way, *my* worldview." He also took pleasure, he admitted, in finding the "runt" of any group of new recruits to make an example of him. It was brought to his attention that he was the least popular of all station chiefs, to which he responded, "I don't want them to like me."

Recently divorced due to "irreconcilable differences," Ron spoke little of his personal life outside of work, noting only that his ex-wife "just couldn't butch up; I tried, but there's just so many times I can scream abuse for panties all over the shower curtain and messes in the kitchen. Hell, I don't let my recruits live like that, why the hell should I let my wife live like that." He briefly touched on his childhood, only in responding to direct questions, that he was the youngest of four brothers, and he was not close with any of them. "To me," he explained, "if you get too close, you can sometimes actually ruin the relationship." In his spare time, he liked to "hole up" in his cabin, where he lived by himself, and paint. Most of his paintings, he said, were of solid architecture, as he liked the form and feel of impermeable structures.

Initial Impressions

Along with the malevolent antisocial, *tyrannical sadists* such as Ron are among the most frightening and cruel of the personality disorder subtypes. Both subtypes relate to others in an attacking, intimidating, and overwhelming way; both are accusatory and abusive and almost invariably destructive. At times Ron was crudely assaultive and distressingly vulgar, and at other times he was physically restrained yet unrelentingly critical and bitter. There was a verbally or physically overbearing character to his assaults, and even minor resistances or weaknesses stimulated him, encouraging his attack rather than deterring and slowing him down. He frequently intentionally heightened and dramatized his surly, abusive, inhumane, and unmerciful behaviors. Although tyrannical sadists such as Ron often embody the purest form of the psychopathic sadist, they often exhibit some features of other personality types, most notably the negativistic and the paranoid. In Ron's case, he primarily exhibited patterns of the latter, along with his sadistic personality structure. In contrast to the explosive sadist, for whom hostility serves primarily as a discharge of pent-up feelings, Ron employed violence as an intentional instrument to inspire terror and intimidation, thereby securing cooperation and obeisance from his victims. Quite frequently, he displayed a disproportionate level of abusiveness and intimidation to impress not only the victim but those who observed his unconstrained power. Moreover, he could self-consciously observe and reflect on the consequences of his violence, and do so with a deep sense of satisfaction. Many other sadists, by contrast, would experience second thoughts and feel a measure of contrition about the violence they had produced.

Much of what motivated Ron was his fear that others may recognize his inner insecurities and low sense of self-esteem. To overcome these deeply felt inner weaknesses, he learned that he could feel superior by overwhelming others by the force of his physical power and brutal vindictiveness.

Immediate attention needed to be focused on drawing Ron into the process of treatment, as he was undoubtedly going to be quite resistant. Highly concrete, structured strategies would be the most appropriate choice, in initial stages, to develop a therapeutic alliance by working in a manner and voice in which he was highly accustomed. A second order of techniques to follow would address his constitutional anger, examine and correct his perpetuating need to dominate *others,* and acclimate him to appreciate the difficult experience of the people around him. It would be necessary to work toward a dissipation of his *active-pain* orientation, as well as an augmentation of his empathy for *others.* Clearly, anger management concepts were to be used throughout the course of treatment as a useful tool to achieve these goals.

Domain Analysis

Apparently intimidated by the psychologist's setting, Ron asserted a kind of overconfidence in completing various assessment measures. The following are the results of the combined MCMI-III Grossman Facet Scales and MG-PDC highlights:

Cognitively Dogmatic: Ron could be described as unbending and authoritarian, demanding from others an allegiance to his way of thinking; he was well aware of subtleties of thought and expression in others, and did his best to exploit these weaknesses to make others more amenable to his worldview.

Interpersonally Abrasive: One of Ron's favorite sayings was "I'm not trying to make them like me." He reveled in intimidating and humiliating others and expressing abusive comments and acts. It gave him a great deal of satisfaction to feel interpersonal power in this regard.

Inviolable Self-Image: This domain, shared with the paranoid prototype, seemed to capture Ron's sense of self-importance and aggrandizement, as well as his refusal to show any vulnerability. This, of course, was likely reflective of his tendency to feel as though he could be attacked at any given time.

Therapeutic Course

Not surprisingly, Ron actively resisted exploring his motives. Although he did not start out as an active and willing participant in therapy, a strong, directive approach adopted by his psychologist spoke his language and drew him into the therapeutic process. He submitted to therapy under the pressure of a job demand, but he gradually became more open to reframing his attitudes as well as the possible benefits of doing so. A circumscribed focus was optimally suited for Ron. Directive *cognitive techniques,* such as those of Meichenbaum (1977) and Ellis (1979), were used to confront him with the obstructive and self-defeating nature of his *dogmatic* expectations of the world around him. With Ron, this took the form of a cognitive reorientation and restructuring, highlighting more effective and rational approaches to his belief system in tandem with denoting deficiencies in his usual expectations. An inroad such as this, tied deeply to a concrete and indisputable logic, was the most effective means for gaining Ron's investment in the process.

Formal *behavior modification* methods were fruitfully explored to achieve greater consistency and interpersonal harmony in his social behavior. Although the deeply rooted character of these problems impeded the effectiveness of most therapeutic procedures, it was fruitful to explore the more confrontive and incisive techniques of both cognitive and *interpersonal* therapies (e.g., Benjamin, Kiesler). In support of short-term interpersonal techniques, *family* treatment methods were utilized to focus on the complex network of relationships that sustained his personality style. Together with cognitive restructuring procedures, this proved to be among the most useful techniques in addressing his *abrasive interactions,* helping him recognize the source of his own hurt and angry feelings and to appreciate how he provoked hurt and anger in others. With these methods, Ron learned not to assume that a problem was always traceable to another person's stupidity or laziness. As he found it possible to accept a measure of responsibility for his difficulties, he refrained from concluding that the therapist tricked him into admitting it. This was a decent start to introducing Ron to the idea that it may be okay to occasionally express vulnerability (i.e., introducing less directive, more *supportive/humanistic* techniques to address his rigid and *inviolable self-image*). However, noting that at that point he had completed his obligatory number of sessions and had taken valuable information from the sessions, he said, "I'll be finishing up now. Thanks for everything." Ron thus ended the treatment before moving into this final modality, but it might be anticipated that had he been more self-motivated to continue, the more directive beginning may have fostered productivity in more client-defined ending stages of treatment.

It is important to note that Ron did not start out a willing participant in therapy, and he agreed to treatment under the pressure of vocational difficulties. A strong and determined attitude overcame his desire to outwit the therapist by setting up situations to test the therapist's skills, to catch inconsistencies, to arouse ire, and, if possible, to belittle and humiliate the therapist. For the therapist, restraining the impulse to express a condemning attitude was not a difficult task. Goal-directed in a brief treatment program, the therapist was able to check any hostile feelings, keeping in mind that Ron's difficulties were not fully under his control. Nevertheless, Ron may have actively impeded his progress toward conflict resolution and goal attainment, undoing what good he had previously achieved in treatment. A combination of cognitive and interpersonal techniques were employed with behavioral anger management to counteract his contrary feelings and his inclination to retract his more kindly expectations of others and quickly rebuild the few advances that he and the therapist had struggled to attain. A committed and professional approach prevented relapses by confronting the ambivalence that stood to rob him of what steps he had secured toward progress.

Case 6.3, Ray P., 53

An Assertive/Sadistic Personality: Enforcing Type (Sadistic with Compulsive Features)

Presenting Picture

Complaints from employees prompted an employee assistance program visit for Ray, a midlevel supervisor for a debt-collection agency; however, Ray refused to see anyone "directly associated with the company." Therefore, an outside referral was made, bringing him to our attention. Ray presented as entirely smug and mused that the visit was a plot designed by his boss to give him a "bad rap." According to Ray, his boss was fearful of Ray's taking his job, "and well he should be," for this was clearly Ray's intent and he had every confidence that he would, in fact, succeed. When asked how he perceived himself as a supervisor, he wasted no time in stating, "Tough but entirely fair." He *expected* a full workday out of everyone, with no slacking off, chatter, coming in late, or excuses for not getting tasks done. "I check 'em *in,* and I check 'em *out*. Every day!" he emphasized with pride that had an undertone of hostility. He refused to work with "problem" employees; he simply fired them, as they probably did not have what it took for his line of work. Debt collection was something Ray was very proud of. He said that he loved the power of his job, the aspect of telling others what to do, but he most enjoyed collecting debt. With immense satisfaction, he described one case where he prompted a debtor to run, then chased her clear across the country, doing anything he saw fit to prolong the chase. Eventually, he caught up with her in California, where, as he described it, "I kept her guessing for weeks and finally just embarrassed the hell out of her in front of her family out there, during a get-together." With a laugh, he added, "My guy said he'd never saw so many 'deer-in-headlights' eyes. It was one of the most satisfying moments of my life."

Initial Impressions

Ray represented a subtype we term the *enforcing sadist,* a pattern he shared with some military sergeants, police officers, university deans, court judges, clergy members, and others whose hostile inclinations are employed ostensibly in the public interest. He was an individual who felt he had the right to control and punish others, determine when rules had been broken, and decide how these violators should be dealt with, even violently and destructively. Operating under the guise of sanctioned roles to meet the common interest, the deeper motives that spurred his actions were of questionable legitimacy owing to the extraordinary force with which he meted out condemnation and punishment. As a socially sanctioned referee, he searched out rule breakers and perpetrators of incidental infractions that fell within his societally endorsed role and exercised whatever powers he possessed to the most severe degree. In this sense, Ray presented some of the major features of the compulsive personality, one who was a stickler for rules, but who, as an enforcing sadist, could openly discharge his otherwise deeply repressed anger against the weak and condemnable.

To meet Ray was to do so at one's peril. Because his position had been authorized by society, he could execute within his immense domain the means to prevail over and destroy others. In carrying out his duties, he treated others in an inhumane and destructive manner. Despite his responsibility to be fair and balanced, he did not feel a need to put limits on the emotions that drove his sadistically vicious behaviors. What differentiated Ray from other sadists was his built-in and socially sanctioned power base, which allowed him to exert any and all forms of control over others.

Underpinning Ray's need to "seek justice" in this most extreme manner was an extremely volatile collection of anger and hostility which would need to be dispelled in order to begin work. As a modicum of peacefulness would be established (less *active* orientation), and Ray's tension would dissipate, it would be possible to address several basic assumptions that served to create this embittered personal context. This would also remedy the confusion regarding his reversed *pleasure–pain* continuum. As some of these basic assumptions would come into question, and his perpetuating circles would be disrupted, a stronger *other* orientation would be stimulated to develop healthier socialization and, together with behavioral methods, to establish a basic set of emotional and behavioral controls derived from a healthier characterologic context.

Domain Analysis

Not entirely surprisingly, Ray's administration of the MCMI-III produced a questionably valid protocol, as his overall presentation emphasized his "being in the right" in all affairs. Domains were discernable, however, from the

Grossman Facet Scales and the MG-PDC, with the following areas presenting as most salient:

Interpersonally Abrasive: More than anything, Ray seemed driven by a need to intimidate, scorn, and humiliate others, using abusive means to beat others into submission, to "tow the line," and to "fess up to their depravity and irresponsibility."

Temperamentally Hostile: Underlying all of Ray's actions was a vitriolic and caustic hostility that was mostly left unbridled, except when necessary to keep it under wraps to effectively scheme for an attack.

Cognitively Constricted: Ray constructed his worldview in concrete terms of "right and wrong," "bad and good," "acceptable and unacceptable," and the like. He ascribed to the "morally righteous" ways of being, condemning most others (especially debtors) as subhuman and unworthy of living life without their "much deserved" fear.

Therapeutic Steps

From the beginning, the therapist was always cognizant of Ray's inclination to be spoiling for a fight, as it would be a source of satisfaction to him to tangle with the therapist to prove his strength and test his powers. A first focus was to counter Ray's omnipresent undertone of anger and resentment, which perpetuated his expectations that the therapist would be devious or scheming. This took a synergistic approach to initial interventions, starting with a potentiated pairing of modalities, all aimed at addressing his *temperamental hostility.* Several *pharmacologic agents* were explored to modulate the threshold and intensity of Ray's reactivity. Although not often effective in similar circumstances, it was highly worthwhile to explore this option, as it did downgrade the frequency and depth of his hostile feelings, thereby decreasing some of the self-perpetuating consequences of his aggressive behavior. Well-directed *behavioral* approaches provided Ray with opportunities to further vent his anger. Once drained of hostility or having it more benignly channeled, he was able to explore his habitual expectations and attitudes and was guided through various *cognitive* and *emotion-based* techniques (e.g., Beck, Greenberg) into less destructive perceptions and outlets. By confronting and then venting these feelings, Ray was able to dilute his inclination to repeatedly distort incidental remarks and actions of the therapist so that they appeared to deprecate and vilify him. Similarly, a worthy brief therapeutic goal was to undo his habit of misinterpreting what he saw and heard and magnifying minor slights into major insults and slanders.

Following Ray's de-escalation of anger and cognitively adjusting his perceptions of others (as modeled with his therapist), as noted, it was then efficacious to change the content of the cognitively based interventions to those aimed at cognitive distortions, specifically, those that *constricted* his thought patterns to conceptualize much of the world in dichotomous thinking. This was further facilitated by the use of self-actualizing techniques such as *experiential* methods of sensitizing Ray to prodromal cues and *gestalt* procedures to enable him to see the other's point of view. Following in catalytic sequence were *interpersonal* techniques (e.g., Klerman, Benjamin) that were fruitful in curbing his more *abrasive* relational style and teaching him more acceptable social behavior. Although he declined this option and terminated early, *group* methods may have also been productive, as Ray may have become a useful catalyst for group interaction and possibly improved various constructive social skills and attitudes. However, the downside to this possibility was the potential risk that he would intrude on and disrupt therapeutic functions.

Case 6.4, Clayton B., 39

An Assertive/Sadistic Personality: Spineless Type (Sadistic with Avoidant Features)

Presenting Picture

In great detail, Clayton described frequently being pushed around as a child, both by other children and by his father. But "I don't have that problem any more," he explained, due to various tactics he had since embraced. He was a small child who was adopted at age 6, went through a late onset of puberty, and always sought to "be a man." His father, a Marine, was always disgusted by him and frequently insulted and attacked him. As an adult in therapy, however, Clayton stated that this was all under control, as he *had* become a man, had gone through military training, and would be the first to "make it clear" that he would not allow *anyone* to threaten him, "not even that old son-of-a-bitch." He was a gun enthusiast and worked in a gun and ammunition store, where he often fired into the ceiling to shake up "suspicious" customers, usually those of different ethnic backgrounds. He was court-ordered to treatment, in fact, following what he called "just everything blown out of proportion and a bunch of do-gooders trying to be politically correct." What had happened was that a bullet he shot into the air ricocheted and lodged into a Hispanic man's leg.

Very defensive and extremely bigoted, Clayton seemed *extremely* discomforted by anyone who appeared to be different, or who appeared to threaten his freedom or his expression of it. He did disclose that he relied on the fact that he would never "come to blows" with anyone, for as long as he showed he was tougher, "then the 'other guy' is really the coward." Not surprisingly, he lived a very guarded, prisonlike life, which is anything but the free life he worshipped, and showed many other signs of cowardly, underhanded behavior.

Clinical Assessment

Clayton was deeply insecure and irresolute, often faint-hearted and cowardly, in fact. His sadistic actions were responses to perceived dangers and fears. His aggression signified an effort to show others that he was *not* anxious, nor ready to succumb to the inner weaknesses and external pressures he experienced. When necessary, he committed violent acts as a means of overcoming his fearfulness and need to secure refuge. He was basically an insecure and cowardly person whose venom and cruelty were essentially a counterphobic act. Anticipating real danger, projecting his hostile fantasies, he struck first, hoping thereby to forestall antagonism. An analysis of his psychic structure indicated that his overt hostility and abuse mapped onto a covert pattern of avoidant personality characteristics; this is a pattern we have termed the *spineless sadist*. The fearful nature of his actions was seen in an amalgam of preemptive strikes, whereas a more *avoidant* person would likely withdraw. When Clayton's fantasy was peopled with powerful and aggressive enemies, when he felt precariously undefended, he gained moments of peace by counteracting the dangers he saw lurking about him. To ward off panic, he counteracted his assailants by engaging in the very acts he deeply feared. Subjected early on to repeated physical brutality and intimidation, Clayton had learned to employ these instrumentalities of destruction and turn them against those who seemed threatening and abusive, as a message to others that he was neither anxious nor intimidated. Not only did this mechanism serve to enable him to master his personal fears, but it served to divert and impress the public with a false sense of confidence and self-assurance. As with many other sadists, public aggressiveness is not a sign of genuine confidence and personal strength, but a desperate means to try to feel superior and self-assured.

Clayton's self-perpetuations were situated in a constant state of protectiveness, and his constitutional proclivity was to ward off, in hex sign fashion, any possible perceived threat with a false macho demeanor (an ineffective *active-pain* construct). A first measure would be to question Clayton's logic behind his characterological fears and suspicions, as well as alleviate long-developed hostilities. As a more reasonable understanding of these fears became established, it would be possible to work toward greater understanding of and empathy for *others,* as well as develop effective and more satisfying interactional skills and contexts.

Domain Analysis

Clayton refused to complete any psychological tests and would not accede to the clinician's use of the MG-PDC. Therefore, the following domains could not be empirically supported, but in his clinician's best judgment, they appeared to be the most important areas for intervention:

Fantasy Mechanism: This avoidant characteristic fueled Clayton's fears and created justification for his sporadic outbursts. Consistently, Clayton found himself fantasizing about the dangers and potential slights he might experience from otherwise innocuous individuals in his presence.

Combative Self-Image: Although this was decidedly untrue, Clayton liked to think of himself as unflinching and ultimately powerful as a man, ready to utilize any violent or destructive means necessary to ensure his sense of freedom, safety, and persona, and continually projecting an image of toughness to ward off difficulties.

Cognitively Dogmatic: Clayton was persistent and unbending in his bigoted beliefs, categorizing all differences according to surface qualities and perceived dangers, and insistent that despite any evidence to the contrary, his view of people, places, and problems was inviolably correct.

Therapeutic Steps

From the outset, it should be noted that owing to the volatility of Clayton's emotions, it was well advised to be alert for signs of decompensation and to be prepared to intervene *biophysically,* had it become necessary. It was important to counter Clayton's feeling that the therapist's efforts to encourage him to assume responsibility and self-control were a sign of rejection or denigration, as this would likely reinforce his *fantasy mechanism,* giving him further undue substantiation of his already exaggerated sense of the harmfulness of other people. A warm, trusting, and empathic atmosphere was established to prevent disappointment, dejection, and even rage. These potential reactions were anticipated, given his characteristic style, and they needed to be responded to with equanimity if fundamental changes were to be explored and relapses prevented. As a sound and secure therapeutic alliance was established, Clayton gradually learned to tolerate his contrary feelings and dependency anxieties. Learning how to face and handle his unstable emotions were then coordinated with the strengthening of healthier attitudes through *cognitive* methods such as those of Beck and Meichenbaum. In large part, these methods began to loosen his overly rigid and *dogmatic* views. Additionally, the therapist served as a model to demonstrate how feelings, conflicts, and uncertainties could be approached and resolved with reasonable equanimity and foresight. As implied, by his affective instability and self-deprecation, Clayton avoided confronting and resolving his real interpersonal difficulties. His coping maneuvers were a double-edged sword, relieving passing discomfort and strains but perpetuating faulty attitudes and strategies.

Special care was called for in this treatment regimen to counteract the possibility that Clayton's hold on reality could disintegrate and his capacity to function wither. Similar care was taken when the attention and support that he required were withdrawn and when his strategies proved wearisome and exasperating to others, precipitating their anger. *Pharmacologic agents* were used, as he at one point began to succumb to depression. Particular attention was given to anticipate and quell the danger of suicide during this time. A major concern during this period was the forestalling of a persistent decompensation process. Among the early signs of such a breakdown were marked discouragement and melancholic dejection. At this phase, *supportive* therapy was called for, and cognitive reorientation methods were actively implemented. Efforts were made to boost Clayton's sagging morale, to encourage him to continue in his usual sphere of activities, to build his self-confidence, and to deter him from being preoccupied with his melancholy feelings. Although this approximated crisis intervention mode, it did provide an opportunity for these *supportive* methods to begin to examine Clayton's overly *combative self-image* and make appropriate adjustments to many of his self-assumptions. He could not be pressed beyond his capabilities, however, for his failure to achieve any goals would only strengthen his conviction of his incompetence and unworthiness. Properly executed cognitive methods oriented to correcting erroneous assumptions and beliefs were especially helpful.

Resistances and Risks

The assertive/sadistic pattern will not be readily altered because mistrust is both chronic and deep. Moreover, these individuals will resist exploring their motives, and their defenses are resolute. One of the major challenges the therapist faces is to gain collaboration. It is an understatement to say that these personalities are not willing participants in therapy. The submissive and help-seeking role of patient is anathema to these power-oriented people. When they submit to therapy it is usually under the press of severe marital discord or work conflicts. For example, they may be in a jam as a consequence of aggressive or abusive behavior on their job, or as a result of incessant quarrels and brutality toward their spouse or children. Rarely do they experience guilt or accept blame for the turmoil they cause. To them, the problem can always be traced to the other person's stupidity, laziness, or hostility. Even when they accept a measure of responsibility for their difficulties, one senses an underlying resentment of their "do-gooder" therapist, who tricked them into admitting it.

Not uncommonly, these personalities will challenge therapists and seek to outwit them. They will set up situations to test the therapist's skills, to catch inconsistencies, to arouse ire, and, if possible, to belittle and humiliate the therapist. It is no easy task for the therapist to restrain the impulse to do battle or to express a condemning attitude; great effort must be expended at times to check these counterhostile feelings. Therapists must avoid getting in a power struggle with these patients. Beck et al. (2003) note that the therapist may actually gain credibility by acknowledging the patient's skill in manipulating others, including the therapist. Therapists may have to remind themselves that these patients' plight was not of their own doing, that they were the unfortunate recipients of a harsh upbringing, and that only by a respectful and sympathetic approach can they be helped to get on the right track.

To accomplish this goal therapists must not only be ready to see things from the patient's point of view but must convey a sense of trust and create a feeling of sharing an alliance. It is important, however, that the building of rapport not be interpreted by the patient as a sign of the therapist's capitulation, of the therapist's having been intimidated by bluff and arrogance. Attempts to build rapport must not exceed personal boundaries, and the therapist must set clear limits. A balance of professional firmness and authority, mixed with tolerance for the patient's less attractive traits, must be maintained. By building an image of being a fair-minded and strong authority figure, the therapist may encourage these patients to change their expectancies. Through quiet and thoughtful comments, the therapist may provide a model for learning the mix of power, reason, and fairness. By this process, patients may develop more wholesome attitudes toward others and be led to direct their energies more constructively than in the past.

CHAPTER 7

Personalized Therapy for the Conscientious/ Compulsive Personality Patterns

The most prominent features of the conscientious/compulsive personality are excessive emotional control and interpersonal reserve, preoccupation with matters of order, organization and efficiency, indecisiveness, and a tendency toward being overly moralistic and judgmental. It is our belief that much of the personality organization of the compulsive individual arises in reaction to marked feelings of interpersonal ambivalence (Haslam, Williams, Kyrios, McKay, & Taylor, 2005; Mancebo, Eisen, Grant, & Rasmussen, 2005; Warner et al., 2004). Like passive-aggressive (negativistic) personalities, compulsive personalities are torn between their leanings toward submissive dependence on the one hand and defiant autonomy on the other (Millon, 1969/1985, 1981, 1996b). Unlike the overt emotional lability and chronic vacillation of negativists, however, compulsive personalities bind and submerge their rebellious and oppositional urges through a rigid stance of overcompliance, conformity, and propriety (Koldobsky, 2005). By clinging grimly to rules of society and insisting on regularity and uniformity in relationships and life events, these individuals help restrain and protect themselves against their own aggressive impulses and independent strivings. Although this behavioral and cognitive rigidity may effectively shield the individual from intrapsychic conflict as well as social criticism, it may also preclude growth and change, cause alienation from inner feelings, and interfere with the formation of intimate and warm relationships.

To others, conscientious/compulsives appear to be industrious and efficient but lacking in flexibility, imagination, and spontaneity (Mudrack, 2004). They may also be viewed as stubborn or stingy and picayune, with a tendency to get lost in the minutiae, rather than appreciate the substance of everyday life (Guo-Qiang, Ya-Lin, Zao-Huo,

Yu-Ping, & Hong-Geng, 2006; Holaway, Heimberg, & Coles, 2006). Compulsives are easily upset by the unfamiliar or by deviations from their accustomed routines. Their perfectionistic standards and need for certainty may result in a tendency toward indecisiveness and procrastination. Although the social behavior of compulsives is typically polite and formal, there is a definite tendency to relate to others on the basis of their rank or status. Compulsives require considerable reassurance and approval from their superiors and consequently may relate to them in a deferential, ingratiating, and even obsequious manner (Battle et al., 2004). In contrast, they may be quite autocratic and condemnatory with subordinates, using their authority and the rules they represent to justify the venting of considerable hostility and criticalness.

Compulsives devalue self-exploration and exhibit little or no insight into their motives and feelings (Bhar & Kyrios, 2005; Borton, Markowitz, & Dieterich, 2005). They are beset with deep ambivalence and contrary feelings, and extensive defensive maneuvers must be employed to transmute or seal off frightening urges from conscious awareness. While rigid moralism and behavioral conformity bind much of their hidden feelings of defiance and anger, these individuals also find it necessary to compartmentalize or isolate their emotional responses to situations. They may particularly attempt to block or otherwise neutralize reactions to stressful events for fear that signs of emotional weakness may become apparent and lead to embarrassment or disapproval.

Despite their elaborate defensive strategies, conscientious/compulsives tend to be among the personality styles that are most troubled by clinical syndromes (Villemarette-Pittman, Stanford, Greve, Houston, & Mathias, 2004). Their cognitive and behavioral organization makes them particularly susceptible to anxiety and affective disorders of virtually every type (Albert, Maina, Forner, & Bogetto, 2004; J. G. Johnson, Cohen, Kasen, & Brook, 2006; Rassin & Muris, 2005). Plagued by their own exacting standards, as well as the high expectations that they perceive others to hold for them, compulsives frequently feel as though they have fallen short of their criteria for acceptable performance. Although angry at themselves for being imperfect and resentful toward others for their unyielding demands, compulsives dare not expose either their own shortcomings or their anxious hostility toward others. Rather than voicing their defiance or venting their resentment and thereby being subject to social rebuke, they turn their feelings inward, discharging their anger toward themselves. In this regard, the compulsive's propensity toward experiencing guilt, expressing self-reproach, and acting contrite serves as a form of expiation for hidden, unacceptable feelings while preventing humiliation or condemnation from others (Grilo, Skodol, et al., 2004). The anger-guilt, anxiety, and self-degradation sequence may occur quite frequently in compulsives, resulting in a chronic, mild depression or Dysthymic Disorder. Major depressive states may be quite common among compulsives in later life, usually following a period of reflection and self-evaluation. At such times, compulsives are confronted with the realization that their lofty life goals and long-held standards of excellence have not been attained, and further, that rigid conformity to external values has yielded a rather barren existence with the denial of a multitude of potentially satisfying experiences.

Severe clinical syndromes in compulsives tend to have an agitated and apprehensive quality, marked by feelings of guilt and a tendency to complain about personal sin and unworthiness. Eating disorders are quite common (Grilo, 2004; Halmi, 2005; Sansone, Levitt, & Sansone, 2005). The tense and anxious coloring of their symptoms may be a reflection of their struggle to contain their hostility and resentments, as well as their fear that contrition and despondency will prompt derision and condemnation from others (Grisham, Frost, Steketee, Kim, & Hood, 2006).

As with other personality disorders, conscientious/compulsive personality traits have held a prominent place in the psychoanalytic literature. Kolb, in his 1968 revision of Noyes's (1939) original text, provides the following description of the premorbid personality of a depressed-type manic-depressive:

> Many have been scrupulous persons of rigid ethical and moral standards, meticulous, self-demanding, perfectionistic, self-depreciatory, prudish, given to self-reproach, and sensitive to criticism. Their obsessive-compulsive tendencies have doubtless been defensive mechanisms for handling hostility, which characteristically they cannot express externally. (Kolb, 1968, pp. 372–373)

An important distinction must be made between compulsive personality traits and obsessive-compulsive symptoms as they occur in depression. Although there is some evidence that obsessions, ruminative worry, and compulsive behaviors are more likely to occur in individuals with "obsessive" or compulsive premorbid personalities (Vaughan, 1976; Videbech, 1975), these same symptoms are frequent accompaniments of syndromal episodes in a variety of other personality types. Studies that have attempted to carefully tease apart clinical symptomatology from enduring characterologic traits, however, have revealed considerable differences with respect to the intensity and duration of obsessive-compulsive symptoms (Grilo, Sanislow, et al., 2004).

Of particular interest is the suggestion in some of these studies that obsessional symptoms and traits serve as a defense against depression (Shea et al., 2004). Wittenborn and Maurer (1977) hypothesize that intensification of obsessing and denial of anger at the onset of a clinical episode may serve a defensive function among individuals feeling overwhelmed by environmental stressors and sensing an impending loss of control. Kendell and Discipio (1970) suggested that marked premorbid obsessing seemed to offer protection against the development of manic episodes. Von Zerssen (1977), in his review of the literature, postulated that many of the obsessive traits resulted from the tendency to build defenses against the negative emotions involved in depression. He cites as an example the melancholic's strivings toward self-confirmation in performance as a strategy to avoid a lack of self-esteem. Consistent with this line of thought, Akiskal (1980), notes that the psychoanalytical literature has suggested that the anankastic traits of orderliness, guilt and concern for others are a defense against the depressive's tendency for hostility and self-preoccupation.

A brief summary of the obsessive-compulsive personality pattern as interpreted by the evolutionary model is portrayed in the polarity schema of Figure 7.1. Notable

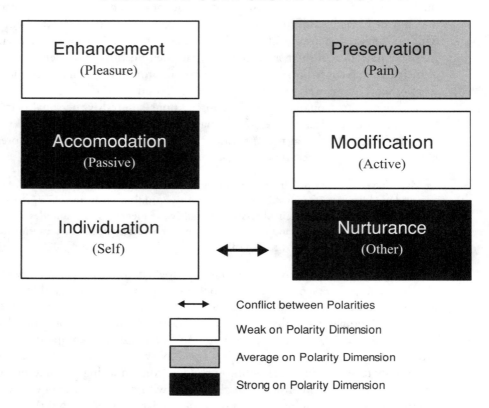

FIGURE 7.1 Status of the conscientious/compulsive personality prototype in accord with the Millon polarity model.

here is the dominance of the passive (accommodating) and other (nurturing) polar extremes. Worthy of note also is the arrow between the "self" and "other" boxes, which signifies the conflict experienced between these two orientations. As has been described previously, and as will be elaborated in later pages, the compulsive is one of two "ambivalent" personality disorders; both compulsives and negativists struggle between doing the bidding of others versus making their own choices. The compulsive resolves this conflict by submerging all indications of self-interest and instead devoting all efforts toward meeting the desires of others. The weak intensity seen in the self–individuating polarity and the contrasting strong intensity in the other–nurturing polarity represents this resolution. To ensure that their unconscious self-desires do not become overtly manifest, compulsives are extraordinarily accommodating, never taking the initiative in matters, always awaiting signals from others as to what they should do (Whiteside & Abramowitz, 2004). Notable also in the polarity figure is the relative strength of the preservation focus over that of enhancement. This difference signifies the strong interest on the part of compulsives to protect themselves against potential harm and criticism, and a contrasting indifference to the experience of pleasure and joy; it is here where we can see the grim and cheerless demeanor that typifies these personalities.

Clinical Picture

Our analysis of the characteristics of the obsessive-compulsive personality may be usefully differentiated in several ways, notably in accord with the several domains in which this pathology is manifested and in the several subtypes in which the prime features are displayed (see Figure 7.2).

The major characteristics of the compulsive personality are organized in terms of the usual eight clinical domain grouping.

Disciplined Expressive Behavior

The grim and cheerless demeanor of compulsives is often quite striking. This is not to say that they are invariably glum or downcast but rather to convey their characteristic air of austerity and serious-mindedness. Posture and movement reflect their underlying tightness, a tense control of emotions. Most significant, their emotions are kept in check by a regulated, highly structured, and carefully organized life. They appear

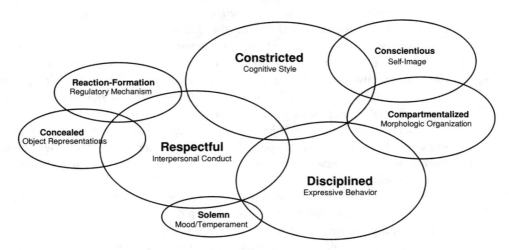

OBSESSIVE-COMPULSIVE PROTOTYPE

FIGURE 7.2   Salience of prototypal conscientious/compulsive domains.

emotionally tight, displaying features that signify an inner rigidity and control. There is a tendency for them to speak precisely, with clear diction and well-phrased sentences. Clothing is formal and proper, consistent with current fashions, but restrained in color and style. Perfectionism limits the alternatives they consider in their everyday actions, often interfering with their ability to make choices and complete ordinary tasks.

Respectful Interpersonal Behavior

Compulsives display an unusual adherence to social conventions and proprieties, preferring to maintain polite, formal, and "correct" personal relationships. Most are quite scrupulous in matters of morality and ethics. In a similar vane, they usually insist that subordinates adhere to their personally established rules and methods of conduct. The social behavior of conscientious/compulsives may be characterized as formal. They relate to others in terms of rank or status; that is, they tend to be authoritarian rather than egalitarian in their outlook. This is reflected in their contrasting behaviors with "superiors" as opposed to "inferiors." Compulsive personalities are deferential, ingratiating, and even obsequious with their superiors, going out of their way to impress them with their efficiency and serious-mindedness. Many seek the reassurance and approval of authority figures, experiencing considerable anxiety when they are unsure of their position. These behaviors contrast markedly with their attitudes toward subordinates. Here the compulsive is quite autocratic and condemnatory, often appearing pompous and self-righteous. This haughty and deprecatory manner is usually cloaked behind regulations and legalities. Not untypically, compulsives will justify their aggressive intentions by recourse to rules or authorities higher than themselves.

The compulsive person is extraordinarily careful to pay proper respect to those in authority (Fullana et al., 2004). These individuals are not only correct and polite but ingratiating and obsequious. Their conduct is beyond reproach; they are ever punctual and meticulous in fulfilling the duties and obligations expected of them. These behaviors serve a variety of functions beyond gaining approval and the avoidance of displeasure. For example, by allying themselves with a "greater power" compulsives gain considerable strength and authority for themselves. Not only do they enjoy the protection and the prestige of another, but by associating their actions with the views of an external authority, they relieve themselves of blame should these actions meet with disfavor. Of course, by submerging their individuality and becoming chattels of some other power or person, compulsives alienate themselves, preclude experiencing a sense of true personal satisfaction, and lose those few remnants of personal identity they may still possess.

As noted, compulsives are usually uncompromising and demanding in relationships with subordinates. In this way they bolster their deep feelings of inadequacy. Disrespect and disloyalty on the part of subordinates remind them all too painfully of their own inner urges and weaknesses. Moreover, this power over others provides them with a sanctioned outlet to vent hostile impulses. Should the others fail to live up to their standards, they feel just in reprimanding and condemning them.

Constricted Cognitive Style

The thinking of compulsive personalities is organized in terms of conventional rules and regulations as well as personally formulated schedules and social hierarchies. They tend to be rigid and stubborn about adhering to formal schemas for constructing and shaping their lives. Notable also is the ease with which they can be upset by having to deal with unfamiliar customs and novel ideas (Jovev & Jackson, 2004). In these circumstances, conscientious/compulsives feel unsure of what course of action should be taken, often ending up immobilized and indecisive. Especially concerned with matters of propriety and efficiency, compulsives tend to be rigid and unbending about regulations and procedures. These behaviors often lead others to see them as perfectionistic, officious, and legalistic.

Compulsives are contemptuous of those who behave "frivolously and impulsively"; emotional behavior is considered immature and irresponsible. To them, people must be judged by "objective" standards and by the time-proven rules of an organized society. Reactions to others must be based on established values and customs, not on personal judgments. What compulsives invariably fail to recognize is that they seek to judge others in accord with rules that they themselves unconsciously detest. They impose harsh regulations on others largely to convince themselves that these rules can, in fact, be adhered to. If they succeed in restraining the rebellious impulses of others, perhaps they can be confident of successfully restraining their own.

Compulsives are viewed by others as industrious and efficient, though lacking in flexibility and spontaneity. Many consider them to be stubborn, stingy, possessive, uncreative, and unimaginative. As noted previously, they tend to procrastinate, appear indecisive, and are easily upset by the unfamiliar or by deviations from routines to which they have become accustomed. Content with their nose to the grindstone, many work diligently and patiently at activities that require being tidy and meticulous. Some judge these behaviors to be a sign of being orderly and methodical; others see it as reflecting a small-minded and picayune nature (see Table 7.1).

Conscientious Self-Image

These personalities see themselves as devoted to work, as industrious, reliable, meticulous, and efficient individuals. They tend to minimize the importance of recreational and leisure activities in favor of those that signify productive efforts. Fearful of being viewed as irresponsible or slack in their efforts, as well as being seen as one who fails to meet the expectations of others or is error-prone, compulsives overvalue those aspects of their self-image that signify perfectionism, prudence, and discipline.

Compulsives are good "organization men," typifying what we have termed the bureaucratic personality type. The compulsive's self-image is that of a conscientious, selfless, loyal, dependable, prudent, and responsible individual. Not only do these individuals willingly accept the beliefs of institutional authorities, but they believe that these authorities' demands and expectations are "correct." Compulsives identify with these strictures, internalizing them as a means of controlling their own repressed

Table 7.1   Clinical Domains of the Conscientious/Compulsive Personality Prototype

Behavioral Level:

(F) **Expressively Disciplined** (e.g., maintains a regulated, highly structured, and strictly organized life; perfectionism interferes with decision making and task completion).

(F) **Interpersonally Respectful** (e.g., exhibits unusual adherence to social conventions and proprieties, as well as being scrupulous and overconscientious about matters of morality and ethics; prefers polite, formal, and correct personal relationships, usually insisting that subordinates adhere to personally established rules and methods).

Phenomenological Level:

(F) **Cognitively Constricted** (e.g., constructs world in terms of rules, regulations, schedules, and hierarchies; is rigid, stubborn, and indecisive and notably upset by unfamiliar or novel ideas and customs).

(S) **Conscientious Self-Image** (e.g., sees self as devoted to work, industrious, reliable, meticulous, and efficient, largely to the exclusion of leisure activities; fearful of error or misjudgment, and hence overvalues aspects of self that exhibit discipline, perfection, prudence, and loyalty).

(S) **Concealed Objects** (e.g., only those internalized representations, with their associated inner affects and attitudes, that can be socially approved are allowed conscious awareness or behavioral expression; as a result, actions and memories are highly regulated, forbidden impulses sequestered and tightly bound, personal and social conflicts defensively denied, kept from awareness, maintained under stringent control).

Intrapsychic Level:

(F) **Reaction Formation Mechanism** (e.g., repeatedly presents positive thoughts and socially commendable behaviors that are diametrically opposite own deeper contrary and forbidden feelings; displays reasonableness and maturity when faced with circumstances that evoke anger or dismay in others).

(S) **Compartmentalized Organization** (e.g., morphologic structures are rigidly organized in a tightly consolidated system that is clearly partitioned into numerous, distinct, and segregated constellations of drive, memory, and cognition, with few open channels to permit interplay among these components).

Biophysical Level:

(S) **Solemn Mood** (e.g., is unrelaxed, tense, joyless, and grim; restrains warm feelings and keeps most emotions under tight control).

Note: F = Functional Domains; S = Structural Domains.

impulses and employing them as a standard to regulate the behavior of others. Their vigorous defense of institutional authorities often brings them commendation and support, rewards that serve to reinforce their inclination toward public obedience and moral self-righteousness.

It is characteristic of compulsives to be as harsh in their self-judgments as they are with others. In addition, they voice a strong sense of duty to others, feeling that they must not let the others down and, more significantly, not engage in behaviors that might provoke others' displeasure. Although compulsives feel self-doubt or guilt for failing to live up to some ideal, they have no awareness that it is often their own ambivalence about achieving, their own unconscious desire to defy authority, that blocks them from attaining their public aspirations. They may rationalize their indecisiveness by the "wisdom" of looking before they leap, of delaying action until they are sure of its correctness, and of aiming for high standards, which, of course, demand the most careful and reflective appraisal. These philosophical clichés merely cloak an unconscious desire to undo the rigid mold into which compulsives have allowed their life to be cast.

Concealed Object Representations

It is of special importance to the compulsive that only those internalized representations of the past that are socially acceptable be permitted into conscious awareness or given expression behaviorally. Inner impulses and attitudes, as well as residual images and memories, are all highly regulated and tightly bound. Forbidden impulses are sequestered in the unconscious. Similarly, current personal difficulties and social conflicts anchored to past experiences are defensively denied, kept from conscious awareness and maintained under the most stringent of controls.

Compulsives take great pains to avoid recognizing the contradictions between their unconscious impulses and their overt behaviors. This they do by devaluing self-exploration. Thus, compulsives often exhibit little or no insight into their motives and feelings. To bolster this defensive maneuver, they demean the personal equation, claiming that self-exploration is antithetical to efficient behavior and that introspection only intrudes on rational thinking and self-control. Protectively, then, they avoid looking into themselves and build a rationale in which they assert that analyses such as these are signs of immature self-indulgence, traits that they view as anathema to civilized life.

Reaction-Formation Regulatory Mechanism

Compulsives engage in numerous mechanisms of defense to keep a tight rein on their contrary feelings and dispositions. More than any other personality, they actively exhibit a wide range of regulatory actions. Most distinctive, perhaps, is their use of reaction-formation. This is seen in their repeated efforts to present a positive spin on their thoughts and behaviors, to engage in socially commendable actions that are, in fact, diametrically opposite their deeper forbidden and contrary feelings. Hence, they tend to display publicly a mature reasonableness when faced with circumstances that would evoke dismay or irritability in most persons. The ingratiating and obsequious manner of many conscientious/compulsives, especially in circumstances that normally evoke frustration and anger in others, may be traced to a reversal of their hidden and oppositional urges. Not daring to expose their true feelings of defiance and rebelliousness, they bind these feelings so tightly that their opposite comes forth.

Two of the most effective techniques for transforming negative impulses, yet finding outlets for them at the same time, are identification and sublimation. If compulsives can find a punitive model of authority to emulate, they can "justify" venting their hostile impulses toward others and perhaps receive commendation as well. For example, in one case, the author observed that a child identified with his parents' strict attitudes by tattling and reproaching his brother; this enabled the child to find a sanctioned outlet for his otherwise unacceptable hostility. Much of the compulsive's self-righteous morality reflects the same process. Mechanisms of sublimation serve similar functions. Unconscious feelings of hostility that cannot be tolerated consciously are often expressed in socially acceptable ways through occupations such as judge, dean, soldier, or surgeon. Fiercely moralistic fathers and loving but overcontrolling, mothers are more common ways of restraint that often camouflage hidden hostility.

There are two other intrapsychic mechanisms—isolation and undoing—that do not provide an outlet for submerged rebellious impulses but do serve to keep them in check. Compulsive individuals also compartmentalize or isolate their emotional response to a situation. They block or otherwise neutralize feelings that are normally aroused by a stressful event and thereby ensure against the possibility of reacting in ways that might cause embarrassment and disapproval. Should conscientious/compulsives trespass the injunctions of authority figures or fail to live up to their expectations, they may engage in certain ritualistic acts to undo the evil or wrong they feel they have done. In this manner, they seek expiation for their sins, and they thereby regain the goodwill they feared may be lost.

Compartmentalized Morphologic Organization

The structure of the compulsive's mind is rather distinctive among the personality patterns. To keep oppositional feelings and impulses from affecting one another and to keep ambivalent images and contradictory attitudes from spilling forth into conscious awareness, the organization of compulsives' inner world must be rigidly compartmentalized. There is a tightly consolidated system that is clearly partitioned into numerous, distinct, and segregated constellations of dispositions, memories, and feelings. Crucial is that these compartments be tightly sealed, hence precluding any open channels through which these components can interrelate.

Appearing deliberate and poised on the surface, compulsives sit atop this tightly constrained but internal powder keg. They are beset by deep ambivalences and conflicts, and their inner turmoil threatens to upset the balance they have so carefully wrought throughout their lives. They must preserve that balance and protect themselves against the intrusion into both conscious awareness and overt behavior of their intensely contrary impulses and feelings. They must carefully avoid events that could dislodge and unleash these forces, causing them to lose favor with those in authority. Having opted for a strategy in which rewards and security are granted to those in power, they must, at all costs, prevent losing the powerful's respect and protection. To achieve this they must take no risks and operate with complete certainty that no unanticipated event will upset their equilibrium. Avoiding external disruptions is difficult enough, but their greatest task is that of controlling their own emotions, that is, restraining the impulses that surge from within and from which they cannot escape. Their only recourse for dealing with these intrusive and frightening urges is either to transmute them or to seal them off. As noted previously, they do this by the extensive use of intrapsychic mechanisms. Because of the depth of their ambivalence and the imperative nature of its control, compulsive personalities employ more varied defensive mechanisms than any of the other pathological patterns.

A major force behind the tightly structured world of conscientious/compulsives is their fear of disapproval and their concern that their actions will be not only frowned upon, but severely punished. This fear can be understood given their likely history of exposure to demanding, perfectionistic, and condemnatory parents. One would assume that by toeing the line and behaving properly and correctly, compulsives could put this concern aside and be relaxed and untroubled. But this does not prove to be possible because their conformity and propriety are merely a public façade behind which lurks deeply repressed urges toward defiance and self-assertion. The ever-present threat that their rebellious and angry feelings will break into the open intensifies their fear of provoking condemnation. At some level, they sense the pretentiousness and insincerity of their public behavior. Thus, their fantasies may be a constant reminder of the disparity that exists between the front they present to others and the rebelliousness they feel beneath. No matter how perfect their behavior may be in fact, no matter how hard they may attempt to prove themselves, this inner ambivalence remains. They must be alert to the possibility of detection at all times. Condemnation is a constant threat because their true feelings may be readily uncovered. To cope with both their fears and their impulses, compulsives engage in the characteristic control mechanisms and formal interpersonal behaviors that have been addressed in previous sections.

Solemn Mood/Temperament

Compulsives typically are unrelaxed, tense, joyless, and grim. Most restrain warm and affectionate feelings, keeping their emotions under firm control. Some compulsives exhibit a marked diminution in activity and energy, attributable in all probability to their lifelong habit of constraint and inhibition. Few evidence a lively or ebullient manner; most are rigidly controlled and emotionally tight, and their failure to release pent-up energies is likely to dispose them to psychophysiologic disorders. Any speculation that the ambivalence of compulsives might reflect some intrinsic antagonism between opposing temperamental dispositions would seem presumptuous. Yet we do observe an opposition between intense fear and intense anger among these individuals. Both tendencies may be great and may account in part for compulsives' frequent indecisiveness and immobilization. Given their grim and joyless quality, we might also conjecture that many possess a constitutionally based anhedonic temperament. Translating these notions into tangible substrates, it might be hypothesized that regions of the limbic system associated with both fear and anger may be unusually dense or well branched; conflicting signals from these areas might underlie the hesitancy, doubting, and indecisive behaviors seen in these patients. Similarly, the substrate for experiencing pleasure may be poorly developed, leading to the compulsive's typical stern countenance. Speculations such as these are highly conjectural.

Self-Perpetuation Processes

As in previous chapters, this section addresses the features that perpetuate the personality style—that is, are themselves pathogenic of the pattern—followed by a brief exploration of some of the remedial steps that may prove useful in modifying the problem (see Table 7.2).

Given the conflicts and anxieties engendered by their strategy, why do compulsives resist exploring alternative coping methods? One answer, of course, is that they experience less pain by continuing, rather than changing, their style of behavior. Thus, uncomfortable as the strategy may be, it is less anguishing and more rewarding than any other they can envisage. Another answer is that much of what they do is merely due to the persistence of habit, the sheer continuation of what they have learned in the past. Thus, compulsives persevere, in part at least, not because their behavior is instrumentally so rewarding but because it is deeply ingrained, so much so that it persists automatically. None of this is unique to the compulsive personality; it is true of all personality patterns. Each style fosters a *vicious* circle such that the individual's adaptive strategy promotes conditions similar to those that gave rise initially to that strategy.

Table 7.2   Self-Perpetuating Processes: Conscientious/Compulsive Personality

Pervasive Rigidity
  Repeats the familiar and approved
  Imagination incompatible with mechanical lifestyle
  Resists exposure to novel events

Guilt and Self-Criticism
  Lifestyle constrained by punitive introjects
  Persecutes self for deviant thoughts
  Persistent doubt prevents exploration of the new

Creates Rules and Regulations
  Uncovers tangential legalities and standards
  Irrelevant precepts shrink choices
  Excessive structure counters fear of losing control

Pathological personality traits are traps, self-made prisons that are perniciously self-defeating in that they promote their own continuation. The following looks at three of these self-perpetuating processes.

Pervasive Rigidity

Compulsives dread making mistakes and fear taking risks lest they provoke disapproval. Defensively, they learn to restrict themselves to situations with which they are familiar and to actions they feel confident will be approved. They keep themselves within narrow boundaries and confine themselves to the repetition of the familiar. Rarely do they wander or view things from a different perspective than they have in the past. Moreover, conscientious/compulsives are characteristically single-minded, have sharply defined interests, and can stick to "the facts" without deviation. To avoid the unknown—that is, the potentially dangerous—they maintain a tight and well-organized approach to life. They hold onto the tried and true and keep their nose to old and familiar grindstones. The price paid for this rigid and narrow outlook is high. Subtle emotions and creative imagination are simply incompatible with the deliberate and mechanical quality of the compulsive's style. Further, the repetitious and dull routine prevents these persons from experiencing new perceptions and new ways of approaching their environment. By following the same narrow path, compulsives block their chances of breaking the bonds of the past. Their horizons are confined as they duplicate the same old grind.

Guilt and Self-Criticism

By the time compulsives attain adolescence, they are likely to have fully incorporated the strictures and regulations of their elders. Even if they could get away with it and be certain that no external power would judge them severely, they now carry within themselves a merciless internal conscience, an inescapable inner gauge that ruthlessly evaluates and controls them, one that intrudes relentlessly to make them doubt and hesitate before they act. The proscriptions of "proper" behavior have been well learned, and they dare not deviate irresponsibly. The onslaughts of guilt and self-recrimination are adamant and insidious. External sources of restraint have been supplanted with the inescapable controls of internal self-reproach. Compulsives are now their own persecutor and judge, ready to condemn themselves not only for overt acts but for thoughts of transgression as well. These inner controls stop them from exploring new avenues of behavior and thereby perpetuate the habits and constraints of the past.

Creation of Rules and Regulations

Most persons strive to minimize the constraints that society imposes. Laws are the price for a civilized existence, but we prefer as few as necessary. Compulsives are different. Not only do they live by rules and regulations, but they go out of their way to uncover legalities, moral prescriptions, and ethical standards to guide themselves and judge others. This attitude is understandable, deriving from their intense struggle to control raging impulses toward defiance that well up within them. The more restrictive the injunctions they find in legalities and external authority, the less effort they must expend on their own to control these contrary urges. Once more they trap themselves in a self-defeating circle. By creating or discovering new percepts to heed, they draw the noose even tighter around themselves and shrink their world into an ever-narrowing shell. Opportunities for learning new behaviors, or to view the world afresh and more flexibly, are further curtailed. Their own characteristic habits have increasingly narrowed their boundaries for change and growth.

Interventional Goals

Compulsive personalities often seek therapy as a result of psychophysiologic discomforts. These symptoms are the psychosomatic manifestations of the difficulty compulsives have in discharging internal tensions caused by repressed emotions that churn within them. Symptoms often include attacks of anxiety, spells of immobilization, sexual impotence, and excessive fatigue. The therapist is enlisted to help the compulsive cope as the symptoms begin to be perceived as a threat to the efficient and responsible lifestyle that defines the compulsive's identity. This is not to say, however, that compulsives believe their symptoms are of a psychological nature. Compulsives are in fact so well defended against distressing emotions that they are typically oblivious to the possibility that internal ambivalence and repressed resentments exist, much less that they underlie the very symptoms they genuinely believe to be caused by an isolated (if unidentifiable) "disease."

Given the complex and ambivalent character of the compulsive's inclinations, what goals should the therapist keep in mind to guide his or her strategies?

Compulsives' subconscious conviction about the dire consequences of facing desires and discontent leads them to repress "inappropriate" feelings. This serves to keep the compulsive stable, but it also makes the emotional insight needed to reestablish balance in the self–other polarity and the active–passive dimension difficult for the therapist to elicit in the patient. Focused and steady work on countering emotional and behavioral rigidities that perpetuate problems and lead to clinical domain dysfunctions can ultimately lead to the self-examination and risk taking that can help provide increased balance in the personality structure (see Table 7.3).

Reestablishing Polarity Balances

What polarity imbalances underlie the compulsive's difficulties? A typical early learning history of being punished for rule transgressions and praised for virtually nothing results in compulsives operating from the basic premise that their own wishes and desires are "wrong" and that expressing them leads to intimidation and punishment. Unlike the negativistic personality style, whose resentment at having to concede to the wishes of others is at times all too clear, the compulsive personality internalizes others' strictures as "true." Feelings of hostility about having wishes and desires conflict with those of powerful others and are unconsciously repressed in an attempt to avoid further social

Table 7.3 Therapeutic Strategies and Tactics for the Prototypal Conscientious/ Compulsive Personality

Strategic Goals

Balance Polarities

Identify and stabilize self-other conflict

Encourage decisive actions

Counter Perpetuations

Loosen pervasive rigidity

Reduce preoccupation with rules

Moderate guilt and self-criticism

Tactical Modalities

Alter constricted *cognitive* style

Adjust perfectionistic *behaviors*

Brighten solemn-downcast *mood*

disapproval and punishment. The conflict between turning to others versus oneself for approval has been termed the "ambivalent pattern." Normal personalities more or less balance their efforts at securing rewards between both alternatives. The compulsive, who deals with ambivalence by forcing it out of consciousness, exhibits ambivalence passively. Although they are characterized by overt diligence and conscientious work patterns, most compulsives' efforts are a response to the demands and expectations of others, real or imagined. Compulsives are almost exclusively reactive (passive) in relation to their environment. Initiative to actively change their circumstances is rarely exhibited due to their excessive fear of making a mistake. Because of this obsessive need to achieve perfection, tasks are often turned into paralyzing chores marked by indecision and delay. Even more fundamental to the passive style of compulsives is being out of touch, not only with their unconscious oppositional feelings, but with most of their emotions. Even if hesitation were not a behavioral obstacle to self-exploration, the inability to identify what they really feel and want certainly would be.

To reestablish balance in the self–other polarity, conscientious/compulsives must work to establish an identity that differentiates their own feelings and desires from those they judge are expected of them. Before this can be accomplished, repressed anger and fear of disapproval must become conscious and emotionally worked through. Ultimately, both the expectations of others and the one's own needs should be recognized and taken into consideration as valid. The resurrection of a personal self composed of genuine feelings and desires can set the groundwork for a shift in the active–passive polarity. Once wishes are acknowledged as acceptable, only perfectionism stands between the compulsive and a more active, goal-seeking style. Therapeutic work undermining impossibly high standards can help put an end to inertia.

Countering Perpetuating Tendencies

The compulsive decides early on in life that making mistakes leads to punishment. The only way to avoid disapproval is to be "perfect." By the time a compulsive comes to the attention of a therapist, parental injunctions have been internalized and the simple yet foolproof mechanism of potential guilt prevents any deviation from the firmly entrenched rules. Self-criticism functions in much the same manner; by engaging in internal reprimands, compulsives believe that they "prove" their good intentions and obviate the need for disapproval from external sources. In familiar or straightforward situations, they can ward off anxiety and self-reprisals by "doing the right thing." In new or ambiguous situations, however, they are paralyzed by indecision and anxiety because the consequences of different potential responses are unknown. At best, the compulsive can decide how to react based on an educated guess, but this does not satisfy his or her need for complete control. To avoid anxiety-provoking ambiguity, compulsives become pervasively rigid. As they stick to a well-rehearsed routine, they encounter few confusing stimuli. Even thinking becomes limited to the realm of the tried and "acceptable" and does not evoke guilty intrusions of conscience. To further ensure that they are not caught off-guard in an unknown (threatening) situation, compulsives become extraordinarily sensitive to conventions, regulations, laws, and rules that can help them control unacceptable impulses, guide thinking, dictate behavior, and ensure that they are always beyond reproach.

These behavioral patterns, although allowing compulsives to control their guilt and anxiety over social disapproval, severely narrow their thinking and limit their experiences. The compulsive has no opportunity to explore new ways of approaching and integrating stimuli in his or her environment and thus adaptive learning cannot occur. More personally satisfying habits cannot be acquired, and relationships remain restricted. Helping compulsives loosen their unattainable standards of perfection for themselves and others is a basic therapeutic goal that lays the foundation for experimentation with more spontaneous behavior and mental ventures into uncharted "dangerous" cognitive territory. As the constant fear of making a mistake dissipates, restrictive behavior patterns can be varied and more profitable modes can be discovered. Overreliance on rules can be restricted, and creativity, given freer rein, allows for flexible behavior that can prove to be gratifying in and of itself. The possibility of enjoying non-task-oriented activities, including relationships, may then open up.

Identifying Domain Dysfunctions

The compulsive personality is characterized by primary dysfunctions in the domains of cognitive style, expressive behavior, and interpersonal conduct. The compulsive handles life's ambiguities and internal anxieties by adopting a constricted cognitive style that relies on rules, regulations, schedules, and hierarchies for their resolution. Unfortunately, unfamiliar situations and ideas are emotionally and cognitively disruptive because creative mental processes are not available to deal with and integrate novel stimuli. Exploratory therapies that examine the historical development of cognitive rigidities, as well as cognitive approaches that confront the validity of the compulsive's assumptions, can help the patient develop a more fluid and creative cognitive style that allows both more adaptive and more rewarding interaction with the environment.

More fluid thinking can also help compulsives recognize that their disciplined expressive acts lead to limited experiences. Rather than make the most of each situation, compulsives adhere to structured and organized life patterns, regardless of whether they are optimally suited to the context. Insisting that all those around them behave in the same way ensures that exposure to alternative ways of doing or thinking about things is minimal. Once again, exploratory work that challenges internalized strictures and that helps dissolve fears about the "terrible consequences" of making a mistake can help patients experiment with alternative behaviors.

Overly respectful interpersonal relations again reflect the compulsive's reliance on rules; propriety guarantees that the compulsive is always beyond reproach. Lack of interpersonal imagination, however, also leads others to find the compulsive boring and uptight, and the compulsive rarely enjoys rich and rewarding interpersonal feedback. As fears about being judged and punished decrease, the therapist may be able to convince the compulsive to try more spontaneous and potentially gratifying interaction styles, despite initial anxiety. Couples and sex therapy approaches can be particularly effective as an adjunct to individual therapy in helping the compulsive develop a healthier and more fruitful relationship.

Improvements in functioning in the primary dysfunctional domains can be bolstered by therapeutic intervention in the domains of self-image and object representations. The compulsive's self-image is conscientious; the self is seen as industrious, reliable, meticulous, and efficient. Fear of making an error and making a bad impression leads the patient to fixate on discipline, perfection, prudence, and loyalty. Exploratory work can help the patient get in touch with deep-seated aspects of the self that have been repressed, and cognitive work can help the compulsive realize that although these traits are indeed attractive and valuable, other repressed tendencies can balance them and lead to a more functional, healthy, and appealing persona.

Similarly, object representations are concealed, and only socially approved affects, attitudes, and actions are acknowledged. As a wider range of internal experiences come to be tolerated, the therapist can encourage a wider range of expressive communication and sociability. Intrapsychic coping mechanisms can get stronger as compulsives acknowledge the existence of the deeper emotional experiences they have been unconsciously repressing. The compulsive deals with these ("unacceptable") feelings by using the regulatory mechanism of reaction formation, and thus will display exactly the opposite emotion. For example, a compulsive who believes that anger is a weakness will suppress the feelings even when it would be appropriate.

As work in the other domains helps these patients develop an individual identity, they will no longer need to present themselves in a socially proper light. The compartmentalized morphologic organization of the compulsive's personality may also become more fluid and integrated; distinct and segregated memories, cognitions, and drives can be drawn on in various contexts and profitably applied. The typically solemn emotional affect should become sunnier as the need to control every aspect of behavior and environment diminishes. Decreased obsessive behavior and lessened concern with outcomes can increase the patient's enjoyment of the process of living.

Selecting Therapeutic Modalities

As he or she does in all of life's undertakings, the compulsive wants to perform "perfectly" in therapy. To this end, he or she may desire highly structured therapeutic approaches that provide a yardstick against which to measure "progress." Successful intervention with this personality style, however, entails the encouragement of open and spontaneous communication (Magnavita, 2005). Not only does this approach provide no specific procedural framework, but spontaneity terrifies the compulsive, in itself resulting in a host of possible resistances and transference reactions with which the therapist must cope. As the compulsive's deep-seated fear of "losing control" is inevitably kindled by the therapy process (which threatens to disequilibrate the much labored-for balance the patient has achieved), so is the ever-present rage that is activated by the pressure to maintain (unattainable) perfection. Some patients may express their resentments and anger by becoming openly critical of themselves, the therapy, or the therapist; justification for all interventions may be demanded of the therapist. Patients who view anger as an unacceptable form of expressing displeasure may become so "busy" at work that they are "forced" to miss sessions. In either case, as Benjamin (1993, 2003) points out, therapists can make use of the compulsive's intellectual curiosity to secure cooperation where emotional guardedness would cause the patient to flee. A therapist's initial kindly and logical discussion of some of the patient's behaviors and their causes, if they ring true to the patient, can foster the trust in the therapist that is an essential requirement for success (Vogel, Hansen, Stiles, & Götestam, 2006). Without this trust, very few compulsives are likely to accept as viable such therapeutic goals as increasing interpersonal openness and warmth (Bender, 2005).

What methods and procedures are likely to be most efficacious with these personalities?

Behavioral Techniques

Behavioral methods are useful in treating many of the undesirable manifestations of the compulsive personality disorder, particularly phobic avoidance and ritualistic or highly restrictive and rigid behavior. Treatment involves desensitizing the patient to the anxiety-provoking stimuli (whatever they may be for the particular compulsive) that promote the problematic behavior. The first step involves establishing a hierarchy of stimuli within a relevant context, followed by relaxation training (Vogel, Stiles, & Götestam, 2004). Covert desensitization can then be carried out. Other effective techniques used with these disorders, according to Salzman (1989), include flooding, modeling, response prevention, satiation training, and thought-stopping. Important in this regard also is a clear-cut agenda, such as prioritized problem specifics, and a systematic problem-solving approach designed to overcome indecisiveness and procrastinating behaviors. Also useful are formal relaxation procedures to modulate underlying tensions and anxieties. However, Turkat (1990) concluded that behavioral techniques alone are usually not sufficient to undo the long-term habit system of these patients. A measure of social skills training, combined with a effort to reduce their commitment to constant work, may occasionally be efficacious.

Interpersonal Techniques

Obsessive-compulsive personalities possess traits that create difficulties in all forms of therapeutic technique. Developing a collaborative relationship may be difficult to achieve owing to their high level of rigidity, their persistent defensiveness, their resistance to emotional expression, and their tendency to devalue interpersonal relationships that are not based on a clear hierarchy of status. Progress on interpersonal approaches therefore will require the establishment of rapport, contingent largely on the patient's respect for the therapist's competence and genuineness.

One treatment technique to work on causative factors is the *interpersonal* approach. Benjamin (1993, 2005) assumes that the majority of conscientious/compulsive patterns are acquired as a response to a cold and demanding parent that the child must placate to avoid verbal or physical punishment. Constant frustration of the desire for parental love and approval is transformed into an identification with the critical parent, followed by the internalization of self-criticisms. The first step toward emotional healing is to enable the patient to openly recognize the character of these early learning experiences and to develop a measure of empathy, if not compassion, for the child he or she once was. Perfection and absolute control need to be exposed and accepted as the unrealizable aims that they are. More realistic and less frustration-producing standards can then be integrated. The inevitable anxiety produced by failing to live up to such lofty early goals can then begin to dissipate. Benjamin also suggests employing cognitive techniques (outlined later in this discussion) to help the compulsive recognize that values and relationships are best seen as variegated and multidimensional rather than black-and-white phenomena.

Couples therapy is also recommended as useful (Links et al., 2004a). The sexual arena is one in which many of the compulsive's patterns can be easily identified. Power struggles manifest themselves in the female compulsive's inability to give up sexual control (and frequent consequent anorgasmia). The male compulsive patient will be likely to interpret any lack of submission to his sexual overtures as a seizure of control, if not rejection, on the part of his partner. The therapist can help mediate communication and clarify that sexual (as well as other) reluctance can in fact result from differences in desire, and not necessarily from a will to control or put down. Sexual therapy may help some compulsives interact in a less controlling and more open way through the practice of sexual exercises. Prescribed by the therapist, these procedures require the patient to follow instructions (which the compulsive is good at) and thus paradoxically yield control to his or her partner (as the doctor ordered!).

A common aim of compulsive patients is to finally come to an understanding with their critical parent. *Family* therapy generally represents an attempt to bring members together, straighten out misunderstandings, and allow for the expression of long-stifled sentiments. Most often, satisfactory resolution of long-standing issues does not occur. Talking about relationship difficulties can be problematic here, as compulsives have a tendency to dominate other family members, and problems may even be aggravated. The compulsive needs to give up the wish for harmonious understanding before any structural changes in personality can occur. A different form of family therapy can occur in the compulsive's current family. Better success may be had where playful contact is encouraged between the patient and his or her spouse and children in an effort to emphasize the rewards inherent in even non-task-oriented activity and in being warm and spontaneous.

Group therapy can prove to be virtually fruitless with many compulsive patients, as they will often ally themselves with the therapist, refusing to participate wholeheartedly with other group participants. Unable to share thoughts and feelings spontaneously, compulsives have been termed "monopolists" by Yalom (1985), a designation to signify their tendency to dominate and control group discussions. Group leaders may be called on to modulate power struggles in which the compulsive patient seeks to assume a stance of authority in the peer relationship. On the other hand, group therapy may successfully diffuse the compulsive person's tedious and problematic impact. Also of value are opportunities to explore the compulsive's real problems, rather than just talking about them. A useful model proposed by Wells and Giannetti (1990) has been designed to obviate certain contraindications for this approach among compulsives, as well as to resolve developmental issues that often lie at the core of their difficulties. Nevertheless, compulsives often develop contempt for the other patients in the group, or suffer extreme anxiety if forced to relinquish their defenses and expose their feelings in front of others.

Cognitive Techniques

Cognitive reorientation methods are particularly well suited to the compulsive, who tends to overintellectualize in an effort to ward off emotional reactivity. The cognitive therapy approach offered by Beck et al. (2003) suggests that helping these patients alter their basic cognitive assumptions about themselves and the world will lead to a therapeutic shift in emotions and behaviors. These assumptions include the following: "There are right and wrong behaviors, decisions, and emotions"; "To make a mistake is to have failed, to be deserving of criticism"; "Failure is intolerable"; "I must be perfectly in control of my environment as well as of myself; loss of control is intolerable and dangerous"; "I am powerful enough to initiate or prevent the occurrence of catastrophes by magical rituals or obsessional ruminations"; and "Without my rules and rituals, I'll collapse into an inert pile." At the onset of therapy the patient is taught the cognitive theory of emotion, and specific goals related to the compulsive's difficulties are established (Vogel et al., 2004). Goals are ranked according to solvability and importance; some easily resolved difficulties should be put at the top of the list to motivate the patient with experiences of therapeutic success. The automatic thoughts that interfere with the attainment of goals should be identified (Sookman, Abramowitz, Calamari, Wilhelm, & McKay, 2005). Thoughts, feelings, and behaviors related to specific goals are monitored during the week so that the conscientious/compulsive can become aware of anxiety-provoking stimuli and the cognitive assumption they elicit. Finally, after the negative consequences of these assumptions have been grasped, patient and therapist can work at refuting them in a way that makes sense to the patient.

Self-Image Techniques

If the main goal of therapy is to help patients stabilize following unsettling circumstances, the therapist may wish to help them identify the troublesome consequences of their actions, but also to help them refute their role in creating them, and thereby regain a sense of control. A procedure of cognitive dissonance and reorganization may be well received by compulsive persons owing to their preference for structured and problem-centered solutions, their focus on the here and now, and their characteristic defenses.

One of the more useful behavioral approaches is teaching patients how to truly relax (Vogel et al., 2004). A common problem in convincing compulsives to make use of helpful relaxation techniques is that they are perceived as a waste of productive time. Adopting a stance of short-term behavioral experimentation, where patients assess the helpfulness of relaxation exercises in their lifestyles, helps overcome resistances. If a patient is afraid of giving up worrying due to an irrational conviction that it is somehow useful in preventing disaster, he or she may agree to try limiting worry behavior to a particular time of the day. Beck and Freeman (1990) also suggest that patients be warned about the likelihood of relapse and the probable need for booster sessions; in this way, it may be possible to minimize these patients' tendency to want to be perfect, thereby avoiding feelings of shame over their "failure" that may prevent them from requesting a needed session.

Rogers's (1967) procedures may be helpful in showing the patient that the therapist, an authority figure, displays a measure of high self-regard and a willingness to permit the patient to express his or her deeper feelings of hostility and not be repudiated for them. Of value also are experiential procedures that may be a first step in illustrating for patients how readily their defensive façade can be pierced by deep feelings of an implicit character. Equally valuable among experiential techniques is their anti-intellectual character, their focus on the concrete realities of subtle feelings and emotions.

Intrapsychic Techniques

Psychodynamic approaches focus on interpreting displaced and repressed elements that result in overt symptoms. Compulsive patients strongly resist abandoning their defenses initially, fearing a loss of control and the upsurge of untoward thoughts and emotions. Slowly, as they become aware of the therapist's support and their increasing confidence in themselves, compulsives may not only abandon their defensive patterns, but begin to recognize that they may function more effectively without their protective façade. Progress is usually evident as patients learn to decrease their self-expectations and to supplant them with worthy but realistic and achievable goals. Rather than intellectualize and discuss matters cognitively, an effort should be made to promote an increase in risk taking and emotionally based decision making. Here, the therapist's task is to undo the patient's need for absolutes and certainties.

The transference relationship can be used as a starting point for exploring earlier relationships that may have been causative in the development of symptoms. Early traumas may be investigated. Dreams and free association can be helpful in getting past the patient's intellectual guard to deep-seated fears and feelings; often the patient is surprised at the blatant and emotionally revealing content of his or her dreams. The patient's fantasies about a relaxed and flexible approach to life can also be explored. As fears and feelings of shame become conscious they can be productively worked through. While the valuable aspects of compulsivity need to be acknowledged by the therapist, its creativity-blocking and frequently inefficient aspects need to be pointed out.

Pharmacologic Techniques

Pharmacological intervention with compulsive patients, if indicated, usually involves the use of anxiolytic and antidepressant medications, but only as an adjunct to psychotherapy. Relieving the anxiety and depression that help maintain compulsive symptoms often leads to more cooperative patients, enabling therapists to make inroads into the rigid structure of this personality. The utility of various medications with the Axis I obsessive-compulsive syndromes does not extend to the Obsessive-Compulsive Personality Disorders of Axis II (Jenike, 1991; Mancebo et al., 2005).

Making Synergistic Arrangements

How can therapies best be combined and sequenced to optimize therapeutic progress?

After establishing treatment goals and a solid alliance with the patient, behavioral techniques such as relaxation training, desensitization, and thought-stopping can prove to have good early results as an adjunct to the cognitive or interpersonal individual therapies. The possible benefits of anxiolytic or antidepressant medication can then be evaluated for the specific individual, as premature administration can lead, as with every personality disorder, to temporary alleviation of emotional symptoms and termination before longer term reconstructive work can be done. Once some initial insight and behavior change is achieved by the patient in the course of individual treatment, the therapist may decide that couple, sex, or, less commonly, family therapy may further

Table 7.4   Conscientious/Compulsive Personality Disorder Subtypes

Conscientious: Rule-bound and duty-bound; earnest, hardworking, meticulous, painstaking; indecisive, inflexible; marked self-doubts; dreads errors and mistakes. (Pure Compulsive Subtype)

Parsimonious: Miserly, niggardly, tight-fisted, ungiving, hoarding, unsharing; protects self against loss; fears intrusions into vacant inner world; dreads exposure of personal improprieties and contrary impulses. (Mixed Compulsive/Schizoid Subtype)

Bureaucratic: Empowered in formal organizations; rules of group provide identity and security; is officious, high-handed, unimaginative, intrusive, nosy, petty, meddlesome, trifling, closed-minded. (Mixed Compulsive/Narcissistic Subtype)

Bedeviled: Ambivalences unresolved; feels tormented, muddled, indecisive, befuddled; beset by intrapsychic conflicts, confusions, frustrations; obsessions/compulsions condense and control contradictory emotions. (Mixed Compulsive/Negativistic Subtype)

Puritanical: Austere, self-righteous, bigoted, dogmatic, zealous, uncompromising, indignant, and judgmental; grim and prudish morality; must control and counteract own repugnant impulses and fantasies. (Mixed Compulsive/Paranoid Subtype)

increase self-understanding and help provide environmental conditions that bolster the process of reorganizing the functional structure of the compulsive personality.

Illustrative Cases

With perhaps three or four notable exceptions (antisocials, borderlines), compulsives have been found to blend with almost every other personality type. The variants described in these cases reflect these combinations in part, but they are mostly accentuations of a number of the more prominent clinical domains of the prototypal obsessive-compulsive personality (see Table 7.4).

Case 7.1, Mark T., 42

A Compulsive Personality: Conscientious Type (Compulsive with Dependent Traits)

Presenting Picture

Mark, a driver's license examination site supervisor, sought therapy after a colleague, one day in frustration, made the comment, "You need help," which Mark took to mean, "Something must be dreadfully wrong with me." Regimented and automated in his mannerisms and work ethics, he was entirely rule-bound and driven by a desire to make everything in his life conform to a set of self-imposed rules and regulations in his constant quest to please the higher-ups. It was insufficient, he said, that he kept a smooth-running operation at his job; rather, he made sure that he was the first to arrive and the last to leave every day, took his lunch break at his desk, and triple-checked the other examiners' assignments to ensure that everyone knew precisely what they were doing each day. Mark admitted that the others were quite experienced and competent in their work, assuring that "any problem always gets nipped in the bud," yet he kept an extensive schedule of rotations and flow charts for the unit, taking absolute responsibility for everyone and everything involved with the site. To Mark, this was doing the bare minimum expected of him; to his colleagues, however, this was far beyond protocol, crossing well into obsessiveness. However, on the rare occasions that situations would arise calling for autonomous or flexible thought or action, Mark was almost abominably ineffectual, clinging desperately to "the way things are supposed to be," rather than attempting to maneuver in a way that might resolve difficult situations. So long as absolute order was maintained at all times, Mark would derive much satisfaction from his work, but it was one of these unusual situations, where Mark effectively blocked problem resolution with his rigid adherence to rules and regulations, that prompted his colleague's comment.

Initial Impressions

This behavior of the *conscientious compulsive* is typified, more than any other compulsive type, by a conforming dependency, compliance to rules and authority, and a willing submission to the wishes and values of others. In essence, Mark's personality pattern combines with features associated primarily with the dependent personality. Mark had a tendency to be self-effacing and noncompetitive, as well as a fear of independent self-assertion and a surface compliance to the expectations and demands of others. He voiced a strong sense of duty, feeling that others must not have their expectations unmet. His self-image, on the surface, was that of being a considerate, thoughtful, and cooperative person, prone to act in an unambitious and modest way. He possessed deep feelings of personal inadequacy, as he tended to minimize attainments, underplay tangential attributes, and grade his abilities by their relevance to fulfilling the expectations of others. Dreading the consequences of making errors or mistakes, he reacted to situations that were unclear or ambiguous by acting indecisively and inflexibly, evincing marked self-doubts and hesitations about taking any course of action. The fear of failure and of provoking condemnation created considerable tension, as well as occasional expressions of guilt. Submissive behavior with those in authority may also be traced to a reversal of hidden rebellious feelings. Lurking behind the front of propriety and restraint may be intense contrary feelings that occasionally break through their controls. Therefore, there was a marked denial of discordant emotions and a tendency to neutralize feelings normally aroused by distressful events.

Mark's extreme self-doubts and deflated sense of self-esteem were given support by attaching himself to an institutional organization. In this way, he sought to associate his actions by identifying them with those in authority. He made efforts to maintain a behavioral pattern that was consistent and unvarying, one in which independent actions were restrained and the strictures of approved rules were rigidly complied with. The conscientious tendency to perfection and a preoccupation with minor irrelevancies distracted his attention from deeper sources of anxiety, inadequacy, and anticipated derogation.

For Mark, a focus on immediate manifestations would be in order, but as always, from a systematic, personologic perspective. It would be necessary, first, to work toward adjusting his anxieties regarding possible "slip-ups" and the consequences of imperfections (decrease *pain* orientation). As his vigilance became diminished, it would then be useful to address, in a nonconfrontive manner, his self-perpetuations that established rules are infallible and that he must rely on and abide by these constructs in all circumstances (a rigid *passive-other* orientation). Additionally, it would be necessary to enhance his rather meager sense of self, as his self-deprecating attitudes continually enforced the notion that he lacked the mere ability to function with any free will. An approach melding these interventions in a synergistic manner would help to achieve a more *active-other* personal style.

Domain Analysis

Mark was eager to complete assessment measures, as he saw this as a well-justified means to measuring and precisely addressing current concerns and difficulties, for which he admitted, "I had always thought things were going along swimmingly, until this point." Highlighted domains of the MCMI-III Grossman Facet Scales and the MG-PDC were as follows:

Expressively Disciplined: Mark held true to the adage "A dollar's work for a dollar's pay," maintaining a rigid, regulated course of action well beyond work to most aspects of his life, where just rewards, no more nor less, would come by virtue of conscientious and measured effort and task completion.

Cognitively Constricted: There was no room for deviation from the expectations of others, according to Mark; he became notably upset with any straying from expectation or protocol and with any novel means of completing assigned tasks.

Inept Self-Image: Mark saw himself as intrinsically inadequate, and he lacked any sense of self-confidence, especially when it came to autonomous action or decision. It was no surprise that Mark vested himself in the auspices of an established agency in order to adopt and carry out well-defined tasks and earn self-esteem through fulfilling an extrinsic agenda.

Therapeutic Steps

Short-term *supportive* measures were the major initial vehicle for treating Mark. Although it would become necessary to more directly address difficulties in self-image, it would not be prudent to begin with these. Instead, gradual rapport building without challenge or confrontation, combined with tangible *behavioral* goal setting, was the first order. Among Mark's reasons for seeking therapy were unanticipated attacks of anxiety, spells of immobilization, and excessive fatigue. Because symptoms such as these threatened his public style of efficiency and responsibility (his *expressive discipline*), it was especially useful to begin by employing circumscribed and focused methods of treatment aimed at these issues. As Mark viewed his symptoms more as products of an isolated physical disease rather than recognizing that they may have represented the outcropping of his inner psychological dynamics (e.g., ambivalence and repressed resentments), a less expressive and more concise approach suited him best for this early stage. Certainly, for every piece of defensive armor removed, the therapist had to bolster Mark's confidence twofold. To remove more defenses than he could tolerate would have prolonged the treatment plan extensively. Fortunately, Mark was well guarded, such that careful inquiries by the therapist fostered growth without a problematic relapse. Caution was the byword with this patient.

Owing to his anxious conformity and his fear of public ridicule, Mark viewed therapy as a procedure that would expose his feelings of inadequacy. Tense, grim, and cheerless, he preferred to maintain the status quo rather than confront the need to change. His defensiveness was honored, and probing and insight proceeded at a careful pace. Once a measure of trust and confidence had developed in the relationship, the therapist used *cognitive* and *experiential* methods to stabilize anxieties and foster change. Because Mark preferred to restrict his actions and thoughts to those to which he was accustomed, therapeutic procedures did not confront more than he could tolerate. Goals of this nature focused on changing assumptions, noted by Beck and others, such as the fear that any deviation from expected protocol would result in a catastrophe (*constricted cognitions*) or that not performing at the highest level would result in a humiliating failure (*inept self-image*). Unless his problematic beliefs were explicitly addressed, he may have voiced pseudo-insights, but this would have been a façade to placate the therapist. His habitual defenses were so well constructed that general insight-based interpretations were likely to be temporary at best. Genuine progress necessitated brief, focused techniques to modify problematic self-statements and assumptions. Without these concrete and short-term techniques, Mark would have paid lip service to treatment goals, expressing shame and self-condemnation for his past shortcomings, but he may not have readily relinquished his defensive controls. Empathy alone may likewise have been only modestly useful because of his evasiveness and his discomfort with emotion-laden materials. Owing to his need to follow a rigid and formalized lifestyle, he was likely to respond better to short-term cognitive or interpersonal methods that were specific in their procedures rather than to more expressive or *nondirective* techniques. To diminish the occurrence of setbacks, efforts were made to strengthen his will to give up maladaptive beliefs such as unrelenting self-criticism and the unyielding correctness of authority-based rules and regulations.

Case 7.2, Norma S., 24

A Conscientious/Compulsive Personality: Puritanical Type (Compulsive with Paranoid Features)

Presenting Picture

Norma, a church youth group leader, was troubled by both insomnia and "impure thoughts" that someone like her, a self-proclaimed "God-fearing Christian," should "certainly not have." Quite high-strung and seemingly at her wit's end, Norma broke into tears at the recollection of a slip-up in front of the youth group adolescents (in this case, accidentally using a "foul" word). She acknowledged and detailed that any minor deviation from perfect order in and around her environment was enough to ruin her entire day's schedule, create recurring thoughts and feelings of guilt, and make her "feel sick to my stomach." For example, the thought of a dish towel not replaced in the rack after she had left for a therapy appointment constituted her dwelling being in "complete and total disarray," and she was left with an agitation over the decision of whether to right this "terrible" wrong, or to be punctual for her appointment.

Norma had learned certain routines that helped combat insomnia prior to starting therapy, but it seemed as though "nothing" could possibly help with her impure thoughts: "I just shouldn't be having them, but sometimes, I feel like, maybe I like them." Norma had a boyfriend, also a youth group leader, "but I know he doesn't take the work as seriously as me." She noted that her boyfriend had made gestures that suggested he wished to come into her apartment, possibly to spend the night. "That's out of the question, even if we're engaged. But sometimes . . . oh, this is bad, this is bad . . . sometimes, I think I want him to stay." She could not bring herself to speak her impure thoughts, for she feared the result would be to act on them. Equally troubling for her was the fact that she was seeing a therapist, something that she thought to be immoral, and something that she did in absolute secrecy. Norma's most salient vulnerability seemed to be her fear of being *shamed*, whether to herself or in front of her fellow congregants.

Initial Impressions

Norma, a *puritanical compulsive* sharing some of the zealous, dogmatic, and bigoted qualities of the paranoid personality, could be described as possessing an austere, self-righteous, highly controlled, but deeply conflictful conformity to the conventions of propriety and authority. Her intense anger and resentment were given sanction, at least as she saw it, by virtue of the fact that she was on the side of righteousness and morality. Evident were periodic displays of suspiciousness, irritability, obsessional ideation, and severe judgmental attitudes. There was a tendency toward denial, with an extreme defensiveness about admitting emotional difficulties and psychosocial problems. However, despite the preceding efforts, there were clear signs that Norma was unusually tense and high-strung. As she anticipated public exposure and humiliation, periods of self-deprecation and self-punishment gave way to outbursts of extrapunitive anger and persecutory accusations. This conflictual struggle against expressing emotions and directing anger endangered her efforts at maintaining control. But beneath her cooperative and controlled façade were marked feelings of personal insecurity, and Norma was vigilantly alert to avoid social transgressions that may have provoked humiliation and embarrassment. She avoided situations that may have resulted either in personal censure or derision, and she dreaded making mistakes or taking risks, lest these provoke disapproval. By adhering vigorously to propriety and convention, by following the straight and narrow path, she sought to minimize criticism and punitive reactions, particularly from persons in authority.

Beneath the surface, Norma felt the pressure of irrational impulses, including what she judged to be repugnant impulses and sexual desires. Her puritanical attitudes had developed as a protection against her own as well as the world's uncontrollable passions. Rather than allowing these impulses to wreak public havoc, should they ever have been let loose and allowed expression, Norma kept them tightly under control, resisted their emergence, and ensured that such emotions be kept from desirable objects. Progressing over time from acts of an impersonal propriety and politeness, she deteriorated into an acerbic dogmatism, a harsh and opinionated style that sought constantly to fix the mistakes of others and to endlessly criticize as inadequate or improper what others had done. Not only did she have to prove others wrong and immoral, but she judged them as deserving of punishment.

As a first measure, it would be necessary to modify Norma's proclivities toward tense hypervigilance against imperfections and its resultant anger and disillusionment (decrease *pain* orientation). Measures to adjust self-perpetuations would follow, specifically addressing the ambivalent schemas that constantly thwarted disapproval (a rigid *passive-other* orientation). Norma's statute-centered morality routinely set up impossible catch-22 conflicts and perceived antagonisms, such that she could never measure up to her imposed standards, and this characterological flaw fed into an already depleted sense of *self*. Furthermore, she lived in constant fear of acting out based on these conflicts. This therapeutic progression would focus on less stressful, healthier interactions and would foster a greater *active-self* personologic style.

Domain Analysis

Norma often voiced her disapproval of the therapeutic enterprise as "shamefully self-centered and obsessed with bad humanity," and she balked at several of the items on various psychometric measures, particularly those with sexual content. However, her MCMI-III results did confirm prominent compulsive and paranoid patterns in the disordered range. Highlights from the MG-PDC and Grossman Facet Scales included the following domains:

Temperamentally Irascible: Generally sullen in her demeanor, Norma displayed a humorlessness with decidedly edgy and brittle tendencies, taking offense to innocuous remarks and presenting visible and marked tensions at the mere suggestion of wrongdoing.

Concealed Objects (Intrapsychic Content): Norma allowed only positive, socially approved thoughts and feelings conscious expression, although she had become aware of those "other" thoughts that were becoming irrepressible.

Interpersonally Respectful: This domain reflected Norma's pressure to conduct herself morally and righteously, holding herself to an unrealistically conscientious standard for interactions, and demanding a socially polite, nonargumentative, morally sanctioned, and formal quality to her relationships.

Therapeutic Steps

Supportive therapy was necessary to begin this process with Norma, with an adjustment period of 2 to 3 sessions which served to allow her to "put everything out on the table" in a safe manner. She, of course, resisted this at first, until the therapist was able to fully assure her that "what we put out here on our imaginary table in front of us is only for you and I to see and sort through; we can discard anything that simply doesn't seem right." This approach allowed Norma to gradually become comfortable with sharing uncomfortable material. A *psychopharmacologic* agent was helpful during this early stage in treatment, after some deliberation and hesitancy over the "moral implications" of such an intervention. Here, it was useful to provide a concrete and thorough discussion of the physiological reasoning behind the use of this drug for her to accept this treatment. As Norma was able to establish a baseline of comfort with these "unusual" (from her perspective) conditions, her *irascible* mood began to show a modicum of flexibility.

Norma sought therapy because she felt ineffectual in her life; her preoccupations with perfection and purity in every conceivable facet of her life had, in effect, undermined her capacity to perform those duties she expected of herself. She was now stricken with chronic panic attacks, periods of emotional and effectual paralysis, and excessive fatigue. Because these symptoms were at odds with her public persona, it was most practical to utilize those methods focused on pronounced expectations and admitted conflicts. We are speaking, here, of her *concealed objects,* which is a concept bordering the conscious and unconscious realms. Norma was not oriented toward exploring her difficulties as a manifestation of troubled or repressed internal psychological functions; rather, she viewed these symptoms as physical ailments that needed to be fixed. Fortunately, in terms of treatment, the conflicts had become more conscious, with troubling content becoming less concealed. As she would have strongly resisted extensive *insight-oriented* therapies that were at odds with her considerable moral and religious investment, it was best to work from a concise milieu, in this case, using aspects of *motivational interviewing* (e.g., Hettema, Steele, & Miller, 2005) to identify her intentions and explore, in a supportive/humanistic manner, more fluid coping skills and defenses. Even with this cautious and targeted intervention, defenses did have to be removed, and the therapist needed to keep the old therapeutic axiom in mind: "Don't take anything away unless you have something to replace it." Norma, by nature, was quite well-guarded, and appropriate, nonintrusive probings and suggestions provided for positive motion and limited setbacks in treatment.

Owing to her zealous conformity and her terror at the thought of being "shamed," Norma had a tendency to view therapy as an instrument whose inherent design was to uncover and humiliate her by proving her inadequate. Consistently wrought up with worry, she was not oriented toward fundamental change, but toward alleviation of difficulty with minimal personal modification. This desire was honored, and inquiries and suggestions were undertaken carefully. As the therapeutic relationship was built and began to gain effectiveness, the therapist used *cognitive* and *interpersonal* methods to effect the necessary changes, as well as alleviate sources and manifestations of anxiety. Norma's tolerance was always kept in mind when more confrontive measures were employed, as it was only safe for her to work with familiar behaviors and attitudes. As noted by Beck and others, tangible goals in this realm included disputing fears such as the inevitability of a particular shortcoming resulting in a catastrophe, or that performing at less than perfection would result in devastating failure. In Norma's language, this translated to, "If I have to do something that is morally reprehensible and not *interpersonally respectful,* I will perish." Explicitly addressing these problematic assumptions and self-statements with concrete and short-term techniques short-circuited most attempts to placate the therapist with false insights and empty talk. Although the early employment of these focused methods were effective, the therapist needed to continue to be alert for half-hearted expressions of culpability, as Norma tended to use this tactic to obscure and salvage unrelinquished defensive controls. A caveat should be issued, as well, that empathy by itself would have fostered evasiveness, and most likely would have been ineffective due to her uneasiness with more personal, affective issues. In sum, her quite rigid style was best suited to focused cognitive or interpersonal methods, rather than nondirective, expressive modalities.

Case 7.3, Julie V., 34

A Conscientious/Compulsive Personality: Parsimonious Type (Compulsive with Schizoid Features)

Presenting Picture

Julie was the head of the billing department for a large law firm and lived her life with seemingly no other intent than to plan for a rainy day. Although she took pride in her hard work, she also matter-of-factly stated, "I don't know that I necessarily have to *like* the work to do it well," and that at least she didn't *dislike* it. Julie's life was devoid of pleasure or excesses, as there really was "no room" for such nonsense; her entire being was focused on making sure that what she had achieved was not lost, with an unusual and enigmatic emphasis on her finances. For example, in her daily commute, she would walk two miles from the train stop to the office, her only intention being to save the bus fare. At first, this impressed her colleagues, and for a time, she was actually admired for this initiative. Others joined her, but she didn't seem to take particular notice. However, as the winter months ensued, Julie seemed oblivious to the cold and continued, without remark, to save the $1.00 fare by walking the two miles. At this point, her colleagues, who had since given up, began to make fun of her. Again, she was oblivious to the involvement of others. On a related note, she kept the vast majority of her money in a safe in her basement and would open a bank account only after interviewing the president of the bank. She noted that she faced some problems in that her company was initiating a "direct-deposit only" policy for paychecks, but Julie refused to participate, noting that she wanted to keep track of the physical paper associated with the tangible pay stub.

Although Julie stated that she was happy with her particular lifestyle, there was a notable dearth of enthusiasm, as if to say that relative safety was the only necessity of life, and true happiness was something best left alone. However, her sister pointed out to her that "it just isn't normal for you to feel *nothing!*," describing her apparent pervasive apathy. At the insistence of her sister, who also offered to pay for therapy services and assure confidentiality, Julie acquiesced to treatment.

Initial Impressions

What was most notable in Julie, a *parsimonious compulsive* (sharing aspects of the schizoid pattern), was her miserliness, the protective wall she placed between herself and the outer world, keeping tight to that which she possessed, being ungiving and unsharing, thereby effectively disengaging and distancing from others with a cool self-protectiveness from external intrusion. Her parsimony, as we viewed it, reflected wariness against the possibility of loss, a self-protective stance in which exposure permitted the possibility of loss. Just as she learned in her struggle with parental restrictions to find a small sphere of behavior that was safe and above reproach, so too did she, as an adult, gather and hold tight to her limited body of rights and possessions. As Fromm (1947) put it, she would hoard and protect against all intrusions those few prized belongings she had struggled to acquire for herself. Having been deprived of so many wishes and desires in childhood, she nurtured and protected what she had achieved. She fortified herself and staved off those whom she imagined wished to deprive her of her resources. These fortifications, though, truly represented a deeper and more devious need for her possessions and privacy to be secure. She dared not permit anyone to explore the emptiness of her inner self, the truly barren quality of her attainments and competencies. Of even greater import, she dreaded that others would uncover her rebellious urges, or any angry and defiant feelings that lurked beneath her cloak of respectability and propriety. She had to quickly stop others from exploring and possibly exposing the pretense of her very existence. Respect was a way of maintaining distance, then, a means of hiding what she must keep from others and from herself.

Rigid adherence to the status quo was an intractable rule in Julie's life, along with a distaste for sharing or interacting (*passive* orientation), and these principles needed to be respected throughout the course of therapy, with interventions and increasingly confrontive measures proceeding at *her* pace. It would be most beneficial to begin with a supportive perspective, gradually broaching the possibilities of more targeted perspectives and tactics. As her considerably fortified barriers would relax, she would become more prepared to begin exploring her self-perpetuations. Again, at *her* pace, the focus would be on such assumptions as that everyone else was either incompetent or antagonistic, or that some possible flaw in herself would inevitably lead to catastrophe (*pain* orientation, conflicting and salient *self–other* imbalance). As some attitudes were clarified, it would be possible to adjust self-imposed barriers, encourage socialization, and work toward a new appreciation of enjoyment (increase *pleasure*).

Domain Analysis

When asked to complete self-report measures, Julie stated, "That's okay; I respectfully decline." She did agree to her therapist's use of the MG-PDC after she explained to Julie how she would be using it and that she would discuss all results with her. Highlights from this assessment included the following domains:

Interpersonally Unengaged: Julie seemed indifferent and remote from others, as well as unresponsive to attempts to engage her in interpersonal interactions; this domain had some self-protective qualities of a more avoidant nature, but largely these were more characteristically disinterested and passively removed, in line with schizoid manifestations.

Expressively Disciplined: Highly organized, although insular, Julie attended to details and was extremely fastidious in carrying out expectations; this domain seemed to be motivated by a need to be beyond reproach and to ward off inquisition.

Temperamentally Solemn: Julie appeared to have fought impulses to express emotion throughout her adult life, and quite possibly throughout much of childhood as well. What manifested, then, was a clamping-down expressed in a joyless, grim, and restrained temperament seemingly devoid of much feeling.

Therapeutic Steps

A *supportive therapy* approach was useful in initiating treatment, as it set the stage for a less disconcerting therapeutic atmosphere and helped desensitize Julie to currently discomforting and anxiety-provoking situations. Introduction of a *psychopharmacologic agent,* in a suitable dosage that did not intrude on her effectiveness in daily tasks, also proved beneficial in preparing Julie for more confrontive methods that would follow, as well as provided a modicum of relaxation and freer expression, temperamentally, thus combating her tense, controlled *solemnity.* Julie was unlikely, at the outset, to accept the notion that any difficulty she faced might stem from inner psychological dynamics (e.g., ambivalence and repressed resentments); rather, she was convinced that these were symptoms analogous to a singular physical disease, if not a direct manifestation of a physical problem. Therefore, a less exploratory and more direct plan suited this case best. As the combined supportive and pharmacologic initiation proved successful in alleviating some of her characteristic guardedness and stifling, *behavioral modification* techniques could be employed, which took on the quality of experimenting with a less rigid, less *hyperdisciplined* approach to tasks and expectations. Of course, as the therapist removed Julie's troublesome coping strategies, she needed to provide extra measures of support and help her replace those obsolete strategies with more effective skills. She exercised caution consistently with Julie, as removing more defenses than she could tolerate would have been extremely counterproductive. Hypervigilance to Julie's sensitivities was *not* necessary, however, as her well-established defenses were able to tolerate careful inquiries and appropriate disputes.

Julie's *interpersonal disengagement,* on the other hand, was primarily geared toward avoiding any vulnerability to expose her inadequacy and dulling any affective need for close interpersonal contact. She was rigid and implacable, and any thoughts of fulfillment were overshadowed by a need to maintain the status quo. This defensive nature was respected, and more intrusive and expressive approaches were avoided in the earlier stages. As the therapeutic relationship developed and a more genuine trust emerged, short-term *cognitive* and *interpersonal* methods began to be employed. As Julie preferred to maintain her usual boundaries and regulations, these procedures proceeded at a comfortable pace, as determined by her. During this period, the work focused on modifying beliefs and schemas (e.g., imperfection begets catastrophe, half-hearted performance results in failure and denigration). One of Julie's habitual coping strategies was to voice pseudo-insights in attempts to cloak the need for change, and this required a watchful eye on the part of the therapist. Her defenses were rather immutable, unlikely to have been swayed by her own or the therapist's insights. A *nondirective* approach, relying primarily if not solely on the therapist's empathic posture, would have been only modestly useful, as Julie would have most likely used her evasive tactics in dodging emotionally charged issues. Genuine progress required tangible methods that worked rapidly enough in modifying problematic assumptions to provide consistent incentive to remain invested in therapy. She responded best to short-term cognitive and interpersonal methods that were specific in their procedures, as abstraction, pondering, and exploring were an ill fit for her regimented style.

Case 7.4, Bryan G., 27

A Conscientious/Compulsive Personality: Bedeviled Type (Compulsive with Negativistic Features)

Presenting Picture

Bryan, a young executive who prided himself on "finding the straight and narrow path to success, amidst my peers who do nothing but party and keep being screwups," was referred for therapy by his physician after an inexplicable bout of nightmares that would wake him up, screaming, on a nightly basis, thereby waking his wife and two children.

Exceedingly tense and agitated, Bryan seemed to always be in conflict with himself, expressing desires for emotional outlets, yet convinced that such outlets just couldn't exist "within the logical order." He had trouble outlining what this "logical order" was, or where it originated, but insisted that he could not deviate from it. Stopping short of considering deviations from the norm "absolute disasters," Bryan did explain, "I'm just not built for the angst that that would cause." He then explained that he was "the only person who could do certain things" in his role at work, and he emanated the sense that this fact carried forth into his role in his home life and society overall. However, Bryan was not without fantasies. He could vividly describe the "ideal vacation," one that would take him across the country at high speeds in a foreign sports car, and one could see the pleasure and temporary relaxation that permeated his tense being, the rigidity and upset manifest through bodily tautness simply melting away. He was swiftly brought back into his "reality," however, as the fantasy approached feasibility. That is, the therapist pointed out in the initial interview that such a vacation was quite possible and that many people do, in fact, take cross-country trips as he described. Bryan, however, gave numerous rationalizations and carefully worded explanations as to why "this might be a possibility for some, but not for me." He cited his work responsibilities, his belief that such an endeavor would be wasteful, and his considerable time constraints, just to name a few of his reasons, seemingly becoming more resentful as he named the numerous objections to his fantasy plan. He was trapped between very powerful desires and the need to keep "compartmentalized" for the greater sake of order.

Clinical Assessment

As with some variants of both negativistic and compulsive ambivalent personality types, Bryan, a *bedeviled compulsive,* possessed an amalgamation of both prototypes. He experienced a deep struggle beneath the surface between the need to comply with the wishes of others and the desire to assert his own interests. Contending quite unsuccessfully with this ambivalence was what undermined him. For the most part, the strategy of self-denial works reasonably well for most compulsives, as long as their defenses are in place and no major disruption of the status quo occurs; they simply submerge any oppositional desires and put forth a proper and correct front. For a bedeviled subtype such as Bryan, however, this strategy did not hold. Although he appeared on the surface to be in psychic control, underneath he was going around in circles, unable to decide which course to follow, increasingly unsure of who he was and what he wanted to do. When he was expected to act decisively, he oscillated and procrastinated, felt tormented and befuddled, became cautious and timid, delaying decisions and using complex rationales to keep his inner confusion under control. Unable to get a hold of who he was, feeling great pressure to meet his obligations, he began to doubt what it was that he believed and what it was that he wanted. Caught in his upsurging ambivalence, with one part of himself accelerating in one direction, and the other part resisting movement, Bryan became exhausted, grumpy, and discontent, but, more than anything else, perplexed and confused, driven by thoughts and impulses that could no longer be contained and directed. The persistence of these oscillating directions resulted in Bryan's tendency to engage in *self-torture,* to create a self-punitive resolution that sought to undo the powerful emotions that bedeviled him. Unable to acknowledge what was upsetting him, that is, the ambivalences of his inner life, he sought through obsessions and compulsions to provide an outlet for his contradictory emotions, hoping thereby that these irreconcilable feelings would not undermine or overwhelm him. Most troublesome during this time was the recognition that he might be driven by temptations that would overwhelm his moral strength. Constrained and deformed by these contradictory tendencies, he felt as though he was on the edge of psychic dissolution.

Though Bryan would be prone to avoid change, as is characteristic of the prototypal compulsive personality, an important feature in this case was his emerging realization that there indeed was a *need* for treatment, as the therapist would be able to draw on the momentum inherent in this quality. Prior to countering and disputing Bryan's perpetuations, it would be necessary to alleviate his most salient agitations and anxieties (hypervigilance to avoiding *pain*). As Bryan's ambivalence regarding therapy dissipated, the next phase of treatment would be directively confronting such faulty and conflicting beliefs as his need to conform, juxtaposed against his desire to release (strong and conflictual *passive-active* stance), and to correct relational imbalances (less salient, but still conflictual *self–other*), such as a strong tendency to distrust and devalue others mixed with a negative and condemning self-view. As these conflicts became clarified, the therapist would be able to strengthen Bryan's *pleasure* orientation, a construct that was present but thoroughly denied.

Domain Analysis

Bryan was very inquisitive throughout treatment, wanting to know details regarding treatment technique, assessment procedures, and measurements of progress. Therefore, he was very amenable to assessment, although his profile did show a great deal of conflict in terms of response style (i.e., he showed moderately high tendencies toward both *desirability* and *debasement*). The most salient domains uncovered with the Grossman Facet Scales were as follows:

Reliable Self-Image: It was very dangerous for Bryan to imagine himself relaxing, disengaging from tasks, or otherwise enjoying himself: "Life's not about enjoyment, it's about attainment and doing what's expected; I learned that long ago."

Cognitively Constricted: Just as it was dangerous to consider relaxation, it was equally dangerous for Bryan to think independently, for he considered anything not entirely in line with traditional values or procedures to be utterly iconoclastic.

Expressively Resentful: His resentment manifest less in action than in attitude, Bryan curtailed the more active and open assault-style resentment of the negativist, but evidenced caustic expressions regarding the "hedonism" of others "and how everyone's ruining it for the hard workers who have to pick up the slack." This emanated from Bryan's apparent inability to engage in a simple fantasy of his own without guilt.

Therapeutic Steps

Bryan was not initially fully cooperative in therapy, although he paid immense lip service to being very attuned to the therapeutic process. Although he was, at heart, committed to therapy, he did show resistance to actively and fully participating in more vulnerable areas by intellectualizing and testing the therapist. These resistances played in a somewhat passive-aggressive manner at first, with Bryan ostensibly going along with some therapeutic suggestion, then undermining that very strategy. A strong and determined attitude on the part of the therapist overcame Bryan's desire to outwit her by setting up situations to test her skills, to catch inconsistencies, and to arouse ire. For the therapist, restraining the impulse to express a condemning attitude was facilitated by keeping in mind that Bryan's difficulties were not fully under his conscious control. Several *motivational interviewing* techniques were employed to counteract his contrary feelings regarding treatment and to clarify his intention for this intervention. As it turned out, Bryan's conflictual style (as was evident in assessment) seemed to highlight for him that he, in essence, felt *undeserving* of those more pleasurable aspects of life, and that his overcommitment to work was a form of self-flagellation. A committed and professional approach prevented relapses by confronting these ambivalences that often robbed him of what steps he could secure toward progress.

As these ambivalences cleared, it was possible to begin a sequence of interventions aimed at resolution of problematic domains, and therefore, symptom relief. A circumscribed focus was the most optimally suited treatment for Bryan, as therapy became more targeted. *Interpersonal* methods (e.g., Magnavita, Benjamin), as well as formal *behavioral modification* procedures, were productive in achieving greater consistency and interpersonal harmony in his social behavior. With the ammunition for learning the *origins* of his behavioral/interpersonal *resentfulness* gleaned from the earliest stages of treatment, it was much easier to begin using direct behavioral modalities as replacement skills for his subtle *resentful behaviors* and *attitudes*. In this sense, beginning with these interventions without having the context (i.e., starting therapy directly with such behavioral interventions) would have likely fallen on ill-prepared ears and would not carry the same meaning; conversely, by focusing these tasks within the framework of Bryan's understanding of his self-punitive tendencies, there was greater understanding and tolerance for initial discomforts in the building of new skills.

Directive *cognitive techniques,* such as those of Meichenbaum and Ellis, were used to confront Bryan with the obstructive and self-defeating character of his expectations and his personal relations, such as his resentful attitudes, and were further augmented to include reframing and reorientation in regard to his *constricted* thought patterns. This modality was used to reconstruct specific beliefs, such as his feelings of guilt over simple fantasizing of relaxation. In sequence, this was easier, given that Bryan no longer felt a strong need to punish himself; therefore, his overreliance on constricted cognitions as an avoidance behavior against possible thoughts of fulfillment became less relevant. Possibilities, such as open-ended thoughts, were gradually introduced into his repertoire, and he began recognizing that not all deviant lines of thought were a pathway to disaster. This introduced the possibility of more *existential/humanistic* approaches to treatment, which were employed toward the end of treatment to explore alternatives to his dependency on his *reliable self-image*.

A thorough reconstruction of personality was not the only means of altering his deeper pathologies. In support of the aforementioned individual techniques, *family* treatment methods were also of clinical utility and were rather successful in examining the complex network of relationships that sustained his personality style. Together with individual procedures, these methods proved to be among the most useful in helping him recognize the source of his own hurt and angry feelings and in appreciating how he provoked hurt and anger in others.

Resistances and Risks

In the early phases of treatment it is particularly important for the therapist to keep in mind that compulsives, even more than other personality-disordered patients, perceive change as a possible route to danger and increased vulnerability. Security and stability for them depend on a simple and well-ordered life. Should the unanticipated occur, or should stress supersede their defenses, equanimity may falter. They may vacillate among diffuse anxiety, explosive outbursts, expressions of doubt and contrition, and any number of bizarre compulsions. If pressure mounts or continues over prolonged periods, compulsives may decompensate into a florid disorder.

Compulsive personalities are likely to regard therapy as an encroachment on their defensive armor. They seek to relieve their symptoms, but at the same time want desperately to prevent self-exploration and self-awareness. The patient's defensiveness is deeply protective and must be honored by the therapist; probing should proceed no faster than the patient can tolerate. Only after building trust and self-confidence may one chance bringing to the open the patient's anger and resentment. It is important for therapists who are trying to establish rapport with compulsive patients in the initial phases of therapy not to push a close emotional relationship too quickly. Although this is a valid therapeutic technique for the later phases of treatment, anything but a respectful, problem-focused manner may cause the compulsive enough discomfort to lead to premature termination.

Insight may be a first step, but not a guarantee, toward consenting to take risks, both in and out of therapy. For every piece of defensive armor removed, the therapist must be sure to bolster the patient's autonomy twofold. To remove more defenses than the patient can tolerate is to invite disaster. Fortunately, compulsives themselves are usually so well guarded that precipitous movement by the therapist is often ignored or intellectualized away. The therapist's best recourse against excessive hesitation is to reiterate often that life offers no guarantees, and that taking risks, though opening one up to the possibility of pain, disappointment, and failure, is also the only chance one has at real reward and success. Discussion of how the patient would cope were things to turn out badly may give the patient a modicum of security even in the face of threatening new situations.

Therapists often experience exasperation at a compulsive patient's focus on detail, particularly when the details come to obscure the larger picture. Sometimes the patient is perceived as boring and dry. Frustration often results from the compulsive's tendency to avoid significant emotional issues; rather than examine the anxiety that underlies their actions, compulsives often justify their behavior as the best response to confusing goals, or, alternatively, to the psychological problems of others. Anger is a common reaction when the patient's need for control manifests itself through the patient's passive refusal to do assignments. The astute therapist will manage to use his or her own reactions as a tool in understanding the patient's resistances, and will keep in mind that a power struggle will do little to help the patient. Polarity conflicts and perpetuating tendencies should always remain the focus of therapy.

CHAPTER 8

Personalized Therapy for the Skeptical/ Negativistic Personality Patterns

The overt picture of the *DSM-IV*'s skeptical/negativistic syndrome, formerly called the passive-aggressive personality, is strikingly *dissimilar* from that of the conscientious/compulsive personality (Wetzler & Morey, 1999). According to Millon (1969/1985, 1981, 1990, 1996b), however, both share an intense and deeply rooted ambivalence about themselves and others. Compulsives deal with this ambivalence by vigorously suppressing the conflicts it engenders, and they appear as a consequence to be well controlled and single-minded in purpose; their behavior is perfectionistic, scrupulous, orderly, and quite predictable. In contrast, the skeptical/negativist fails either to submerge or to otherwise resolve these very same conflicts; as a consequence, the ambivalence of negativists intrudes constantly into their everyday life, resulting in indecisiveness, fluctuating attitudes, oppositional behaviors and emotions, and a general erraticism and unpredictability. They cannot decide whether to adhere to the desires of others as a means of gaining comfort and security *or* to turn to themselves for these gains, whether to be obediently dependent on others *or* defiantly resistant and independent of them, whether to take the initiative in mastering their world *or* to sit idly by, passively awaiting the leadership of others. They vacillate, then, like the proverbial donkey, moving first one way and then the other, never quite settling on which bale of hay is best (Cramer, Torgersen, & Kringlen, 2003; Sprock & Hunsucker, 1998).

The erratic pattern of behaviors observed among the negativistic is similar to that employed by young children who explore, through trial and error, various actions and strategies in the hope of discovering which ones succeed for them (Coid, 1999). In this exploratory phase, children display considerable spontaneity, shifting in an almost random fashion from assertion to submission, to avoidance, to exploitation, to obstinacy, and so on. Most children meet with fairly stable parental responses to their varied behaviors, and, as a consequence, most learn to discern which actions and attitudes are acceptable and so achieve their goals. This predictability in gauging the consequences of one's behaviors is not learned by future negativists, for these children experience little in the way of parental consistency (J. G. Johnson, Cohen, Chen, Kasen, & Brook, 2006; J. J. Johnson, Smailes, Cohen, Brown, & Bernstein, 2000). Because they cannot discern a clear pattern of consequences for their behaviors, they continue on an erratic, childish course. The persistence of these childlike and capriciously unpredictable behaviors accounts in part for the frequency with which these personalities are referred to in adulthood as "emotionally immature."

Referring to this pattern as the "negativistic personality," some noted these individuals' general contrariness and disinclination to doing things that others wish or expect of them (Ritzler & Gerevitz-Stern, 2006). But beyond this passive resistance there is a capricious impulsiveness, an irritable moodiness, a grumbling, discontented, sulky, unaccommodating, and fault-finding pessimism that characterizes their behaviors. They not only obstruct but dampen everyone's spirits as sullen malcontents and perennial complainers whose very presence demoralizes others. Although anguished and discontent with themselves, they never appear satisfied with others either. Even in the best of circumstances, they always seem to seek the dark lining in the silver cloud. If they find themselves alone, they would prefer to be with others; if they are with others, they prefer to be alone. If someone gives them a gift, they dislike being obligated; if they fail to receive one, they feel slighted and rejected. If they are given a position of leadership, they complain bitterly about the lack of support they get from others; if they are not allowed to lead, they become critical and unsupporting of those who are (McIlduff & Coghlan, 2000).

The broader formulation of the passive-aggressive or negativistic personality taken here is consistent with the "oral sadistic melancholic" described in the writings of early psychoanalysts (Kasen et al., 2001). Characterized by deep-seated and pervasive ambivalence, consequent to difficulties arising in the oral biting stage, these individuals have been described as spiteful, petulant, and overdemanding, with a pessimistic mistrust of the world (Menninger, 1940).

The characteristic vacillation, discontentment, and socially maladaptive behaviors of passive-aggressive personalities almost inevitably result in varying states of interpersonal conflict and frustration as well as emotional confusion and distress (Farmer, Nash, & Dance, 2004; Fossati et al., 2000; Sinha & Watson, 2006). Consequently, such individuals are highly susceptible to psychiatric symptomatology, including anxiety, somatoform disorders, and especially depression. Although major depressive episodes are not uncommon, passive-aggressive personalities are probably most likely to experience chronic forms of Dysthymic Disorder. Typically, these individuals display an agitated form of dysphoria, shifting between states of anxious futility, self-deprecation, and despair to demanding irritability and bitter discontent. They may struggle between their desire to act out defiantly and their social sense that they must curtail their resentments. Although passive-aggressive personalities are accustomed to directly venting their feelings, anger will be restrained and turned inward should they sense that such expression might result in rejection or humiliation. Their grumbling, moody complaints and sour pessimism, however, serve as a vehicle of tension discharge, relieving them periodically of mounting inner- and outer-directed anger. A secondary but important function of these behaviors is to intimidate others and induce guilt, which provides the negativist with some sense of retribution for the miseries others have caused him or her in the past. After a time, however, the sullen moodiness and complaining of the passive-aggressive may tend to annoy and alienate others. Although the piteous distress of these depressed individuals may inhibit others from directly expressing their frustration and annoyance, their exasperation is readily perceived by the hypersensitive negativist and taken as further evidence of the low esteem others hold for him or her (Grilo et al., 1998).

A final commentary in this introductory section on the skeptical/negativistic personality turns our attention to the evolutionary model and the polarity characterization represented in Figure 8.1. Little stands out in this portrayal, other than the element of conflict and ambivalence signified by the double-pointed arrow between the self and other polarities. This indicates the inability of negativistic personalities to find a comfortable ground between acting on their own behalf and doing so for others. They cannot find a consistent, single-minded purpose. As a consequence, they shift erratically back and forth, manifesting fluctuating attitudes and unpredictable behaviors (Joiner & Rudd, 2002). If they move toward the fulfillment of what others desire, they become irritated and annoyed with themselves for doing so, quickly shifting their thoughts and feelings in favor of doing their own thing. In so doing, however, they jeopardize the security and support they need from others, leading them quickly to become contrite and to reverse their position again. Negativists are active, not passive, shifting from one moment to the next in their behaviors, thoughts, and feelings. Little joy is experienced in this process; fear and self-preservation predominate (Fava et al., 2002; Lilienfeld & Penna, 2001). Whichever direction they take, there are discomforting consequences to pay. It is this unsettled character of the self–other orientation that keeps negativists in a perpetual state of discontent and dysphoria.

Clinical Picture

This section provides the reader with several perspectives on the negativistic personality. As in prior chapters, we first organize clinical data sources in line with the eight domains (see Figure 8.2).

This section discusses the central features of the so-called skeptical/negativistic pattern, detailing these characteristics in accord with the major domains of clinical analysis utilized in earlier chapters. As noted previously, the traits of the negativist are more broadly conceived here than in the *DSM-IV* appendix, and it is thereby conceptualized as a comprehensive personality disorder. This extended formulation is guided

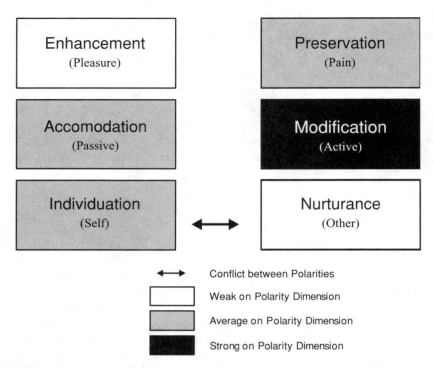

FIGURE 8.1 Status of the skeptical/negativistic (passive-aggressive) personality prototype in accord with the Millon polarity model.

by the personality pattern described as the "negativistic" type by Millon in 1969 (see Table 8.1).

Resentful Expressive Behavior

One of the problems that arise when focusing on the distinctive characteristics of a pathological personality type is that the reader is led to believe, incorrectly, that these individuals always display the features that have been described. This is not the case. Most personalities behave "normally" much of the time; that is, their behaviors are appropriate to the reality conditions of their environment. What a text such as this seeks to stress are those features that, by virtue of their frequency and intensity, *distinguish* certain personalities. Thus, "resentfulness" may be used as a descriptor to characterize the negativist (Vereycken, Vertommen, & Corveleyn, 2002). But almost everyone behaves resentfully sometimes, and the negativist is not resentful much of the time. What distinguishes negativists is the ease with which they can be made to act in a resentful manner and the regularity with which this behavior is manifested. With

NEGATIVISTIC PROTOTYPE

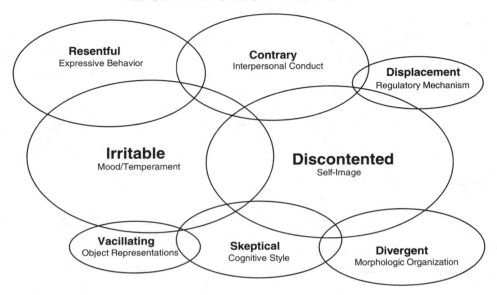

FIGURE 8.2 Salience of prototypal skeptical/negativist domains.

this qualification in mind, the discussion turns to a brief note of the resentful feature as typically found in the negativist.

As seen in these personalities, resentfulness is manifested in a variety of forms that signify their resistance to fulfilling the expectancies of others. Thus, they exhibit procrastination, inefficiency, obstinacy, and contrary and socially irksome behaviors. These actions also reflect the gratification that negativists feel in demoralizing and undermining the pleasures and aspirations of others.

Contrary Interpersonal Conduct

Most persons acquire styles of relating to others that enable them to achieve an optimal level of satisfaction and security, as well as to maintain a reasonable degree of self-harmony. So-called normals may be differentiated from pathological personalities by the variety and character of the strategies they employ to achieve these goals. Healthy personalities draw on their strategies flexibly as they face changing demands and pressures. Psychologically impaired individuals, however, tend to be inflexible. They approach different events as if they were the same and utilize the same strategies they acquired in childhood, even though these are presently inappropriate. Once they have learned a particular style that has worked for them, they continue to use it as if it were a sacred rulebook for navigating the future.

Table 8.1   Clinical Domains of the Skeptical/Negativistic Personality Prototype

---

Behavioral Level:

(F) Expressively Resentful (e.g., resists fulfilling expectancies of others, frequently exhibiting procrastination, inefficiency, and obstinacy, as well as contrary and irksome behaviors; finds gratification in demoralizing and undermining the pleasures and aspirations of others).

(F) Interpersonally Contrary (e.g., assumes conflicting and changing roles in social relationships, particularly dependent and contrite acquiescence and assertive and hostile independence; conveys envy and pique toward those more fortunate, as well as actively concurrently or sequentially obstructive and intolerant of others, expressing either negative or incompatible attitudes).

Phenomenological Level:

(F) Cognitively Skeptical (e.g., is cynical, doubting, and untrusting, approaching positive events with disbelief and future possibilities with pessimism, anger, and trepidation; has a misanthropic view of life, is whining and grumbling, voicing disdain and caustic comments toward those experiencing good fortune).

(S) Discontented Self-Image (e.g., sees self as misunderstood, luckless, unappreciated, jinxed, and demeaned by others; recognizes being characteristically embittered, disgruntled, and disillusioned with life).

(S) Vacillating Objects (e.g., internalized representations of the past comprise a complex of countervailing relationships, setting in motion contradictory feelings, conflicting inclinations, and incompatible memories that are driven by the desire to degrade the achievements and pleasures of others, without necessarily appearing so).

Intrapsychic Level:

(F) Displacement Mechanism (e.g., discharges anger and other troublesome emotions either precipitously or by employing unconscious maneuvers to shift them from their instigator to settings or persons of lesser significance; vents disapproval by substitute or passive means, such as acting inept or perplexed, or behaving in a forgetful or indolent manner).

(S) Divergent Organization (e.g., there is a clear division in the pattern of morphologic structures such that coping and defensive maneuvers are often directed toward incompatible goals, leaving major conflicts unresolved and full psychic cohesion often impossible by virtue of the fact that fulfillment of one drive or need inevitably nullifies or reverses another).

Biophysical Level:

(S) Irritable Mood (e.g., frequently touchy, temperamental, and peevish, followed in turn by sullen and moody withdrawal; is often petulant and impatient; unreasonably scorns those in authority and reports being annoyed easily or frustrated by many).

Note: F = Functional Domains; S = Structural Domains.

The problem that faces negativists (and borderlines also) is quite different from that of most pathological personalities. Their difficulties stem *not* from the rigid character of their coping style but from its exaggerated fluidity. They are actively and overtly ambivalent, unable to find a satisfactory direction or course for their behavior. They vacillate and cannot decide whether to be dependent on or independent of others and whether to respond to events actively or passively. Their dilemmas do not arise from an overcommitment to one strategy but from a lack of commitment. As a consequence, they vacillate indecisively in a tortuous and erratic manner from one mood and one course of action to another. They behave by fits and starts, shifting capriciously down a path that leads nowhere and precipitates them into endless wrangles with others and disappointments with themselves.

The contrary character seen in this domain of the negativistic personality takes the form of changing and conflicting social relationships. Most notable is the contrast between dependent and contrite acquiescence, on the one hand, and assertive and hostile independence, on the other. They exhibit envy and pique toward those whom they see as more fortunate, and are actively obstructive toward those with whom they must relate regularly, expressing either critical or incompatible attitudes toward them.

It would appear from the foregoing that the ambivalence and erratic course of skeptical/negativists would fail to provide them with any satisfactions or security. If this were the case, we would expect them to decompensate quickly. Few do. Hence, we are forced to inquire as to what gains and supports these individuals do achieve in the course of behaving in their vacillating and ambivalent manner.

Quite simply, being "difficult," quixotic, unpredictable, and discontent will produce certain rewards and avoid certain discomforts. The following are examples, drawn from the sphere of marital life, of the ingenious, though unconscious, mechanisms these personalities employ.

A negativistic man, who is unwilling or unable to decide whether to grow up or remain a child, explodes emotionally whenever his wife expects "too much" of him. Afterward, he expresses guilt, becomes contrite, and pleads forbearance on her part. By turning toward self-condemnation, he evokes her sympathy, restrains her from making undue demands, and maneuvers her into placating rather than criticizing him.

A woman, feeling the ambivalence of both love and hate for her husband, complains bitterly about his loss of interest in her as a woman. To prove his affections, he suggests that they go on a second honeymoon, that is, take a vacation without the children. To this proposal she replies that his plan only proves that he is a foolish spendthrift; in the same breath, however, she insists that the children come along. No matter what he does, he is wrong. She has not only trapped him but confused him as well. Her ambivalence maneuvers him, first one way and then the other. It forces him to be on edge, always alert to avoid situations that might provoke her ire, yet he can never quite be sure that he has succeeded.

The negativist's inconsistent strategy, of being discontent and unpredictable, of being both seductive and rejecting, and of being demanding and then dissatisfied, is an effective weapon not only with an intimidated or pliant partner but with people in general. Switching among the roles of the martyr, the affronted, the aggrieved, the misunderstood, the contrite, the guilt-ridden, the sickly, and the overworked is a tactic of interpersonal behavior that gains negativists the attention, reassurance, and dependency they crave, while at the same time allowing them to subtly vent their angers and resentments. For all its seeming ineffectuality, vacillation recruits affection and support, on the one hand, and provides a means of discharging the tensions of frustration and hostility, on the other. Interspersed with self-deprecation and contrition, acts that relieve unconscious guilt and serve to solicit forgiveness and reassuring comments from others, this strategy proves *not* to be a total failure at all.

Skeptical Cognitive Style

It is typical for negativists to be cynical, doubting, and untrusting, approaching most events in their life with a measure of disbelief and skepticism. Future possibilities are viewed with a degree of trepidation, if not pessimism and suspicion. Most negativists display a misanthropic view of life, tend to appraise matters in a whining and grumbling manner, and voice disdain and caustic comments about circumstances and persons that appear to be experiencing good fortune.

It should also be noted that negativists are usually quite articulate in describing their subjective discomforts. Only rarely, however, are they willing to explore or to admit any insight into its roots. In talking about their sensitivities and difficulties, they will *not* recognize that these reflect, in largest measure, their own inner conflicts and ambivalences. Self-reports alternate between preoccupations with personal inadequacies, bodily ailments, and guilt feelings, on the one hand, and social resentments, frustrations, and disillusionments, on the other. They will voice dismay about the sorry state of their life, their worries, their sadness, their disappointments, their "nervousness," and so on. Although most will express a desire to be rid of distress and difficulty, they seem unable, or perhaps unwilling, to find any solution.

Ambivalence also characterizes the thinking of these persons. No sooner do they see the merit of approaching their problems one way than they find themselves saying "But...." Fearful of committing themselves and unsure of their own desires and competencies, they find their thoughts shifting erratically from one solution to another. Because of their intense ambivalences, they often act precipitously, on the spur of the moment. Any other course for them would lead only to hesitation or vacillation, if not total immobility.

Discontented Self-Image

Negativists often assert that they have been trapped by fate, that nothing ever works out for them, and that whatever they desire runs aground. These negativistic persons express envy and resentment over the "easy life" of others. They are frequently critical and cynical with regard to what others have attained, yet covet these achievements themselves. Life, skeptical/negativists claim, has been unkind to them. They feel cheated and unappreciated. Whatever they have done has been for naught. Their motives and behaviors have always been misunderstood, and they are now bitterly disillusioned. The obstructiveness and pessimism that others have attributed to them are only a reflection, they feel, of their sensitivity or the pain they have suffered from physical disabilities or the inconsiderateness that others have shown toward them. But here again, the negativist's ambivalence intrudes. Perhaps, they say, it has all been a consequence of their own unworthiness, their own failures, and their own bad temper. Maybe it is their own behavior that is the cause of their misery and the pain they have brought to others. Among these personalities, the ambivalent struggle between feeling guilt and feeling resentment permeates every facet of thought and behavior.

Vacillating Object Representations

The inner templates of the past among negativistic personalities are composed of complexly conflicting images and memories. Few components of this template are composed of internally consistent qualities. Most internalized objects are associated with contradictory feelings, countervailing inclinations, and incompatible memories. Hence, the foundation of dispositions that serve to organize the negativist's ongoing perceptions and personal relationships is divergently oriented and in a constant state of flux. Adding to these internally vacillating objects is the fact that they are generally colored by negative emotions, resulting in a disposition to undermine the pleasures and achievements of self and others, without necessarily appearing to do so.

The behaviors of these overtly ambivalent personalities are even more erratic and vacillating than we might expect from their reinforcement history. They appear to have labored under a double handicap. Not only were they deprived of external consistency and control in childhood, but, as a consequence of these experiences, they never acquired the motivation and competencies of internal control. Unsure of what their environment expects of them and unable to impose self-discipline and order, these persons seem adrift in their environment, bobbing up and down erratically from one mood to another.

As has been noted in previous books (Millon, 1981, 1996b), these individuals failed to experience consistent parental discipline. What they did acquire was largely through implicit modeling. In essence, they imitated the contradictory or capricious style of their parents. Deprived of conditions for acquiring self-control and modeling themselves after their opposing or erratic and ambivalent parents, these personalities never learn to conceal their moods for long and cannot bind or transform their emotions. Whatever inner feelings well up within them—be it guilt, anger, or inferiority—they spill quickly to the surface in pure and direct form.

Displacement Regulatory Mechanism

A distinguishing clinical feature of negativists is their paucity of intrapsychic controls and mechanisms. Their moods, thoughts, and desires tend not to be worked out internally. Few unconscious processes are employed to handle the upsurge of feelings, and, as a consequence, these come readily to the surface, untransformed and unmoderated. These negativistic persons are like children in that they often react spontaneously and impulsively to passing emotions. As a result, there is little consistency and predictability to their reactions.

Perhaps the most consistent mechanism seen among negativists is their use of displacement, that is, their tendency to shift their anger both precipitously and unconsciously from their true targets (e.g., persons or settings) to those of lesser significance. Thus, through their passive-aggressive maneuvers, negativists will vent their resentments by substitute means, such as acting inept or perplexed or behaving in a forgetful or indolent manner.

Displacement, and the confusion of attitudes and feelings that this creates, is paralleled by a variety of other, often erratic and contradictory mechanisms. Sometimes patients will turn their externally directed, hostile feelings back toward themselves, a mechanism termed by some "introjection," the converse of projection. For example, the hatred they feel for others may be directed toward themselves, taking the form of guilt or self-condemnation. True to form, however, the negativist will alternate between introjection and projection. At one time, by projection, these persons will ascribe their destructive impulses to others, accusing the others, unjustly, of being malicious and unkind to them (Coid, 2003). At other times, by introjection, they will reverse the sequence, accusing themselves of faults that justifiably should be ascribed to others.

Thus, even in the use of unconscious mechanisms, the negativist behaves in a vacillating and contradictory manner. Those at the receiving end of these seemingly bizarre intrapsychic processes cannot help but conclude that the person is behaving in an irrational way and exhibiting uncalled for outbursts and emotional inconsistencies.

Divergent Morphologic Organization

The pattern of morphological structures in the skeptical/negativistic personality exhibits a clear division among its components. Hence, controls and defensive maneuvers are often employed to achieve incompatible goals and purposes. Major conflicts may remain unresolved, therefore, and full psychic cohesion may become impossible to achieve by virtue of the fact that the fulfillment of one goal or purpose will nullify or undo and reverse another.

Weakness of intrapsychic control would not prove troublesome if the negativist's feelings were calm and consistent, but they are not (Coolidge, Thede, & Jang, 2001). Rooted in deep personal ambivalences, negativists experience an undercurrent of perpetual inner turmoil and anxiety. Their equilibrium is unstable. Their inability to anticipate the future as consistent or predictable gives rise to a constant state of insecurity. The frustration and confusion they feel turn readily to anger and resentment. Guilt often emerges and frequently serves to curtail this anger. In short, the actively ambivalent suffers a range of intense and conflicting emotions that, because of weak controls and lack of self-discipline, surge quickly and capriciously to the surface.

Irritable Mood/Temperament

The personality pattern is best characterized by the rapid succession of changing behaviors and moods. Much of the time, these patients seem restless, unstable, and erratic in their feelings. They are easily nettled, offended by trifles, and readily provoked into being sullen and contrary (Coolidge, DenBoer, & Segal, 2004). There is often a low tolerance for frustration (Craig, 2003). Many are chronically impatient and irritable and fidgety unless things go their way. There are periods when they vacillate from being distraught and despondent at one moment, to being petty, spiteful, stubborn, and contentious the next. At other times they may be enthusiastic and cheerful, but this mood is usually short-lived. In no time, they are again disgruntled, critical, and envious. They often begrudge the good fortunes of others and are jealous, quarrelsome, and easily piqued by signs of indifference or minor slights. They wear their emotions on their sleeves. Many are excitable and impulsive. Others suddenly burst into tears and guilt at the slightest upset. Still others often discharge anger or abuse at the least provocation. The impulsive, unpredictable, and often explosive reactions of these personalities make it difficult for others to feel comfortable in their presence or to establish rewarding and enduring relationships with them. Although there will be periods of pleasant sociability and warm affection, most acquaintances of these personalities often feel on edge, waiting for them to display a sullen and hurt look or become obstinate or nasty.

Negativists do not exhibit a distinctive or characteristic level of biologic activation. However, there is reason to believe that they may possess an intrinsic irritability or hyperreactivity to stimulation. They seem easily aroused, testy, high-strung, thin-skinned, and quick-tempered. Minor events provoke and chafe them. They become inflamed and aggrieved by the most incidental and insignificant acts of others. Of course, these hypersensitivities could stem from adverse experiences as well as constitutional proclivities. We may speculate further that these personalities possess some unusual mixture of temperaments. Their behavioral ambivalences may reflect the back-and-forth workings of conflicting dispositions and result in the erratic and contradictory emotional reactions they characteristically display. The reader must note that there is no substantive evidence to warrant placing confidence in these biogenic conjectures.

The negativistic pattern may be more prevalent among women than among men. Although speculative as a thesis, because women are subject to hormonal changes during their menstrual cycles that could regularly activate marked, short-lived, and variable moods, such rapid changes in affect may set into motion erratic behaviors and interpersonal reactions that lead to both the acquisition and perpetuation of an ambivalently oriented pattern. Whereas obstreperous and uncontrolled characteristics among men are likely to be judged signs of being tough-minded, these very same characteristics among women may be viewed as being bitchy and negativistic. Note again that conjectures such as these are no more than unconfirmed speculations.

Self-Perpetuation Processes

Most pathological personalities feel some measure of stability and self-content with the lifestyle they have acquired. This is not typical among negativistic personalities. Their feelings, attitudes, and behaviors allow for little internal equilibrium or consistent

Table 8.2   Self-Perpetuating Processes: Skeptical/Negativistic Personality

Unpredictable and Negative Behaviors
Erratic actions scatter efforts
Inconstant behavior impedes progress
Sulking goads exasperation

Anticipation of Disappointment
Good fortune will end abruptly
Jumps the gun to avoid disillusionment
Vented discontentment provokes hostility

Re-creation of Disillusioning Experiences
Striving followed by testing behavior
Ultimately drives others to anger
Creates vicious circles of expected betrayal

external gratification. They frequently live in a phenomenological state of discontent and self-dissatisfaction. Their irritability provokes them to behave unpredictably and to appear restless, sullen, and obstructive much of the time. Not only do they suffer an ever-present sense of inner turmoil, but they act out their discontent for all to see.

The following describes three aspects of the negativistic style that perpetuate and intensify the troublesome behaviors and attitudes acquired in childhood (see Table 8.2).

Negativistic and Unpredictable Behaviors

Acting erratically, vacillating from one course to another, is a sheer waste of energy. By attempting to achieve incompatible goals, these persons scatter their efforts and dilute their effectiveness. Caught in their own crosscurrents, they cannot commit themselves to one clear direction, swinging indecisively back and forth, performing ineffectually, and experiencing a sense of paralyzing inertia or exhaustion (Sinha & Watson, 2001).

In addition to the wasteful nature of ambivalence, negativists may actively impede their own progress toward conflict resolution and goal attainment. Thus, they frequently undo what good they previously had done. Driven by contrary feelings, they retract their kind words to others and replace them with harshness, or they undermine achievements they struggled so hard to attain. In short, their ambivalence often robs them of what few steps they secured toward progress. This inconstant behavior, blowing hot and cold, precipitates others into reacting in a parallel capricious and inconsistent manner. By prompting these reactions, negativists re-create the very conditions of their childhood that fostered the development of their unstable behaviors in the first place.

Most people weary of the sulking and stubborn unpredictability of these actively ambivalent personalities. Others are frequently goaded into exasperation and confusion when their persistent efforts to placate the negativist so frequently meet with failure. Eventually, everyone is likely to express both anger and disaffiliation, reactions that serve only to intensify the negativist's dismay and anxiety.

Anticipating Disappointment

Not only do negativists precipitate real difficulties through their negativistic behaviors, but they often perceive and anticipate difficulties where none in fact exist. They have learned from past experience that good things don't last, that positive feelings and attitudes from those whose they seek love will end abruptly and capriciously and be followed by disappointment, anger, and rejection (Craig & Bivens, 2000; Franken & Hendriks, 2000; King, 1998).

Rather than be disillusioned and embittered, rather than allowing themselves to be led down the primrose path to suffer the humiliation and pain of having their hopes dashed again, it would be better to put a halt to illusory gratifications and to the futility and heartache of short-lived pleasures. Protectively, then, negativists may refuse to wait for others to make the turnabout. Instead, they jump the gun, pull back when things are going well, and thereby cut off experiences that may have proved gratifying had they been completed. The anticipation of being set back and left in the lurch prompts negativists into a self-fulfilling prophecy. By their own hand, they defeat their chance to experience events that could have promoted change and growth.

By cutting off the goodwill of others and by upsetting their pleasurable anticipations, negativists gain the perverse and negative gratification of venting hostility and anger. These acts, however, prove to be Pyrrhic victories; not only do they sabotage their own chances for rewarding experiences, but they inevitably provoke counterhostility from others and increased guilt and anxiety for themselves. Their defensive action has instigated responses that perpetuate the original difficulty, setting into motion a vicious circle in which they feel further discontent and disappointment (Kantor, 2002).

Re-creating Disillusioning Experiences

As noted earlier, interpersonal vacillation does gain partial gratification for the negativist. And partial reinforcements, as we know from experimental research, strengthen habits and cause them to persist and recur. In the negativist this appears to take the form of unconscious repetition compulsions in which the individual re-creates disillusioning experiences that parallel those of the past.

Despite their ambivalence and pessimistic outlook, negativists operate on the premise that they can overcome past disappointments and capture, in full measure, the love and attention they only partially gained in childhood. Unfortunately, their search for complete fulfillment can no longer be achieved for they now possess needs that are in fundamental opposition to one another; for example, they both want and do not want the love of those on whom they depend. Despite this ambivalence, negativists enter new relationships as if a perfect and idyllic state could be achieved. They go through the act of seeking a consistent and true source of love, one that will not betray them as their parents and others have in the past. They venture into new relationships with enthusiasm and blind optimism; this time, all will go well. Despite this optimism, they remain unsure of the trust they really can place in others. Mindful of past betrayals and disappointments, they begin to test their newfound loves to see if they are loyal and faithful. They may irritate others, frustrate them, and withdraw from them, all in an effort to check whether they will prove as fickle and insubstantial as those of the past. Soon these testing operations exhaust the partner's patience; annoyance, exasperation, and hostility follow. The negativist quickly becomes disenchanted; the idol has proved to be marred and imperfect, and the negativist is once more disillusioned and embittered. To vent their resentment at having been naive, these persons may turn against their "betrayers," disavow and recoil from the affections they had shown, and thereby complete the *vicious* circle. These experiences recur repeatedly, and with each recurrence, negativists further reinforce their pessimistic anticipations. In their efforts to overcome past disillusionment, they have thrown themselves into new ventures that have led to further disillusion.

Interventional Goals

The impression that negativists convey is that of childlike rebellion. They are likely to come to therapy at the request of others because their oppositional behavior has interfered with their marital, parental, or occupational responsibilities. Relationships with authority figures tend also to be problematic. This personality's characteristic negative outlook on life is likely to extend to therapy as well; therefore, it is improbable that negativists have entered the therapeutic arena voluntarily. Convinced that others are to blame for their misfortunes, they avoid taking responsibility for altering their provocative behaviors.

Progress in therapy is not promising. These personalities appear compliant on the surface, yet covertly they resist and manage to undermine the therapist's efforts. It may be difficult for these patients to see the therapist as a collaborator rather than an adversary.

The goals of therapy are to guide negativistic patients to recognize the source and character of their ambivalences toward self and others and to reinforce a more consistent approach to life. Treatment must further attempt to mitigate their tendency to overreact in an obstructive and sullen manner. Recognition of the factors that foster the cyclical and recurrent nature of their interactions with others will assist in planning interventions, especially those oriented to the mood/temperament and self-image domains (see Table 8.3).

Reestablishing Polarity Balances

The conflictual coping style of the negativistic personality is manifested by extreme vacillations between submission to others and gratification of self-needs. They may seek to obtain nurturance from others without examining their own adaptive capabilities.

Table 8.3 Therapeutic Strategies and Tactics for the Prototypal Skeptical/ Negativistic (Passive-Aggressive) Personality

Strategic Goals

Balance Polarities

Diminish self-other conflict

Stabilize erratically changing actions

Counter Perpetuations

Reduce anticipation of disappointment

Moderate unpredictable behaviors

Prevent creation of disillusionment

Tactical Modalities

Reverse discontented self-image

Moderate irritable *moods*

Alter skeptical *cognitive* style

Undo contrary/resentful *behaviors*

Not uncharacteristically, they may shift gears and quickly turn against those from whom they sought assistance. This self–other conflicted orientation provokes others to respond angrily in return. Assisting these patients in finding a comfortable balance within these bipolar orientations should be considered a major goal of therapy. Negativists need to learn to differentiate between the self and others and to adopt coping mechanisms that will allow them to move flexibly from fulfilling their own desires, without guilt, to being oriented toward others, without resentment.

Unlike the obsessive-compulsive, who is overly controlled and represses urges to act out, the negativist employs an active mode of adaptation, displaying both erraticism and hyperreactivity. In these efforts to avoid distress, these personalities enact behaviors that not only upset others but also harm themselves. The observed imbalance in the active–passive polarity must be attenuated. It would be beneficial for negativists to take a more passive stance, especially in ambiguous situations where carefully exploring options and gathering more evidence when needed are more adaptive than reacting impulsively and erratically.

Countering Perpetuating Tendencies

The inconsistencies to which negativists were exposed in childhood reinforced the belief that disappointments are inevitable in life. In anticipation of this, they may withdraw prematurely from potentially gratifying experiences, upsetting their focus and changing their goals, only to repeat the same dysfunctional cycle. This behavior not only alienates others but also induces guilt in themselves. To interrupt this pattern, negativists must learn to commit to a specified plan of action and to actively follow through. Acquiring control over their impulses is a paramount therapeutic goal.

Through their erratic and oppositional behaviors, negativistic personalities place themselves in double-bind situations, vacillating between incompatible goals and unable to commit and fulfill personal needs. Scornful, moody, and unpredictable emotional displays tend to exasperate others, causing them to react in a similar fashion. This, in turn, intensifies their belief that others cannot be relied on and will generate new conflictual behaviors. A major goal of personologic therapy with this disorder is to temper the volatile expression of behaviors and affect. When these patients learn to appropriately express their discontent, resentful encounters will give way to more mature interactions.

It is in the realm of interpersonal relations that the erratic cycle is played out in its full form. Not knowing whether they can rely on their partner, negativists proceed to test his or her fidelity and trustworthiness, eventually exasperating even the most compliant partner. Unable to find security and disillusioned once again, they will turn to their next victim. To prevent this recapitulation of past experiences, the dyadic relationship between the therapist and the patient may serve as a stable model to emulate, a starting block from which the patient can learn new ways of connecting.

Identifying Domain Dysfunctions

Central to this disorder are dysfunctions in the mood/temperament and self-image domains. Negativists feel that the world does not understand them and fear that there is little hope they will ever receive fair treatment. Their discontent is manifested through fickle and volatile emotional displays. Therapeutic efforts must be directed toward balancing the emotional seesaw, helping these patients gain control over the expression of negative affects. These personalities vacillate between blaming others and attributing the cause of their woes to themselves. Therapeutic goals include strengthening a consistent self-image, as well as improving their perceptions of the real basis of their misfortunes.

Negativists have a very pessimistic outlook on life, believing that good things don't last. This skepticism often leads them to pull back and choose an opposite course of action when things seem to be going their way, thereby causing their predictions to come true. Therapy must assist these patients to challenge the faulty assumptions and allow them to actively test reality. This negative outlook expresses itself particularly in interpersonal relationships. Believing that personal needs will never be met satisfactorily and that they will not be treated fairly, negativists develop a conflictual interpersonal style. They also resent others' good fortune, feeling personally deprived when observing what others may have received. Therapy must strive to help patients regulate contrary behaviors and develop tolerance for others so that their social behaviors will be more charitable and consistent.

Problems in relatedness began early in life and characterize their domain of inner object representations. Experiences from the past have left a residue of internalized dispositions that are essentially ambivalent. Intervention must work toward replacing these conflictual and vacillating objects with more stable, dependable ones.

When expressing discontent and troublesome feelings, the skeptical/negativist quite often fails to recognize their original and primary unconscious source. More direct and consciously assertive ways of voicing discontent should be explored in real life. As noted, the internal morphological structures of negativists are divergent, consisting of coping mechanisms that are directed toward incompatible goals. The ultimate therapeutic objective in this area is a more consistent coping strategy, as well as a commitment to follow through in achieving its goal, that of psychic cohesion.

Selecting Therapeutic Modalities

The therapist must seek to demonstrate the effectiveness of therapy to these patients whose skeptical nature is likely to discount the possibility of progress ever being achieved. When everything seems to be moving along well and progress is made steadily, these patients may suddenly decide to discontinue therapy, stating that it was a waste of time. Major life issues that were brought up just prior to the end of the previous session may be discounted by the next meeting. The therapist will have to go with the flow, so to speak, keeping in mind his or her plan of action, not giving in to countertransference feelings or reactions. Much therapy time will be devoted to exploring resistances, and a slow pace of progression with many ups and downs can be expected.

Behavioral Techniques

Formal *behavior modification* methods may be fruitfully explored to achieve greater consistency in social behaviors. Lacking appropriate role models in childhood, some negativists may have learned that goals may be achieved only through indirect means. The thought of dealing with matters in a straightforward way is anxiety-arousing. During the course of therapy, negativists will be asked to engage in behaviors that are likely to raise anxiety levels. Teaching anxiety-management techniques can help them tolerate the expected discomforts and frustrations that normally would cause them to change their mode of action.

Controlling untimely expressions of anger may require impulse control and assertiveness skills training. These patients need to learn to count to 10. By learning to directly express appropriate anger, the negativist will be less inclined to displace resentments onto substitute objects. Within the therapeutic context, role-playing and videotaped playback of interactions may facilitate an understanding of the negativist's dysfunctional interpersonal style. A functional analysis will reveal that there are contextual determinants to the negativist's behavior. Stimulus control procedures, such as removal of environmental pressures that aggravate the patient's anxieties, may be explored and appropriate modifications should be made.

Engaging the patient in behavioral contracting at the outset of treatment may foster compliance with therapy. Contracts should initially be short term and concise to avoid giving the negativist an opportunity to use ambiguity as an excuse for not following through. Accomplishing the stated goals in the contract will help the patient develop a view of the self as competent. Self-management procedures are generally contraindicated as a first approach because these patients believe that others are to blame for their misfortunes.

Interpersonal Techniques

Interpersonal techniques can be used to help these patients gain insight into the origin of their destructive behaviors and how these early learning experiences are played out in their current relationships. The transference reactions manifested in therapy will shed light on these patterns. Gradually, the therapist can start pointing out possible connections between the patient's early experiences and his or her current style of interacting. It is vital that the therapist point out the commonalities between the patient's behavior in the family of origin and his or her behavior in treatment, so that therapy will not recapitulate the childhood experiences or end in premature termination (Benjamin, 1993; Benjamin & Cushing, 2004). Most important is to establish a collaborative therapeutic relationship, one in which the patient is permitted to act out capriciously, if not assertively, without the fear of provoking therapeutic retribution. Discussions can be centered on the patient's habit of seeking help but then refusing it when offered. Care must be taken on the part of the therapist to protect against his or her own countertransference reactions to a patient who has provoked and felt neglected by former caregivers. Little progress should be expected until the negativist's hidden agenda of therapeutic abuse and incompetence has been relinquished.

As noted, interpersonal work with negativists is a slow and arduous process. Benjamin states that in order for negativists to recognize their maladaptive patterns, they must be partly adept at blocking these cycles and must have some desire to give up their mode of interaction. Successfully working through the obstructive behaviors in therapy will provide a corrective emotional experience. The therapist may be the first person who has not expressed criticism or counterreacted with hostility.

Because *family* and *marital* treatment methods focus on the complex network of relationships that often sustain this personality style, these may prove to be among the most useful techniques available (Carlson, Melton, & Snow, 2004; Slavik, Carlson, & Sperry, 1998). When negativists come in for marital therapy, it is not unusual for the identified patient in the dyad to be the victim of misplaced hostility. Quite commonly, however, each partner has his or her own conflicts and dysfunctional style and in turn perpetuate each other's pathology. The negativist often projects undesirable traits onto the marital partner and subsequently expresses dismay, yet proceeds to behave in a manner that actually generates this behavior in the partner. In couples therapy it is not uncommon that improvement in one member of the dyad may result in increased symptomatology in the other. The therapist must be attuned to this possibility.

Group methods may be fruitfully employed to assist the patient to acquire more self-control and consistency in social situations. When group members share their reaction to the obstructiveness of the negativistic person, self-recognition of pathological patterns may be facilitated. Unfortunately, premature dropout may ensue, especially in the early phases. Because their interactions are consistently negative, these patients do not usually receive positive responses from others. Yalom (1985) describes these patients as "help-rejecting complainers," as other participants experience repeated confusion and frustration in response to the vacillating patterns of the negativist. According to Yalom, negativists are among the most difficult group therapy patients. Care must be taken by the therapist to restrain his or her role as a rescuer, that is, to avoid expressions of encouragement and giving explicit advice. By opening up the floor to reactions from other group members, negativists can be led to recognize their behaviors' effect on others. Of course, negativists may intentionally or inadvertently hold others responsible for their own misfortunes, or may speak or act in other ways to sustain the pattern. Therapists should be especially alert when group members occasionally combine forces against the negativist.

Cognitive Techniques

More directive *cognitive* techniques may be used to confront these patients with the obstructive and self-defeating character of their interpersonal relations. Cognitive approaches must be handled with caution, however, lest the patient become unduly guilt-ridden, depressed, and suicidal. The greatest benefit derived through these approaches is to stabilize these patients, to set them straight, and to put reins on their uncontrollable vacillations of mood and behavior, very much like what must be done with borderline personalities.

Beck et al. (2003) highlight a number of cognitive interventions with this disorder. From the outset, patients need to be engaged in a collaborative and practically oriented series of tasks. Because they are extremely resistant to external control, the therapist must take special care to actively involve skeptical/negativists in treatment planning, reinforcing the autonomy they so desire. The therapist must avoid challenging the accuracy of their dysfunctional beliefs too directly or prematurely.

Important in this therapeutic technique is assisting patients to become more aware of the assumptions and expectancies that shape their dysfunctional thoughts and behaviors (Morse et al., 2002). Central to this model is an analysis and reorientation of their conflicting cognitive schemas about autonomy and self-interest versus submissiveness and other-focus. Also important is that clear-cut rules and limits be set and maintained consistently. Another cognitive approach recognizes the skeptical/negativist's inclination to defy authority and to engage in meaningless power struggles. Here, it is wise to lead the patient to recognize that he or she is making cognitive selections and choices, rather than being externally abused and manipulated by others. As Beck and Freeman (1990) note, the therapist should encourage patients to select in-session topics for discussion. Also useful are cognitive experiments that can be tested in reality to examine the accuracy of the patient's beliefs and assumptions.

Self-Image Techniques

Typical automatic thoughts of the negativistic person include the following: "Nothing ever works out for me in life"; "I never get what I deserve"; and "How dare others tell me how to lead my life?" These faulty statements can be explored and subsequently challenged. A dysfunctional thought record will be useful to help identify the automatic thoughts and accompanying emotions. The validity of the negativist's thinking can then be determined by setting up alternative hypotheses and trials to test them. Reality testing will provide these patients with more precise information about the probability of anticipated misfortune, hence taking the edge off their skepticism.

Another important strategy is maintaining consistency in treatment. Negativists will inevitably try to blame lack of progress on the therapist, but by setting strict rules, structuring sessions, and giving clear rationales for each intervention, the ambiguity that provides an excuse for their lack of responsibility should be reduced via Glasser's (1965) reality/control procedures. It is also important to examine which of the negativist's assumptions contribute to his or her success in obtaining satisfaction from others, exploring both pros and cons as well as short-term versus long-term gains. A Rogerian model, one that permits patients to listen to their own verbalizations, may lead them to recognize the character of their own inner struggles, thereby opening up the opportunity to develop a coherent rather than conflictual sense of self.

Intrapsychic Techniques

Because of the deeply rooted character of these problems and the high probability that unconscious resistances will impede the effectiveness of other therapeutic procedures, it may be necessary to explore the more extensive and prolonged techniques of *psychodynamic* therapy. On the other hand, working with negativists is often so toxic for many therapists that they readily refer them to others who may be more tolerant or less likely to express negative countertransferences (e.g., anger, annoyance). The talent of these patients to criticize and rebut the therapist's efforts serves as a major defense against deeper self-awareness. As the negativist becomes more willing to accept guidance from the therapist, a searching exploration may begin to trace the early roots of the negativist's conflictual psyche that developed in childhood, inconsistently rewarding at times and frequently punishing. Most notable in this personality disorder is how these patients undermine themselves repeatedly. As Gabbard (1990) suggests, the therapist should deliver a frank statement about the consequences to themselves of these patients' behaviors, for example, "I sense you are trying to make me angry with you."

A thorough reconstruction of personality may be the only means of altering the pattern. An awareness of the origins of his or her paradoxical behavior should enhance the negativist's understanding of how the same behaviors are played out in negative transference responses to the therapist. The neutrality of responses with which the therapist engages the patient can be a major corrective force. Once these personalities see that they can express their anger overtly, without disapproval and rejection from this authority figure, a more consistent model and self-image may then be internalized. Replacement of the vacillating objects with stable ones will allow negativists to view their interactions with others as consistent and on safe ground.

Unless there is a greater harmony in the negativist's internal structural elements, coping and defensive maneuvers will continue to be used to fulfill contradictory goals. The therapist must help the patient understand that his or her behavior actually serves to exacerbate conflicts. Encouraging patients to make sense of the confused mix of emotions they carry inside will help them get in touch with internal stimuli. Once they understand these feelings, the internal confusion may no longer be overwhelming. The patient can then sort through his or her internal reserves to select appropriate coping mechanisms.

Stone (1993) notes that dream analysis can be helpful to get at the heart of the central conflicts. If the therapist can work through the patient's resistance, underlying feelings of impotence and unworthiness may be exposed and examined. Stone further points out that the patient has received primarily conditional love in the past and enters treatment with the belief that the therapist will not be much different. When the therapist communicates an understanding of the issues important to the patient and provides support rather than telling the patient what to do, the negativistic personality can start to develop a more secure self-image.

Pharmacologic Techniques

As noted previously, negativists are quite vulnerable and react with strong emotional feelings when under stress (anxiety, depression). Their internal conflicts comprise feelings of inadequacy as well as hostility toward those on whom they are dependent. Intense anxieties frequently preoccupy the patient in the early phases of treatment. *Pharmacological* anxiolytic agents may prove helpful in their relief. If depressive features predominate, antidepressant drugs may be prescribed. However, the therapist must be aware of the potential for the misuse of medication, such as the patient's inclination to be oppositional and noncompliant. Attention should also be given to the proclivity of these patients to suicide via the use of medications.

Making Synergistic Arrangements

What combinations and sequences should be taken to optimize the effectiveness of the various domain-oriented techniques described previously?

Therapy must initially help the negativistic personality to settle down and calm his or her erratic emotions. Supportive techniques may be used as a first approach, especially if combined with pharmacological intervention. Without first curtailing the patient's emotional lability, other interventions are not likely to prove beneficial. Behavioral techniques can be of use to desensitize the patient to established anxiety-arousing stimuli. These methods should promote increasingly autonomous behavior, allowing the patient to feel more in control. This will subsequently decrease the resentfulness and contrariness displayed in interpersonal situations. Concurrent modifications in the patient's cognitive style will help him or her attend in more detail to attitudes and assumptions about self and others.

Throughout the therapy process, the use of interpersonal techniques will facilitate negativists' recognition of their interactive patterns. Understanding their own contributions to interpersonal difficulties may pave the way for a transition in object-relatedness. Only when therapy has progressed for some period of time will dynamic techniques be able to help these patients get in touch with their innermost fears and contradictions. Understanding and acknowledgment of these feelings will significantly reduce the need for displacement and other externalizing defenses. Gradually, the careful application of the techniques described earlier can result in psychic cohesion.

Illustrative Cases

In contrast to the *DSM-III* and *DSM-III-R* formulations, the passive-aggressive/ negativistic personality has been introduced into the appendix of *DSM-IV* to represent a comprehensive pattern of traits. This wider ranging concept of the disorder will result in part in overlaps and combinations with other personality disorders. As such, we should anticipate finding amalgams and mixtures that display the features of several personalities, a number of which are described in the following cases (see Table 8.4).

Table 8.4   Skeptical/Negativistic Personality Disorder Subtypes

Circuitous: Opposition displayed in a roundabout, labyrinthine, and ambiguous manner (e.g., procrastination, dawdling, forgetfulness, inefficiency, neglect, stubbornness); indirect and devious in venting resentment and resistant behaviors. (Mixed Negativistic/Dependent Subtype)

Vacillating: Emotions fluctuate in bewildering, perplexing, and enigmatic ways; difficult to fathom or comprehend own capricious and mystifying moods; wavers, is in flux, and is irresolute both subjectively and intrapsychically. (Mixed Negativistic/Borderline Subtype)

Discontented: Grumbling, petty, testy, cranky, embittered, complaining, fretful, vexed, and moody; gripes behind pretense; avoids confrontation; uses legitimate but trivial complaints. (Mixed Negativistic/Depressive Subtype)

Abrasive: Contentious, intransigent, fractious, and quarrelsome; irritable, caustic, debasing, corrosive, and acrimonious; contradicts and derogates; few qualms and little conscience or remorse. (Mixed Negativistic/Sadistic Subtype)

Case 8.1, Barry K., 36

A Skeptical/Negativistic Personality: Circuitous Type (Negativistic with Dependent Traits)

Presenting Picture

Barry, a substitute high school math teacher, was always one step behind in life, a trait he traced back to childhood. He noted that he always felt that he was the least talented in his family of four talented siblings and overachieving parents. His wife was a successful corporate lawyer and made a very substantial living, providing she and Barry and their son what Barry called "a pretty cushy life, when it's all said and done." For the past 3 years, since the birth of their son, Barry had relegated himself to the role of "Mister Mom," working only occasionally as a substitute teacher, and he had felt that everything was working out well. Recently, though, his wife had given Barry an ultimatum: Get help! Barry was very surprised at her ire after he lost a substantial amount of her money to his passive hobby of playing the stock market online during one of his nonworking days. "I've made money, too. I don't know what she's so upset about," he said. Highly dependent on her for income, Barry enjoyed the freedom inherent in substitute teaching, though he indicated that he might take a permanent job "for the rest of the year, anyway," to appease his wife.

Complaints he heard from his wife, as well as school administrators, included repressed hostility, grumbling, a habit of giving incomplete answers, and forgetful ("incompetent") resistance to finishing even simple tasks. He admitted that there was a shred of truth there, as "you can keep your work load minimized by being smart and acting a little stupid." Currently, Barry admitted that there was a "woman friend" at the school where he was thinking about taking a semipermanent job, though he gave ambiguous statements when asked about the nature of this new friendship.

Initial Impressions

Barry was an example of what we have termed the *circuitous* subtype of the Negativistic Personality Disorder, closely corresponding to the classification previously labeled the Passive-Aggressive Personality Disorder. Here we saw a prominent, if not singular, feature that was characterized by a resistance to the expectations of others, a resistance that was expressed indirectly rather than directly. Despite the passive nature of his resentments, Barry clearly was grumbling and oppositional, habitually angry at those who demanded of him a level of performance that he was deeply unwilling to carry out. As noted, his oppositional behaviors were displayed indirectly and, as the descriptive label suggests, in a circuitous fashion through maneuvers such as procrastination, dawdling, stubbornness, forgetfulness, and a general but intentional inefficiency. Barry was largely a psychic blend of both negativistic and dependent traits. Unwilling or fearful of expressing resentments directly and overtly, he often fulfilled the requirements set forth by others, but with foot-dragging slowness and a bumbling inefficiency. He was not consciously aware of the problems he had caused. He resisted facing the guilt feelings and interpersonal conflicts he would have to deal with were he not protecting himself against conscious awareness. Moreover, by maintaining a high degree of repression, his neglectfulness and disagreeable behaviors could remain impervious to efforts to pressure him to change. He usually expressed resistance in ways that did not appear to be intentionally oppositional; hence, he could not readily be criticized for his behavior. Despite these frequently successful maneuvers at self-protection, he had effectively, if unconsciously, sacrificed his own opportunities for achievement. He retaliated against the rejection and depreciation he had felt in the past in a way that ultimately undid him in the future.

Because of Barry's pessimism and lack of feelings of competence, a safe and empathic environment would need to be established, along with measures to ensure that familiar but ineffective relationship patterns would not become troublesome in the context of therapy. As these patterns emerged, however, it would be possible to address them in a manner creating a concurrent intellectual understanding and personal resonance. Self-perpetuating issues that followed and needed to be confronted in a similar manner would include strong tendencies toward *active* and *passive* orientations (e.g., expending much energy scheming to be inefficient, lazy, bumbling), as well as conflicting *self–other* tendencies (e.g., expressing more negative feelings by letting others down, yet ruining his own interests in so doing). As these deeply conflictual characterologic strategies became clarified, it would be beneficial to employ measures that afford the opportunity to build and implement more effective strategies.

Domain Analysis

Barry completed the MCMI-III, the MG-PDC, and several other assessment instruments without incident. Although his modifying indices were slightly ambivalent, demonstrating some conflict in desirability/debasement and a relatively low level of disclosure, he did produce a valid protocol. Highlights of his domain analysis from the MG-PDC and Grossman Facet Scales were as follows:

Interpersonally Contrary: Unresolved in terms of whether he wished to be dependent and contrite or assertive and hostile, Barry would unwittingly display interpersonal acts that had, as their cumulative effect, tendencies to frustrate and even infuriate others by virtue of his supposed incompetent responses and inept presentations.

Cognitively Naive: Barry was often described as "having his head in the sand" when it came to recognizing and responding to potential or actualized difficulties; he routinely glossed over problems, denied conflicts of any nature, and questioned, with frequency, "What's everyone so upset about?"

Expressively Resentful: Often procrastinating or resisting expectations, colleagues had said, "Barry will plot for an hour to get out of five minute's worth of work." He often irked others and seemed to get a kind of reinforcement from successfully seeing tasks not completed or thwarted, not recognizing his involvement in their failure.

Therapeutic Steps

A primary goal of treatment with Barry was to aid him in reducing his intense ambivalence and growing resentment of others. With an empathic and brief focus, it was possible to sustain a productive, therapeutic relationship. With a therapist who could convey genuine caring and firmness, Barry was able to overcome his tendency to employ maneuvers to test the sincerity and motives of the therapist. Although he was slow to reveal his resentment because he disliked being viewed as an angry person, it was brought into the open and dealt with in a kind and understanding way. He was not inclined to face his ambivalence, but his mixed feelings and attitudes were a major focus of treatment. To prevent him from trying to terminate treatment before improvement occurred and to forestall relapses, the therapist employed techniques to counter Barry's expectation that supportive figures would ultimately prove disillusioning. Circumscribed *interpersonal* approaches (e.g., Benjamin, Kiesler) were used to deal with the seesaw struggle enacted by Barry in his relationship with the therapist. His *contrary* style was exhibited through ingratiating submissiveness and a concealed yet evident taunting attitude. Similarly, he solicited the therapist's goodwill, but when it was expressed, he rejected it, voicing doubt about the genuineness of the therapist's feelings. Inconsistencies such as these were dealt with by introducing *cognitive confrontations.* It was important to keep those inconsistencies in focus or Barry may have appreciated the therapist's perceptiveness verbally but not altered his attitudes. Involved in an unconscious repetition compulsion in which he re-created disillusioning experiences that paralleled those of the past, Barry came to recognize the expectations *cognitively,* thus setting the stage for further work toward building a less *naive* approach to his self-view. He was also taught to deal with the enactment of expectations interpersonally.

Despite his ambivalent outlook and *resentful behaviors,* there was good reason to operate on the premise that Barry could overcome past disappointments. To capture the love and attention only modestly gained in childhood could not be achieved, although habits that precluded partial satisfaction could be altered in the here and now. Toward that end, the therapist helped him disentangle needs that were in opposition to one another. For example, he both wanted and did not want the love of those on whom he depended. Despite this ambivalence, he entered new relationships, such as in therapy, as if an idyllic state could be achieved. He went through the act of seeking a consistent and true source of love, one that would not betray him as he believed his parents and others did in the past. Despite this optimism, he remained unsure of the trust he could place in others. Mindful of past betrayals and disappointments, he began to test his new relationships to see if they were loyal and faithful. In a parallel manner, he attempted to irritate and frustrate the therapist to check whether he would prove to be as fickle and insubstantial as others had in the past. It was here that the therapist's warm support and firmness, combined with *behavior modification* techniques, played a significant role in reintegrating Barry's expectations and in exhibiting consistency in relationship behavior. The therapist did not set goals too high because Barry may not have been able to tolerate demands or expectations well. Brief therapeutic efforts were directed to build his trust, to focus on positive traits, and to enhance his confidence and self-esteem.

Case 8.2, Claire B., 31

A Skeptical/Negativistic Personality: Abrasive Type (Negativistic with Sadistic Traits)

Presenting Picture

Claire was referred to an employee assistance program following several coworker complaints regarding her interpersonal attitude; an emotional break occurred in one of the appointments, and Claire was referred to outside treatment. She explained, "No one really likes me at work, or really, anywhere." One coworker reported being frightened by her aggressive, critical demeanor. Despite glowing reports regarding the quality of her work, the report stated that her job was in jeopardy owing to her harsh interpersonal manner, her inability to work constructively with others, and her tendency to "snap." "Everyone annoys me and I get angry," Claire explained. "What am I supposed to do? Not react?" The idea of being friendly or establishing some kind of camaraderie with people in her work environment seemed a very foreign notion to her, if not something she would simply reject outright. Reporting very few friends outside of work, no history of relationships that had become substantial, and living alone, Claire also stated that even her cat annoyed her. "He's always getting sick, so I stop feeding him and he doesn't get sick all over the place." Questions regarding her childhood and family of origin met the expected aggressive defense of "What does this have to do with my job?" She did mention, however, that she was the younger of two siblings of elderly parents, her father had died when she was young, and her mother, who had also passed away recently, spent her life constantly disgruntled and annoyed by the fact that she had to work so hard to support her daughter at her more advanced age. "I mean, she told me, I don't know how many times, I was an accident and I prevented her from retiring."

Initial Impressions

In contrast to Barry, who exhibited his struggle between doing what others wish and doing what he wishes in an oblique, if not somewhat passive, manner, Claire, an *abrasive negativist* acted in an overtly and directly contentious and quarrelsome way. To Claire, everything and anyone served as a sounding board for discharging her inner irritabilities, readily available objects for assaulting. More than merely irritable in a general way, she was intentionally abrasive and antagonistic. Not surprisingly, Claire exhibited features usually associated with the sadistic personality prototype. She had incessant discords with others that magnified every minor friction into repeated and bitter personal struggles. She insisted that her quarrelsomeness was dedicated to certain high principles; though a kernel of truth may be found in her belief, these higher principles corresponded to positions she herself held, never those held by others. Others were unquestionably wrong; she was unquestionably right. She was fault-finding and dogmatic and found her greatest satisfaction not so much in the legitimacy and logic of her arguments as in the fact that arguing served to demean others and retaliate against them. The hostile and opposing manners of an abrasive negativist such as Claire were part of the core of her being. Her knack of belittling and denigrating anyone in the name of whatever principle she happened to espouse was well-rehearsed and persistent. Derogation of others was "good for them." Believing that she got no personal satisfaction in telling people off or in having ulterior motives for doing so, she felt unconstrained, free to say and do anything she pleased "to set people right."

It was evident to those with whom Claire related that her pretensions of principled behavior were but a thin veneer. Faced with any opposition, especially from persons she considered of lesser stature than herself, she would spew forth bitter complaints of how she had been ill treated by others and how unappreciated she was. As a result of these direct attacks, the deeper origins of her personality style were reactivated. Recriminations and counteractions were refueled. She claimed that anything personal she had done to others did not really reflect her character, but was merely a justified reaction to the uncaring treatment to which she had been exposed. Initially, Claire did not accede to a therapeutic focus that would seek to explore aspects of herself, as she rejected the premise that she was responsible for current difficulties. She would need to establish a less impulsive style of interacting (balance toward diminishing *active* and encouraging *passive* style), which would be a pragmatic and concrete goal with which she could resonate. This would serve as a preamble to focus on countering perpetuations such as her perception that she needed to be defensive and antagonistic in response to what she felt was ambivalent and perhaps harmful treatment from others, and what was most likely brought on by her abrasive style (clarification of *self–other* conflict). From here, it would be useful to explore less caustic relational styles, which would encourage empathy and alleviate her salient *pain* orientation.

Domain Analysis

Claire was not compliant in taking personality assessments, leaving self-report measures unfinished. The MG-PDC was used to complete her domain analysis, which revealed these three most salient domains:

Expressively Resentful: Claire seemed to derive a sense of satisfaction from undermining others, thwarting their more positive experiences and accomplishments with demoralizing statements and vitriolic acts. She regularly acted in a socially irksome manner, where resentfulness was more the rule than the exception.

Cognitively Dogmatic: Though they were a thin veil for her true motivations and beliefs, which had to do more with her inner feelings of hurt and disappointment, Claire routinely grasped at "higher principles" and social imperatives as a justification for her bitterness and often spiteful acts and statements.

Interpersonally Abrasive: Claire could often be vicious and abusive in her interactions with others, and although she did not admit to a sense of pleasure from this, she did derive a great deal of satisfaction in intimidating and humiliating those she deemed flawed or compromised.

Therapeutic Steps

A circumscribed and focused approach was optimally suited for Claire, as she was loath to deeper introspective measures. She was hardly a willing participant in therapy initially, agreeing to treatment only under the pressure of vocational difficulties. For the therapist, a most important aspect of the therapeutic relationship was restraining any impulse to express more negative attitudes. Nevertheless, Claire did actively impede early progress toward conflict resolution and goal attainment, often undoing what was accomplished in treatment by the next session. The therapist's committed and professional approach prevented relapses by confronting the ambivalence that often robbed Claire of what steps she had secured toward progress. Formal *behavior modification* methods were fruitfully explored to combat inconsistencies in her expressions, and she did learn to see the benefits of altering *resentful acts* and the consequences of doing so. Through observation of simple behavioral changes, practiced in vivo first in her office, and then in more personal contexts, she noted changes in the reactions of others and a greater sense of satisfaction than could be achieved via her older coping strategies. This opened the door for a *catalytic sequence* to directive *cognitive* techniques, such as those of Meichenbaum and Ellis. These were productively employed to confront Claire with the obstructive and self-defeating character of her expectations and her personal relations. For example, she was facing difficulty as a consequence of aggressive behavior and incessant quarrels, but each of these was diminished when she viewed her behavior differently and acquired other means of fulfilling the needs that drove them. With the addition of confrontive methods aimed at loosening her *dogmatic* attitude, she learned not to assume that a problem could always be traced to another person's stupidity, laziness, or hostility.

Although the deeply rooted character of Claire's problems impeded the effectiveness of most therapeutic procedures, it was beneficial to explore the more incisive techniques of *interpersonal* therapies (e.g., Benjamin, Kiesler). A thorough reconstruction of personality was not necessarily the only means of altering her deeper pathologies. In support of these interpersonal techniques, a *group therapy* setting was also used to focus on the *abrasive* pattern that sustained her personality style by providing reinforcement through surface satisfaction from undermining others, but ultimately left her feeling unfulfilled and lonely. Together with cognitive reframing procedures, this combination proved to be highly useful in helping Claire recognize the source of her own hurt and angry feelings and to appreciate how she provoked hurt and anger in others. As she found it possible to accept a measure of responsibility for her difficulties, she did not find it necessary to conclude that she had been tricked into admitting it.

Throughout the entirety of the process, the therapist conveyed a sense of trust and a willingness to develop a constructive alliance. A balance of professional authority and tolerance was useful in diminishing the probability that Claire would relapse or impulsively withdraw from treatment.

Case 8.3, Pam S., 34

A Skeptical/Negativistic Personality: Discontented Type (Negativist with Depressive Traits)

Presenting Picture

When Pam presented for her first therapy appointment at her husband's insistence, she quickly became fully exasperated with basic interview questions. Almost immediately turning on the therapist when asked what she felt was most important to address, she barked, "Listen, first of all, *you're* the doctor, *I* don't even know what's going on, and I'm not a shrink, that's your job!" With some effort and rapport building, she then regained some control of her affect, and she admitted, contritely, that she really wanted to fix her relationship with her husband, "with whatever it takes. I don't care. Just, I don't know, do your voodoo that you do."

Pam claimed that she couldn't gain any emotional space in her marriage, although she did admit that it wasn't her husband who was too "clingy" or demanding; it was she. She then mused, "I must drive him crazy, but that's me!" She then detailed several episodes when she had set up impossible and frustrating situations to which her husband would inevitably succumb. That, she explained, was where she came in. "I don't know what makes me do it, but I'd see him bumble and then I'd be totally disgusted with him and I'd kind of let him know it, but knowing he couldn't possibly do right. But I didn't care." She seemed to show little concern that her corrosive behaviors and antagonism might cause unrest for anyone else but herself. Very defensive and unwilling to cooperate in responding to very general questions, Pam stated bitterly, "You get personal, *fast.*" It was immediately apparent that she was entirely ill at ease with exploring any aspects of her needs or behaviors, and she would inevitably see it as a huge burden to be asked to modify any of her own viewpoints or expectations.

Initial Impressions

From the foregoing, it was clear that Pam exhibited features akin to depressive personalities, especially those of the ill-humored subtype. Pam's pattern, termed the *discontented negativist,* often shows embitterment, complaints, and pessimism, but unlike many other negativists, she was neither indirect in her expression of disillusion and displeasure, nor was she consciously contentious and abrasive. This negativist is the consummate griper. She did not assault others in a harsh and brutal fashion; rather, she attacked under cover, from behind some pretense from which she took piecemeal potshots. She would leave her object of criticism somewhat unprotected, often with no clear response to make. Her complaints essentially reflected her hidden resentments and her deep discontents about life. She wouldn't provide real solutions to the problems she would gripe about; in fact, she often instigated the problem. Hence, her apparently worthwhile observations were merely sly ways to discharge her personal dissatisfactions, ways that ultimately intensified problems rather than resulting in their resolution. Pam did not risk open battles and confrontations. Rather, she sought to undercut her adversaries, to make them look inept or ridiculous, hence reaffirming the correctness of her own views, without directly endangering herself or being overwhelmed by the counteractions of others. She used the cover of minor and tangential slights to avoid being exposed. Whereas some negativists (e.g., the circuitous subtype) hide completely behind the veneer of seeming indifference and passivity, Pam was open, but not confrontational, using small cuts rather than coarse and abrasive actions. Her complaints were merely safe ploys to discharge her deeper discontents, struggles, and conflicts. She acted as if she were exasperated with the problems at hand, giving evidence thereby of being a person of goodwill and good intentions who has had to struggle with the inefficiencies and ineptitude of others. Hence, there was a sense of puzzlement, if not bewilderment, among those who perceptively recognized her underlying anger. Should they try to examine the legitimate problems about which Pam had complained, or should they confront her for being an annoyingly persistent crank and grumbler? She was skilled in complaining about the characteristics of associates and relatives, accusing them of being incompetent and negativistic, precisely those attributes she possessed herself. Not able to fulfill her own wishes successfully, nor to discharge her resentments directly, Pam demeaned the power and stature of competing others, and thereby appeared to rise up in relative stature. She claimed that it was others who had fallen short; she, personally, was blameless and innocent.

Pam was caught in a conflict between her need for self-expression and her resentment of those who had achieved it. This further intensified the inner conflict that gave rise to her fundamental problem between self and other. Early treatment would focus on establishing a trusting, empathic, and supportive environment, as the source of much of Pam's discontent was perceived shortcomings. As more directed interventions were called for, a note of caution would be prudent, as she would be likely to suffer setbacks and possible depressive episodes if her usual coping strategies were altered too quickly. It would be wise to implement modalities aimed at alleviating disgruntled moods and establishing more effective social skills. From there, it would be appropriate to alter such perpetuations as chronic pessimism and creation of disillusionment and resentfulness toward others (reduction of *pain* orientation), along with strengthening her troubled social environment by creating more satisfying interactions. In other words, this would constitute a clarification of *self–other* issues, as well as enhance *pleasure*.

Domain Analysis

Although she initially was unreceptive to testing, Pam did eventually accede to the domain assessment, which revealed the following most salient domains:

Displacement Mechanism: Pam indirectly discharged her anger onto others by either finding and exploiting minor faults or problems, or by more actively orchestrating situations whereby others would fail to meet her expectations, giving her license to disapprove or grumble without reproach.

Cognitively Pessimistic: Most of Pam's thought content revolved around viewing events negatively, finding hopelessness in otherwise innocuous situations, and even creating self-fulfilling prophecies in which she could find reinforcement in "proving" how terrible or upsetting others were to her.

Discontented Self-Image: Maneuvers such as those just described were a thinly veiled strategy for hiding Pam's innate sense of personal failure, unachieved wishes, and lack of fulfillment, as well as her feelings of being unappreciated and denigrated throughout much of her life.

Therapeutic Steps

Because of an intense ambivalence between her desire for reassurance and nurturance and her fear of trusting an unknown person, Pam required an early warm and attentive attitude on the part of the therapist. As the therapist was able to engage her early on, she was not disposed to employ repetitive maneuvers to test the sincerity and motives of the therapist. Toward the goal of reducing the likelihood of decompensation, the therapist did not set goals too high or press changes too quickly. A watchword of this intervention was caution; should Pam feel overwhelmed by losing innate strategies such as her *displacement mechanism* too quickly, whether at earlier or later stages of treatment, she may have left therapy abruptly, with possibly an even greater sense of aggravation regarding the motives and actions of others. To this end, initial efforts were directed to build Pam's trust before planting the seed for any deeper personality-restructuring efforts.

To begin, *client-centered* principles and procedures designed to orient her attention to her positive traits and to enhance her confidence and self-esteem were implemented to explore personal *discontentment* in a manner that was less threatening. Here, she was able to identify and subsequently avoid environmental pressures that aggravated her anxieties and dejection, as well as begin to acknowledge and have validated her concerns about her own self-worth. This was an essential building of confidence in this procedure, which would provide a foundation to be able to address much harder, self-reflective questions that would follow regarding her social and familial interactions and her habitual routines that kept interpersonal conflict and friction in place. Notably, attention needed to be directed toward anticipating quasi-suicidal gestures in moments where she felt personally vulnerable or when significant realizations became apparent. Pam could be impulsive either when she felt guilty or when she sought a dramatic form of retribution. The therapist helped her recognize the sources and character of her ambivalence and reinforced a more realistic and optimistic outlook on life. Because she entered treatment in an agitated state, the reduction of these anxieties and guilt was an early goal of treatment.

As Pam gained trust in the therapeutic relationship and was able to independently voice and address her self-generated conflicts, it was possible to begin incorporating several more focused, directive techniques to begin changing expectations and frustrating transactions. Deeper *insight-oriented* approaches were not necessary and may even have been counterproductive, as Pam appeared to need greater evidence to change more benevolent beliefs about herself and the people around her. Therefore, "new experience before new insight" (e.g., Strupp & Binder, 1984) was a strong paradigm in which to work. First, circumscribed *behavior modification* methods were explored to focus on social behavior that could be strengthened in a relatively short time period, with *cognitive* techniques following to confront Pam with the obstructive and self-defeating character of her *pessimistic* beliefs and expectations. Her relations with significant others were strengthened by employing a number of *interpersonal* treatment techniques (e.g., Klerman, Benjamin). These combined approaches evidenced the benefits of changed perspectives and actions and left Pam wondering, "What was the upset all about?" A final stage saw the implementation of preliminary *object-relations* work to give Pam an opportunity to find explanatory concepts for her perpetual *displacement* of anger and guilt and to create self-derived solutions for these perplexities. Such approaches were handled cautiously, however, lest she succumb to feelings of failure or become unduly guilt-ridden or depressed. Of great benefit was to stabilize Pam and help her control her vacillations of mood and behavior. In this way, the possibility of setbacks or deterioration in her condition was diminished.

Environmentally, throughout the course of treatment, efforts were made to reduce the stressors of her home life. Working with family members was necessary. Had they not been optimally motivated, treatment may have called for more intensive techniques to reduce the possibility of setbacks. There was also the possibility of Pam's withdrawal from treatment should she resist facing the humiliation of confronting painful memories and feelings. With a nurturant and empathic attitude, the therapist was able to overcome her fear of reexperiencing false hopes and disappointments. The warmth and understanding of the therapist moderated Pam's expectation that others would be rejecting, which would have led her to pull back, thereby cutting off experiences that might have proved gratifying had they been completed. It was important to decrease her anticipation of loss, which may have prompted her into a self-fulfilling prophecy. Without focused attention, she may have defeated the chance to experience events that could promote change and growth.

Case 8.4, Liz J., 29

A Skeptical/Negativistic Personality: Vacillating Type (Negativistic with Borderline Traits)

Presenting Picture

At first, it seemed hard to believe that Liz, a returning college student, was presenting for therapy because of "ferocious arguments that bordered on the violent" with her husband, although she stated, "I really don't see it that way. I mean, I'm usually a very happy person, but I have my moments." Rather charming and friendly at the outset of the interview, Liz had an ingratiating smile and a sense of comfort, although it soon became apparent that her beguiling presentation would not consistently sustain. Currently, Liz was studying art and enjoying her course of study considerably. Her guardedness and impulsive defensiveness first struck when the therapist asked about her pursuit of a bachelor's at a nontraditional age; her smile dissipated quickly and she said matter-of-factly, "That's none of your damned business." A moment later, she was apologizing for her harshness, recanting and saying, "Yeah, I guess, actually, it *is* your business."

Liz swayed often between several different moods without provocation. Her elongated college career was a result of many changes in major courses of study. She would start very enthusiastically, but as she reached more advanced coursework and varying moods struck, she would lose interest and even become somewhat agitated with the "stupidity" of the work. She also found the tight schedule of the "nine-to-five" world, in which she currently worked as a customer service representative, entirely frustrating because it lacked the flexibility for what she described as her "off-times"—those times where she "can't handle dealing with other people." Although she had found contentment in studying art, where adherence to a schedule was a secondary consideration, mood swings prompted her husband's request for her to visit the therapist's office. She admitted that she often took her frustrations and sour moods out on him, but then, "I'd always make it up to him." He was always bewildered after what he called "one of Liz's episodes," and he was complaining that as a very laid-back individual, he was experiencing too much stress stemming from Liz's unpredictability.

Initial Impressions

Although Liz's primary characteristics are seen among most negativists, the quality of rapid fluctuation from one emotional state or interpersonal attitude to another is particularly notable in *vacillating negativists*. Liz was experienced by others, particularly her husband, as upsetting and frustrating because of her sharp and frequent reversals of mood and behavior. At times she was affectionate, predictable, and interesting and charming. But in the blink of an eye, she became irritable, oppositional, and disagreeable. The next moment, she was self-assured, decisive, and competent; then she reverted to being dependently clinging and childlike. Tantrums were quite common, frequently moving to the foreground and evidencing her characteristic recalcitrant behaviors and emotional instabilities. She could become almost childlike in other ways: being disagreeably disobedient one moment, and submissively conforming the next. Most characteristic, however, was her bewildering and enigmatic emotions, her inability to fathom her own capricious and mystifying moods, and her subjective wavering and intrapsychic fluctuations.

Liz was actively ambivalent. Her oscillation was rapid, with extremes of emotion. What made her difficult to grasp was that her behaviors and emotional states were unpredictable, changing from one moment to the next for no obvious reason. Her ambivalence was not only a matter of public appearance, but also belied internal conflict. For example, her self-image shifted rapidly: She disparaged herself at one moment and acted pleased and superior the next. In many ways, Liz's vacillating negativistic personality is a dilute variant of the borderline personality. However, the ambivalence of the borderline is exhibited in all spheres of expression, between being passive or active, between seeking pleasure or pain, and being self-focused one moment and other-focused the next. By contrast, Liz's struggle was centered largely on the polarity of self versus other. As a result, her intrapsychic ambivalence was more limited in its underlying scope and makeup, resulting in a less severe form of pathology than seen in the borderline.

Before more directive methods could be utilized, Liz needed to view the therapeutic environment as a safe and trusting atmosphere, and an empathic but steadfast posture from the therapist would help her begin to interact in a way that would not require her characteristic defenses and hostilities. As her comfort in session increased, therapy would address beliefs that stood to undermine her confidence and perpetuate her erratic and impulsive emotions. Her social strategies would be examined in tandem with these thought structures to further clarify her conflicts between *self* and *other,* as well as to lessen her very *active* stance in continually expecting disappointment and disillusionment and warding off these difficulties with impulsive and inefficient tactics.

Domain Analysis

Following her early expression of frustration in the initial interview, Liz became contrite and eager to please, and she cooperated fully in her domain analysis. She did, however, produce a profile that suggested minor "faking good," and score adjustments were made. The MG-PDC illuminated the following areas as salient domains:

Interpersonally Contrary/Paradoxical: Both conflictual and manipulative in her interpersonal behavior, Liz effectively kept people off-guard by her unpredictability. She was very labile in her interactions, with this tendency demonstrating an overtly instrumental quality. The severity of her self–other conflict suggested negativistic and borderline interpersonal qualities.

Cognitively Capricious: Liz's perceptions of her environment experienced vacillations, inconsistencies, and fluctuations, usually tied to immediate stimuli, whether external events or personal reflections; the quality of these cognitions generally reflected more extreme, nonsubtle viewpoints emphasizing the most potent possible meaning.

Discontented Self-Image: Unlike the borderline's uncertain identity, Liz had a fairly clear, though pessimistically skewed, self-view of being luckless, jilted, misunderstood, and passed over. Because of much of this perceived unfair treatment, she had begun to internalize this phenomenological perception as less worthy and undeserving, facets she felt she had to make up for by acting pleasant and charming.

Therapeutic Steps

Early goals in this intervention included the facilitation of autonomy, the building of confidence, and the overcoming of fears of self-determination. As anticipated, there was a period of intermittent resistance. The therapist needed to encourage a more independent and self-assured perspective, even from the beginning, but this needed to be accomplished in a manner that Liz would not perceive as rejection.

Trust-building measures were taken in the context of a directive, humanistic approach utilizing *motivational interviewing* principles (Hettema et al., 2005) to engage Liz in discovering her ambivalent motivations and resolving inconsistencies revolving around her *discontented self-image*. These initial measures also helped to prevent disappointment, dejection, and even rage in the therapeutic relationship, as even this supportive, empathic approach included unfamiliar self-challenges. These potential reactions were to be expected, given Liz's characteristic style, and they needed to be responded to with equanimity if fundamental changes were to be explored and relapses prevented. When a sound and secure therapeutic alliance was established, the patient learned to tolerate many of her more contrary and conflictual feelings, setting the foundation for later social skill-building and thought modification measures.

Learning how to face and handle her unstable emotions needed to be coordinated with the strengthening of more stable, less *capricious* attitudes through *cognitive* methods such as those of Beck et al. (2003) and associates, as well as those of Ellis. Primary among these methods were measures aimed at correcting specific cognitive distortions such as dichotomous thinking and "awfulizing," learning that there is a spectrum of degrees of intensity to any given event. Further, as Liz began to acknowledge these shades of gray, she spontaneously began making the observation that a single event often has both positive and negative qualities, but this does not have the inevitability of corrosive conflict. Building on these cognitive skills, the therapist was then able to work in *interpersonal* procedures such as those of Kiesler and Benjamin, and also was able to serve as a model to demonstrate how feelings, conflicts, and uncertainties could be approached and resolved with reasonable equanimity and foresight. In this regard, Liz learned alternatives to the *contrary* and often *paradoxical* social behaviors she had come to rely on. Also beneficial, after some headway was made in this modality, was *couples therapy* with her husband, implemented, in part, to test these newly learned attitudes and strategies in a more natural setting than that found in individual treatment.

Resistances and Risks

Negativistic patients frequently decompensate into anxiety and depressive disorders. Therapists must be on guard to anticipate suicidal attempts as ambivalent personalities can act quite impulsively when they feel guilty, need attention, or seek a dramatic form of retribution. Because these patients often enter treatment in an agitated state, an early treatment task is to calm their anxieties and fears. Relieved of tension, many will lose the incentive to continue treatment. Motivating them to pursue a more substantial course of therapy may call for considerable effort on the part of the therapist as these personalities are deeply ambivalent about dependency relationships. They desire to be nurtured and loved by a powerful parental figure, but such submission poses the threat of loss and undermines the desire to maintain independence.

A seesaw struggle is often enacted between patient and therapist; the negativist is likely to exhibit an ingratiating submissiveness on one occasion, and a taunting and demanding attitude on another. Similarly, these patients may solicit the therapist's affections, but when these are expressed, the patient rejects them, voicing doubt about the genuineness of the therapist's feelings. When the therapist points out these contradictory attitudes, patients may verbally appreciate the therapist's perceptiveness but not alter their attitudes at all.

It becomes clear that the roundabout tactics negativists employ to air their grievances can take many different forms in the therapeutic setting. Delaying payments, late arrivals, forgetting appointments, not remembering to do homework, poor boundaries, and anger projection are just a few examples of the many resistances encountered. These patients are likely to use the ambiguity inherent in the therapeutic setting as an excuse for withdrawing or enacting passive-aggressive maneuvers.

If therapy has moderated the negativist's pathology to the point where he or she can satisfactorily fulfill social and occupational obligations without causing friction, treatment should be considered successful. Only in select cases can therapy become a major corrective force for more fundamental personality change.

REFERENCES

Abraham, K. (1968). Notes on the psychoanalytic investigation and treatment of manic-depressive insanity and allied conditions. In *Selected papers of Karl Abraham*. London: Hogarth. (Original work published 1911)

Abramson, L., Seligman, M., & Teasdale, J. (1978). Learned helplessness in humans: Critique and reformulation. *Journal of Abnormal Psychology, 87*, 49–74.

Affsprung, E. H. (1998). Closet narcissistic disorder and the college student. *Journal of College Student Psychotherapy, 13*, 5–19.

Agass, D. (2000). Aspects of narcissism in a once-weekly psychotherapy. *British Journal of Psychotherapy, 17*, 37–50.

Aizawa, N. (2002). Grandiose traits and hypersensitive traits of the narcissistic personality. *Japanese Journal of Educational Psychology, 50*, 215–224.

Akiskal, H. S. (1980). External validating criteria for psychiatric diagnosis: Their application in affective disorders. *Journal of Clinical Psychiatry, 41*(12 Sec 2).

Alarcon, R. D. (1996). Personality disorders and culture in *DSM-IV:* A critique. *Journal of Personality Disorders, 10*, 260–270.

Albert, U., Maina, G., Forner, F., & Bogetto, F. (2004). *DSM-IV* obsessive-compulsive personality disorder: Prevalence in patients with anxiety disorders and in healthy comparison subjects. *Comprehensive Psychiatry, 45*, 325–332.

Arkowitz, H. (1992). Integrative theories of therapy. In D. K. Freedhein & H. J. Freudenberger (Eds.), *History of psychotherapy: A century of change* (pp. 261–303). Washington, DC: American Psychological Association.

Arkowitz, H. (1997). Integrative theories of therapy. In P. L. Wachtel & S. B. Messer (Eds.), *Theories of psychotherapy: Origins and evolution* (pp. 227–288). Washington, DC: American Psychological Association.

Arntz, A., Dreessen, L., Schouten, E., & Weertman, A. (2004). Beliefs in personality disorders: A test with the Personality Disorder Belief Questionnaire. *Behavior Research and Therapy, 42*, 1215–1225.

Bandura, A., & Walters, R. H. (1959). *Adolescent aggression*. New York: Ronald.

Battle, C. L., Shea, M. T., Johnson, D. M., Yen, S., Zlotnick, C., Zanarini, M. C., et al. (2004). Childhood maltreatment associated with adult personality disorders: Findings from the Collaborative Longitudinal Personality Disorders Study. *Journal of Personality Disorders, 18*, 193–211.

Beck, A. T. (1974). *Coping with depression*. New York: Institute for Rational-Emotive Therapy.

Beck, A. T., Butler, A. C., Brown, G. K., Dahlsgaard, K. K., Newman, C. F., & Beck, J. S. (2001). Dysfunctional beliefs discriminate personality disorders. *Behavior Research and Therapy, 39*, 1213–1225.

Beck, A. T., & Freeman, A. (1990). *Cognitive therapy of personality disorders*. New York: Basic Books.

Beck, A. T., Freeman, A., & Davis, D. D. (2003). *Cognitive therapy of personality disorders* (2nd ed.). New York: Guilford Press.

Bender, D. S. (2005). The therapeutic alliance in the treatment of personality disorders. *Journal of Psychiatric Practice, 11*, 73–87.

Benjamin, L. S. (1990). Interpersonal analysis of the cathartic model. In R. Plutchick & H. Kellerman (Eds.), *Emotion: Theory, research, and experience* (Vol. 5, pp. 209–229). San Diego, CA: Academic Press.

Benjamin, L. S. (1993). *Interpersonal diagnosis and treatment of personality disorders*. New York: Guilford Press.

Benjamin, L. S. (2005). Interpersonal theory of personality disorders: The structural analysis of social behavior and interpersonal reconstructive therapy. In M. Lenzenweger & J. Clarkin (Eds.), *Major theories of personality* (2nd ed.). New York: Guilford Press.

Benjamin, L. S., & Cushing, G. (2004). An interpersonal family-oriented approach to personality disorder. In M. M. MacFarlane (Ed.), *Family treatment of personality disorders: Advances in clinical practice* (pp. 41–69). Binghamton, NY: Haworth Clinical Practice Press.

Benning, S. D., Patrick, C. J., Blonigen, D. M., Hicks, B. M., & Iacono, W. G. (2005). Estimating facets of psychopathy from normal personality traits: A step toward community epidemiological investigations. *Assessment, 12*, 3–18.

Bergin, A. E., & Lambert, M. J. (1978). The evaluation of therapeutic outcomes. In S. L. Garfield & A. E. Bergin (Eds.), *Handbook of psychotherapy and behavior change* (2nd ed.). New York: Wiley.

Berk, S., & Rhodes, B. (2005). Maladaptive dependency traits in men. *Bulletin of the Menninger Clinic, 69*, 187–205.

Bhar, S. S., & Kyrios, M. (2005). Obsessions and compulsions are associated with different cognitive and mood factors. *Behavior Change, 22*, 81–96.

Bienvenu, O. J., & Brandes, M. (2005). The interface of personality traits and anxiety disorders. *Primary Psychiatry, 12*, 35–39.

Binder, J. (1979). *Choosing the appropriate form of time-limited dynamic psychotherapy*. Charlottesville: University of Virginia Medical Center.

Binder, J. L. (2004). *Key competencies in brief dynamic psychotherapy: Clinical practice beyond the manual*. New York: Guilford Press.

Birbaumer, N., Veit, R., Lotze, M., Erb, M., Hermann, C., Grodd, W., et al. (2005). Deficient fear conditioning in psychopathy: A functional magnetic resonance imaging study. *Archives of General Psychiatry, 62*, 799–805.

Blackburn, R. (1993). *The psychology of criminal conduct.* Chichester, England: Wiley.

Blackburn, R., Logan, C., Renwick, S. J. D., & Donnelly, J. P. (2005). Higher-order dimensions of personality disorder: Hierarchical structure and relationships with the five-factor model, the interpersonal circle, and psychopathy. *Journal of Personality Disorders, 19,* 597–623.

Blair, R. J. R. (2005). Applying a cognitive neuroscience perspective to the disorder of psychopathy. *Development and Psychopathology, 17,* 865–891.

Blair, R. J. R., Mitchell, D. G. V., Peschardt, K. S., Colledge, E., Leonard, R. A., Shine, J. H., et al. (2004). Reduced sensitivity to others' fearful expressions in psychopathic individuals. *Personality and Individual Differences, 37,* 1111–1122.

Blair, R. J. R., Peschardt, K. S., Budhani, S., Mitchell, D. G. V., & Pine, D. S. (2006). The development of psychopathy. *Journal of Child Psychology and Psychiatry, 47,* 262–275.

Blatt, S. (1974). Levels of object representation in anaclitic and introjective depression. *Psychoanalytic Study of the Child, 29,* 107–157.

Blatt, S. (2004). *Experiences of depression.* Washington, DC: American Psychological Association.

Blatt, S. J., & Shichman, S. (1983). Two primary configurations of psychopathology. *Psychoanalysis and Contemporary Thought, 6,* 187–254.

Blizard, R. A. (2001). Masochistic and sadistic ego states: Dissociative solutions to the dilemma of attachment to an abusive caretaker. *Journal of Trauma and Dissociation, 2,* 37–58.

Blonigen, D. M., Hicks, B. M., Krueger, R. F., Patrick, C. J., & Iacono, W. G. (2005). Psychopathic personality traits: Heritability and genetic overlap with internalizing and externalizing psychopathology. *Psychological Medicine, 35,* 637–648.

Bolognini, M., Plancherel, B., Laget, J., Halfon, O., Corcos, M., & Jeammet, P. (2003). Depression and dependency: Which relationship? *Psychology: Journal of the Hellenic Psychological Society, 10,* 270–278.

Bornstein, R. F. (1998). Implicit and self-attributed dependency needs in dependent and histrionic personality disorders. *Journal of Personality Assessment, 71,* 1–14.

Bornstein, R. F. (1999). Histrionic personality disorder, physical attractiveness, and social adjustment. *Journal of Psychopathology and Behavioral Assessment, 21,* 79–94.

Bornstein, R. F. (2004). Integrating cognitive and existential treatment strategies in psychotherapy with dependent patients. *Journal of Contemporary Psychotherapy, 34*(4), 293–309.

Bornstein, R. F., Hilsenroth, M. J., Padawer, J. R., & Fowler, J. C. (2000). Interpersonal dependency and personality pathology: Variations in Rorschach Oral Dependency scores across Axis II disorders. *Journal of Personality Assessment, 75,* 478–491.

Borton, J. L. S., Markowitz, L. J., & Dieterich, J. (2005). Effects of suppressing negative self-referent thoughts on mood and self-esteem. *Journal of Social and Clinical Psychology, 24,* 172–190.

Brašic, J. R. (2002). A creative senior citizen with likely bipolar II disorder and likely histrionic personality disorder expresses herself. *German Journal of Psychiatry, 5,* 5–23.

Britton, R. (2004). Narcissistic disorders in clinical practice. *Journal of Analytical Psychology, 49,* 477–490.

Burnette, M. L., & Newman, D. L. (2005). The natural history of conduct disorder symptoms in female inmates: On the predictive utility of the syndrome in severely antisocial women. *American Journal of Orthopsychiatry, 75,* 421–430.

Cale, E. M., & Lilienfeld, S. O. (2002). Histrionic personality disorder and antisocial personality disorder: Sex-differentiated manifestations of psychopathy? *Journal of Personality Disorders, 16,* 52–72.

Cale, E. M., & Lilienfeld, S. O. (2006). Psychopathy factors and risk for aggressive behavior: A test of the "threatened egotism" hypothesis. *Law and Human Behavior, 30,* 51–74.

Callaghan, G. M., Summers, C. J., & Weidman, M. (2003). The treatment of histrionic and narcissistic personality disorder behaviors: A single-subject demonstration of clinical improvement using functional analytic psychotherapy. *Journal of Contemporary Psychotherapy, 33,* 321–339.

Carlson, J., Melton, K. A., & Snow, K. (2004). Family treatment of passive-aggressive (negativistic) personality disorder. In M. M. MacFarlane (Ed.), *Family treatment of personality disorders: Advances in clinical practice* (pp. 241–272). Binghamton, NY: Haworth Clinical Practice Press.

Cartwright, D. (2002). The narcissistic exoskeleton: The defensive organization of the rage-type murderer. *Bulletin of the Menninger Clinic, 66,* 1–18.

Chabrol, H., & Leichsenring, F. (2006). Borderline personality organization and psychopathic traits in nonclinical adolescents: Relationships of identity diffusion, primitive defense mechanisms and reality testing with callousness and impulsivity traits. *Bulletin of the Menninger Clinic, 70,* 160–170.

Cleckley, H. (1941). *The mask of sanity.* St. Louis, MO: Mosby.

Cogswell, A., & Alloy, L. B. (2006). The relation of neediness and Axis II pathology. *Journal of Personality Disorders, 20,* 16–21.

Coid, J. W. (1999). Aetiological risk factors for personality disorders. *British Journal of Psychiatry, 174,* 530–538.

Coid, J. W. (2003). The co-morbidity of personality disorder and lifetime clinical syndromes in dangerous offenders. *Journal of Forensic Psychiatry and Psychology, 14,* 341–366.

Cooke, D. J., Michie, C., Hart, S. D., & Clark, D. A. (2004). Reconstructing psychopathy: Clarifying the significance of antisocial and socially deviant behavior in the diagnosis of psychopathic personality disorder. *Journal of Personality Disorders, 18,* 337–357.

Cooke, D. J., Michie, C., Hart, S. D., & Clark, D. A. (2005). Searching for the pan-cultural core of psychopathic personality disorder. *Personality and Individual Differences, 39,* 283–295.

Coolidge, F. L., DenBoer, J. W., & Segal, D. L. (2004). Personality and neuropsychological correlates of bullying behavior. *Personality and Individual Differences, 36,* 1559–1569.

Coolidge, F. L., Thede, L. L., & Jang, K. L. (2001). Heritability of personality disorders in childhood: A preliminary investigation. *Journal of Personality Disorders, 15,* 33–40.

Craig, R. J. (2003). Use of the Millon Clinical Multiaxial Inventory in the psychological assessment of domestic violence: A review. *Aggression and Violent Behavior, 8,* 235–244.

Craig, R. J., & Bivens, A. (2000). MCMI-III scores on substance abusers with and without histories of suicide attempts. *Substance Abuse, 21,* 155–161.

Craighead, L. W., Craighead, W. E., Kazdin, A. E., & Mahoney, M. J. (Eds.). (1994). *Cognitive and behavioral interventions: An empirical approach to mental health problems.* Boston: Allyn & Bacon.

Cramer, V., Torgersen, S., & Kringlen, E. (2003). Personality disorders, prevalence, sociodemographic correlations, quality of life, dysfunction, and the question of continuity. *PTT: Persönlichkeitsstörungen Theorie und Therapie, 7,* 189–198.

Crawford, T. N., Cohen, P., & Brook, J. S. (2001a). Dramatic-erratic personality disorder symptoms: Pt. I. Continuity from early adolescence into adulthood. *Journal of Personality Disorders, 15,* 319–335.

Crawford, T. N., Cohen, P., & Brook, J. S. (2001b). Dramatic-erratic personality disorder symptoms: Pt. II. Developmental pathways from early adolescence to adulthood. *Journal of Personality Disorders, 15,* 336–350.

Dadds, M. R., Fraser, J., Frost, A., & Hawes, D. J. (2005). Disentangling the underlying dimensions of psychopathy and conduct problems in childhood: A community study. *Journal of Consulting and Clinical Psychology, 73,* 400–410.

Davidson, K., & Tyrer, P. (1996). Cognitive therapy for antisocial and borderline personality disorders: Single case study series. *British Journal of Clinical Psychology, 35*(3), 413–429.

DeMatteo, D., Heilbrun, K., & Marczyk, G. (2006). An empirical investigation of psychopathy in a noninstitutionalized and noncriminal sample. *Behavioral Sciences and the Law, 24,* 133–146.

Dickinson, K. A., & Pincus, A. L. (2003). Interpersonal analysis of grandiose and vulnerable narcissism. *Journal of Personality Disorders, 17*(3), 226–236.

D'Silva, K., Duggan, C., & McCarthy, L. (2004). Does treatment really make psychopaths worse? A review of the evidence. *Journal of Personality Disorders, 18,* 163–177.

Edens, J. F. (2006). Unresolved controversies concerning psychopathy: Implications for clinical and forensic decision making. *Professional Psychology: Research and Practice, 37,* 59–65.

Edens, J. F., Marcus, D. K., Lilienfeld, S. O., & Poythress, N. G., Jr. (2006). Psychopathic, not psychopath: Taxometric evidence for the dimensional structure of psychopathy. *Journal of Abnormal Psychology, 115,* 131–144.

Eldridge, N., & Gould, S. (1972). Punctuated equilibria: An alternative to phyletic gradualism. In T. Schopf (Ed.), *Models in paleobiology.* San Francisco: Freeman.

Ellis, A. (1979). *Theoretical and empirical foundations of rational-emotive therapy.* Monterey, CA: Brooks/Cole.

Farmer, R. F., Nash, H. M., & Dance, D. (2004). Mood patterns and variations associated with personality disorder pathology. *Comprehensive Psychiatry, 45,* 289–303.

Farrington, D. P. (2005). The importance of child and adolescent psychopathy. *Journal of Abnormal Child Psychology, 33,* 489–497.

Fava, M., Farabaugh, A. H., Sickinger, A. H., Wright, E., Alpert, J. E., Sonawalla, S., et al. (2002). Personality disorders and depression. *Psychological Medicine, 32,* 1049–1057.

Fenichel, O. (1945). *The psychoanalytic theory of neurosis.* New York: Norton.

Fernando, J. (1998). The etiology of the narcissistic personality disorder. *Psychoanalytic Study of the Child, 53,* 141–158.

Fernando, J. L. (2000). Superego analysis in narcissistic patients with superego pathology. *Canadian Journal of Psychoanalysis, 8,* 99–117.

Flanagan, E. H., & Blashfield, R. K. (2003). Gender bias in the diagnosis of personality disorders: The roles of base rates and social stereotypes. *Journal of Personality Disorders, 17,* 431–446.

Forouzan, E., & Cooke, D. J. (2005). Figuring out la femme fatale: Conceptual and assessment issues concerning psychopathy in females. *Behavioral Sciences and the Law, 23,* 765–778.

Fossati, A., Feeney, J. A., Donati, D., Donini, M., Novella, L., Bagnato, M., et al. (2003). Personality disorders and adult attachment dimensions in a mixed psychiatric sample: A multivariate study. *Journal of Nervous and Mental Diseases, 191,* 30–37.

Fossati, A., Maffei, C., Bagnato, M., Donati, D., Donini, M., Fiorilli, M., et al. (2000). A psychometric study of *DSM-IV* passive-aggressive (negativistic) personality disorder criteria. *Journal of Personality Disorders, 14,* 72–83.

Frances, A. J., Clarkin, J. F., & Perry, S. (1984). *Differential therapeutics in psychiatry.* New York: Brunner/Mazel.

Franken, I. H. A., & Hendriks, V. M. (2000). Early-onset of illicit substance use is associated with greater Axis-II comorbidity, not with Axis-I comorbidity. *Drug and Alcohol Dependence, 59,* 305–308.

Freud, S. (1925). Some character-types met with in psychoanalytic work. In J. Strachey (Ed. & Trans.), *The standard edition of the works of Sigmund Freud* (Vol. 14, pp. 310–333). London: Hogarth. (Original work published 1916)

Freud, S. (1932). *The interpretation of dreams* (3rd ed.). New York: Macmillan.

Frick, P. J., & Dantagnan, A. L. (2005). Predicting the stability of conduct problems in children with and without callous-unemotional traits. *Journal of Child and Family Studies, 14,* 469–485.

Frick, P. J., & Morris, A. S. (2004). Temperament and developmental pathways to conduct problems. *Journal of Clinical Child and Adolescent Psychology, 33,* 54–68.

Fromm, E. (1941). *Escape from freedom.* New York: Rinehart.

Fromm, E. (1947). *Man for himself.* New York: Holt, Rinehart and Winston.

Fullana, M. A., Mataix-Cols, D., Caseras, X., Alonso, P., Menchón, J. M., Vallejo, J., et al. (2004). High sensitivity to punishment and low impulsivity in obsessive-compulsive patients with hoarding symptoms. *Psychiatry Research, 129,* 21–27.

Fung, M. T., Raine, A., Loeber, R., Lynam, D. R., Steinhauer, S. R., Venables, P. H., et al. (2005). Reduced electrodermal activity in psychopathy-prone adolescents. *Journal of Abnormal Psychology, 114,* 187–196.

Gabbard, G. O. (1990). *Psychodynamic psychiatry in clinical practice.* Washington, DC: American Psychiatric Press.

Gabbard, G. O. (1994). *Psychodynamic psychiatry in clinical practice (2nd Ed.).* Washington, DC: American Psychiatric Press.

Geberth, V. J., & Turco, R. N. (1997). Antisocial personality disorder, sexual sadism, malignant narcissism, and serial murder. *Journal of Forensic Sciences, 42,* 49–60.

Geiser, F., & Lieberz, K. (2000). Schizoid and narcissistic features in personality structure diagnosis. *Psychopathology, 33,* 19–24.

Glancy, G., & Saini, M. (2005). An evidenced-based review of psychological treatments of anger and aggression. *Brief Treatment and Crisis Intervention, 5*(2), 229–248.

Glasser, M. (1997). Problems in the psychoanalysis of certain narcissistic disorders. *Psychoanalytic Psychotherapy in South Africa, 5,* 35–50.

Glasser, W. (1961). *Mental health or mental illness? Psychiatry for practical action.* New York: Harper.

Glasser, W. (1965). *Reality therapy.* New York: Harper & Row.

Glasser, W. (1990). *The control theory–reality therapy workbook.* Canoga Park, CA: Institute for Reality Therapy.

Glickauf-Hughes, C. (1997). Etiology of the masochistic and narcissistic personality. *American Journal of Psychoanalysis, 57,* 141–148.

Goldberg, D. A. (2003). Impact of narcissism: The errant therapist on a chaotic quest. *Psychoanalytic Quarterly, 72,* 837–841.

Goldstein, K. (1940). *Human nature in the light of psychopathology.* Cambridge, MA: Harvard University Press.

Greenberg, L. S., & Safran, J. D. (1987). *Emotion in psychotherapy.* New York: Guilford Press.

Grilo, C. M. (2004). Diagnostic efficiency of *DSM-IV* criteria for obsessive compulsive personality disorder in patients with binge eating disorder. *Behavior Research and Therapy, 42,* 57–65.

Grilo, C. M., McGlashan, T. H., Quinlan, D. M., Walker, M. L., Greenfeld, D., & Edell, W. S. (1998). Frequency of personality disorders in two age cohorts of psychiatric inpatients. *American Journal of Psychiatry, 155,* 140–142.

Grilo, C. M., Sanislow, C. A., Gunderson, J. G., Pagano, M. E., Yen, S., Zanarini, M. C., et al. (2004). Two-year stability and change of schizotypal, borderline, avoidant, and obsessive-compulsive personality disorders. *Journal of Consulting and Clinical Psychology, 72,* 767–775.

Grilo, C. M., Skodol, A. E., Gunderson, J. G., Sanislow, C. A., Stout, R. L., Shea, M. T., et al. (2004). Longitudinal diagnostic efficiency of *DSM-IV* criteria for obsessive-compulsive personality disorder: A 2-year prospective study. *Acta Psychiatrica Scandinavica, 110,* 64–68.

Grisham, J. R., Frost, R. O., Steketee, G., Kim, H., & Hood, S. (2006). Age of onset of compulsive hoarding. *Journal of Anxiety Disorders, 20,* 675–686.

Grotjahn, M. (1984). The narcissistic person in analytic group therapy. *International Journal of Group Psychotherapy, 34,* 234–256.

Gude, T., Hoffart, A., Hedley, L., & Ro, O. (2004). The dimensionality of dependent personality disorder. *Journal of Personality Disorders, 18,* 604–610.

Gunderson, J. G., & Ronningstam, E. (2001). Differentiating narcissistic and antisocial personality disorders. *Journal of Personality Disorders, 15,* 103–109.

Guo-Qiang, W., Ya-Lin, Z., Zao-Huo, C., Yu-Ping, C., & Hong-Geng, Z. (2006). [A study on clinical characteristics and defense mechanism of obsessive compulsive disorder diagnosted Early]. *Chinese Journal of Clinical Psychology, 14,* 126–128.

Hale, L. R., Goldstein, D. S., Abramowitz, C. S., Calamari, J. E., & Kosson, D. S. (2004). Psychopathy is related to negative affectivity but not to anxiety sensitivity. *Behavior Research and Therapy, 42,* 697–710.

Halmi, K. A. (2005). Obsessive-compulsive personality disorder and eating disorders. *Eating Disorders: Journal of Treatment and Prevention, 13,* 85–92.

Hare, R. D., Cooke, D. J., & Hart, S. D. (1999). Psychopathy and sadistic personality disorder. In T. Millon, P. H. Blaney, & R. D. Davis, (Eds.), *Oxford textbook of psychopathology* (pp. 555–584). New York: Oxford University Press.

Haslam, N., Williams, B. J., Kyrios, M., McKay, D., & Taylor, S. (2005). Subtyping obsessive-compulsive disorder: A taxometric analysis. *Behavior Therapy, 36,* 381–391.

Hersoug, A. G., Bogwald, K., & Hoglend, P. (2004). Changes of defensive functioning: Does interpretation contribute to change? *Clinical Psychology and Psychotherapy, 12*(4), 288–296.

Hettema, J., Steele, J., & Miller, W. (2005). Motivational interviewing. *Annual Review of Clinical Psychology, 1,* 91–111.

Hicks, B. M., Markon, K. E., Patrick, C. J., Krueger, R. F., & Newman, J. P. (2004). Identifying psychopathy subtypes on the basis of personality structure. *Psychological Assessment, 16*, 276–288.

Hicks, B. M., & Patrick, C. J. (2006). Psychopathy and negative emotionality: Analyses of suppressor effects reveal distinct relations with emotional distress, fearfulness, and anger-hostility. *Journal of Abnormal Psychology, 115*, 276–287.

Hingley, S. (2001). Psychodynamic theory and narcissistically related personality problems: Support from case study research. *British Journal of Medical Psychology, 74*(1), 57–72.

Hirose, S. (2001). Effective treatment of aggression and impulsivity in antisocial personality disorder with risperidone. *Psychiatry and Clinical Neurosciences, 55*(2), 161–162.

Holaway, R. M., Heimberg, R. G., & Coles, M. E. (2006). A comparison of intolerance of uncertainty in analogue obsessive-compulsive disorder and generalized anxiety disorder. *Journal of Anxiety Disorders, 20*, 158–174.

Holmbeck, G. N., & Durlak, J. A. (2005). Comorbidity of dependent personality disorders and anxiety disorders: Conceptual and methodological issues. *Clinical Psychology: Science and Practice, 12*, 407–410.

Holt, S. E., Meloy, J. R., & Strack, S. (1999). Sadism and psychopathy in violent and sexually violent offenders. *Journal of the American Academy of Psychiatry and the Law, 27*, 23–32.

Horowitz, M. J. (1997). Psychotherapy of histrionic personality disorder. *Journal of Psychotherapy Practice and Research, 6*, 93–107.

Huprich, S. K., Clancy, C., Bornstein, R. F., & Nelson-Gray, R. O. (2004). Do dependency and social skills combine to predict depression? Linking two diatheses in mood disorders research. *Individual Differences Research, 2*, 2–16.

Imbesi, L. (1999). The making of a narcissist. *Clinical Social Work Journal, 27*, 41–54.

Imbesi, L. (2000). On the etiology of narcissistic personality disorder. *Issues in Psychoanalytic Psychology, 22*, 43–58.

Ivey, G. (1999). Transference-counter-transference constellations and enactments in the psychotherapy of destructive narcissism. *British Journal of Medical Psychology, 72*, 63–74.

Jenike, M. (Ed.). (1991). *Understanding obsessive-compulsive disorder (OCD): An international symposium held during the eighth World Congress of Psychiatry, Athens, Greece, October 1989*. Lewiston, NY: Hogrefe & Huber.

Johansson, P., Kerr, M., & Andershed, H. (2005). Linking adult psychopathy with childhood hyperactivity-impulsivity-attention problems and conduct problems through retrospective self-reports. *Journal of Personality Disorders, 19*, 94–101.

Johnson, J. G., Cohen, P., Chen, H., Kasen, S., & Brook, J. S. (2006). Parenting behaviors associated with risk for offspring personality disorder during adulthood. *Archives of General Psychiatry, 63*, 579–587.

Johnson, J. G., Cohen, P., Kasen, S., & Brook, J. S. (2006). Personality disorders evident by early adulthood and risk for anxiety disorders during middle adulthood. *Journal of Anxiety Disorders, 20*, 408–426.

Johnson, J. J., Smailes, E. M., Cohen, P., Brown, J., & Bernstein, D. P. (2000). Associations between four types of childhood neglect and personality disorder symptoms during adolescence and early adulthood: Findings of a community-based longitudinal study. *Journal of Personality Disorders, 14*, 171–187.

Johnson, S. M. (1987). *Humanizing the narcissistic style*. New York: Norton.

Joiner, T. E., Jr., & Rudd, M. D. (2002). The incremental validity of passive-aggressive personality symptoms rivals or exceeds that of other personality symptoms in suicidal outpatients. *Journal of Personality Assessment, 79,* 161–170.

Joseph, S. (1997). *Personality disorders: Symptom-focused drug therapy.* New York: Haworth Press.

Jovev, M., & Jackson, H. J. (2004). Early maladaptive schemas in personality disordered individuals. *Journal of Personality Disorders, 18,* 467–478.

Kaminer, D., & Stein, D. J. (2001). Sadistic personality disorder in perpetrators of human rights abuses: A South African case study. *Journal of Personality Disorders, 15,* 475–486.

Kantor, M. (2002). *Passive-aggression: A guide for the therapist, the patient and the victim.* Westport, CT: Praeger Publishers.

Kasen, S., Cohen, P., Skodol, A. E., Johnson, J. G., Smailes, E., & Brook, J. S. (2001). Childhood depression and adult personality disorder: Alternative pathways of continuity. *Archives of General Psychiatry,* 58, 231–236.

Kendell, R. E., & Discipio, W. J. (1970). Obsessional symptoms and obsessional personality traits in patients with depressive illnesses. *Psychological Medicine, 1,* 65–72.

Kernberg, O. F. (1967). Borderline personality organization. *Journal of the American Psychoanalytic Association, 15,* 641–685.

Kernberg, O. F. (1975). *Borderline conditions and pathological narcissism.* Northvale, NJ: Aronson.

Kernberg, O. F. (1986). *Severe personality disorders: Psychotherapeutic strategies.* New Haven, CT: Yale University Press.

Kernberg, O. F. (1992). *Aggression in personality disorders and perversions.* New Haven, CT: Yale University Press.

Kernberg, O. F. (1998). Narcissistic personality disorders. *Journal of European Psychoanalysis,* 7–18.

Kernberg, O. F. (2001). Die narzisstische persönlichkeit und ihre beziehung zu antisozialem verhalten und zu perversionen [The narcissistic personality and its relationship to antisocial behavior and to perversion]. *PTT: Persönlichkeitsstörungen Theorie und Therapie, 5,* 137–171.

Kiehl, K. A., Bates, A. T., Laurens, K. R., Hare, R. D., & Liddle, P. F. (2006). Brain potentials implicate temporal lobe abnormalities in criminal psychopaths. *Journal of Abnormal Psychology, 115,* 443–453.

Kiehl, K. A., Smith, A. M., Mendrek, A., Forster, B. B., Hare, R. D., & Liddle, P. F. (2004). Temporal lobe abnormalities in semantic processing by criminal psychopaths as revealed by functional magnetic resonance imaging. *Psychiatry Research: Neuroimaging, 130,* 27–42.

Kiesler, D. J. (1986). Interpersonal methods of diagnosis and treatment. In J. O. Cavenar (Ed.), *Psychiatry* (Vol. 1, pp. 1–23). Philadelphia: Lippincott.

King, A. R. (1998). Relations between MCMI-II personality variables and measures of academic performance. *Journal of Personality Assessment, 71,* 253–268.

Klerman, G. L. (1974). Treatment of depression by drugs and psychotherapy. *American Journal of Psychiatry, 131,* 186–191.

Klerman, G. L. (1984). Ideologic conflicts in combined treatments. In B. Beitman & G. L. Klerman (Eds.), *Combining pharmacotherapy and psychotherapy in clinical practice* (pp. 17–34). New York: Guilford Press.

Klerman, G. L., Weissman, M. M., Rounsaville, B. J., & Chevron, E. S. (1984). *Interpersonal psychotherapy of depression.* New York: Guilford Press.

Klonsky, E. D., Jane, J. S., Turkheimer, E., & Oltmanns, T. F. (2002). Gender role and personality disorders. *Journal of Personality Disorders, 16,* 464–476.

Kohut, H. (1971). *The analysis of the self.* New York: International Universities Press.

Kolb, L. (1968). *Noyes' Modern clinical psychiatry.* Philadelphia: Saunders.

Koldobsky, N. M. S. (2005). El trastorno obsesivo compulsive de la personalidad, realidad e interés clínico [Obsessive compulsive personality disorder, reality and clinical interest]. *Revista Argentina de Clínica Psicológica, 14,* 7–18.

Kotler, J. S., & McMahon, R. J. (2005). Child psychopathy: Theories, measurement, and relations with the development and persistence of conduct problems. *Clinical Child and Family Psychology Review, 8,* 291–325.

Kraus, G., & Reynolds, J. (2001). The "A-B-C's" of the Cluster B's: Identifying, understanding, and treating Cluster B personality disorders. *Clinical Psychology Review, 21*(3), 345–373.

Kraus, J., & Sheitman, B. (2005). Clozapine reduces violent behavior in heterogeneous diagnostic groups. *Journal of Neuropsychiatry and Clinical Neurosciences, 17* (1), 36–44.

Kurtz, R. R. (1997). Treating the narcissistic personality from a narrative family systems perspective. *Journal of Psychological Practice, 3,* 7–19.

Lacroix, L., Peterson, L., & Verrier, P. (2001). Art therapy, somatization, and narcissistic identification. *Art Therapy, 18,* 20–26.

Lahey, B. B., Loeber, R., Burke, J. D., & Applegate, B. (2005). Predicting future antisocial personality disorder in males from a clinical assessment in childhood. *Journal of Consulting and Clinical Psychology, 73,* 389–399.

Larsson, H., Andershed, H., & Lichtenstein, P. (2006). A genetic factor explains most of the variation in the psychopathic personality. *Journal of Abnormal Psychology, 115,* 221–230.

Lazarus, A. A. (1981). *The practice of multimodal therapy: Systematic, comprehensive, and effective psychotherapy.* New York: McGraw-Hill.

Liebowitz, M. R., & Klein, D. F. (1979). Case I: assessment and treatment of phobic anxiety. *Journal of Clinical Psychiatry, 40*(11), 486–492.

Lilienfeld, S. O., & Penna, S. (2001). Anxiety sensitivity: Relations to psychopathy, *DSM-IV* personality disorder features, and personality traits. *Journal of Anxiety Disorders, 15,* 367–393.

Links, P. S., & Stockwell, M. (2002). The role of couple therapy in the treatment of narcissistic personality disorder. *American Journal of Psychotherapy, 56,* 522–538.

Links, P. S., Stockwell, M., & MacFarlane, M. M. (2004a). Indications for couple therapy: The paradox of the histrionic/obsessive-compulsive couple. *Journal of Family Psychotherapy, 15,* 73–88.

Links, P. S., Stockwell, M., & MacFarlane, M. M. (Ed.). (2004b). Is couple therapy indicated for patients with dependent personality disorder? *Journal of Family Psychotherapy, 15,* 63–79.

Livesley, W. J., Jackson, D. N., & Schroeder, M. L. (1989). A study of the factorial structure of personality pathology. *Journal of Personality Disorders, 3,* 292–306.

Llanes, S. J., & Kosson, D. S. (2006). Divided visual attention and left hemisphere activation among psychopathic and nonpsychopathic offenders. *Journal of Psychopathology and Behavioral Assessment, 28,* 9–18.

Loas, G., Atger, F., Perdereau, F., Verrier, A., Guelfi, J., Halfon, O., et al. (2002). Comorbidity of dependent personality disorder and separation anxiety disorder in addictive disorders and in healthy subjects. *Psychopathology, 35,* 249–253.

Lobbestael, J., Arntz, A., & Sieswerda, S. (2005). Schema modes and childhood abuse in borderline and antisocial personality disorders. *Journal of Behavior Therapy and Experimental Psychiatry, 36,* 240–253.

Lynam, D. R., & Gudonis, L. (2005). The development of psychopathy. *Annual Review of Clinical Psychology, 1,* 381–407.

Magnavita, J. J. (2005). *Personality-guided relational psychotherapy.* Washington, DC: American Psychological Association.

Mancebo, M., Eisen, J., Grant, J., & Rasmussen, S. (2005). Obsessive compulsive personality disorder and obsessive compulsive disorder: Clinical characteristics, diagnostic difficulties, and treatment. *Annals of Clinical Psychiatry, 17*(4), 197–204.

Mann, J. (1973). *Time-limited psychotherapy.* Cambridge, MA: Harvard University Press.

Marmorstein, N., & Iacono, W. G. (2005). Longitudinal follow-up of adolescents with late-onset antisocial behavior: A pathological yet overlooked group. *Journal of the American Academy of Child and Adolescent Psychiatry, 44,* 1284–1291.

Martens, W. H. J. (2004). 14 ways to disturb the treatment of psychopaths. *Journal of Forensic Psychology Practice, 4,* 51–60.

Martens, W. H. J. (2005). Multidimensional model of trauma and correlated antisocial personality disorder. *Journal of Loss and Trauma, 10,* 115–129.

Massion, A. O., Dyck, I. R., Shea, M. T., Phillips, K. A., Warshaw, M. G., & Keller, M. B. (2002). Personality disorders and time to remission in generalized anxiety disorder, social phobia and panic disorder. *Archives of General Psychiatry, 59,* 434–440.

May, B., & Bos, J. (2000). Personality characteristics of ADHD adults assessed with the Millon Clinical Multiaxial Inventory: Pt. II. Evidence of four distinct subtypes. *Journal of Personality Assessment, 75,* 237–248.

McCann, M. E. (1994). Mourning accomplished by way of the transference. In R. Frankiel (Ed.), *Essential papers on object loss* (pp. 449–467). New York: New York University Press.

McCown, W. G., & Carlson, G. (2004). Narcissism, perfectionism and self-termination from treatment in outpatient cocaine users. *Journal of Rational-Emotive and Cognitive Behavior Therapy, 22,* 329–340.

McCray, J., & King, A. (2003). Personality disorder attributes as supplemental goals for change in interpersonal psychotherapy. *Journal of Contemporary Psychotherapy, 33*(2), 79–92.

McIlduff, E., & Coghlan, D. (2000). Reflections: Understanding and contending with passive-aggressive behavior in teams and organizations. *Journal of Managerial Psychology, 15,* 716–732.

McLaughlin, K. A., & Mennin, D. S. (2005). Clarifying the temporal relationship between dependent personality disorder and anxiety disorders. *Clinical Psychology: Science and Practice, 12,* 417–420.

Meichenbaum, D. (1977). *Cognitive-behavioral modification: An integrative approach.* New York: Plenum Press.

Meloy, J. R. (1988). *The psychopathic mind.* Northvale, NJ: Aronson.

Menninger, K. (1940). Character disorders. In J. F. Brown (Ed.), *The psychodynamics of abnormal behavior* (pp. 384–403). New York: McGraw-Hill.

Messer, S. B. (1986). Eclecticism in psychotherapy: Underlying assumptions, problems, and trade-offs. In J. C. Norcross & M. R. Goldfried (Eds.), *Handbook of eclectic psychotherapy* (pp. 379–397). New York: Brunner/Mazel.

Messer, S. B. (1992). A critical examination of belief structures in integrative and eclectic psychotherapy. In J. C. Norcross & M. R. Goldfried (Eds.), *Handbook of psychotherapy integration* (pp. 130–165). New York: Basic Books.

Messer, S. B. (1996). Concluding Comments. *Journal of Psychotherapy Integration, 6,* 135–137.

Miliora, M. T. (1998). JFK: A narcissistic political leader. *Psychohistory Review, 27,* 19–36.

Miller, W. R., & Rollnick, S. (2002). *Motivational interviewing: Preparing people for change* (2nd ed.). New York: Guilford Press.

Millon, T. (1969). *Modern psychopathology: A biosocial approach to maladaptive learning and functioning.* Philadelphia: Saunders. (Reprinted 1985, Prospect Heights, IL: Waveland Press)

Millon, T. (1981). *Disorders of personality: DSM-III, Axis II.* New York: Wiley-Interscience.

Millon, T. (1984). On the renaissance of personality assessment and personality theory. *Journal of Personality Assessment, 48,* 450–466.

Millon, T. (1988). Personologic psychotherapy: Ten commandments for a post eclectic approach to integrative treatment. *Psychotherapy, 25,* 209–219.

Millon, T. (1990). *Toward a new personology: An evolutionary model.* New York: Wiley-Interscience.

Millon, T. (1999). *Personality-guided therapy.* New York: Wiley.

Millon, T. (2002). Assessment is not enough: The SPA should participate in constructing a comprehensive clinical science of personality. *Journal of Personality Assessment, 78,* 209–218.

Millon, T. (2004). *Masters of the mind: Exploring the stories of mental illness from ancient times to the new millennium.* Hoboken, NJ: Wiley.

Millon T., Bloom, C., & Grossman, S. (in press). *Personalized Assessment.* New York: Guilford Press.

Millon, T., & Davis, R. D. (1996a). *Disorders of personality: DSM-IV and beyond.* New York: Wiley.

Millon, T., & Davis, R. D. (1996b). *Personality and psychopathology: Building a clinical science.* New York: Wiley-Interscience.

Millon, T., & Grossman, S. D. (2006). Millon's evolutionary model for unifying the study of normal and abnormal personality. In S. Strack (Ed.), *Differentiating normal and abnormal personality* (2nd ed., pp. 3–46). New York: Springer.

Millon, T., & Grossman, S. D. (in press). *Millon-Grossman personality domain checklist,* Coral Gables, FL: Dicandrien.

Millon, T., Millon, C., Davis, R. D., & Grossman, S. D. (2006). *Millon Clinical Multiaxial Inventory—III Manual* (3rd ed.). Minneapolis, MN: NCS Pearson Assessments.

Millon, T., Simonsen, E., Birket-Smith, M., & Davis, R. (Eds.). (1998). *Psychopathy: Antisocial, criminal, and violent behavior.* New York: Guilford Press.

Mitchell, D. G. V., Avny, S. B., & Blair, R. J. R. (2006). Divergent patterns of aggressive and neurocognitive characteristics in acquired versus developmental psychopathy. *Neurocase, 12,* 164–178.

Montagne, B., van Honk, J., Kessels, R. P. C., Frigerio, E., Burt, M., van Zandvoort, M. J. E., et al. (2005). Reduced efficiency in recognising fear in subjects scoring high on psychopathic personality characteristics. *Personality and Individual Differences, 38,* 5–11.

Morse, J. Q., Robins, C. J., & Gittes-Fox, M. (2002). Sociotropy, autonomy, and personality disorder criteria in psychiatric patients. *Journal of Personality Disorders, 16,* 549–560.

Mudrack, P. E. (2004). Job involvement, obsessive-compulsive personality traits, and workaholic behavioral tendencies. *Journal of Organizational Change Management, 17,* 490–508.

Mulder, R. (1996). Antisocial personality disorder: Current drug treatment recommendations. *CNS Drugs, 5*(4), 257–263.

Murphy, C., & Vess, J. (2003). Subtypes of psychopathy: Proposed differences between narcissistic, borderline, sadistic, and antisocial psychopaths. *Psychiatric Quarterly, 74,* 11–29.

Murray, E. J. (1983). Beyond behavioural and dynamic therapy. *British Journal of Clinical Psychology, 22,* 127–128.

Murrie, D. C., Cornell, D. G., & McCoy, W. K. (2005). Psychopathy, conduct disorder, and stigma: Does diagnostic labeling influence juvenile probation officer recommendations? *Law and Human Behavior, 29,* 323–342.

Muscatello, C. F., & Scudellari, P. (2000). Anger and narcissism: Between the void of being and the hunger for having. *Psychopathology, 33,* 227–232.

Myers, W. C., Burket, R. C., & Husted, D. S. (2006). Sadistic personality disorder and comorbid mental illness in adolescent psychiatric inpatients. *Journal of the American Academy of Psychiatry and the Law, 34,* 61–71.

Ng, H. M., & Bornstein, R. F. (2005). Comorbidity of dependent personality disorder and anxiety disorders: A meta-analytic review. *Clinical Psychology: Science and Practice, 12,* 395–406.

Noyes, A. P. (1939). *Modern Clinical Psychiatry (2nd ed.).* Philadelphia & London: W.B. Saunders Company.

Ogloff, J. R. P. (2006). Psychopathy/antisocial personality disorder conundrum. *Australian and New Zealand Journal of Psychiatry, 40,* 519–528.

O'Neil, R., & Bornstein, R. (2001). The dependent patient in a psychiatric inpatient setting: Relationship of interpersonal dependency to consultation and medication frequencies. *Journal of Clinical Psychology, 57*(3), 289–298.

Ornstein, A. (1998). The fate of narcissistic rage in psychotherapy. *Psychoanalytic Inquiry, 18,* 55–70.

Overholser, J. C., Stockmeier, C., Dilley, G., & Freiheit, S. (2002). Personality disorders in suicide attempters and completers: Preliminary findings. *Archives of Suicide Research, 6,* 123–133.

Paris, J. (2004). Personality disorders over time: Implications for psychotherapy. *American Journal of Psychotherapy, 58,* 420–429.

Patrick, C. J., Hicks, B. M., Krueger, R. F., & Lang, A. R. (2005). Relations between psychopathy facets and externalizing in a criminal offender sample. *Journal of Personality Disorders, 19,* 339–356.

Patton, M. J., & Meara, N. M. (1996). Kohut and counseling: Applications of self psychology. *Psychodynamic Counseling, 2,* 328–355.

Perry, J. D., & Perry, J. C. (1996). Reliability and convergence of three concepts of narcissistic personality. *Psychiatry: Interpersonal and Biological Processes, 59,* 4–19.

Pfiffner, L. J., McBurnett, K., Rathouz, P. J., & Judice, S. (2005). Family correlates of oppositional and conduct disorders in children with attention deficit/hyperactivity disorder. *Journal of Abnormal Child Psychology, 33,* 551–563.

Pica, M., Engel, S., & Welches, P. (2003). An experiential approach to the inpatient anger management group. *International Journal of Group Psychotherapy, 53*(2), 177–200.

Pietrzak, R. H., & Petry, N. M. (2005). Antisocial personality disorder is associated with increased severity of gambling, medical, drug and psychiatric problems among treatment-seeking pathological gamblers. *Addiction, 100,* 1183–1193.

Pincus, A. L., & Wilson, K. R. (2001). Interpersonal variability in dependent personality. *Journal of Personality, 69,* 223–251.

Pinel, P. (1798). *Nosographie philosophique.* Paris: Richard, Caille, & Ravier.

Plakun, E. M. (Ed.). (1990). *New perspectives on narcissism.* Washington, DC: American Psychiatric Press.

Porter, S., & Woodworth, M. (2006). Psychopathy and aggression. In C. J. Patrick (Ed.), *Handbook of the psychopathy* (pp. 481–494). New York: Guilford Press.

Rado, S. (1969). *Adaptational psychodynamics.* New York: Science House.

Raine, A., Ishikawa, S. S., Arce, E., Lencz, T., Knuth, K. H., Bihrle, S., et al. (2004). Hippocampal structural asymmetry in unsuccessful psychopaths. *Biological Psychiatry, 55,* 185–191.

Rasmussen, P. R. (2005). *Personality-guided cognitive-behavioral therapy.* Washington, DC: American Psychological Association.

Rassin, E., & Muris, P. (2005). To be or not to be . . . indecisive: Gender differences, correlations with obsessive-compulsive complaints, and behavioral manifestation. *Personality and Individual Differences, 38,* 1175–1181.

Reich, W. (1949). *Character analysis (3rd ed.).* New York: Farrar, Straus and Giroux. (Original work published 1933)

Reid, W. (1978). *The psychopath: A comprehensive study of antisocial disorders and behaviors.* New York: Brunner/Mazel.

Reid, W., & Gacono, C. (2000). Treatment of antisocial personality, psychopathy, and other characterologic antisocial syndromes. *Behavioral Sciences and the Law, 18*(5), 647–662.

Riesenberg-Malcolm, R. (1996). "How can we know the dancer from the dance?": Hyperbole in hysteria. *International Journal of Psycho-Analysis, 77,* 679–688.

Ritzler, B., & Gerevitz-Stern, G. (2006). Rorschach assessment of passive-aggressive personality disorder. In S. K. Huprich (Ed.), *Rorschach assessment of the personality disorders* (pp. 345–369). Mahwah, NJ: Erlbaum.

Rivas, L. A. (2001). Controversial issues in the diagnosis of narcissistic personality disorder: A review of the literature. *Journal of Mental Health Counseling, 23,* 22–35.

Rocca, P., Villari, V., & Bogetto, F. (2006). Managing the aggressive and violent patient in the psychiatric emergency. *Progress in Neuro-Psychopharmacology and Biological Psychiatry, 30*(4), 586–598.

Rogers, C. R. (1967). *The therapeutic relationship and its impact.* Madison: University of Wisconsin Press.

Romano, D. M. C. (2004). A self-psychology approach to narcissistic personality disorder: A nursing reflection. *Perspectives in Psychiatric Care, 40,* 20–28.

Ronningstam, E. F. (Ed.). (1998). *Disorders of narcissism: Diagnostic, clinical, and empirical implications.* Washington, DC: American Psychiatric Press.

Rovik, J. O. (2001). Overt and covert narcissism: Turning points and mutative elements in two psychotherapies. *British Journal of Psychotherapy, 17,* 435–447.

Rutter, M. (2005). Commentary: What is the meaning and utility of the psychopathy concept? *Journal of Abnormal Child Psychology, 33,* 499–503.

Sacks, O. (1973). *Awakenings.* New York: Harper & Row.

Salekin, R. T., Leistico, A. R., Trobst, K. K., Schrum, C. L., & Lochman, J. E. (2005). Adolescent psychopathy and personality theory: The interpersonal circumplex—Expanding evidence of a nomological net. *Journal of Abnormal Child Psychology, 33,* 445–460.

Salzman, L. (1989). Compulsive personality disorder. In T. Karasu (Ed.), *Treatments of psychiatric disorders* (pp. 2771–2782). Washington, DC: American Psychiatric Press.

Sansone, R. A., Levitt, J. L., & Sansone, L. A. (2005). The prevalence of personality disorders among those with eating disorders. *Eating Disorders: Journal of Treatment and Prevention, 13,* 7–21.

Schoenewolf, G. (1997). Soiling and the anal-narcissistic character. *American Journal of Psychoanalysis, 57,* 47–62.

Schwartz, R. C. (2001). "Psychotherapeutic diagnosis and treatment of histrionic personality disorder": Reply. *Annals of the American Psychotherapy Association, 4,* 4.

Sharp, C., van Goozen, S., & Goodyer, I. (2006). Children's subjective emotional reactivity to affective pictures: Gender differences and their antisocial correlates in an unselected sample of 7 to 11-year-olds. *Journal of Child Psychology and Psychiatry, 47,* 143–150.

Shea, M. T., Stout, R. L., Yen, S., Pagano, M. E., Skodol, A. E., Morey, L. C., et al. (2004). Associations in the course of personality disorders and Axis I disorders over time. *Journal of Abnormal Psychology, 113,* 499–508.

Sifneos, P. E. (1972). *Short-term psychotherapy and emotional crisis.* Cambridge, MA: Harvard University Press.

Sigmund, D., Barnett, W., & Mundt, C. (1998). The hysterical personality disorder: A phenomenological approach. *Psychopathology, 31,* 318–330.

Simonoff, E., Elander, J., Holmshaw, J., Pickles, A., Murray, R., & Rutter, M. (2004). Predictors of antisocial personality: Continuities from childhood to adult life. *British Journal of Psychiatry, 184,* 118–127.

Sinha, B. K., & Watson, D. C. (2001). Personality disorder in university students: A multitrait-multimethod matrix study. *Journal of Personality Disorders, 15,* 235–244.

Skeem, J. L., Edens, J. F., Camp, J., & Colwell, L. H. (2004). Are there ethnic differences in levels of psychopathy? A meta-analysis. *Law and Human Behavior, 28,* 505–527.

Slater, L. (1998). *Prozac diary.* New York: Random House.

Slavik, S., Carlson, J., & Sperry, L. (1998). The passive-aggressive couple. In J. Carlson & L. Sperry (Eds.), *The disordered couple* (pp. 299–314). Philadelphia: Brunner/Mazel.

Slavinska-Holy, N. (Ed.). (1988). *Borderline and narcissistic patients in therapy.* Madison, CT: International Universities Press.

Slavson, S. R. (1943). *An introduction to group therapy.* New York: Commonwealth Fund.

Sochos, A. (2005). Attachment and representational change in cognitive analytic therapy: Developing a taxonomy. *Counselling Psychology Review, 20,* 15–30.

Sookman, D., Abramowitz, J. S., Calamari, J. E., Wilhelm, S., & McKay, D. (2005). Subtypes of obsessive-compulsive disorder: Implications for specialized cognitive behavior therapy. *Behavior Therapy, 36,* 393–400.

Soyer, R. B., Rovenpor, J. L., Kopelman, R. E., Mullins, L. S., & Watson, P. J. (2001). Further assessment of the construct validity of four measures of narcissism: Replication and extension. *Journal of Psychology: Interdisciplinary and Applied, 135,* 245–258.

Sperry, L. (1995). *Handbook of diagnosis and treatment of the* DSM-IV *personality disorders.* New York: Brunner/Mazel.

Sprock, J. (2000). Gender-typed behavioral examples of histrionic personality disorder. *Journal of Psychopathology and Behavioral Assessment, 22,* 107–122.

Sprock, J., & Hunsucker, L. (1998). Symptoms of prototypic patients with passive-aggressive personality disorder: *DSM-III-R* versus *DSM-IV* negativistic. *Comprehensive Psychiatry, 39,* 287–295.

Stewart, J. R. (1997). Implications of narcissistic personality disorder for rehabilitation counseling and education. *Rehabilitation Education, 11,* 337–351.

Stone, M. H. (1993). Long-term outcome in personality disorders. In P. Tyrer & G. Stein (Eds.), *Personality disorder reviewed.* London: Gaskell.

Stone, M. H. (1998). Sadistic personality in murderers. In T. Millon, E. Simonsen, M. Birket-Smith, & R. D. Davis (Eds.), *Psychopathy: Antisocial, criminal, and violent behavior* (pp. 346–355). New York: Guilford Press.

Stone, M. H. (2005). Violence. In J. M. Oldham, A. E. Skodol, & D. S. Bender (Eds.), *The American Psychiatric Publishing textbook of personality disorders* (pp. 477–491). Washington, DC: American Psychiatric Publishing.

Strand, S., & Belfrage, H. (2005). Gender differences in psychopathy in a Swedish offender sample. *Behavioral Sciences and the Law, 23,* 837–850.

Straton, D. (2004). Iatrogenic dependency disorder. *Australasian Psychiatry, 12,* 69–71.

Strupp, H. H., & Binder, J. L. (1984). *Psychotherapy in a new key: A guide to time-limited dynamic psychotherapy.* New York: Basic Books.

Stuart, G. L., Moore, T. M., Gordon, K. C., Ramsey, S. E., & Kahler, C. W. (2006). Psychopathology in women arrested for domestic violence. *Journal of Interpersonal Violence, 21,* 376–389.

Teusch, L., Böhme, H., Finke, J., & Gastpar, M. (2001). Effects of client-centered psychotherapy for personality disorders alone and in combination with psychopharmacological treatment. *Psychotherapy and Psychosomatics, 70,* 328–336.

Timmerman, I. G. H., & Emmelkamp, P. M. G. (2005). Parental rearing styles and personality disorders in prisoners and forensic patients. *Clinical Psychology and Psychotherapy, 12,* 191–200.

Tringone, R. F. (1991). Construction of the Millon Personality Diagnostic Checklist-III-R and personality prototypes. *Dissertation Abstracts International, 51* (10-B).

Tringone, R. F. (1997). The MPDC: Composition and Clinical Applications. In T. Millon (Ed.), *The Millon Inventories: Clinical and personality assessment.* New York: Guilford Press.

Turkat, I. D. (1990). *The personality disorders.* New York: Pergamon Press.

Tweed, R. G., & Dutton, D. G. (1998). A comparison of impulsive and instrumental subgroups of batterers. *Violence and Victims, 13,* 217–230.

Tyrer, P., Morgan, J., & Cicchetti, D. (2004). The Dependent Personality Questionnaire (DPQ): A screening instrument for dependent personality. *International Journal of Social Psychiatry, 50,* 10–17.

Valliant, P., Hawkins, T., & Pottier, D. (1998). Comparison of psychopathic and general offenders in cognitive behavioral therapy. *Psychological Reports, 82*(3, Pt. 1), 753–754.

Vasey, M. W., Kotov, R., Frick, P. J., & Loney, B. R. (2005). The latent structure of psychopathy in youth: A taxometric investigation. *Journal of Abnormal Child Psychology, 33,* 411–429.

Vaughan, M. (1976). The relationship between obsessional personality, obsessions in depression, and symptoms of depression. *British Journal of Psychiatry, 129,* 36–39.

Vereycken, J., Vertommen, H., & Corveleyn, J. (2002). Authority conflicts and personality disorders. *Journal of Personality Disorders, 16,* 41–51.

Videbech, T. (1975). The psychopathology of anancastic endogenous depression. *Acta Psychiatrica Scandinavica, 52,* 336–373.

Vien, A., & Beech, A. R. (2006). Psychopathy: Theory, measurement, and treatment. *Trauma, Violence, and Abuse, 7,* 155–174.

Villemarette-Pittman, N. R., Stanford, M. S., Greve, K. W., Houston, R. J., & Mathias, C. W. (2004). Obsessive-compulsive personality disorder and behavioral disinhibition. *Journal of Psychology: Interdisciplinary and Applied, 138,* 5–22.

Vincent, G. M. (2006). Psychopathy and violence risk assessment in youth. *Child and Adolescent Psychiatric Clinics of North America, 15,* 407–428.

Vogel, P., Hansen, B., Stiles, T., & Götestam, K. (2006). Treatment motivation, treatment expectancy, and helping alliance as predictors of outcome in cognitive behavioral treatment of OCD. *Journal of Behavior Therapy and Experimental Psychiatry, 37*(3), 247–255.

Vogel, P., Stiles, T., & Götestam, K. (2004). Adding cognitive therapy elements to exposure therapy for obsessive compulsive disorder: A controlled study. *Behavioral and Cognitive Psychotherapy, 32*(3), 275–290.

Von Zerssen, J. (1977). Premorbid personality and affective psychosis. In G. D. Burrows (Ed.), *Handbook of depression.* Amsterdam: Excerpta Medica.

Walker, R. (1992). Substance abuse and B-cluster disorders: Pt. II. Treatment recommendations. *Journal of Psychoactive Drugs, 24,* 233–241.

Warner, M. B., Morey, L. C., Finch, J. F., Gunderson, J. G., Skodol, A. E., Sanislow, C. A., et al. (2004). The longitudinal relationship of personality traits and disorders. *Journal of Abnormal Psychology, 113,* 217–227.

Warren, J. I., & South, S. C. (2006). Comparing the constructs of antisocial personality disorder and psychopathy in a sample of incarcerated women. *Behavioral Sciences and the Law, 24,* 1–20.

Warren, M. P., & Capponi, A. (1996). The place of culture in the aetiology of the narcissistic personality disorder: Comparing the United States, Japan, and Denmark. *International Journal of Communicative Psychoanalysis and Psychotherapy, 11,* 11–16.

Waska, R. T. (1996). The wandering soul: Narcissism and the failure to integrate the self-soothing function. *Journal of Clinical Psychoanalysis, 5,* 445–475.

Wells, R., & Giannetti, V. (Eds.). (1990). *Handbook of brief psychotherapies.* New York: Plenum Press.

West, M. (2004). Identity, narcissism and the emotional core. *Journal of Analytical Psychology, 49,* 521–551.

Westen, D., & Weinberger, J. (2004). When clinical description becomes statistical prediction. *American Psychologist, 59,* 595–613.

Westermeyer, J., & Thuras, P. (2005). Association of antisocial personality disorder and substance disorder morbidity in a clinical sample. *American Journal of Drug and Alcohol Abuse, 31,* 93–110.

Wetzler, S., & Morey, L. C. (1999). Passive-aggressive personality disorder: The demise of a syndrome. *Psychiatry: Interpersonal and Biological Processes, 62,* 49–59.

Whiteside, S. P., & Abramowitz, J. S. (2004). Obsessive-compulsive symptoms and the expression of anger. *Cognitive Therapy and Research, 28,* 259–268.

Wise, E. A. (2001). The comparative validity of MCMI-II and MMPI-2 personality disorder scales with forensic examinees. *Journal of Personality Disorders, 15,* 275–279.

Witte, T. H., Callahan, K. L., & Perez-Lopez, M. (2002). Narcissism and anger: An exploration of underlying correlates. *Psychological Reports, 90,* 871–875.

Wittenborn, J. R., & Maurer, H. S. (1977). Persisting personalities among depressed women. *Archives of General Psychiatry, 34,* 968–971.

Yalom, I. D. (1985). *The theory and practice of group psychotherapy.* New York: Basic Books.

INDEX